PSYCHOLOGY SURVEY 6

EDITED BY
HALLA BELOFF & ANDREW M. COLMAN

PSYCHOLOGY SURVEY

EDITED BY
HALLA BELOFF AND ANDREW M. COLMAN

The British
Psychological Society

© The British Psychological Society, 1987

First edition published in 1987 by the British Psychological Society, St Andrews House, 48 Princess Road East, Leicester, LE1 7DR, UK.

Available in the UK, Europe, Africa, Asia and Australasia from:

> The British Psychological Society
> The Distribution Centre
> Blackhorse Road
> LETCHWORTH
> Hertfordshire
> SG6 1HN
> UK

Available in North and South America, Canada, the Philippines, US dependencies and Japan from:

> The MIT Press
> 28 Carleton Street
> Cambridge
> MA 02142
> USA

British Library Cataloguing in Publication Data:
  Psychology Survey 6
  1. Psychology
  I. Beloff, Halla   II. Colman, Andrew M.
  III. British Psychological Society
  150   BF121

ISBN 0 901715 58 1

Library of Congress Cataloguing in Publication Data:
  Psychology survey. no. 1-   1978-
    1. Psychology—Periodicals.   I. British Psychological Society.
  BF1.P853   150'.5   79-647880
                                            MARC-S
  Library of Congress   79[8607r85]rev

  0-2 62-02261-3

Printed and bound in Great Britain by A. Wheaton & Co. Ltd., Exeter

CONTENTS

Preface

1 Experiments and Experience: Usefulness and Insight in Psychology   1
  Keith Oatley

2 Face Recognition   28
  Andrew W. Young

3 Emotion: Cognitive Approaches   55
  Brian Parkinson

4 Reasoning   74
  Jonathan St B.T. Evans

5 Identity   94
  Glynis M. Breakwell

6 Language, Social Identity and Health   115
  Caroline Dryden and Howard Giles

7 The Psychology of Eating and Eating Disorders   140
  P. Wright

8 Human Organic Memory Disorders   170
  Andrew Mayes

9 The Concepts of Sociobiology   192
  John Lazarus

10 The Ethics and Politics of Animal Experimentation   218
  Jeffrey A. Gray

11 Hypnosis 234
  Graham F. Wagstaff

12 Psychology and Computer Design 255
  David J. Oborne

13 The Psychological Influences of Television 276
  Barrie Gunter

Index 305

PREFACE

Psychology Survey is now a well-established publication, presenting in each volume a selection of topics that are currently generating significant interest and research activity. Each chapter, written by someone who is in the thick of things, seeks to provide a critical and, at times, provocative – although perforce succinct – evaluation of the state of the art in one particular field of interest.

The *Survey* can be used as a supplement to textbook and specialist reading. We hope that students will find the chapters useful as critical reviews to supplement their own reading of primary sources. (They may also be used as examination cribs, of course; but this is not recommended by the editors, because the chapters are designed to stimulate thought and further reading rather than to be swallowed uncritically.) Other psychologists – professionals and academics – will find the *Survey* useful for updating their knowledge of problems outside their own specialized fields of expertise fairly painlessly.

As before, we have tried to cover topics over a wide range: basic and applied; experimental and humanistic; closely focused on technical problems and devoted to broader issues of debate; clearly respectable and more maverick. It might be invidious to give our nominations here: readers will make their own selections. But nowhere, we hope, is there a chapter that simply deals with a traditional subject in a routine, computer-aided survey style.

Psychology shows no sign of settling into rutted paths. There are indeed dramatic changes taking place, even in the traditional research areas, and new fields are evolving all the time. That is what has made our editorial work a pleasure, and what will surely make *Psychology Survey 6* a useful addition to any working psychologist's library.

The skill, good humour, and patience of Joyce Collins and Christopher Feeney at the BPS office in Leicester also contributed to our pleasure in editing this volume. Our thanks to them.

HALLA BELOFF

ANDREW M. COLMAN

EXPERIMENTS AND EXPERIENCE: USEFULNESS AND INSIGHT IN PSYCHOLOGY
Keith Oatley

Psychology is unusual in that it aims at both usefulness and insight. As with engineering and medicine, some aspects of psychology are of interest for their practical implications; as with history and literature, some aspects are of interest because they offer insights, extending our understanding and experience of ourselves and others.

In most psychological research one of these aspects is more salient than the other. Difficulties arise because different aims make different methods appropriate. Divisions and factions have grown up, and there are arguments that only some particular way of doing psychology is capable of approaching truth.

Thinking about the two parallel aims of psychology, usefulness and insight, makes it easier to understand the different approaches within the subject; including the functions of experiments on animals and the distinctive contributions that only studies of human subjects can make.

USEFULNESS

What is meant by 'a useful piece of psychology'? Francis Bacon (1605) said that a primary purpose of knowledge was 'the relief of man's estate'. Bacon was a founder of natural scientific investigation, and he refers to that characteristically Western desire to make human life tomorrow better than it has been today, to make knowledge not just a means of showing off but a practical benefit to humanity. In this, science and technology go together. If we can discover causes of events and the properties of things, then we shall in principle be able to shape these properties and apply causes to human ends. Here are two psychological examples, one related to medicine and one to optical engineering.

Stress

First, an example from the research of Ivan Pavlov and his colleagues (Pavlov, 1927) on the classical conditioning of dogs. Dramatic anxiety occurred in a dog that Shenger-Krestovnikova was experimenting on. She was training the dog to perform a discrimination, following the usual procedure – exposure to a stimulus, followed by presentation of food. The dog became conditioned to salivate when it was shown one stimulus, a circle that was always followed by food, but did not salivate when shown an ellipse which was not followed by food. In the experiment the ellipse was made gradually more similar to the circle. When the ratio of length to width of the ellipse reached 9:8, the dog could just discriminate the patterns. After three weeks of sessions with this 9:8 ratio a change occurred. The dog stopped performing at all, even when the task was made easier.

> The hitherto quiet dog began to squeal in its stand, kept wriggling about, tore off with its teeth the apparatus of mechanical stimulation of the skin, and bit through the tubes connecting the animal's room with the observer, a behaviour which never happened before. On being taken into the experimental room the dog now barked violently, which was also contrary to its usual custom (Pavlov, 1927, p.291).

The implications drawn by Pavlov were that the dog was suffering from an acute neurosis. Research continued to discover how this condition developed. Evidently animals were psychologically stressed when signals for the arrival of food were barely sufficient to be discriminated. Pavlov, without the experimental caution that he showed elsewhere, became keen on the idea that bromide acted as a tranquillizer for animals with experimental neuroses (Boakes, 1984).

Pavlov's idea about neurosis might itself be useful and even insightful, but a clear example of how this procedure was put to work is a study of the effects of stress in the presence of an environmental health hazard.

Keehn (1986, quoting Startsev) describes an experiment in this tradition by Petrova in 1946. Coal-tar, a substance suspected of causing cancer, was repeatedly applied to a 10 cm square patch on the backs of nine dogs for two years. After the first year, four of the dogs were subjected to the stress of experimental neurosis, while the other five were not. The stressed dogs developed papillomatosis, a kind of cancer, at the site of the coal-tar application, and two of them also developed cancers elsewhere. The control dogs developed benign papillomata at the site of the coal-tar application, but these disappeared subsequently without a trace.

This kind of experiment was an early clue to understanding how psychological stress and environmental health hazards interact. The animal model is close to our current understandings that stress increases the risk of cancer from physical causes. It is now thought that psychological stresses decrease the efficiency of our auto-immune systems, making them less able to recognize and dispose of growing cancer cells in the body (for example, Ader, 1981). Animal models have been important not only in making possible experiments on the relationship between health and susceptibility to disease of a kind that we could not possibly perform on humans, but also in investigating how we might diminish the damaging effects of stress.

Image enhancement in visual systems

Here, as a second example, is some work from visual psychophysics which has an engineering application. Combining research on human vision and optical equipment is helpful because the visual system and many artificial optical systems have to solve similar problems, and so there is a cross-fertilization of ideas.

In one set of experiments, Geoff Sullivan, Mark Georgeson and I were trying to find out the function of the 'channels' in the human visual system that responded to specific spatial frequencies (Campbell and Robson, 1968). A spatial frequency is the periodicity of elements in a regularly repeating visual pattern. Higher frequency means a larger number of elements per unit of visual angle. Looking down at a zebra crossing one sees a very low spatial frequency: 10 stripes fill up most of the visual field. Holding at arm's length one of the universal product codes, the stripes now printed on most goods in supermarkets, would present a stimulus of high spatial frequency, with many hundreds of stripes to the equivalent visual angle. It was perhaps rather surprising that channels in the human visual system were tuned to specific spatial frequencies.

Sullivan, Georgeson and Oatley (1972) showed that these frequency channels could account for the discrimination of patterns that were not repetitive, for example, small spots or single lines. It seems as if the visual system performs a Fourier analysis. Fourier analysis implies that patterns can be broken down into a set of repetitive spatial frequencies, with the stripes adding and subtracting at different points to produce the pattern. Holograms, for instance, work in this way, with the image distributed into a set of wave patterns. A single dot is made up in the spatial Fourier domain of all possible spatial frequencies of equal amplitude, all adding together in one place and cancelling out elsewhere.

The cochlea in the ear performs a Fourier analysis on incoming sounds, resolving them into time-varying frequencies. These correspond to temporal oscillations, such as those made by the string of a guitar. The mathematics of the analysis and synthesis of spatial and temporal frequencies is the same, so a sharp, discrete sound, a click, can be analysed into a set of all temporal frequencies. In the reverse direction, the click can be synthesized by adding all possible temporal frequencies so that they add at one point in time and cancel elsewhere.

It makes sense for the auditory system to resolve sounds into temporal frequencies as a basis for our perception of pitch. But why should the visual system perform a spatial Fourier analysis? The clue comes from engineering practices of removing blur from images. In the spatial frequency domain, blur is equivalent to attenuation (decreased amplitude) of the higher frequencies. High frequencies are equivalent to fine detail; they contribute to the sharpness of edges. Any optical instrument is limited in the detail it can resolve: in Fourier terms this is a progressive attenuation of higher frequencies. The importance of Fourier analysis here is that if visual information can be transformed into a frequency representation and if the frequency attenuation can be estimated, then any losses due to blur can be compensated for, simply by multiplying the amplitude of those frequencies that have become attenuated.

The principle is familiar to people with high fidelity audio equipment. High frequencies add to the sharpness of sounds. On many audio systems there are controls to amplify selectively any frequencies which have become attenuated, and so improve fidelity. In Fourier terms high fidelity is equivalent to all frequencies being transmitted with exactly their original amplitude, a so-called flat frequency response.

In proposing a spatial Fourier analysis in the visual system, the idea was that the system can compensate actively to achieve a flat frequency response in the spatial frequency domain. Corneal imperfections, lens irregularities and the like make the eye much more blur-producing than even the cheapest camera. We can see the fall-off in the amplitude of the higher spatial frequencies transmitted by the eye in Figure 1A: with more than about 10 stripes per degree the amount of contrast (amplitude from bright to dark) needed to see stripes at threshold has to be progressively increased. Yet above threshold, people see sharply. The hypothesis was that if in any spatial frequency channel the signal is above threshold, and if the amount of attenuation is known by the system, then loss of amplitude due to blur can be compensated for by multiplying the signal in each channel in proportion to the attenuation it has suffered (see, for example, Oatley, 1976). Georgeson and Sullivan (1975) showed that when observers match the contrasts of stripes of different spatial frequencies above threshold, the visual system does indeed do this. It maintains constancy, and gives a flat frequency response in the spatial frequency domain (see Figure 1B) just as the best audio systems do in the temporal frequency domain.

Results of Fourier de-blurring can be seen in Figure 2. The right-hand image of Figure 2 was produced by transforming the very blurred left-hand image into its spatial frequency components by computer and multiplying any frequencies that were attenuated to give a flat frequency response. Resynthesis from these frequency components produced the right-hand image. Though the amount of blur in people with normal vision is not as bad as it is in the left-hand picture, the principle is similar.

This shows how engineering ideas are useful in psychology. In the next step the ideas went the other way, from psychology to engineering. The trouble with Fourier deblurring is that when a signal is multiplied, so too is any noise in the image. Noise is random disturbance of a signal spread across the whole frequency spectrum. It is especially troublesome in the high frequencies, because it degrades fine detail, though in a different way from blur. Fourier deblurring makes any noise much worse. This can be seen in the increased graininess of the right-hand image of Figure 2. So there is a trade-off between blur and noise; the more the blur is corrected, the worse the noise can become.

Now it is known that as well as being blur-prone, the visual system is also very noisy. And yet we do see sharp images, not just blur free, but noise free.

Geoff Sullivan's idea, derived from thinking about psychophysical experiments and theories, was that spatial frequency channels might allow images to be de-noised as well as de-blurred. If the noise in each spatial channel is clipped out of each channel before the signal in that channel is multiplied, then the advantages of de-blurring can be gained without the disadvantages of multiplying the noise. In this way the most troublesome noise can be eliminated from most images, while edge detail is also enhanced by deblurring.

This is a good theory of the function of Fourier channels in the visual system, and it has been demonstrated as an engineering possibility (Baker and Sullivan, 1980). Its applications range from image enhancement in the blurred, noisy data of satellite and aerial photography, to the blurred, noisy data of Computed Axial Tomograms (CAT scans), where this technique would allow the X-ray exposures necessary to take good pictures to be substantially reduced.

6 / Keith Oatley

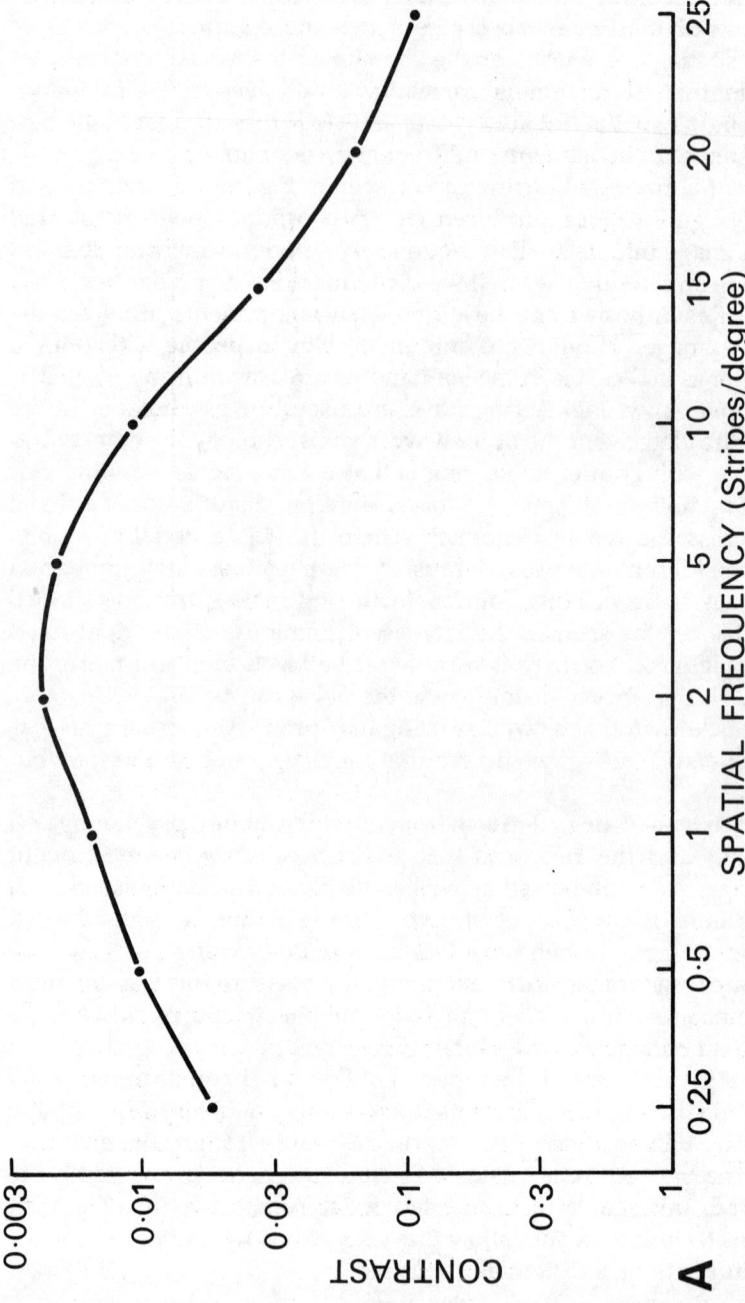

Figure 1. A: A frequency response curve showing attenuation of the higher frequencies from an individual observer's contrast settings for sinusoidal stripes of differing spatial frequency at threshold, where the stripes are only just visible. B: A flat frequency response from the same observer's settings for stripes of different spatial frequencies when matching them to the same contrast as a pattern above threshold that was 5 stripes per degree of visual angle (from Oatley, 1977, after Georgeson and Sullivan, 1975).

Experiments and Experience: Usefulness and Insight in Psychology / 7

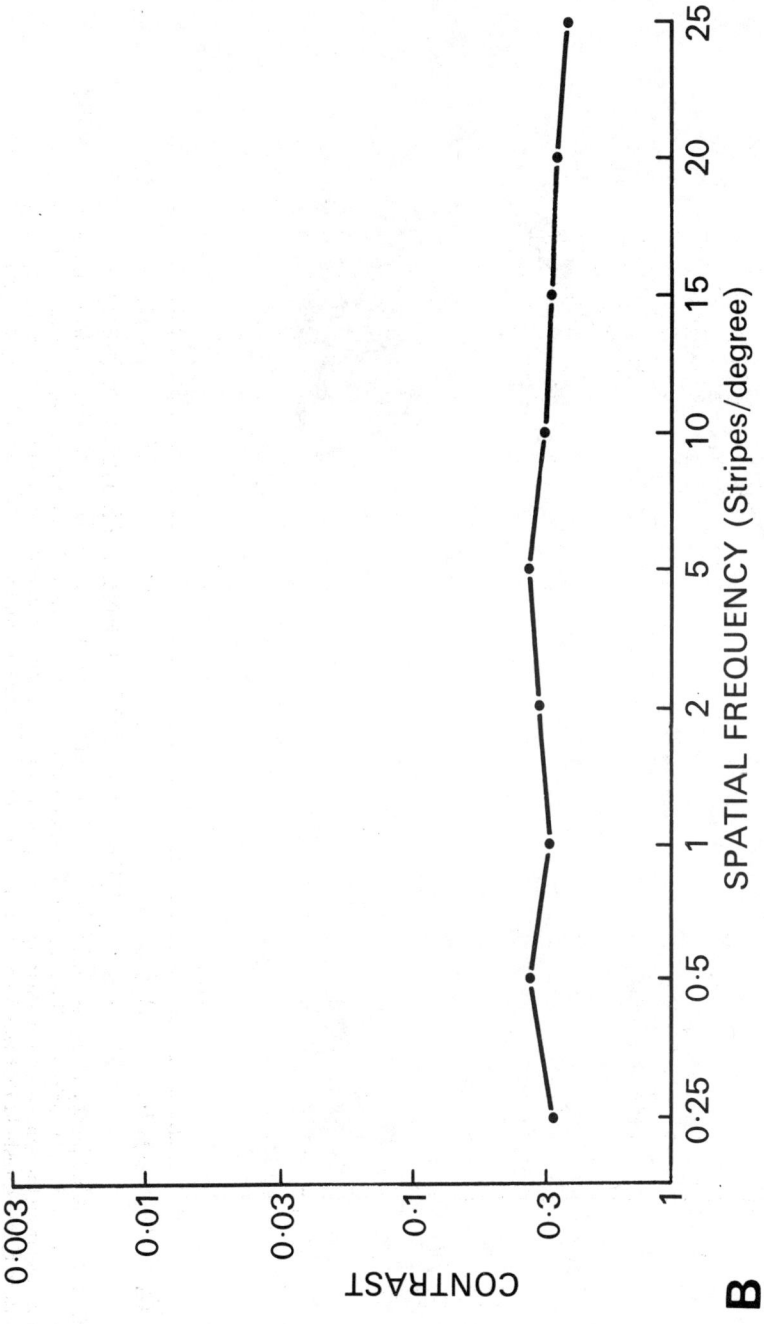

8 / Keith Oatley

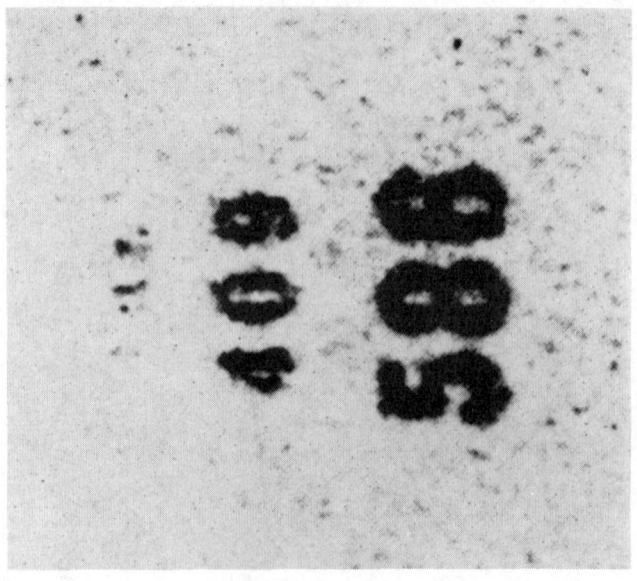

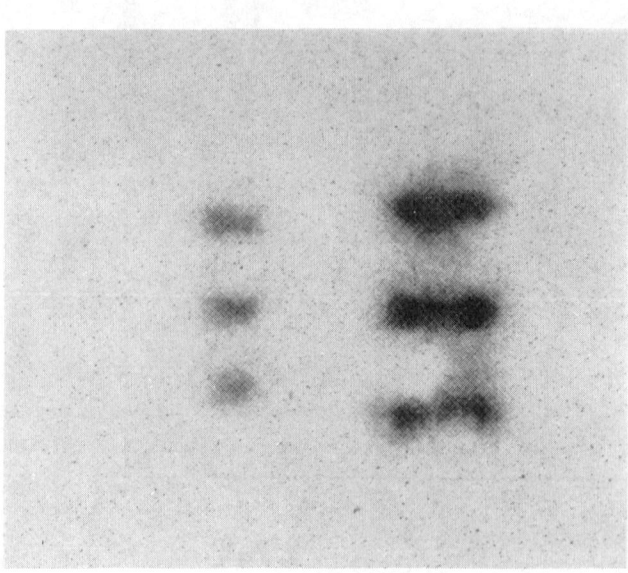

Figure 2. Fourier deblurring of a visual image: the right-hand image was produced from the blurred left-hand image by compensating computationally for the attenuation of higher spatial frequencies (from Gennery, 1973). Reproduced with permission of The Optical Society of America.

Politics and technology

The foregoing examples, along with many others, certainly show psychological research being useful. But while there is a movement towards practical applications of psychology, this usefulness is frequently hampered by more negative considerations.

The use of animals in research on psychiatric and psychosomatic problems often causes suffering to animals, which most people, including researchers, do not want. As Jeffrey Gray describes in his chapter in this volume, demands to abolish research that causes suffering to animals have become a political campaign. One way forward is to agree a system of weighing potential human advantages against the degree of animal suffering, as Bateson (1986) has suggested.

Similarly, engineering applications of information-processing and artificial intelligence can be used for purposes that are not beneficial, or politically agreeable, to everybody. They may, for instance, allow unwelcome types of surveillance, have unexpected military uses or increase unemployment. Again, there are campaigning groups, such as the British Society for Social Responsibility in Science, that seek to inform the public about negative implications that may not be obvious (see, for example, Shallice's, 1973, work on the uses of research on sensory deprivation in interrogation methods).

Political movements in which people seek to regulate research attest to the multiple considerations alive in a complex society. Uses of science and technology need to be assessed, so that we can decide by ordinary political processes what changes really are for 'the relief of man's estate'. In a pluralistic society, even something as apparently straightforward as usefulness can only be decided by debate within a community of interest groups. Both intended effects and unintended side-effects must be considered.

INSIGHT

Psychology as insight seems quite different. Often, practical application is secondary or remote. Yet we can find the more insightful psychological studies immensely fascinating and there is little doubt that they are important. But what is insight?

One of the best descriptions of insight, I think, is by George Eliot (1856).

> Appeals founded on generalizations and statistics require a sympathy ready-made, a moral sentiment already in activity; but a picture of human life such as a great artist can give, surprises even

the trivial and the selfish into that attention to what is apart from themselves, which may be called the raw material of moral sentiment . . . Art is the nearest thing to life; it is a mode of amplifying experience and extending our contact with our fellow-men beyond the bounds of our personal lot.

It is to artists like George Eliot herself that we turn for insights into our own and other's lives, motives and actions. She is arguing that insight has two aspects. One is the empathetic enlivening of our understanding of others, which in turn, of course, reflects back on our understanding of ourselves. This is not just the acquisition of new information, but the engagement of our sympathy, enabling matters other than our more selfish desires to become important to us. The other is the extension of our experience – in Piaget's terms (see Ginsberg and Opper, 1979), the assimilation of experience so that our schemata accommodate, not so much in the physical world but the interpersonal world.

Insight is a form of sight within ourselves or beneath the surface of things. It increases our understanding. Insight may bring to consciousness matters that we might know in some way but be unaware of. Perhaps these are matters which have implications that we did not know about. Perhaps they are things we have not thought of as significant before. Insight also means putting together previously disparate pieces of knowledge.

One difference, which is not always sharp, between technical knowledge and insight is that between learning something quite new and being able to think about familiar things in a new way.

Consider the following remark. 'The mechanical energy of a pea falling from a height of one inch, would, if transformed into luminous energy, be sufficient to give a faint impression of light to every man that ever lived' (Pirenne, 1948, p.78). This is certainly striking, and many people find it interesting. The work of Pirenne on the sensitivity of retinal receptors to just a few photons has been useful in the design of optical equipment and in defining the limits of visual sensitivity. But it is not insightful.

Contrast this with another remark about vision.

Our perception of the outside world is like an inner dream which is in harmony with things outside; and instead of saying that hallucination is false perception of the outside world, we should say that ordinary perception is hallucination that is true (Taine, 1870, tome 1, p.411, my translation).

Taine is arguing that our visual systems construct the visual scenes that we experience. We make these constructions without any retinal input in dreams and hallucinations. What happens when our eyes are open is that retinal data guide this visual constructive process. This idea is not informative in the same way that Pirenne's remark is, but it allows us to understand the world and our visual abilities in a new way. It expands our experience of seeing.

What kind of psychology is insightful? Again, I will give two examples – some observational studies of emotions in animals and children, and an experiment from social psychology.

The expression of emotions

From Charles Darwin's books of 1871 and 1872, in which he first started to write extensively about psychology, there grew an interest in the comparative psychology of animals and humans. Ethology, behaviourism and work on non-verbal communication are among the later offspring of this line (Boakes, 1984). Darwin's book of 1872 is the first scientific study of emotions, and it proposes that emotional expressions are not necessarily useful in accomplishing instrumental tasks. They exist because they have a history. Just as the appendix has been thought to be a vestige of dietary history unrelated to current human diets, so emotional expressions are vestiges of behavioural history.

Evolutionary history suggests that the emotional expression of sneering contempt, in which one lip is raised, is a vestige of animals drawing back a lip in preparation for a biting attack.

Drawing back the lip is no longer useful, since humans now rarely bite each other. On the basis of individual history Darwin argued that, in childhood, screaming was an important means of summoning help from a parent. It required forced evacuation of air from the lungs. This in turn required a compression of the chest, which produced a higher than usual pressure of blood so that delicate tissues such as the retinae had to be protected. They were so protected in screaming and crying, continued Darwin, supplementing his account with photographs, by tightly contracting various muscles round the eyes. Such contractions become habitual and stamped into the nervous system. In adulthood when we are sad we still make facial expressions that are vestiges from infancy. Early influences extend elsewhere, he suggests, so that the bodily contact which we experience as really rather adult in sexual caresses, is itself probably derived from infant habits of touching and clasping our mother. 'Hence we long to clasp in our arms those whom we tenderly love. We probably owe this desire to inherited habit, in association with the nursing and tending of our children' (Darwin, 1872, p.213).

Darwin suggests in such passages some pieces of pure insight. It is scarcely useful to imagine that emotional expressions derive from an animal or infant past, but it does extend our understanding, making links to matters which we might observe, and allowing us to experience the continuity of our adult lives with an evolutionary and infantile ancestry from which we are not emancipated. It has the effect of rocking us a little in our imagination that all adult life is voluntary and rational.

In a study of human ethology, Judy Dunn and Carol Kendrick (1982) have extended these kinds of observation, and studied the childhood origins of love and envy. Here is a piece from one of their transcripts.

> Baby is pulling papers and magazines out of bookcase. Mother to Baby: 'No! Stop!' Elder brother (aged about three) immediately runs over, starts pulling out papers too, looking at Mother. Mother to elder child: 'No Duncan, there's no need for you! You know better – or don't you?' Duncan: 'No!' (p.168)

To gain an insight into this we must do something quite unlike an experiment, we must put ourselves in the position of Duncan, and ask ourselves why we might do this if we were in his position. If we do, we may make a link that Darwin wrote about, seeing a continuity of our own emotions with the actions of childhood. In so far as we can identify with Duncan we might see how important it is to gain the attention of a loved person.

Dunn and Kendrick describe several interactions in which a child tries to gain a mother's attention, or to join in an interaction, when feeling left out. Are such scenes capable of extending our understanding in the same way as the pictures that George Eliot argues that an artist can draw? Yes, I think so. It occurs to me that perhaps Duncan was at a loss, at a loose end, perhaps feeling envious of the kind of care his new sibling had been getting. Could he know he felt envious? Probably not: the baby's action just prompted his action. But as an adult it makes me wonder if not just expressions of emotion, but feelings of envy too derive from such childhood actions. Does envy have to do with wanting to imitate others when there seems something unsatisfactory in what I am doing myself, while simultaneously allowing me to be destructive because I am feeling angry?

Helping people in distress

Here is another example, this time from social psychology. In 1973 John Darley and Daniel Batson published an experiment on helping strangers. The subjects were trainee Christian ministers. They were asked individually to prepare a brief talk which was to be recorded. They were assigned randomly and without their knowledge, as is usual in psychology experiments, to one of two conditions: in one the subject was asked to talk on 'The good Samaritan', a bible story about a traveller who stops to take care of a man who has been beaten and robbed; in the other the subject had to talk on 'Vocational roles for ministers'. There was then another division, again without subjects' knowledge, into three further categories. Subjects in a 'low hurry' condition were asked to walk across to another building for the recording session and told that they had plenty of time. In an intermediate condition subjects were told to go right over. In the 'high hurry' condition subjects were told they were late, that the assistant was waiting and that they should hurry. As each subject walked down an alley to the other building he passed a young man lying in a doorway coughing and groaning, though not actually saying 'I have fallen among thieves'. This was, of course, an accomplice of the experimenters.

The results were that of the subjects in the low hurry condition 63 per cent offered help, of those in the intermediate condition 45 per cent offered help, but only 10 per cent of those in the high hurry condition did so: these differences were statistically significant. Those preparing a talk on 'The good Samaritan' were not much more likely to stop than the others, this difference not being statistically significant.

Though in the form of an experiment, it is not clear that this study is useful. It affords an insight into helpfulness in public places, however. For most of us, the decision to help a stranger lying on the ground causes a conflict in us. The costs of helping are unpredictable and may be great. We might ourselves be mugged, or get involved in some wretched scene, perhaps with someone drunk. Being in a hurry makes helping less likely. But a precept did not have much effect: being reminded of the parable did not substantially increase people's likelihood of helping. Helping others is in theory something we would like to do, but having an appointment is often in practice more pressing.

EXPERIMENTS AND RELIABLE KNOWLEDGE

Making a coarse distinction we might think that properly conducted experiments create reliable knowledge, while observational studies that are insightful might provide us with stimulating ideas but only unreliably. We might also think that since we cannot control most psychological variables in people, the best work on important issues like stress will be on animals, as in Petrova's cancer experiments. Proper experimental research on humans can be done in areas like psychophysics, as in the work on spatial frequency perception. But experiments are not really appropriate to social psychology: those like Darley and Batson's show ingenuity, but may seem more like practical jokes than serious science.

These are common opinions within psychology, and are responsible for the way in which experimental psychology on animals and individual human behaviour is thought to provide reliable and cumulative knowledge comparable, say, to biochemistry. They are also responsible for the lower status in the academic world of psychology that is not experimental.

Though these opinions have some substance, they may be quite misleading, particularly if we remember that psychology is not just technical: not just behavioural engineering, ergonomics and human factors research. We expect psychology to be insightful.

There seems to be a trade-off between certainty and insight. Results of experimental manipulation and technological application properly carried out are universally convincing. But matters that convey insight are not; and they are seldom susceptible to experimentation or technical solutions.

Helmholtz (1866) raised the question of reliability in discussing why visual perception should seem so certain. He said it is because it is like doing an experiment. So, if trying to find out why mercury expands and contracts, we do not passively watch mercury in a tube, correlating its expansion with changes in temperature, barometric pressure, humidity or other variables. Instead we experiment, and choose just when and where to apply a particular influence. This choice allows us to convince ourselves that a specific operation, like applying heat, is a sufficient cause for the mercury to expand. Vision is convincing for the same reason, he continues. We are not passive recipients of visual impressions. If we were, we would never have been able to decipher them. This is shown by the research of Held and Hein (1963), influenced by Helmholtz's ideas, in which kittens reared with only passive vision, and unable to act, become functionally blind. Helmholtz argued that we notice that we get a particular image of a table by moving actively into a particular position. We can make it disappear by shutting our eyes, and make it reappear at will by turning our eyes towards it again. Doing this we gain something like an experimental conviction that the different views of the table are due to our movements.

Experimental method is closely linked to technology. Not only can we perform an experiment which produces knowledge, but we can put the principles to work to make other products which might be useful. We could make a switch with a tube of mercury and use it to operate a relay to control the temperature of a heating system. Where causes are approximately independent of each other, and where a whole process can be decomposed into parts, science and technology are related. In one, operations are applied as questions to extract understanding by analysis. The other runs the operation in the reverse direction, synthetically. It puts together well-understood causal principles to make a useful mechanism. The conjunction of these two operations, scientific and technical, allows us to converge on understandings that are, for practical purposes, certain. A scientific understanding is very often a technical one. Conversely, where we do not have a technical grasp, we often do not have a good scientific one, either.

Although there are non-experimental sciences like geology and astronomy, psychologists have been persuaded that nothing comes quite as close to certainty as the experiment.

Psychology has hoped to succeed by becoming an experimental science, and aspects of it have succeeded in this way, notably those in which Helmholtz did some of the groundwork. For example, we do understand scientifically a lot about colour vision, and this knowledge is put to use in three-colour printing, colour photography and colour television. We also understand some of the applications of Fourier analysis discussed earlier, these, too, being based on Helmholtz's ideas about the function of special sense organs laying out stimulation of different qualities in spatially distributed arrays.

So scientific psychology should be useful. The argument has two parts. One is that experimental psychology with no practical application is insecurely based, and subject to fashions. The other is that we should think about practical purposes in the very process of approaching scientific understanding. Helmholtz put the argument bluntly, saying that this practical sense of understanding is the only sense of truth worth having, of being able confidently to act towards an object in question. This is the only 'escape from the labyrinth of opinions' (Helmholtz, 1866, p.19).

I argue here that Helmholtz is right when we are thinking about mechanisms, but that the idea is incomplete, because it does not take account of psychology as insight. In understanding emotions, for instance, we do not primarily want our understanding to be useful. We want insights. We want to see something about ourselves and others in a way that we had not before and for it to be enlivening, as George Eliot suggested.

VERSTEHEN AND THE EXTENSION OF EXPERIENCE

English-speaking psychologists have been strongly influenced by natural scientific approaches, hence the casting even of social psychological observations and ideas into experimental form, as in the study by Darley and Batson (1973). In Europe, particularly in Germany, however, philosophers have struggled with the question of whether there is anything distinctive about the methods and approach to truth in social and human sciences.

One distinctive attribute of human science, clearly different from anything in natural science and technology, was expounded by Dilthey in the latter part of the last century (see, for example, Dilthey, 1926). It is usually referred to as *Verstehen*, meaning 'understanding', and in this context 'interpretive understanding'. In Dilthey's work it is the imaginative entering into a human event or expression so that we can rethink it or re-experience it ourselves. When we read the incident of Duncan and his baby brother from Dunn and Kendrick (1982), we take the actions of Duncan and his mother as expressions of their life together. We cannot understand them simply as parts of causal sequences (though causal sequences are also at issue). Rather, by empathetically entering into that scene we glimpse what it was like to be Duncan, and his reasons for acting at that time. We could not glimpse what it was like to be a retinal receptor or anything else that was purely mechanism.

Verstehen has become an important idea in social science, especially as developed by Weber (for example, Weber, 1922): what makes human action meaningful is that it is intended, more or less consciously. It is this which sets it apart from mechanical causes, and it is this that requires *Verstehen*. The idea is also implicit in Freud's (for example, Freud, 1912) account of transference in which the analyst uses her or his intuition to understand some of the patient's unspoken thoughts and intentions, especially those that concern the relationship that is developing in therapy. The core of this idea of empathetic understanding was stated by George Eliot in the quotation given earlier, though she did not mention there the important idea that it is actors' intentions that really set human science off from natural science.

In terms of cognitive psychology, we would say that it would be impossible to understand what was going on between Duncan and his mother if we did not have some kind of schema (Bartlett, 1932), which allows us to make inferences about motives that are not directly given in the vignette itself. This schema must itself be based on our own experience of being a child, a parent or a sibling.

Humphrey (1979) has argued that the function of consciousness is to use ourselves and our experience as a model to understand others, to see what it would be like to be in their position. Introspection has evolved as a cognitive means of doing this, as a basis for interpersonal understanding. Humphrey argues that if we knew only the rules of behaviour formulated from the outside, as in behaviourist studies, we would not be able to undertake the simplest human interaction. We would have not the faintest idea what was going on between Duncan and his mother, nor between any other people. Dunn and Kendrick

(1982, p. 211) give an apt quotation from Chekhov, 'People eat their dinner, just eat their dinner, and all the time their happiness is being established or their lives are being broken up.' A Martian without human sympathies or experience of human intentions would only see food ingestion behaviour.

This kind of understanding is close to what we mean by insight, a glimpse of intentions and meanings inside ourselves or others. *Verstehen* is an empathetic understanding of others' lives, used as a distinctive method of study in the social and human sciences.

THE DIFFICULTIES

It is not always stressed that the difficulties with *both* natural science *and* social science in psychology are immense. Neither natural science alone, with its technical applications, nor social science alone, with its interpreted intentions and meanings, seems quite appropriate to the subject matter of psychology.

The reasons are not far to see. Natural science has elaborated procedures to allow our minds to be changed, and hence for our theories to improve when the world does not conform to what we expect. Special instruments, experiments, statistics and so forth become the means for allowing our expectations to be contradicted. Hence Popper's (1963) idea of the importance of refutation in making science reliable. Although the process of improving our theories occurs not quite in the way that Popper supposes, science is a procedure for learning from mistakes. By mistakes we approach more closely to reliability and certainty. This makes it reasonable for people to labour intensively on an experiment, and then export the knowledge to other people, and from a laboratory to a practical application.

There are, however, three crushing disadvantages with natural scientific methods in psychology.

First, being able to measure something or assess reliably whether it has a causal influence is no indication of its importance. The demonstration that an effect is statistically significant does not mean that it is the main influence on what is being measured. Nor does it imply that the data are important. The psychology journals overflow with experimental results, gathered with great care, that are of no interest except to other researchers wanting to publish papers on the same phenomenon. Natural scientific methods help us keep an eye on the facts, but do not help us know whether they are the right facts.

Second, though science is designed to generalize, and to export its results, a laboratory demonstration alone carries no guarantee that an effect will be exportable outside a laboratory. This requires the often even more difficult work of applying the knowledge practically. The difficulty is particularly clear when there is a wish to generalize from animal experiments to human issues. But the problem arises elsewhere, too. British commentators on science are fond of talking about how ideas conceived in Britain are only developed elsewhere, perhaps in the USA or, nowadays, in Japan. Penicillin is a good example. But they forget that an idea is only one step on a long road towards a useful application. If we take Helmholtz more seriously than he perhaps intended, we could say that the way out of the labyrinth of opinion is only gained when we can apply scientific ideas practically.

Third, the methods of natural science are good at uncovering causal chains which operate either one at a time or independently of context, but they are not tuned to discovering influences that are multiple or sensitive to contexts. So, if some human behaviour is affected by genetics, by effects of relationships we have had with people we have loved or admired, by multiple intentions and by idiosyncracies of the meanings that we find in situations, then natural scientific methods are not necessarily the right tools, or at least not the only ones. They are worse where behaviour is overdetermined; if, for instance, a neurotic pattern is not sustained by one process but several alternatives.

Equally, the methods of *Verstehen* in social and human science are subject to disadvantages which many psychologists think are even more disastrous.

First, there is no way of telling whether a particular piece of understanding gained by entering imaginatively into a human event is correct or not. It may be enlivening. We may even get a strong feeling of insight, but its reliability is low, and hence it is not universally convincing. Even from people whom we may greatly respect there is the possibility of false insights. Was Darwin really right when he said that the bodily contact of adult sexual love has bases in infant clasping and cuddling? That is the sort of thing which from the lips of Freud sounds suspect to people who admire Darwin. The possibility of mistaken interpretations is inevitable, and made worse by narrow or biased ranges of sampling, though Darwin and Freud were careful to avoid this in their different ways. Though schemata may accommodate when we achieve a piece of interpretive understanding, there is often not much which will warn of mistakes or inappropriate assimilations.

Second, whereas with proper technical development natural scientific understandings are exportable to other people and other settings, an insight may be confined to the people it concerns. An insight in psychotherapy, for instance, is not easily transmitted to someone else. Even systematic attempts to convey experience, as in history or novels, are chancy. It is at this point that George Eliot was forced to say, rather lamely one may think, that it is only 'great' artists who can manage this.

It is as if natural science and insight stand at opposite poles, with psychology somehow in between. Difficulties for psychology arise at both poles. When straining after the certainties of natural science, but without any real practical purpose, psychology becomes tedious jargon with a strong sense of pointlessness. When questing for insights into what people are really up to, but without the thoughtfulness or touch of an artist, psychology can become implausibly fanciful.

It may be too much to ask for a synthesis of these two modes of enquiry, but the health of psychology depends on it. For too long have we had warring camps, with experimentalists sneering at social and clinical psychologists for the hopelessness of their problems of reliability, and the others sneering back at experimentalists' apparent penchant for triviality so long as it can measured.

In order not to seem merely exhortatory, I will discuss some recent studies of depression to illustrate a more-than-usually fruitful use of different methods in which a synthesis has been achieved; well, almost . . .

THE PSYCHOLOGY OF DEPRESSION

Two empirical approaches have dominated psychological understanding of depression in recent years. One is the work of Seligman and his collaborators. This started with experiments showing that dogs that had experienced inescapable electric shock were unable to learn a new task to avoid shock. These animals, and others in various painful situations of the kind that animal welfare campaigners have objected to, suffered from what Seligman (1975) called 'learned helplessness'. The other approach derives from Brown and Harris's (1978) investigation of life events and difficulties in people's ordinary lives. (Both approaches are attempts to understand so-called 'reactive' depression, not the much rarer 'endogenous' depression in which there is no relation to life circumstances, and which may be more physiologically based.)

Learned helplessness

Helplessness theory is unusual among psychological theories in jumping the gap from the laboratory to the outside world. It has made contact with our intuitions about what it is like to be depressed. To be succesful, animal models need this kind of support, a human *Verstehen* comparable to Pavlov's idea of 'experimental neurosis' and Darwin's idea of humans as continuous with the animals. When this is confirmed by other methods, all is well. If not, one is in danger of what is unkindly called 'anthropomorphizing'.

Though intuitively appealing, the early helplessness theory of depression was only partly successful in generalizing outside the laboratory. The theory was therefore reformulated by Abramson, Seligman and Teasdale (1978), adding to the animal-based idea of helplessness some principles from attribution theory. We become helpless following a failure if we make so-called internal, global and stable attributions: the reason for failure is oneself and not something else (internal); it applies not just to this event but to all others (global); and will apply in the future, not just at this time (stable).

The current popularity of cognitive psychology contributes to the success of this idea. So does its similarity to Beck's theory of depression as a state of hopelessnes (Beck et al., 1979), with its links to the practical application of cognitive therapy for depression (see, for example, Blackburn, 1984).

The core of the idea is that depression is a distortion of normal thought. Just as dogs become helpless when, really, they could escape, so people make things worse than they are. Internal, stable and global attributions systematically distort their interpretations of their failure. Cognitive therapy might then work by helping the depressed person to overcome these cognitive errors.

According to this hypothesis, failures are liable to cause a dejected mood. Attributing a failure globally and stably to oneself makes one vulnerable to escalating this mood change into depression. But much of the evidence for the helplessness hypothesis has been from reactions to failure in laboratory tasks set by experimenters, such as failing to solve impossible anagrams. More recently, doing less well than expected in mid-term college exams has been studied (Metalsky et al., 1982; see also Peterson and Seligman, 1984, for the most recent review of the work of this group). Such events, however, although upsetting, are not severe in the spectrum of human experience. While failures at laboratory tasks and mid-term exams can result in dejected mood, as shown by adjective checklists, they have not been shown to result in clinically significant depression.

Severe life events

Brown and Harris's evidence is of a different kind. Coming from outside the laboratory, they found that severely threatening life events and difficulties, not distortions thinking about milder events, provoke most episodes of clinically significant depression in ordinary people.

So, does either of these approaches explain depression? Or are they each wandering in the labyrinth of opinion?

Brown and Harris found that only events rated as severe were capable of provoking depression. Of 458 randomly selected women voters in Camberwell, London, eight per cent had become clinically depressed in the year before interview. (Data from a further nine per cent of women in the sample who had been clinically depressed for more than a year were not analysed, because the study was of what causes onset of depression.) Clinical depression was diagnosed using a carefully standardized measure and was defined as equivalent to the pattern typically seen in psychiatric out-patients clinics, the so-called 'case level' at which the person has suffered a breakdown and can no longer cope. Of the women who had recent onsets of depression at the case level, 89 per cent had suffered at least one severe event or major difficulty before her breakdown. Only 30 per cent of women who were not depressed had suffered such a severe event or difficulty.

Severe events included bereavement, a child getting into trouble with the police, the family's only breadwinner becoming involuntarily unemployed with no prospect of a future job, the break-up of an established love relationship or marriage and the like. These events were, therefore, severe in ordinary human terms. Severe events had occurred 3.7 times more frequently in depressed than in non-depressed women, whereas for non-severe events there was an approximately equal rate in depressed and non-depressed women. It is, therefore, only severe events that increase the risk of clinical depression at the case level as it actually occurs in the community. Non-severe events, though upsetting, were not associated with increased risk of clinically significant depression at all.

Seligman had found measurable effects on mood that were statistically significant in laboratories and other restricted settings. The work of Brown and Harris raised the question of whether statistical significance in the laboratory had clinical significance outside the laboratory. Though one has little doubt that the animal and human analogue experiments were reliable, there remained a doubt about whether they were valid models of clinical depression.

One of the most creative aspects of Brown and Harris's research was in the *Verstehen* procedure they used to judge the severity of events. Interviewers asked the women whether each of an extensive list of threatening events had occurred to them in the year before the interview, and then collected more detailed information about each event that had happened. The interviewer later described each event to the research team.

The interviewer might say to the research team something like: 'Mrs

Windsor lives in a one-bedroom basement flat with her husband and three small children. Three months before the interview her husband was made redundant, and has not been able to find work . . . ' The interviewer then goes on to give more detail – exactly what happened, whether there was any warning of the event, who was there, what the consequences were and so forth. Importantly, the research team listening to the account of the event make their judgments in a manner that is unbiased, because they do not know whether the woman was depressed or not, nor what her own reaction to it was. The team use their intuitions of what it is like in our society for that event to occur. Helped by a set of rules they make a consensus rating on a four-point scale of how threatening that event would be to the average woman living in those circumstances. The ratings of the research team, made purely on the basis of the context of the event, are called 'contextual threat' ratings.

Contextual threat ratings in the study were very close to the woman's own account of how severely she judged the events. The implication is that the women thought about the events in much the same way as unbiased researchers who had not themselves suffered them. Though cognitive distortions may make mood worse after less severe setbacks, there was no evidence that systematic cognitive distortions cause clinical depressions.

Even with a severe event or major difficulty as a provoking agent, most people do not get depressed. Brown and Harris found that only a fifth of the women suffering one of these became depressed at the case level. To account for why all the women experiencing a provoking agent did not become depressed they postulated four vulnerability factors. The most important was lack of an intimate, supportive relationship. When both severe events and vulnerability factors were taken into account, Brown and Harris could explain a high proportion of the breakdowns that occurred. Contextual threat and vulnerability factors have been more successful in explaining the incidence of depression in our society than any other approach so far.

An interaction effect, in the statistical sense of the rate of depression being higher in the combined presence of a provoking agent and lack of social support than with the sum of effects of provoking agent and lack of social support acting alone, has now been demonstrated in nine of the 10 studies with adequate methodology so far published. These studies determined that events were severe, and did not just use the sum of several less severe events, as occurs with life event checklists like Holmes and Rahe's (1967). Oatley and Bolton (1985) give a full review of this work. A number of these studies have also found that low social support can increase risk of depression independently of life events.

In addition, an interaction effect has been found in a prospective study (Bolton and Oatley, 1986). We studied effects of a single type of severe event by following up for eight months a group of men who had recently become unemployed, and comparing them with a matched comparison group of employed men. We found that there was a significant statistical interaction: men who became clinically depressed were those who became and stayed unemployed, *and* had significantly less social contact with family and friends outside work. Low social contact had no effect on the employed men. It was as if the unemployed men who became depressed had located their sense of themselves in work. The unemployed men who did not become depressed had more contact with family and friends outside working hours.

We postulated (Oatley and Bolton, 1985) that vulnerability is not cognitive distortion, but lack of alternatives for experiencing oneself as worthwhile. While they were employed, none of the men in our study had psychiatric symptoms at clinically significant levels. Lack of social interaction outside working hours made some of them vulnerable, but this vulnerability had its effect only when they became unemployed. It is likely that underlying the small amount of social contact these men had outside their work was a disposition to rely on external structure to provide social interaction for them. While it did so, they were well, but when it was lost, they became depressed.

Instrumental failure or social loss

As well as the issue of severity, the two kinds of approach implicate different kinds of event in depression. In the work on helplessness, failures in an instrumental skill are thought to provoke depression. In work on life events, social losses are thought to be the provoking agents; such losses, in which someone important leaves the scene, have been called 'exit events' (Paykel et al, 1969). Whereas instrumental failures may explain how one might lose a sense of competence, the power of exit events to provoke depression implies the primary importance of relationships.

In theorizing about depression, social psychological issues have often been treated in terms of general instrumental learning principles. But if the evidence is that social losses are the main reasons for depression, this may be a mistake.

Working at a job could be considered instrumental. But employment is also social, as Jahoda (1982) points out. Work enlarges possibilities of social interaction in areas outside the family, it confers collective purpose, together with status and identity. It also structures one's time and requires regular activity. So when a job is lost, it is not only an instrumental failure, and not just an economic matter, important though these considerations are.

The causes of depression are better understood than ever before. The debate between helplessness theory and the social loss theory has been joined. Both have managed to be good psychology in the sense that I have been suggesting. They aim at both insight and usefulness and achieve some of each.

Seligman's group has shown that animal models are productive metaphors for research on depression. The theory was sufficiently clearly formulated to make mistakes, and hence be improved. Some of the theory's mistakes arose from its being insensitive to the epidemiological data on depression. Animal models on their own are not enough. They need to be related to human evidence. The helplessness idea has been taken up, for instance, in investigating why depression is twice as common among women as among men in our society. Dweck et al. (1980) have proposed that this might be due to bias in the kinds of feedback given to girls and boys at school, so that women come to expect less success in instrumental activities.

On the other side, Brown and Harris have shown how *Verstehen* is not just a source of hypotheses to be tested more rigorously in other ways. It can be made reliable. Indeed, it has turned out to be both reliable and to have produced the most convincing psychological hypotheses on the aetiology of depression we have.

In both Seligman's and Brown and Harris's formulations there are practical implications for both prevention and therapy. Brown and Harris's findings have already begun to affect general practitioners in Britain in their approach to the alarmingly common symptoms of depression. Perhaps the most significant practical implication is the recognition of the importance of social support in sustaining mental health. Paradoxically, although technical steps can be taken to improve bad housing, high unemployment and so forth, the creation of a society in which people have adequate social support is not a straightforwardly technical matter.

Having two theories that are different but which cover similar ground is a matter of importance. It opens a properly critical debate, and in the end it is only by publically discussing the evidence that we approach truth. Popper (1963) insisted that mistakes in science are important. But perhaps the biggest obstacle in approaching truth is that when we adopt a theory it becomes too easy for a single individual or a single research group to see the evidence only in the terms of that theory. Indeed to see a new piece of the world through a theory is one of the marks of an insight! We might remember Taine's remark about perception as a kind of hallucination. Popper is not convincing in his suggestion that we should give up a theory whenever there is a mistake. When there is only one theory it is not easy to see mistakes! We tend to hallucinate our theories onto evidence, which then becomes merely data to assimilate. We see mistakes best when there are alternatives, and usually only give up a theory when we find a better one.

In both natural and social science being able to generate alternative theories across a range of the same data is, therefore, of the essence. It allows us to give up less good theories for better ones. Generating alternative theories requires several people: individually we seem better at holding just one theory at a time. Science is successful because it is a social activity, not an individual one.

The vitality of psychology is due in part to its wide variety of methods and also to its subject matter, which is of both immense practical importance and perennial interest for its insights. It is a mere waste of resources for this diversity to be dissipated in scornfully dismissive attitudes between groups of psychologists. In the area of depression, with at least two plausible theories approaching from different directions, the diversity has been converted into a substantial forward movement.

ACKNOWLEDGEMENTS

I thank Geoff Sullivan, Mark Georgeson and Winifred Bolton for their contributions to research described here, and the SERC and MRC for supporting it.

REFERENCES

Abramson L.Y., Seligman, M.E.P and Teasdale, J.D. (1978) Learned helplessness in humans: Critique and reformulation. *Journal of Abnormal Psychology*, 87, 49–74.

Ader, R. (1981) *Psychoneuroimmunology*. London: Academic Press.

Bacon, F. (1605) *The Advancement of Learning*. Edited by A. Johnson (1974). Oxford: Oxford University Press.

Baker, K. and Sullivan, G.D. (1980) Multiple bandpass filters in image processing. *Institute of Electrical Engineers, Proceedings*, 127, part E, no 5. 173–184.

Bartlett, F.C. (1932) *Remembering: A Study in Experimental and Social Psychology*. Cambridge: Cambridge University Press.

Bateson, P. (1986) When to do experiments on animals. *New Scientist*, 20 February, 30–32.

Beck, A.T., Rush, A.J., Shaw, B.F. and Emery, G. (1979) *Cognitive Therapy of Depression*. Chichester: Wiley.

Blackburn, I.M. (1984) Cognitive approaches to clinical psychology. In J. Nicholson and H. Beloff (eds) *Psychology Survey 5*, 290–319.

Boakes, R.A. (1984) *From Darwin to Behaviourism: Psychology and the Minds of Animals*. Cambridge: Cambridge University Press.

Bolton, W. and Oatley, K. (1986) A longitudinal study of social support and depression in unemployed men. *Psychological Medicine* (in press).

Brown, G.W. and Harris, T. (1978) *Social Origins of Depression*. London: Tavistock.

Campbell, F.W. and Robson, J.G. (1968) Application of Fourier analysis to the visibility of gratings. *Journal of Physiology*, 197, 551–566.

Darley, J.M. and Batson, C.D. (1973) 'From Jerusalem to Jericho': A study of situational and dispositional variables in helping behavior. *Journal of Personality and Social Psychology*, 27, 100–108.

Darwin, C. (1871) *The Descent of Man and Selection in Relation to Sex*. London: Murray.

Darwin, C. (1872) *The Expression of the Emotions in Man and Animals*. London: Murray.

Dilthey, W. (1926) The understanding of other persons and their life-expressions. In K. Mueller-Vollmer (ed.) (1985) *The hermeneutics reader*. Oxford: Basil Blackwell.

Dunn, J. and Kendrick, C. (1982) *Siblings: Love, Envy and Understanding*. London: Grant McIntyre.

Dweck, C.S., Goetz, T.E. and Strauss, N.L. (1980) Sex differences in learned helplessness IV: An experimental and naturalistic study of failure generalization and its mediators. *Journal of Personality and Social Psychology*, 38, 441–452.

Eliot, G. (1856) The natural history of German life. In T. Pinney (ed.) (1963) *Essays of George Eliot*. New York: Columbia University Press.

Freud, S. (1912) Recommendations for physicians on the psychoanalytic method of treatment. *Standard Edition of the Complete Psychological Works of Sigmund Freud, Vol. 12*. J. Strachey (ed.) London: Hogarth Press.

Gennery, D.B. (1973) Determination of optical transfer function by inspection of frequency domain plot. *Journal of the Optical Society of America*, 63, 1571–1577.

Georgeson M.A. and Sullivan, G.D. (1975) Contrast constancy: Deblurring in human vision by spatial frequency channels. *Journal of Physiology*, 252, 627–656.

Ginsberg, H. and Opper, S. (1979) *Piaget's Theory of Intellectual Development*, 2nd ed. Englewood Cliffs, N.J.: Prentice-Hall.

Held. R. and Hein, A. (1963) Movement-produced stimulation in the development of visually guided behaviour. *Journal of Comparative and Physiological Psychology*, 56, 872–876.

Helmholtz, H. (1866) *Treatise on Physiological Optics, Vol. III*. Edited by J.P.C. Southall (1962) New York: Dover

Holmes, T.H. and Rahe, R.H. (1967) The Social Readjustment Rating Scale. *Journal of Psychosomatic Research*, 11, 213–218.

Humphrey, N.K. (1979) Nature's psychologists. In B. Josephson and V.S. Ramachandran (eds) *Consciousness and the Physical World*. Oxford: Pergamon Press.

Jahoda, M. (1982) *Employment and Unemployment: A Social-Psychological Analysis*. Cambridge: Cambridge University Press.

Keehn, J.D. (1986) *Animal Models for Psychiatry*. London: Routledge and Kegan Paul.

Metalsky, G.I., Abramson, L.Y., Seligman, M.E.P., Semme, I.A. and Peterson, C. (1982) Attributional styles and life events in the classroom: Vulnerability and invulnerability to depressive mood reactions. *Journal of Personality and Social Psychology, 43,* 612–617.

Oatley, K. (1976) Why isn't the world more fuzzy than it is? *New Scientist,* 12 August, 338–339.

Oatley, K. (1977) How the brain overcomes the eye's defects. *Spectrum: British Science News, no 152,* 2–4.

Oatley, K. and Bolton, W. (1985) A social-cognitive theory of depression in reaction to life events. *Psychological Review, 92,* 372–388.

Paykel, E.S., Myers, J.K., Dienelt, M.N., Klerman, G.L., Lindenthal, J.J. and Pepper, M.P. (1969) Life events and depression: A controlled study: *Archives of General Psychiatry, 22,* 753–760.

Pavlov, I. (1927) *Conditioned Reflexes.* Edited and Translated by G.D. Anrep. Oxford: Oxford University Press.

Peterson, C. and Seligman, M.E.P. (1984) Causal explanations as a risk factor for depression: Theory and evidence. *Psychological Review, 91,* 347–374.

Pirenne, M.H. (1948) *Vision and the Eye.* London: Chapman and Hall.

Popper, K.R. (1963) *Conjectures and refutations: The Growth of Scientific Knowledge.* London: Routledge and Kegan Paul.

Seligman, M.E.P. (1975). *Helplessness: On Depression. Development and Death.* San Francisco: Freeman.

Shallice, T. (1973) The Ulster depth interrogation techniques and sensory deprivation research. *Cognition, 1,* 385–405.

Sullivan, G.D., Georgeson, M.A. and Oatley, K. (1972) Channels for spatial frequency selection and the detection of single bars by the human visual system. *Vision Research, 12,* 383–394.

Taine, H. (1870) *De l'Intelligence.* Paris: Hachette.

Weber, M. (1922) *Economy and Society: An Outline of Interpretive Sociology.* Edited by G. Roth and C. Wittich (1968) Berkeley: University of California Press.

FACE RECOGNITION
Andrew W. Young

Most of us can recognize the faces of people we know with ease. The ability seems so effortless that few of us stop to wonder how face recognition is achieved. Yet it can go spectacularly wrong, as the victims of cases of mistaken identity know only too well.

Face recognition can also go wrong under more ordinary circumstances. Most people can recall incidents in which they addressed a complete stranger because they had mistaken her or his face for that of someone they knew. In such incidents an unfamiliar face is mistakenly thought to be that of a familiar person.

The opposite type of error can also occur, in which a familiar face is mistakenly thought to be unfamiliar. Ellis (in press) mentions that the English clergyman, folksong collector and writer Sabine Baring-Gould, who wrote the words to *Onward, Christian Soldiers*, once lifted up a child and asked 'And whose little girl are you, my dear?' She replied, sobbing, 'I'm yours Daddy.'

I pinched this example from Ellis (in press) because it illustrates so neatly how much we take for granted our ability to recognize faces. We seldom think that we might know someone we have not recognized. Yet our ability to recognize faces is truly remarkable. As Galton (1883) observed, faces form a relatively homogeneous class of visual stimuli, with most having more or less oval shape, two eyes, nose, mouth, hair, ears and chin. Despite these underlying similarities most of us can recognize hundreds, and perhaps thousands, of familiar faces. Often these faces can be remarkably alike, yet it is usually only gifted observers like Courtauld (1982) who notice the resemblance. To the rest of us, the people we know don't seem to look much like each other (Ellis, Young and Hay, in press), though we will often notice that an unfamiliar person resembles a person we already know.

In addition to its instrinsic interest, an understanding of face recognition is also of some practical importance. The most obvious application of knowledge about face recognition is to forensic purposes; knowing when and how to rely on identification evidence, and evaluating face reconstruction techniques such as Photofit (Shepherd, Ellis and Davies, 1981; Davies, 1983). Other applications, however, include the development of automated recognition systems for security purposes, and understanding and rehabilitating the effects of brain injuries (Ellis, in press).

There have been many studies of how face recognition is achieved by normal people, and of the ways in which it can become disordered as a consequence of brain injury. Any review has to be highly selective. In this chapter I examine some of the studies that have helped us to understand what factors make faces special, the nature of the representations used in recognizing faces, how we access semantic information and names from familiar faces, and the different types of face processing ability. The chapter ends with an overview of the main current and likely future directions in investigations of face recognition.

WHAT MAKES FACES SPECIAL?

Faces are very important to us. We use them not only to recognize people we know, but also as one means of assessing the age and sex of people we do not know (Pittenger and Shaw, 1975; Enlow, 1982), to infer moods and feelings (Ekman and Oster, 1979), and to regulate social interaction through eye contact and facial gestures (Argyle, 1975). In addition, we can use the face as a basis for attributing characteristics to people, or relating them to occupational stereotypes (Klatzky, Martin and Kane, 1982). Surprisingly, it has also been shown that hearing adults 'lipread' information about speech phonology from seen faces. Thus McGurk and MacDonald (1976) demonstrated an illusion in which a mismatch between heard and seen (mouthed) phonemes can result in the perceiver 'blending' the two. If, for instance, the sound 'ba' is superimposed on a film of the face of a person saying 'ga', people watching the resulting film find that they hear the sound as 'da'.

Some of these uses of facial information are common to other primate species, and probably have a long evolutionary history (Darwin, 1872). Studies of the monkey brain have, moreover, identified cells that respond to faces (Perrett et al., 1984; Rolls, 1984).

Given this biological background, we should not perhaps be too surprised that very young babies can show remarkable face processing abilities. Goren, Sarty and Wu (1975) demonstrated an innate attentiveness to faces. In their study, infants of median age nine minutes (!) turned their heads and eyes more to follow a moving face-like pattern than to follow scrambled patterns made from the same features. There is also evidence of innate ability to interpret and produce facial expressions. Field *et al.* (1982) found that babies of average age 36 hours were able to discriminate happy, sad and surprised facial expressions, and Meltzoff and Moore (1977, 1983) showed that infants aged up to three weeks or three days imitated facial gestures.

These innate face processing abilities can be seen as primarily serving social and communicative functions (Studdert-Kennedy, 1983). They will, however, also help the baby to build up the information needed for the recognition of individual faces, which is achieved later in infancy (Fagan, 1979).

A number of authors have hypothesized that the significance of faces for humans is such that recognition involves 'special' processing mechanisms. Certainly the capacity to discriminate and recognize faces with ease represents a remarkably sophisticated performance. As Harmon (1973) pointed out, we find it difficult to recognize the members of such other relatively homogeneous stimulus classes as snowflakes and fingerprints, even though we can discriminate between them.

Evidence that face recognition is indeed a special process comes primarily from three sources: inversion effects, studies of cerebral hemisphere differences, and studies of patients with brain injuries who are unable to recognize familiar faces (a condition known as prosopagnosia). Each will be considered in turn.

Inverted (that is upside-down) faces look odd to us, and they can be quite difficult to recognize (see Figure 1). Of course we are used to seeing faces the right way up, but it is known that this is not simply the reason for the difficulty. Yin (1969) showed that other stimuli that we are also used to recognizing in a particular orientation, including pictures of houses, aeroplanes and period costumes, were less affected by inversion than faces. Inversion did have an effect on the recognition of all the types of stimuli that Yin used in his experiments, but its effect was greatest for faces. Thus Yin was able to argue that the difficulty in recognizing inverted faces is caused by a combination of a general familiarity with upright stimuli and a special factor related only to faces.

Yin's (1969) experiments were quite carefully conducted, but they have been greeted with considerable scepticism (Ellis, 1975; Goldstein and Chance, 1981). Valentine and Bruce (in press), however, report experiments that bolster Yin's findings by eliminating some of the criticisms that have been made. Moreover, Phillips (1979) has shown that whereas unfamiliar faces are as well recognized from internal features (eyes, nose, mouth) as from external features (hair, ears, chin), inversion affects recognition from the internal features more than it affects recognition from the external features.

Yin thought that the special difficulty of inverted faces might arise

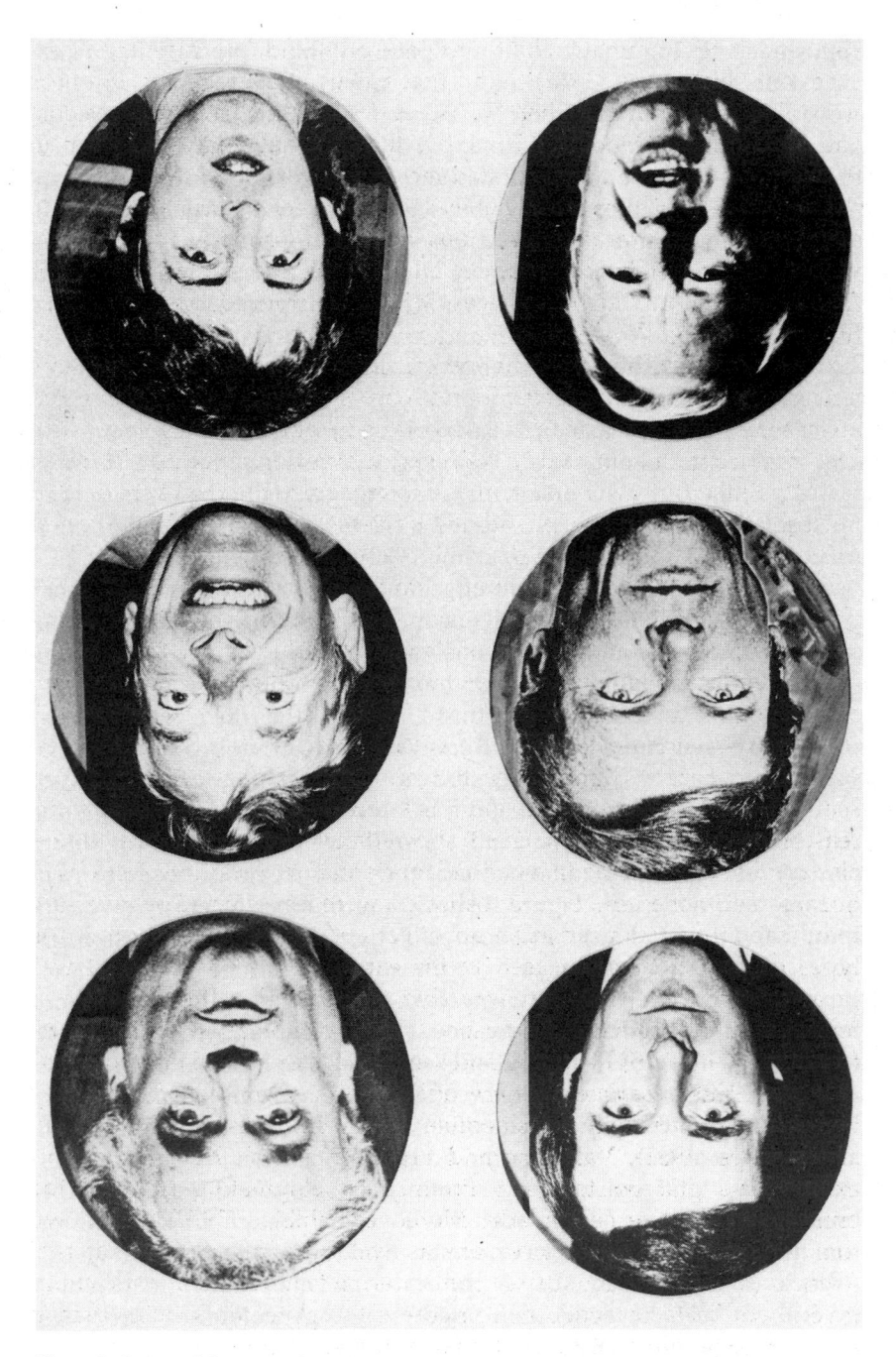

Figure 1. Inverted faces can be difficult to recognize.

from subjects being unable to form a 'personal impression' of them, and cited Köhler's (1940) observation that inverted faces lose their expression. The extent to which inversion interferes with the analysis of facial expression has been demonstrated by Thompson (1980). Figure 2 is an example of the effect he described. The eyes and mouth have been cut out and turned through 180° in each of the faces shown in Figure 2. When the whole face is inverted the effect is not very noticeable, but when the face is the correct way up the expression appears grotesque. Valentine and Bruce (1985) show that this effect actually derives primarily from the relation of the eyes and mouth to each other, since it can occur even when the external features of the face are themselves inverted (see Figure 3).

The effect of inversion on facial expression may help to account for why inverted faces appear slightly odd, but it is not yet clear how it relates to the effect of inversion on recognition. It might be the case that the absence of expression in inverted faces is part of the reason for the difficulty of recognition, as Yin (1969, 1970) thought, or it might be the case that there are independent effects of inversion on expression and recognition. The latter position fits more easily with evidence to be presented later indicating that analyses of facial identity and facial expression are carried out independently of each other.

The strongest evidence supporting Yin's view that the effect of inversion on face recognition is of a different nature to other inversion effects comes from neuropsychological studies. Figure 4 shows data derived from Yin's (1970) investigation of the face recognition abilities of patients with brain injuries. In this study people were given a recognition memory test for faces and houses that they had previously been shown for three seconds each. Figure 4 shows the number of errors made to upright and inverted faces and houses. Patients with posterior lesions of the left cerebral hemisphere and control subjects without cerebral injury show a greater difference between their performance with upright and inverted stimuli for faces than for houses. This is, of course, the pattern described by Yin (1969). For patients with posterior lesions of the right cerebral hemisphere, however, inversion has the same effect for faces and houses. Put crudely, these patients seem to recognize the faces in the same way as they recognize the houses. Notice that the performance levels for upright and inverted houses do not really differ across the three subject groups. The patients with right posterior lesions differ from the others only in their performance on the face recognition tasks.

Previous studies had shown the importance of the right cerebral hemisphere to face recognition (Hécaen and Angelergues, 1962; De Renzi and Spinnler, 1966; Warrington and James, 1967). Yin's (1970) study extended this finding by demonstrating that it is the right hemi-

Face Recognition / 33

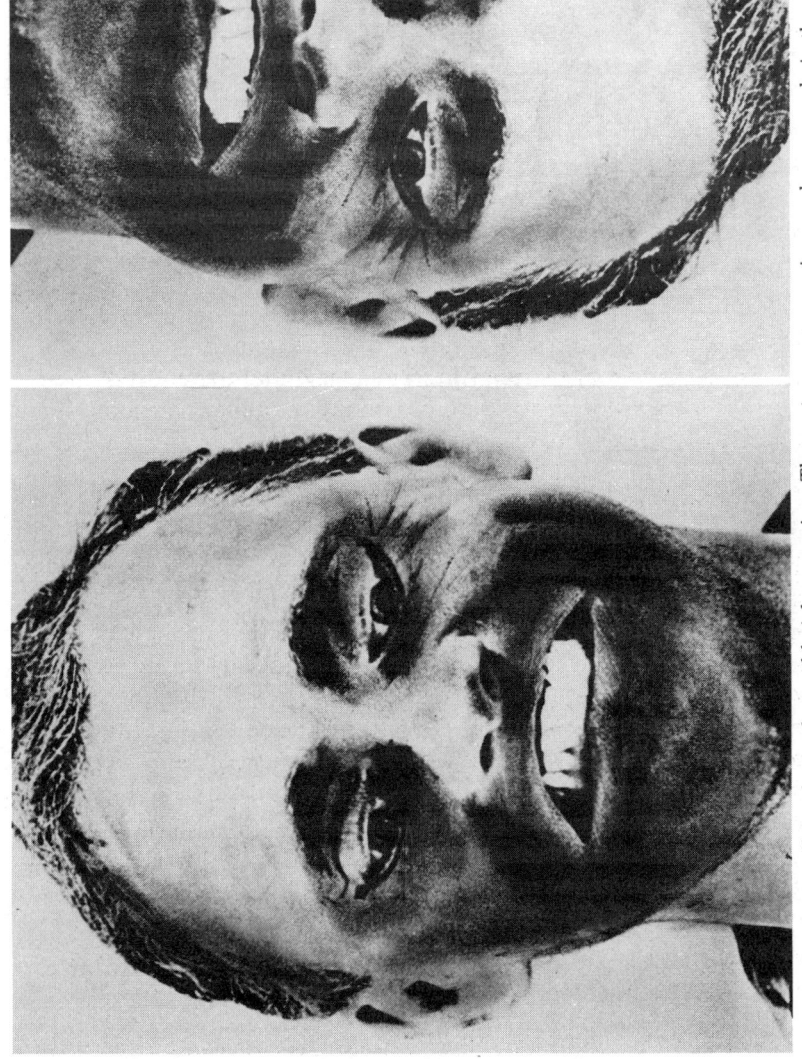

Figure 2. Inversion affects the analysis of facial expression. The grotesque expression can be seen only in the upright face. (Figure adapted from Thompson, 1980.)

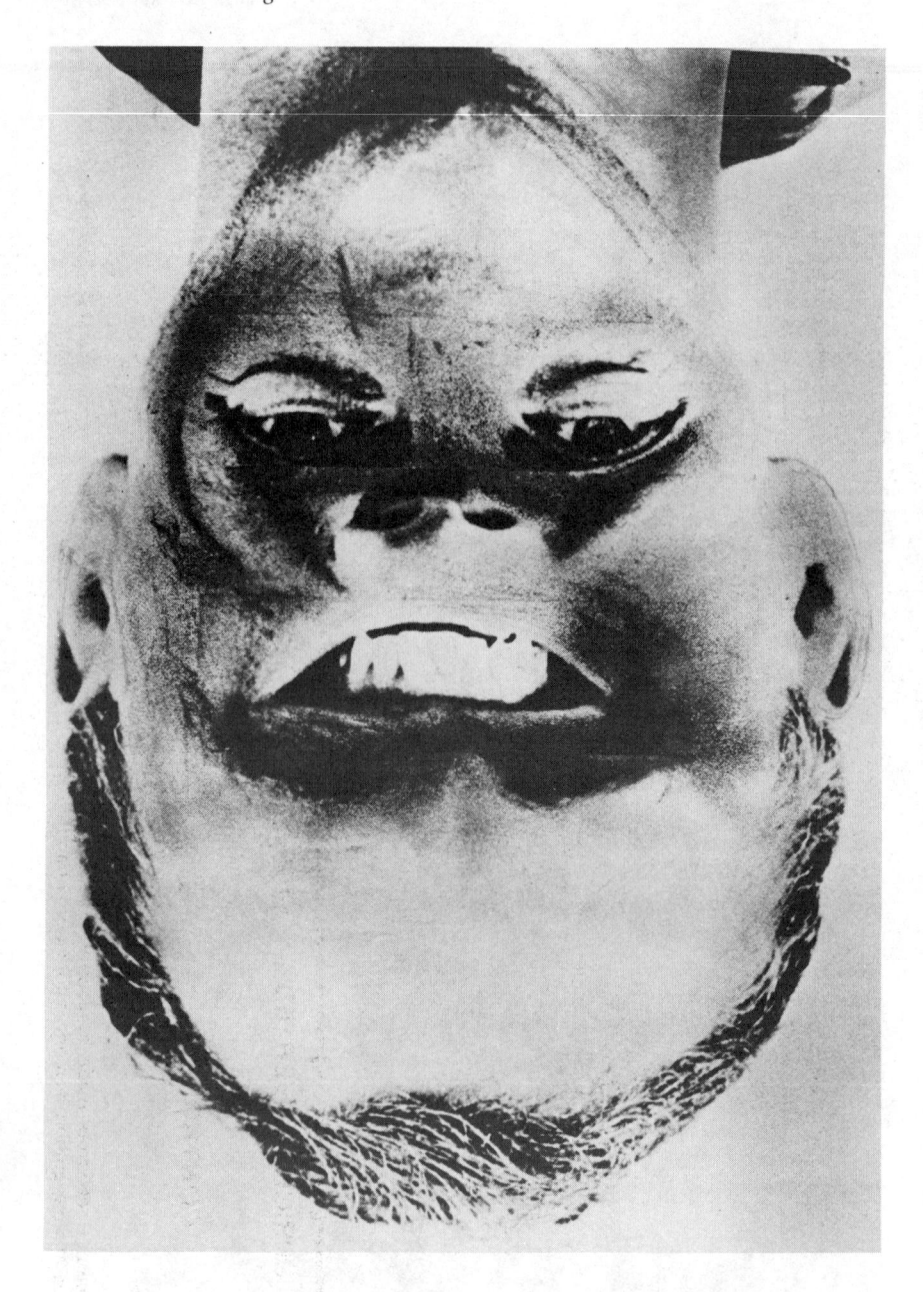

Figure 3. It is the relation of the eyes and mouth to each other that is important to expression analysis. The grotesque expression can be seen even when the external features of the face are themselves inverted. (Figure adapted from Valentine and Bruce, 1985.)

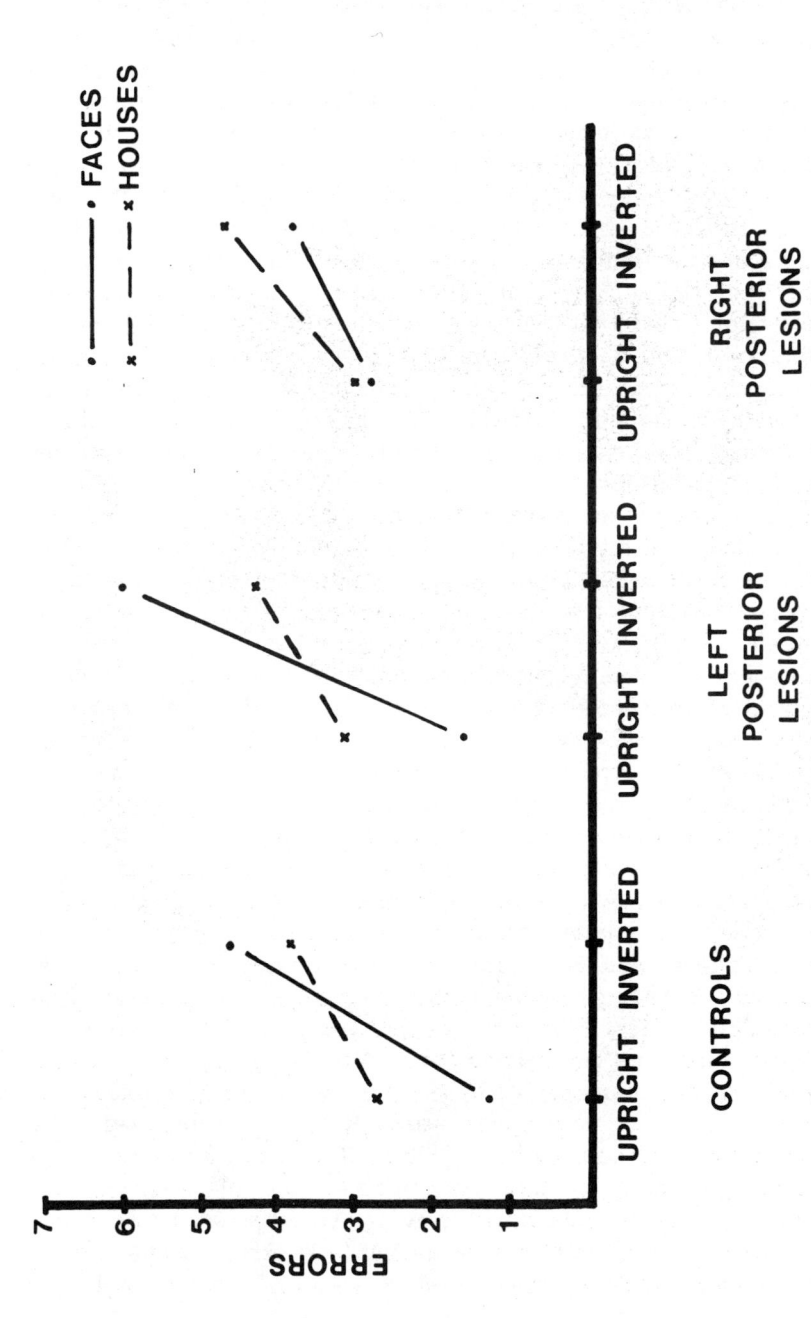

Figure 4. Number of errors made by control subjects and by patients with posterior lesions of the left and right cerebral hemispheres in a recognition memory test for upright and inverted faces and houses. (Data from Yin, 1970.)

sphere's face recognition mechanisms that are particularly sensitive to the face's orientation. When these are damaged, inversion affects faces no more than it affects any other visual stimulus.

Interestingly, a similar point can be demonstrated in studies of normal subjects. Leehey et al. (1978) investigated the recognition of upright and inverted faces presented to right-handed subjects in such a manner that one face fell to the left of the position that the subject was visually fixating and another face fell simultaneously to the right of fixation. The faces presented to the left of fixation are initially projected by the optic nerves to the visual areas of the right cerebral hemisphere, those falling to the right of fixation project initially to the left cerebral hemisphere. Leehey et al. (1978) found that upright faces were better recognized if they were projected to the right cerebral hemisphere, whereas there was no significant hemisphere difference in the recognition of inverted faces.

The most dramatic evidence that there is something special about face recognition has come from investigations of cases of complete inability to recognize previously familiar faces following brain injury. Bodamer (1947) introduced the term 'prosopagnosia' to refer to this condition. Prosopagnosia is by no means a common sequel of brain injury, but it has attracted such interest that there have now been numerous published case reports. Before examining the extent to which the deficit can be restricted to faces, it is necessary to say something about the condition itself.

Although initial reports emphasized the importance of lesions involving posterior areas of the right cerebral hemisphere (Hécaen and Angelergues, 1962), it is now known that prosopagnosia is usually accompanied by bilateral cerebral injuries (Meadows, 1974; Damasio, Damasio and Van Hoesen, 1982). This is probably due to the fact that although the right cerebral hemisphere is important in face recognition, the left hemisphere can also recognize faces to a limited extent. For present purposes, however, the locations of the lesions causing prosopagnosia are less important than the functional deficits observed.

Prosopagnosic patients are often unable to identify any familiar faces, including famous faces, friends, family, and their own faces when seen in a mirror (Hécaen and Angelergues, 1962). They know when they are looking at a face, but have no idea as to who the face might belong to. Recognition of other people has to be achieved by relying on voice, gait, clothing and context. Such methods are not always reliable, and Pevzner, Bornstein and Loewenthal (1962) mention that when he went to court their patient discussed his case with his opponent's attorney (with disastrous consequences) because the two lawyers were similarly clothed.

Despite the inability to recognize familiar faces experienced by prosopagnosic patients, recognition of other types of visual stimuli may remain intact. It is not unusual to find reports of patients who can identify objects or words with ease, yet are completely unable to identify faces. Neither is it the case that prosopagnosia simply involves a breakdown of the most fine visual discriminations, as there are also reports of patients who are able to identify faces but can not identify everyday objects (Hécaen et al., 1974; Albert, Reches and Silverberg, 1975). Thus it seems that there are distinct functional systems subserving face and object recognition.

Some prosopagnosic patients clearly experience impaired perception of faces. The second patient described by Bodamer (1947), for instance, commented that apart from the eyes, faces looked blurred to him. In some other cases, however, face perception appears remarkably intact. Bruyer et al. (1983) describe such a case. Their patient, Mr W, could make exact copies of drawings of faces, could accurately distinguish male from female faces, could determine whether or not photographs of unfamiliar faces (one seen in three-quarter and one in full-face view) showed the same person, and could correctly interpret and mimic facial expressions. Yet he was almost completely unable to identify known faces.

It has been suggested that prosopagnosia involves an inability to determine the individuality of members of a class of stimuli. Certainly, many prosopagnosic patients do have problems in identifying the members of other stimulus classes if these are themselves fairly similar to each other (Blanc-Garin, 1984). Bornstein (1963), for instance, described a prosopagnosic patient who had lost the ability to identify species of birds which had previously been well known to her. She commented that 'All the birds look the same'. Similarly, Bornstein, Sroka and Munitz (1969) studied a prosopagnosic farmer who was no longer able to identify his own livestock.

For other patients, however, the recognition deficit can be relatively restricted to faces. Mr W (Bruyer et al., 1983) was also a farmer, yet he *could* recognize his livestock. He could also identify flowers and famous buildings. Thus he was not impaired at *any* within-category discrimination. None the less, he did still have problems with coins and with playing cards. De Renzi (1986), however, describes a patient whose impairment did not seem to affect the recognition of members of any stimulus category other than faces. Conversely, Assal, Favre and Anderes (1984) present a case report of a prosopagnosic farmer who was initially unable to recognize his cows as well as being unable to recognize the faces of people that he knew (he was apparently more concerned by his inability to recognize his livestock). This patient later regained the ability to recognize faces, yet remained unable to recognize his cows.

Evidence is thus beginning to accumulate in favour of the view that inability to recognize familiar faces is not inevitably linked to difficulties in making other within-category discriminations. It would seem that recognition problems involving only faces can occur.

It is clear, then, that faces are of great social and biological significance for us, and there is a strong case for there being something special about the recognition mechanisms involved. Hay and Young (1982) suggested that the question as to what is special about face processing can itself be separated into two distinct questions. The first is the question as to whether or not the processing of faces is different in nature from the processing of other visual stimuli; this is the question of *uniqueness*. The second question concerns whether or not the processing of faces is handled by a separate system that deals only with faces; this is the question of *specificity*. The evidence discussed here points clearly towards the idea of specificity to faces of the recognition mechanisms involved, but there is as yet no convincing evidence to suggest that they are unique in nature. It may turn out that face recognition mechanisms share many of the properties of mechanisms used in recognizing other types of visual stimuli, but are organized into a face-specific recognition system in order to achieve better coordination between independent mechanisms involved in recognizing faces and analysing their expressions.

THE NATURE OF THE REPRESENTATIONS USED IN RECOGNIZING FACES

Perhaps the most problematic question concerning face recognition is the nature of the representations used to achieve recognition. Methods and ideas that have proved useful in understanding other types of recognition have contributed surprisingly little in this respect. Thus it is not particularly helpful to know that there is evidence to suggest the importance to face recognition of information conveyed by low, intermediate and high spatial frequencies (Harmon, 1973; Tieger and Ganz, 1979; Fiorentini, Maffei and Sandini, 1983).

In its simplest form the spatial frequency approach is, in any case, clearly of only limited applicability to face perception since it treats the face purely as a complex visual stimulus and can not, in consequence, account for inversion effects. Faces are equally complex visual stimuli whether upright or inverted, and contain information in the same spatial frequencies.

The spatial frequency approach, has, none the less, produced some interesting findings. An example would be the discovery of impaired face perception in some elderly people resulting from raised contrast thresholds at lower spatial frequencies (Owsley, Sekuler and Boldt, 1981).

The approach taken by Marr (1982) also seems to be of limited use in understanding face recognition. The axis-based representation that Marr proposed for object recognition would not be well suited to the fine discriminations needed in face recognition (Bruce and Young, 1986).

Many studies have investigated the saliency of individual features to face perception and recognition, and these have been reviewed by Shepherd, Davies and Ellis (1981). The usual finding is that features from the upper part of the face (hair, eyes) tend to be relied on more than features from the lower part of the face (nose, mouth, chin). More recently, however, investigators have also emphasized the importance of the *configuration* formed by the individual features. Thus Haig (1984) used a computer-driven display system that allowed him to change a picture of a face by moving the eyes up or down, to increase or decrease the distance between the eyes, to move the nose up or down, to widen or narrow the mouth, to move the entire set of internal features (eyes, nose and mouth) up or down with respect to the head, and to narrow or widen the head itself. He found that even quite small changes in the arrangement of features with respect to each other could affect recognition.

It seems likely that both the configuration formed by the facial features and the specific features themselves are important to recognition (Sergent, 1984). This would square with the fact that we know that we can recognize some faces from distinctive features in isolation (for example Mick Jagger's lips) or when such distinctive features are concealed (Mick Jagger with his hand across his mouth). For these reasons Bruce and Young (1986) propose that familiar faces are represented by an interconnected set of descriptions; some describing the configuration of the whole face and some describing the details of particular features.

An important finding is that representations of familiar faces differ from those formed of unfamiliar faces. This was first observed by Ellis, Shepherd and Davies (1979), who noted that familiar faces were better recognized from internal features (eyes, nose, mouth) than from external features (hair, chin, ears), whereas there was no difference between internal and external features in recognition memory for unfamiliar faces. This result has been replicated with Japanese subjects and Japanese faces (Endo, Takahashi and Maruyama, 1984). It has also been shown with a matching task by Young, Hay, McWeeny, Flude and Ellis (1985).

Examples of the stimuli used by Young, Hay, McWeeny, Flude and Ellis (1985, Experiment 1) are shown in Figure 5. Subjects were required to decide whether pairs of simultaneously presented photographs showed the same face or different faces. The photographs had to be matched on internal or external facial features. It was found to be easier to match familiar faces than to match unfamiliar faces on internal features (mean reaction times 1,228 vs 1,435 milliseconds), whereas there was no difference between familiar and unfamiliar faces for external feature matches (mean reaction times 1,253 vs 1,286 milliseconds).

We are able, then, to form a more effective representation of the internal features of familiar than of unfamiliar faces. This may happen because in recognizing familiar faces it is important to rely on the part of the face that will not be affected by changes in hairstyle, or it may happen because we spend a lot of time looking at the internal features of familiar faces to determine their expressions and pick up other social signals.

Although some progress has been made towards understanding the nature of the representations used to effect face recognition, there is clearly much more to be found out. In this respect, however, the study of face recognition is no different from word or object recognition, where the same fundamental problem remains unsolved. Because it is unlikely that a satisfactory solution can be achieved at present, a number of researchers have adopted a somewhat different approach. Hay and Young (1982), Bruce (1983), Ellis (1986) and Bruce and Young (1986) have suggested that it may be useful to think of the recognition of familiar faces as involving a 'recognition unit' for each known face. This face recognition unit is held to contain a stored description of the known face, and it will be activated when a seen face resembles the stored description. Activation of the recognition unit will occur to any view of the known face, and signals that the face is familiar. Following activation of the face recognition unit, stored semantic information relating to the person seen can be accessed. The face recognition unit is thus held to act as a link between a description of the seen face's appearance and stored information about that person.

This recognition unit metaphor was initially taken from Morton's (1969, 1979) theory of word recognition, though the version given here has been modified in ways that now make it rather different from Morton's conception. A similar idea of a stored visual template that acts as an interface between perception and relevant stored information has been put forward on the basis of neuropsychological studies by Damasio, Damasio and Van Hoesen (1982).

The advantage of the recognition unit metaphor is that it sidesteps the difficult issue as to *how* recognition is achieved, and instead directs attention towards the functional properties of the recognition system. Investigations of these functional properties can be carried out using

Face Recognition / 41

Same **Different**

Internal

External

Figure 5. Examples of stimuli used by Young, Hay, McWeeny, Flude and Ellis (1985, Experiment 1). The subject's task is to determine whether or not the pairs of photographs show the same person. Matches must be based on internal or external facial features.

conventional experimental techniques, and some interesting findings have been made.

The simplest prediction deriving from a recognition unit model of the type outlined here is that people should be faster at deciding whether or not faces are familiar than they would be at deciding whether or not they belong to people with a given occupation. It should be easier to decide that Margaret Thatcher's face is familiar than to decide that it is a politician's face. This is because the familiarity decision can be based on the face recognition units themselves, whereas the occupation (semantic) decision requires the additional access of semantic information concerning the person seen. Young, McWeeny, Hay and Ellis (1986) showed that this prediction is valid, and that different factors affect reaction times for familiarity and semantic decisions, as the recognition unit idea would predict.

More sophisticated techniques for investigating the properties of recognition units involve priming effects. Bruce and Valentine (1985) investigated identity priming, in which recognition of a face is faster if that face has been seen recently. They showed that we are quicker to recognize a photograph of a face as a familiar person if we have recently seen another photograph of the same person, but that we are no faster at recognizing a photograph of a face as a familiar person if we have recently read that person's name. Thus, you will recognize Robert Redford's face more quickly if you have seen a photograph of his face within the last half-hour or so, but you will be no quicker to recognize his face if you have recently read the name 'Robert Redford'.

This identity priming effect is clearly not one of conscious expectation that Robert Redford might come up again in the course of the experiment, for if it were due to expectation both the name 'Robert Redford' and the face of Robert Redford should produce an equal facilitation. It is, however, readily accounted for in terms of residual activation in the face recognition unit for Robert Redford, produced by the recently seen photograph. The *face* recognition unit for Robert Redford would not, of course, be activated by the sight of Robert Redford's name.

This interpretation of identity priming is supported by Bruce and Valentine's (1985) finding that the size of the priming effect was not related to the degree of difference between the photographs used. This is consistent with the idea that the recognition unit will be activated by any view of the appropriate face. If the identity priming effect were produced only by a visual memory of the original photograph, the degree of difference between the photographs would be a crucial factor.

Semantic priming effects have also been investigated. Bruce and Valentine (1986) showed that face recognition could be facilitated by the prior presentation of the face of a related person. For example, recognizing Sid Little is facilitated if his face is preceded by the face of Eddie Large. This semantic priming effect occurs even when the first face is presented only 250 milliseconds before the second face, which would again seem to rule out any contribution of conscious expectation.

ACCESSING SEMANTIC INFORMATION AND NAMES

When we recognize a familiar face we usually know who the person is, and her or his name. How are semantic information and names accessed?

One way of approaching this question is to look at the sequence or sequences in which these become available. When we recognize the face of David Steel, do we know that his name is David Steel before we know that he is a politician, or do we know that he is a politician before we know that his name is David Steel?

Existing evidence points to the conclusion that names are accessed from familiar faces via intervening semantic information specifying who the person is. Semantic information is usually derived rapidly and directly from familiar faces. Names, in contrast, can be very difficult to remember.

Consider everyday errors. A common experience is to see a face and know who the person is, where she or he is usually seen, who her or his friends are, and so on, yet to be unable to remember the person's name (Reason and Lucas, 1984). The opposite experience, in which the person's name would be remembered but we would be uncertain as to who she or he is, never seems to happen (Young, Hay and Ellis, 1985). We don't look at a face and think 'I know his name is Clint Eastwood, but who is he?' If people's names are accessed from faces via intervening semantic information, such an error could not be made, since semantic information will always be available before the name is retrieved.

Formal experiments also support this conception. Reaction times to name faces are longer than reaction times for categorizing them by occupation (Young, McWeeny, Ellis and Hay, 1986), as would be expected if semantic information is accessed from a familiar face before the person's name.

Interference experiments can also be used to show that semantic information is readily derived from faces, whereas names are not. The face–name interference paradigm involves the simultaneous presentation of a photograph of a face and a printed name, as in Figure 6. The printed name may belong to the person whose face is presented, or it may belong to a different person. If subjects are asked to ignore the printed name and say the name of the person whose *face* is shown, they find that they experience difficulties; the presence of the printed name slows their responses when it is incorrect for the face seen. In contrast, if subjects are asked to say the printed *name* and ignore the face they experience no difficulty (Young, Hay and Ellis, 1986). In other words, irrelevant printed names interfere with face naming, but irrelevant faces do not interfere with the naming of printed names.

This pattern of interference effects can be reversed, however, by changing to a categorization task. When subjects are asked to say 'Yes' if the *face* is that of a politician, their response times are not significantly affected by the irrelevant printed names. But if they are asked to say 'Yes' if the printed *name* is that of a politician, their responses are slowed when the irrelevant face is that of a person who is not a politician. Irrelevant printed names do not interfere with face categorization, whereas irrelevant faces interfere with the categorization of printed names (Young, Hay and Ellis 1986).

These interference effects are consistent with the view that semantic information is derived rapidly and automatically from familiar faces; hence faces will i.e. interfere with name categorization. Names, however, do not seem to be readily accessed from familiar faces, since there is no interference from faces on the naming of printed names.

DIFFERENT TYPES OF FACE PROCESSING ABILITY

A key issue concerns the way in which recognition of familiar faces relates to other aspects of face processing, such as the analysis of expressions. There is now evidence to suggest that there are different

Figure 6. Example of stimulus for face–name interference experiment.

types of face processing ability, and that at least some of these can be carried out independently of each other.

Bruce (1979), for instance, showed that normal people were able to make visual and semantic analyses of seen faces in parallel. In her second experiment she asked subjects to search for the faces of four familiar politicians in sequences of familiar and unfamiliar faces. She showed that search times were affected by the presence of visually similar distractor faces (people who looked like the targets, but were not politicians) and that search times were also affected by the presence of semantically similar distractor faces (other politicians who did not look particularly like the targets). These effects of visual and semantic similarity were independent of each other.

It is possible to reach much the same conclusion as Bruce (1979) on the basis of the neuropsychological literature. Warrington and James (1967) had found that impairments affecting the recognition of familiar faces and impairments affecting immediate recognition memory of unfamiliar faces did not seem to relate to each other. This observation was extended by Benton and Van Allen (1972). They described a prosopagnosic patient who, despite her inability to identify familiar faces, was none the less able to correctly match photographs of unfamiliar faces. She achieved a normal score on the Benton test of facial recognition. In this test photographs of unfamiliar people have to be matched for identity in full-face views, across differences in pose (full-face vs three-quarter view), and across differences in lighting.

Benton (1980) placed considerable emphasis on this finding of intact matching of unfamiliar faces by a prosopagnosic patient. It is now known that the opposite pattern of impairment can also occur, in which a brain-injured person is no longer able to match unfamiliar faces yet remains able to recognize the faces of familiar people (Malone et al., 1982). There is thus evidence for a double dissociation between impairments affecting familiar face recognition and impairments affecting unfamiliar face matching. When these findings are set alongside those of Bruce (1979), it is difficult to resist the conclusion that processes involved in recognizing familiar faces are independent of the kind of directed visual analysis needed to match views of unfamiliar faces or search for a particular set of visual features.

Other dissociations between different types of face processing ability have also been described. The processes required for the analysis of facial expressions, for instance, seem to be independent of those involved in familiar face recognition. Although it is not unusual to find that prosopagnosic patients can neither identify faces nor understand their expressions (Bodamer, 1947), other patients have been found to be able to interpret facial expressions correctly despite an almost complete inability to identify familiar faces (Hécaen and Angelergues, 1962; Shuttleworth, Syring and Allen, 1982). We have already looked at the case of Mr W (Bruyer et al., 1983), who was one such patient. The opposite dissociation has been described by Bornstein (1963), who noted that some prosopagnosic patients show a degree of recovery of ability to identify familiar faces whilst remaining unable to interpret facial expressions. Similarly, Kurucz and Feldmar (1979) and Kurucz, Feldmar and Werner (1979) found that a group of patients with diffuse brain injuries found it difficult to interpret facial emotions yet were still able to identify photographs of American presidents.

Studies of normal subjects can also be used to support the idea of independence of mechanisms involved in the analysis of facial identity and facial expression. Young, McWeeny, Hay and Ellis (in press) found that when people matched simultaneously presented pairs of photographs for identity (that is to determine whether or not the photographs were of the same person) they were faster at matching familiar than unfamiliar faces (mean reaction times 977 vs 1,045 milliseconds). When people matched the same pairs of photographs on expression (that is to determine whether or not the photographs showed the same expression), however, there was no difference between familiar and unfamiliar faces (mean reaction times 1,110 vs 1,117 milliseconds). The presence of an effect of face familiarity for identity but not for expression matches supports the view that the analysis of facial expressions proceeds independently from the analysis of facial identity.

A further dissociation between expression analysis and ability to 'lipread' speech from seen movements of the mouth and tongue is described by Campbell, Landis and Regard (in press). The dissociation was observed in two patients. One was unable to recognize faces and could not categorize facial expressions correctly. She could, however, correctly judge what phonemes were being mouthed in photographs of faces and was susceptible to the McGurk and MacDonald (1976) illusion (the illusion in which a mismatch between heard and seen phonemes results in the perceiver 'blending' the two). The second patient was impaired at making phoneme judgements to face stimuli and was not susceptible to the McGurk and MacDonald illusion, yet had no difficulties in recognizing faces or facial expressions.

Thus it seems that recognition of familiar faces, directed visual analysis (to match unfamiliar faces or search for particular features), expression analysis, and lipreading involve separable functional components that can operate independently of each other. This is not to deny that all of these different types of face processing ability may be carried out using a common initial representation of the seen face (what Bruce and Young, 1986 term 'structural encoding'). Following the construction of such an initial representation, however, the different types of facial analysis seem to be carried out in parallel.

OVERVIEW

Many of us became interested in face recognition after reading the review by Ellis (1975). Although we are still far from understanding how faces are recognized, it is clear that some ten years of further studies have led to considerable progress from the position that Ellis described.

This progress can be largely attributed to three factors. Firstly, emphasis has been placed on how we recognize *familiar* faces. Much of the literature reviewed by Ellis had been concerned with recognition memory for once-seen unfamiliar faces. Whilst it is undoubtedly important to understand the properties of recognition memory for unfamiliar faces, the concentration of the experimental literature on this topic had been one-sided, and there was an implicit assumption that familiar face recognition would prove to be similar to recognition memory for unfamiliar faces. The crucial point that familiar and unfamiliar faces might actually be processed rather differently was emphasized for the normal literature by Bruce (1979), and for the neuropsychological literature by Benton (1980).

The second reason for progress has been the increasing use of information from neuropsychological studies. These were often dismissed in the past because of the complexity of neuropsychological impairments affecting face processing, and because most brain-injured patients have additional problems. The reason for the upsurge of interest in neuropsychological data has been an increased awareness that striking dissociations can occasionally be observed. This has been linked to a general realization that the fact that different deficits are often associated with each other is not very interesting. The deficits that follow brain injury may be associated for many possible reasons, not all of which have any functional significance. Dissociable deficits, however, clearly demonstrate the existence of separable cognitive processes and are thus of commanding theoretical importance.

The third reason is that serious attempts have been made to develop a coherent theoretical structure to underpin studies of face processing. As Ellis (1975) commented, this was conspicuously absent in the literature he reviewed, which was largely given over to investigating the subject and stimulus 'variables' that influence face discrimination and recognition memory (age, sex, race, attractiveness, presentation time, interstimulus interval, and so on). Functional models of face processing have, however, now been put forward by Hay and Young (1982), Bruce

(1983), Ellis (1983, 1986), Rhodes (1985), and Bruce and Young (1986).

The model suggested by Bruce and Young (1986) is shown in Figure 7. This model is an attempt to delineate the functional components involved in face processing, and their relation to each other. It proposes that structural encoding processes create descriptions of the seen face suitable for expression analysis, facial speech analysis (lipreading), directed visual processing, and face recognition units. Recognition of familiar faces involves a match between the products of structural encoding and previously stored structural codes describing the appearance of a familiar face, held in a face recognition unit. The face recognition unit can then access semantic information about the person seen via a 'person identity node', and finally the person's name. It is also proposed that the cognitive system plays an active role in evaluating information provided by these separate functional components.

A model of this type is by no means a solution to the problem of understanding how we recognize faces. It is, however, a useful step in that it can bring together data from diverse sources including laboratory experiments, studies of everyday errors, and studies of the difficulties experienced by patients with cerebral injuries. All of the findings discussed in this chapter can be accommodated within this model. In addition, such functional models may be used to make comparisons of the similarities and differences between face recognition and the recognition of other types of visual stimuli, including objects and words (Bruce and Young, 1986; Ellis, Young and Hay, in press).

We have come a long way since 1975. But what of the future? I do not keep a crystal ball under my tachistoscope, but I none the less think that there are at least two directions that are likely to be increasingly vigorously pursued.

The first involves computational modelling of various aspects of face recognition. There are already a few computer systems that show some ability to recognize faces (for example Stonham, 1986), though they do not perform this task in the way that we think humans do it. Such systems demonstrate, however, the practicability or limitations of different potential solutions to the problem of face recognition. There is also some more general computational work that may have powerful implications for understanding the nature of the representations used in face processing (McClelland and Rumelhart, 1985).

The second likely direction for future research involves increased interest in faces as three-dimensional structures. Although faces all share some similarities in three-dimensional structure, it is none the less possible to divide them into different facial types (Enlow, 1982). These facial types influence the shapes of the facial features themselves. Thus a face is not made up from random combinations of features, as is

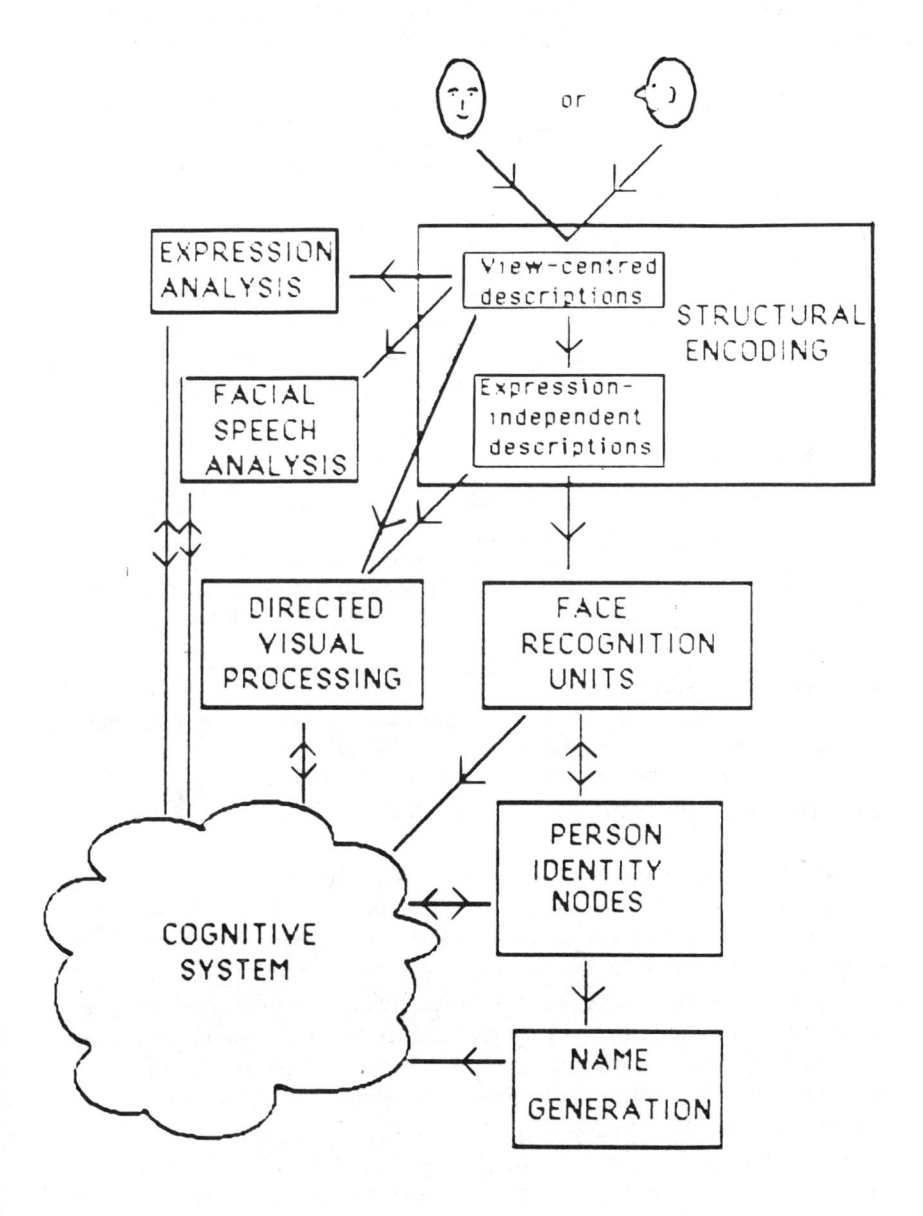

Figure 7. Model of functional components involved in face processing proposed by Bruce and Young (1986).

assumed by techniques such as the Photofit method of constructing likenesses of the faces seen by people who have witnessed crimes. By examining more carefully the different three-dimensional structures that faces can form we may not only be able to improve techniques like Photofit, but should also arrive at a much more detailed understanding of the ways in which a face can provide the information on which age and sex judgements, and perhaps recognition itself, depend.

ACKNOWLEDGEMENTS

I am grateful for the support given by ESRC grants C 0023 2075, C 0023 2246, and C 0023 2323, and to the Press Association for permission to reproduce photographs used in Figure 1, Figure 5, and Figure 6. Figure 7 is reproduced from Bruce and Young (1986) by permission of The British Psychological Society.

REFERENCES

Albert, M.L., Reches, A. and Silverberg, R. (1975) Associative visual agnosia without alexia. *Neurology*, 25, 322–326.
Argyle, M. (1975) *Bodily Communication*. London: Methuen.
Assal, G., Favre, C. and Anderes, J.P. (1984) Non-reconnaissance d'animaux familiers chez un paysan: Zoo-agnosie ou prosopagnosie pour les animaux. *Revue Neurologique*, 140, 580–584.
Benton, A.L. (1980) The neuropsychology of facial recognition. *American Psychologist*, 35, 176–186.
Benton, A.L. and Van Allen, M.W. (1972) Prosopagnosia and facial discrimination. *Journal of the Neurological Sciences*, 15, 167–172.
Blanc-Garin, J. (1984) Perception des visages et reconnaissance de la physionomie dans l'agnosie des visages. *L'Année Psychologique*, 84, 573–598.
Bodamer, J. (1947) Die Prosop-Agnosie. *Archiv für Psychiatrie and Nervenkrankheiten*, 179, 6–53.
Bornstein, B. (1963) Prosopagnosia. In L. Halpern (ed.) *Problems of Dynamic Neurology*. Jerusalem: Hadassah Medical School.
Bornstein, B., Sroka, M. and Munitz, H. (1969) Prosopagnosia with animal face agnosia. *Cortex*, 5, 164–169.
Bruce, V. (1979) Searching for politicians: An information-processing approach to face recognition. *Quarterly Journal of Experimental Psychology*, 31, 373–395.
Bruce, V. (1983) Recognizing faces. *Philosophical Transactions of the Royal Society, London, Series B*, 302, 423–436.
Bruce, V. and Valentine, T. (1985) Identity priming in the recognition of familiar faces. *British Journal of Psychology*, 76, 373–383.
Bruce, V. and Valentine, T. (1986) Semantic priming of familiar faces. *Quarterly Journal of Experimental Psychology*, 38A, 125–150.
Bruce, V. and Young, A.W. (1986) Understanding face recognition. *British Journal of Psychology*, 77.
Bruyer, R., Laterre, C., Seron, X., Feyereisen, P., Strypstein, E., Pierrard, E. and Rectem, D. (1983) A case of prosopagnosia with some preserved covert remembrance of familiar faces. *Brain and Cognition*, 2, 257–284.

Campbell, R., Landis, T. and Regard, M. (in press) Face recognition and lipreading: A neurological dissociation. *Brain*.
Courtauld, E. (1982) Lookalike. *Private Eye*, 539, 10.
Damasio, A.R., Damasio, H. and Van Hoesen, G.W. (1982) Prosopagnosia: Anatomic basis and behavioral mechanisms. *Neurology*, 32, 331–341.
Darwin, C. (1872) *The Expression of Emotions in Man and Animals*. London: Murray.
Davies, G.M. (1983) Forensic face recall: The role of visual and verbal information. In S.M.A. Lloyd-Bostock and B.R. Clifford (eds) *Evaluating Witness Evidence*. Chichester: Wiley.
De Renzi, E. (1986) Current issues on prosopagnosia. In H.D. Ellis, M.A. Jeeves, F. Newcombe and A.W. Young (eds) *Aspects of Face Processing*. Dordrecht: Martinus Nijhoff.
De Renzi, E. and Spinnler, H. (1966) Facial recognition in brain-damaged patients. *Neurology*, 16, 145–152.
Ekman, P. and Oster, H. (1979) Facial expressions of emotion. *Annual Review of Psychology*, 30, 527–554.
Ellis, A.W., Young, A.W. and Hay, D.C. (in press) Modelling the recognition of faces and words. In P.E. Morris (ed.) *Modelling Cognition*. Chichester: Wiley.
Ellis, H.D. (1975) Recognizing faces. *British Journal of Psychology*, 66, 409–426.
Ellis, H.D. (1983) The role of the right hemisphere in face perception. In A.W. Young (ed.) *Functions of the Right Cerebral Hemisphere*. London: Academic Press.
Ellis, H.D. (1986) Processes underlying face recognition. In R. Bruyer (ed.) *The Neuropsychology of Face Perception and Facial Expression*. Hillsdale, N.J.: Lawrence Erlbaum Associates.
Ellis, H.D. (in press) Disorders of face recognition. In K. Poeck (ed.) *Neurology: Proceedings of the 13th World Congress of Neurology*. New York: Springer-Verlag.
Ellis, H.D., Shepherd, J.W. and Davies, G.M. (1979) Identification of familiar and unfamiliar faces from internal and external features: Some implications for theories of face recognition. *Perception*, 8, 431–439.
Endo, M., Takahashi, K. and Maruyama, K. (1984) Effects of observer's attitude on the familiarity of faces: Using the difference in cue value between central and peripheral facial elements as an index of familiarity. *Tohoku Psychologica Folia*, 43, 23–34.
Enlow, D.H. (1982) *Handbook of Facial Growth*, 2nd ed. Philadelphia: W.B. Saunders.
Fagan, J.F. III (1979) The origins of facial pattern recognition. In M.H. Bornstein and W. Kessen (eds) *Psychological Development from Infancy*. Hillsdale, N.J.: Lawrence Erlbaum Associates.
Field, T.M., Woodson, R., Greenberg, R. and Cohen, D. (1982) Discrimination and imitation of facial expressions by neonates. *Science*, 218, 179–181.
Fiorentini, A., Maffei, L. and Sandini, G. (1983) The role of high spatial frequencies in face perception. *Perception*, 12, 195–201.
Galton, F. (1883) *Inquiries into Human Faculty and Its Development*. London: Macmillan.
Goldstein, A.G. and Chance, J.E. (1981) Laboratory studies of face recognition. In G. Davies, H. Ellis and J. Shepherd (eds) *Perceiving and Remembering Faces*. London: Academic Press.
Goren, C.G., Sarty, M. and Wu, P.Y.K. (1975) Visual following and pattern discrimination of face-like stimuli by newborn infants. *Pediatrics*, 56, 544–549.

Haig, N.D. (1984) The effect of feature displacement on face recognition. *Perception*, 13, 505–512.
Harmon, L.D. (1973) The recognition of faces. *Scientific American*, 229, 71–82.
Hay, D.C. and Young, A.W. (1982) The human face. In A.W. Ellis (ed.) *Normality and Pathology in Cognitive Functions*. London: Academic Press.
Hécaen, H. and Angelergues, R. (1962) Agnosia for faces (prosopagnosia). *Archives of Neurology*, 7, 92–100.
Hécaen, H., Goldblum, M.C., Masure, M.C. and Ramier, A.M. (1974) Une nouvelle observation d'agnosie d'objet. Deficit de l'association ou de la categorisation, specifique de la modalité visuelle? *Neuropsychologia*, 12, 447–464.
Klatzky, R.L., Martin, G.L. and Kane, R.A. (1982) Semantic interpretation effects on memory for faces. *Memory and Cognition*, 10, 195–206.
Köhler, W. (1940) *Dynamics in Psychology*. New York: Liveright.
Kurucz, J. and Feldmar, G. (1979) Prosopo-affective agnosia as a symptom of cerebral organic disease. *Journal of the American Geriatrics Society*, 27, 225–230.
Kurucz, J., Feldmar, G., and Werner, W. (1979) Prosopo-affective agnosia associated with chronic organic brain syndrome. *Journal of the American Geriatrics Society*, 27, 91–95.
Leehey, S.C., Carey, S., Diamond, R. and Cahn, A. (1978). Upright and inverted faces: The right hemisphere knows the difference. *Cortex*, 14, 411–419.
McClelland, J.L. and Rumelhart, D.E. (1985) Distributed memory and the representation of general and specific information. *Journal of Experimental Psychology: General*, 114, 159–188.
McGurk, H. and MacDonald, J. (1976) Hearing lips and seeing voices. *Nature*, 264, 746–748.
Malone, D.R., Morris, H.H., Kay, M.C. and Levin, H.S. (1982) Prosopagnosia: A double dissociation between the recognition of familiar and unfamiliar faces. *Journal of Neurology, Neurosurgery and Psychiatry*, 45, 820–822.
Marr, D. (1982) *Vision*. San Francisco: Freeman.
Meadows, J.C. (1974) The anatomical basis of prosopagnosia. *Journal of Neurology, Neurosurgery and Psychiatry*, 37, 489–501.
Meltzoff, A.N. and Moore, M.K. (1977) Imitation of facial and manual gestures by human neonates. *Science*, 198, 75–78.
Meltzoff, A.N. and Moore, M.K. (1983) Newborn infants imitate adult facial gestures. *Child Development*, 54, 702–709.
Morton, J. (1969) Interaction of information in word recognition. *Psychological Review*, 76, 165–178.
Morton, J. (1979) Facilitation in word recognition: Experiments causing change in the logogen model. In P.A. Kolers, M. Wrolstad and H. Bouma (eds) *Processing of Visible Language*, 1. New York: Plenum.
Owsley, C., Sekuler, R. and Boldt, C. (1981) Aging and low-contrast vision: Face perception. *Investigative Ophthalmology*, 21, 362–365.
Perrett, D.I., Smith, P.A.J., Potter, D.D., Mistlin, A.J., Head, A.S., Milner, A.D. and Jeeves, M.A. (1984) Neurones responsive to faces in the temporal cortex: Studies of functional organization, sensitivity to identity and relation to perception. *Human Neurobiology*, 3, 197–208.
Pevzner, S., Bornstein, B. and Loewenthal, M. (1962) Prosopagnosia. *Journal of Neurology, Neurosurgery and Psychiatry*, 25, 336–338.
Phillips, R.J. (1979) Some exploratory experiments on memory for photographs of faces. *Acta Psychologica*, 43, 39–56.

Pittenger, J.B. and Shaw, R.E. (1975) Aging faces as viscal-elastic events: Implications for a theory of nonrigid shape perception. *Journal of Experimental Psychology: Human Perception and Performance, 1,* 374–382.
Reason, J.T. and Lucas, D. (1984) Using cognitive diaries to investigate naturally occurring memory blocks. In J. Harris and P.E. Morris (eds) *Everyday Memory, Actions and Absentmindedness.* London: Academic Press.
Rhodes, G. (1985) Lateralized processes in face recognition. *British Journal of Psychology, 76,* 249–271.
Rolls, E.T. (1984) Neurons in the cortex of the temporal lobe and in the amygdala of the monkey with responses selective for faces. *Human Neurobiology, 3,* 209–222.
Sergent, J. (1984) An investigation into component and configural processes underlying face perception. *British Journal of Psychology, 75,* 221–242.
Shepherd, J.W., Davies, G.M. and Ellis, H.D. (1981) Studies of cue saliency. In G. Davies, H. Ellis and J. Shepherd (eds) *Perceiving and Remembering Faces.* London: Academic Press.
Shepherd, J.W., Ellis, H.D. and Davies, G.M. (1981) *Identification Evidence: A Psychological Evaluation.* Aberdeen: Aberdeen University Press.
Shuttleworth, E.C. Jr, Syring, V. and Allen, N. (1982) Further observations on the nature of prosopagnosia. *Brain and Cognition, 1,* 307–322.
Stonham, T.J. (1986) Practical face recognition and verification with WISARD. In H.D. Ellis, M.A. Jeeves, F. Newcombe and A.W. Young (eds) *Aspects of Face Processing.* Dordrecht: Martinus Nijhoff.
Studdert-Kennedy, M. (1983) On learning to speak. *Human Neurobiology, 2,* 191–195.
Thompson, P. (1980) Margaret Thatcher – a new illusion. *Perception, 9,* 483–484.
Tieger, T. and Ganz, L. (1979) Recognition of faces in the presence of two-dimensional sinusoidal masks. *Perception and Psychophysics, 26,* 163–167.
Valentine, T. and Bruce, V. (1985) What's up? The Margaret Thatcher illusion revisited. *Perception, 14,* 515–516.
Valentine, T. and Bruce, V. (in press) The effect of race, inversion and encoding activity upon face recognition. *Acta Psychologica.*
Warrington, E.K. and James, M. (1967) An experimental investigation of facial recognition in patients with unilateral cerebral lesions. *Cortex, 3,* 317–326.
Yin, R.K. (1969) Looking at upside-down faces. *Journal of Experimental Psychology, 81,* 141–145.
Yin, R.K. (1970) Face recognition by brain-injured patients: A dissociable ability? *Neuropsychologia, 8,* 395–402.
Young, A.W., Hay, D.C. and Ellis, A.W. (1985) The faces that launched a thousand slips: Everyday difficulties and errors in recognizing people. *British Journal of Psychology, 76,* 495–523.
Young, A.W., Hay, D.C., McWeeny, K.H., Flude, B.M. and Ellis, A.W. (1985) Matching familiar and unfamiliar faces on internal and external features. *Perception, 14,* 737–746.
Young, A.W., Hay, D.C. and Ellis, A.W. (1986) Getting semantic information from familiar faces. In H.D. Ellis, M.A. Jeeves, F. Newcombe and A.W. Young (eds) *Aspects of Face Processing.* Dordrecht: Martinus Nijhoff.
Young, A.W., McWeeny, K.H., Ellis, A.W. and Hay, D.C. (1986) Naming and categorising faces and written names. *Quarterly Journal of Experimental Psychology, 38A,* 297–318.
Young, A.W., McWeeny, K.H., Hay, D.C. and Ellis, A.W. (1986) Access to

identity-specific semantic codes from familiar faces. *Quarterly Journal of Experimental Psychology, 38A*, 271–295.

Young, A.W., McWeeny, K.H., Hay, D.C. and Ellis, A.W. (in press) Matching familiar and unfamiliar faces on identity and expression. *Psychological Research*.

EMOTION: COGNITIVE APPROACHES
Brian Parkinson

WHAT IS EMOTION?

The obvious way to start a discussion of psychological research into emotion would be with a definition of the term. Unfortunately, such a beginning presents surprising difficulties. Although lay people apparently have no problems knowing when and how to use emotional terms, psychologists have been hard pressed to agree on the concept's meaning. For example, Kleinginna and Kleinginna (1981) listed 92 distinct definitions. There are good reasons for this complication. First, to the extent that emotional responses are characteristically unplanned and unexpected, they are exactly the kind of phenomena that are difficult to describe in rational terms. In fact, one way of approaching the definitional difficulty is by specifying emotional phenomena as those that are non-rational: it seems that by describing an action as emotional the need for analysis of its reasons is obviated. Part of the meaning of the term is that the phenomenon is of mysterious or unknown cause, something that comes over you. Because of this failure of normal interpretation where emotion is concerned, the problem area represents the true testing ground for any psychology that aims to provide a general theory of human behaviour. The challenge is to provide the specification of processes that by their very nature appear to defy conventional interpretation.

The second reason for the apparent intractability of the problem of definition of emotion is that, as Fehr and Russell (1984) have argued, the structure of the ordinary language category 'emotion' probably depends upon 'family resemblances' (Wittgenstein, 1952) between exemplars rather than necessary and sufficient conditions. The boundary of the set of emotional phenomena is fuzzy rather than a sharp dividing line between cases of emotion and non-emotion. In this view, emotional phenomena cluster around a 'protoype' (Rosch, 1978) which represents the most commonly occurring features of emotional episodes, thereby specifying the essence of what it is to be emotional. Problems of meaning are often reducible to questions about usage of a word, so perhaps the best way to get at a prototypical operational definition of emotion is by surveying the kind of phenomena psychologists study when they say they are doing research on emotion.

Interest has focused on four broad classes of emotional variable. The first and most basic of these factors relates to *cognitive appraisal* of the situation. Individuals apparently react emotionally to stimulus events to the extent that they are perceived as relevant to their current central goals and interests (Lazarus, 1982). These interests may be genetically programmed, for example the need for food, which manifests itself as hunger; or alternatively may be culturally supplied goals, for example striving towards a paper qualification such as a university degree. The second variable of interest in the study of emotion is the body's *internal reaction*, which usually takes the form of a generalized sympathetic arousal response in emotionally provocative situations (Cannon, 1927). This factor underlies the familiar sensations of pounding heart and dry mouth when one is afraid or angry. Thus, the psychophysiological approach to emotion uses measures such as heart rate, muscle tension and skin conductance as indices of emotional response, all of which relate to the body's mobilization of energy in preparation for response. The third factor relates to *overt behaviour*, often considered in terms of approach or avoidance tendencies, which may be intensified as a result of the presence of emotion. For example, the typical reaction to a frightening event is considered to be fight or flight. Finally, researchers have examined the *facial expressive response* to emotional events in accordance with the widely recognized connection between happiness and smiling, anger and scowling and so on.

All these factors are fairly characteristic features of emotional response as conceived by psychologists and lay people alike. However, none of the factors can be considered necessary conditions of emotional experience, so their presence does not provide the material for a classical, logically exclusive definition. It has been argued, for example, that emotion is possible without cognitive appraisal (Zajonc, 1980), that emotion is possible without arousal (Valins, 1966), and it is demonstrable that emotion is possible without facial expression (Leventhal, 1980). Naturally, these assertions too depend upon the definition of emotion adopted by the theorist. The presence of some of the relevant features of prototypical emotion implies probabilistically the presence of the others but does not guarantee it. Emotion is often inferred on the basis of one or two of these indices.

Psychological research into emotion falls into two broad categories. The first examines the antecedents of affective response, and the other considers its consequences. Ever since James's (1884) theory of emotion, which reversed common sense by suggesting that bodily changes precede emotion rather than vice versa, there has been considerable debate about the ordering of the events that lead to an emotional response. In many respects, these controversies are futile because there seems to be no fixed sequence to emotional response. Each of the factors of emotion can serve as either cause or effect, and the sydrome occurs in a structural pattern, with the occurrence of one kind of affective event tending to recruit the other factors. Thus, the classes of variable which have been proposed as potential effects or expressions of emotion often appear also on the list of suggested causes. For example, there is a convincing body of research which confirms common sense ideas about the facial expression of emotion. Ekman, Sorensen and Friesen (1969) have shown that a limited set of facial patterns can be recognized across cultures, suggesting that there is a genetic component to the facial expression of emotion.

The corresponding research into facial movement as a *determinant* of emotion is more counter-intuitive and has produced rather less convincing and less consistent evidence (for example, Tourangeau and Ellsworth, 1979, and see below), but it does seem that the modification of facial expression can also influence the experience of emotion under certain circumstances (Laird, 1984, and see below). Similarly, for the other basic factors of emotional response there has been research examining its occurrence as a symptom of emotion, and as one of its potential causes. Autonomic arousal accompanies several emotional states, and may under certain circumstances contribute to the generation of these same states (Zillmann, 1978), changes in receptivity to certain kinds of cognitive information occur as a result of emotional states (Isen, 1984), and cognitive appraisals are perhaps the most commonly suggested cause of emotion (Lazarus, 1982).

This duality of cause and effect in emotion can be understood using an attributional framework. Individuals may appraise the situation as emotional on the basis of evidence provided by the presence or absence of the characteristic features of emotion. To some extent, they may *decide* to be emotional about an external object because it seems to have caused them to react in ways that are emotional. Subjects' perceived level of arousal, for example, may provide them with *quantitative* information about emotion. Experimental evidence supports this kind of influence. Valins (1966) provided male subjects with feedback of their supposed heart rate while showing them slides of semi-nude females from *Playboy* magazine. The heart rate was prerecorded and programmed to increase in apparent response to the presentation of half of the slides, so that subjects believed they were reacting to these pictures. Valins found that subjects rated these slides coupled with increased heart rate feedback as more attractive than slides which had been presented with stable feedback. This result has been frequently replicated using different kinds of emotional slides (see Parkinson, 1985, for a review). It seems that subjects are prepared to infer emotion on the basis of information about their reactions to stimuli. Laird (1974) conducted a conceptually similar experiment by manipulating facial expressions in connection with various slides. Subjects were told that the activity of facial muscles was being measured using electrodes and that they should relax and contract certain muscles to allow accurate recording. In this way the experimenter was apparently able to induce smiles or frowns in subjects covertly. Laird found that evaluations of the slides were modified in accordance with subjects' facial expressions, so that, if subjects were smiling, they tended to rate the concurrent slide as more emotionally positive. Facial expression, then, may contribute to the available *qualitative* information about emotional response. (Of course, the broadness of a smile, for example, may also provide quantitative information about the emotional state.)

The research that has been conducted on self-attribution of emotion implicitly assumes that individuals engage in fairly protracted cognitive analysis before emotional effects occur. Certainly, in many situations extensive processing is required before the affective implications of a stimulus event become clear. For example, you notice an expensive car parked outside your loved one's house on a Saturday night (when your telephone call earlier apparently only interrupted 'a quiet evening in'), but only become emotional when you remember that it has been mentioned that your most despised rival in romance drives a Porsche. In contrast, some theorists assume a more direct link between the exciting event and the emotional response to it. In this view, special affective processes are attuned to certain stimulus events and produce emotion independently of the cognitive processing of the relevant material. Facial feedback is often thought to affect emotional response in this direct way (Lanzetta, Cartwright-Smith and Kleck, 1976) rather than as a result of the cognitive information it provides the subject (Laird, 1974). The next section surveys recent theories of emotion and examines their assumptions about the role of cognition in the production of affect.

THEORIES OF EMOTION

Theories of emotion can be divided into those that rely on normal psychological principles such as cognitive variables, and those that assume the existence of distinct processes which are specific to emotion, such as facial feedback, or intracranial activity. In this section, examples of both are considered. The aim is not to survey the entire range of available emotion theories (an awesome task given their range; see Strongman, 1978, for brief descriptions of some 28 different approaches). Instead, I will examine the assumptions underlying some of the more recent and influential formulations. First, though, a little retrospection.

The history of psychological emotion theory essentially begins with William James (1884), who suggested that each emotion is characterized by a distinctive pattern of bodily changes which determines the quality of the experienced emotion. The bodily reaction was thought to occur in direct response to the emotional object or event, and it was argued that the perception of these changes as they occurred provided the subjectively felt affect. The special process assumed by James is the unique definition of each emotion by its own distinctive bodily pattern. No cognitive involvement in the production of emotion is postulated but then again there is no specification of the mechanisms whereby the 'exciting fact' results in bodily change.

Cannon (1927) made a convincing case against James's theory by pointing out that the parameters of peripheral physiological response in emotion did not correspond to the known characteristics of emotional reaction. Changes occurred too slowly, in relatively insensitive regions of the body, and artificial induction of these changes was not sufficient in itself to produce emotion. Most crucially, the changes accompanying a wide variety of emotional experiences were found to be broadly similar. Cannon argued, therefore, that the peripheral responses were symptoms rather than causes of emotion, and that special brain processes were responsible for both the subjective experience of emotion and these autonomic changes, which served to prepare the body for whatever response (often fight or flight) that the precipitating situation demanded. Again, Cannon assumed that affective processes arise without direct cognitive involvement but, like James, failed to specify how the external stimulus comes to trigger the emotional response.

The new generation of cognitive theories of emotion was inspired by Schachter's (1964) formulation which seemed to provide a clear pathway through the James–Cannon controversy. Schachter accepted the evidence that peripheral response was essentially equivalent across emotions, and sought another mechanism for differentiation. This, he argued, depended on a cognitive analysis of the current situation in search of a likely explanation for the experienced arousal response. In effect, the quality of emotion was thought to be a function of the subject's attributions as to the cause of the bodily reaction. Thus, cognitive factors were acknowledged as a potential causal factor in the emotion generation process and the door was opened for analyses of affect which did not rely on special mechanisms. It is difficult to overestimate Schachter's influence on the psychology of emotion: since he proposed his theory, the predominant emphasis has been a cognitive one. The focus of Schachter's model is an atypical state of affairs where a subject is unsure about the cause of arousal. As Schachter admitted, however, in the more usual sequence of events, the individual is aware of the precipitating situation prior to the onset of the arousal response, which, in fact, usually takes a second or two to reach consciousness. Thus, it is normally perfectly obvious to the subject which aspects of the situation have initiated emotion and no extensive causal search is needed. However, even here the meaning of the emotion-inducing circumstance requires some cognitive analysis before the emotion can be labelled. According to Schachter, the quantitative aspect of emotion can arise without cognitive mediation, but the qualitative aspect (and presumably the emotional state *per se*) requires prior cognition. This view that affect is postcognitive is now probably the most popular attitude among emotion theorists (Zajonc, 1980, and see below).

Cognitive theories

Cognition can enter into the generation of emotion at a number of stages. First, it is likely to be involved in the appraisal of the external cause of the emotion. Second, assuming Schachter's model is correct, subjects need to notice any arousal present, and then cognitively search the environment for the cause of that arousal. A similar process would occur for other sources of emotional information such as facial movement. Finally the subject decides on a label for the emotion, which incidentally may be subject to continual revision by cognitive reappraisal.

Cognitive theories of emotion usually rely on one or both of the principles of appraisal and attribution. Lazarus's theory (Lazarus, 1968; see also Lazarus, Kanner and Folkman, 1980) provides a typical example of the appraisal position. According to this model, emotion occurs whenever external events are appraised by subjects as having relevance for their central life concerns. The appraisal of threat, for example, initiates various characteristic coping responses, which may be purely cognitive, such as denial or intellectualization of the threat, or may represent active behavioural responses, for example fight or flight. After these responses have been instituted, the threat is reappraised, to check whether further coping is necessary. Benign appraisals of challenge can also occur, accounting for some of the positive emotions. According to Lazarus, the main mechanism for differentiating the various emotions is secondary appraisal which evaluates the alternative coping strategies available. Thus, the quality of an emotion is determined by the individual's evaluations of the behavioural or cognitive responses that the situation requires. Subsequent theories have further examined the appraisal process, and focused on the cognitive algebra involved in generating different emotional states.

One of these models of the cognitive processes determining emotion is provided by Weiner (1985), who drew on his research into attributions about achievement-related behaviour to derive a model which depends on subjects' inferences about the causal structure underlying the emotional event. Weiner assumed that increasingly complex cognitions enter into the differentiation of an emotion over time, so that preliminary reactions to an event relate only to its pleasantness or unpleasantness, and produce an affective tone that is positive or negative but no more. This initial response is modified according to the perceived *causation* behind the event: for instance, when individuals attribute pleasant occurrences to their own ability or effort, pride is experienced.

Weiner tested his theory by asking subjects to recall an occasion when they had experienced pleasant or unpleasant circumstances which seemed to result from various combinations of causes, and report what emotion they had experienced. For instance, subjects asked to recall something bad which they felt had been due to their own lack of effort, consistently reported that the remembered event made them feel shame. The weakness of this kind of study is that it uses subjects' talk about emotion rather than their actual experiences as data. The methodology gives little information about the validity of the system: it offers evidence about subjects' theories and definitions of the various emotional states but not about their real-time appraisal processes. It is interesting to note that Weiner assumed very limited cognitive involvement in the early stages of an emotional response, since the subject has only to decide whether the event is good or bad. Further cognitive work defines the state as a specific emotion. In Weiner's view, then, feeling and thought operate interactively and concurrently.

The attributional approach to emotional experience receives its most difficult test when applied to clinical affective disorders such as depression. Abramson and Martin (1981) put forward a theory of depression based on a grafting of attributional principles to Seligman's (1975) learned helplessness theory. Animal conditioning studies reveal that exposure to prolonged uncontrollable negative reinforcement has demotivational effects on the subject. These effects are not restricted to the original learning situation, but generalize to other tasks. The animal seems to give up trying to obtain reinforcement when it learns that nothing it does makes any difference. According to Seligman, some forms of depression in humans depend on similar processes. It is clear, however, that the experience of inability to control outcomes in one particular situation does not inevitably cause clinical depression in most people.

It seems, therefore, that there must be other factors that underlie the extent of generalization of learned helplessness in humans. Abramson and Martin (1981) suggested that depression occurs only when subjects make certain attributions about their helplessness. Specifically, the symptoms are thought to be most severe when subjects believe that helplessness is caused by factors *internal* to themselves rather than environmental circumstances, when these causes are perceived as *stable* rather than variable, and when they are thought to reflect a *global* deficiency rather than one that is specific to the kind of bad experiences that have happened. In other words, depression occurs when subjects conclude that helplessness is likely to pervade all aspects of their future lives. For example, if you get beaten at Scrabble, you may decide that the game depends on luck, and therefore not feel too bad about it. (Note, however, that consistent losing at Scrabble and other games may change this opinion.) Alternatively, you may think that success at Scrabble is the one true path to assessment of personal worth and so may attribute your failure to something about yourself that is unalterable and that will be reflected in anything else you do. In this case you will get depressed.

The factors underlying depression in this example relate to the personality factor of attributional style, but there is also the possibility that circumstances lead individuals to make these kinds of negative attribution. Clearly, this theory has a certain amount of intuitive validity; we all know people who see the first hint of bad luck as an omen, and expect everything to go wrong from then on. Equally clearly, the analysis seems less relevant to the more extreme forms of psychotic depression, which are seen as stemming from something internal to the person, rather than external circumstances. Accepting this limitation, research into the attributional model of depression has confirmed that attributional processes can influence the severity of emotional response.

The theories considered in this section have only discussed the role of cognition in the appraisal process. They have nothing to say about the role of the other factors of emotion as either cause or effect. In fact they offer no explanation of the structure of an emotional episode, they only characterize the processes that may trigger the various components of the reaction. A second set of cognitive theories of emotion examines the influence of cognition on the operation of these other factors. The pattern of these theories has been mentioned in a previous section. The *causal* impact of bodily responses, facial expressions and overt behaviour may be represented in terms of the subjects' attributions about the cause of these variables, or alternatively the three factors may be seen as sources of emotionally relevant information that feed into the appraisal process. In this view, emotion is the product of the cognitive system just like any other human function. No special processes are implicated in the operation of affect.

Special process theories

Special process theories assume the existence of mechanisms that are specific to emotion, thus explaining its existence as a distinctive category of experience. Often these theories depend upon a substantial unlearned component of emotional responding, and they necessarily assume some independence of cognition and affect. The favourite candidate for a special process underlying emotion is the facial expression factor.

There is no single facial feedback theory, but for ease of exposition, the variants will here be considered together. Many theorists have assumed a causal role for facial expression as part of a wider theory of affect, but the focus in the present section is on the aspects of their theories that relate to this variable (Tomkins, 1962; Izard, 1979; Leventhal, 1984). There is some intuitive validity to the idea that moods can be altered by changing facial expression as evidenced by the popular advice to 'put on a happy face' when things are getting you down ('smile and the world smiles with you'). There are several ways such a strategy might be effective, however, which do not depend on a causal role for facial expression in the experience of emotion. For example, the cognitive decision to adopt a smile itself reflects a positive attitude, and represents the start of a struggle against the bad mood, so it may be the cognitive change rather than the facial change that mediates the improvement of mood. A second possibility is that adopting a smile causes other people to treat you better. It is usually considered preferable to talk to someone who looks happy rather than someone who seems depressed, so smiling tends to encourage attention and pleasantness from other people. Clearly, this can lead to an improvement in mood. Conversely, scowling is likely to confirm any bad feelings about people, because they may start to avoid you.

The attraction of the facial expression variable for the emotion theorist is twofold. First, the face is known to be a channel capable of communicating both quantitative and qualitative information about emotion (see, for example, Ekman and Friesen, 1975), so it represents a variable of some versatility. Second, there is widely accepted evidence that a set of some six or so facial expressions contain innately programmed elements (Ekman, Sorensen and Friesen, 1969). If the additional assumption is made that facial expression *produces* emotional experience as well as expressing it, an explanation of both the causation and the differentiation of the emotions is provided quite easily. The face reacts automatically to the situation and produces the appropriate emotional experience via facial feedback. Of course, no theorist would adopt such an oversimplified view of the emotion generation process, but elements of this reasoning are commonly used. The first problem for such a theory would be the fact that individuals who are unable to express emotion facially still seem to experience it, so there must be some other causal principle apart from facial feedback. Second, the posing of a facial expression does not automatically produce the relevant emotion, so clearly the link between facial responses and emotional experience cannot be a direct one.

The core of the facial feedback hypothesis is that facial expression contributes to emotional experience under some circumstances. This need not imply that it represents either a necessary or a sufficient condition for emotion, but only that it has some influence on subjectively felt affect. The balance of the available experimental evidence supports such an influence (see Laird, 1984), but unfortunately research in this area is plagued by problems of demand characteristics and ambiguity of interpretation. The direct manipulation of facial expression is perhaps impossible to achieve without subjects realizing that the experimenter is trying to get them to smile or frown or whatever, making the purpose of the manipulation transparent, and secondly it is always possible to argue that the expressions achieved using these means are not accurate reflections of naturally occurring facial expressions (see Tomkins, 1981). To be sure, it is most unlikely that any simulation of facial expression could ever *exactly* match the timing and characteristics of a spontaneous expression. An alternative research strategy manipulates facial expression indirectly. The problem here, though, is that the method of modifying expression is also likely to influence emotion directly rather than as a result of the induced facial change. For these reasons it is practically impossible to get definitive evidence for or against the facial feedback hypothesis.

Other special process theories of emotion refer to brain circuits as primary causes of emotion. Cannon's (1927) model represents an early version of this kind of theory. Cannon assumed that emotional processes are excited in the thalamus whenever an emotional stimulus is encountered. The excitation of these processes was thought to occur only in emotional situations generating the distinctive experience of emotion via a neural pathway up to the neocortex, and arousal by downward influence on the autonomic system. The basic problem with all theories of this kind is that they fail to offer any predictions about the kind of stimuli that trigger the special emotional process, nor do they specify how the emotion is acted out behaviourally. Cognitive and social principles are more relevant to these questions. A second point to note is that these theories typically hold that emotion is localized in evolutionarily older regions of the brain, in accordance with the commonly held belief that affect represents a relatively primitive system of behaviour (Averill, 1980). In fact, it can be argued that such a complex and variable phenomenon as emotion cannot be realistically located in any one part of the brain (Lazarus, 1982).

EFFECTS OF EMOTION ON COGNITION

Previous sections have covered the role of cognition in the production of emotion; research into the *effects* of emotional and mood states on cognitive processes is now examined. There is a convincing body of evidence for the existence of these influences, but some uncertainty about their explanation.

First, there are studies which have demonstrated influences of mood on judgement and behaviour. Johnson and Tversky (1983), for example, demonstrated that bad moods initiated by reading about disasters of various kinds made subjects judge the probability of similar and dissimilar disasters occurring in real life to increase. Thus, reading the bad news in the papers may put you in a bad mood which in turn leads you to overestimate the likelihood that you may die of cancer or suffer a fatal road accident. Second, there is evidence that affect influences memory in several ways. The first of these influences is a state-dependent effect (Bower, 1981). This relates to the phenomenon where material learned when in a distinctive mental state, for example, alcoholic intoxication, cannot be remembered (at least not as accurately) unless the individual returns to a similar state. This effect underlies the phenomenon of forgetting where you have put something when you were drunk but finding it again the next time you have a few drinks. Bower argued that emotions can provide a similar contextual cue for memory, so that material learned whilst in one particular emotional state is best remembered in a similar state. Experiments using hypnotically induced affect at the time of learning and recall of word lists have provided demonstrations of this process. If subjects are in a similar emotional state when remembering the words to the one they were in when learning them, then memory is improved. Other influences of affect on memory occur at the time of retrieval. Isen (1984) presented evidence that positive mood increases likelihood as well as speed of recall of pleasant memories. Finally, there are effects of mood at encoding, with subjects showing better memory for pleasantly toned material learnt when they are in a pleasant mood themselves.

Isen argued that the evidence for all these kinds of effect is less consistent in the case of negative emotion than positive emotion, and suggested that there may be a fundamental asymmetry between the two. In this view, happiness and sadness do not represent opposite ends of a single dimension, but may be relatively independent of each other. For example, it might be possible to both like someone and dislike them at the same time (although it seems less plausible that anyone could be both happy and sad simultaneously). Part of the asymmetry in the effects of mood on memory, however, depends on processes of mood-maintenance and mood-repair. When in a positive mood, it is argued, the tendency is to do whatever can be done to stay in that state, so that subjects will tend to 'look on the bright side', and to focus on pleasant rather than unpleasant stimuli; they might, for example, remember pleasantly toned words better afterwards for this reason. In a negative mood-state, however, the desire is to change or repair the mood. This might result in selective inattention to unpleasant material. Despite this tendency, there have been demonstrations that negative mood can sometimes produce state-dependent and other memory effects in just the same way as positive mood. In Bower's experiments, for example, the experimenter told subjects to adopt a negative mood under hypnosis, and in order to obey this instruction to *maintain* an unpleasant state of mind they may have suppressed the usual mechanisms of mood-repair.

The research on effects of emotion on cognition provides further evidence concerning the interrelations between these two categories of experience. In the next section, however, I discuss the opposite view, that affect and cognition operate independently.

AFFECTIVE PRIMACY

Which comes first, thought or feeling? Zajonc (1980) argued that cognition and affect operate as independent systems, and that emotional response may precede cognitive processing under some circumstances. Feelings about an object or event may arise before it is fully interpreted or even recognized. An example of this would be feeling warm toward someone you come across before you are able to recall who they are and how you come to know them. Zajonc contrasted his position with the current trend among theories of emotion to regard affect as the final event of the information processing chain. In this view, feelings arise only after the relevant object or event has been fully appraised and categorized. As the foregoing discussion has revealed, however, there are several cognitive theories of emotion which assume more limited cognitive involvement in the early stages of an emotional reaction (Weiner, 1985). Even Lazarus, who has been the most vocal of Zajonc's opponents on this issue, simply contends that cognitive appraisal at some level always precedes emotion. This does not necessarily imply a thoroughgoing processing of the stimulus, only that some minimal cognitive analysis takes place before emotion can be produced. Indeed, as Leventhal (1984) has pointed out, it is difficult to imagine how an affective response to an object could occur in the absence of any recognition, because, at the very least, the object needs to be distinguishable from other objects, or else emotion would occur indiscriminately.

According to Lazarus (1982), 'emotion results from an evaluative perception of a relationship (actual, imagined, or anticipated) between a person (or animal) and the environment' (p.1023) and as such is necessarily preceded by appraisal of the implications of the stimulus event for the subject's well-being. As Zajonc (1984) has pointed out, however, this analysis evades the empirical question of affective primacy by specifying the presence of cognition in the *definition* of emotion. In effect, Lazarus's argument is that if cognitive appraisal is not involved in generating a particular state, then that state is not an emotion in his terms. Correspondingly, if an emotion has arisen as a consequence of some external event, then that event must necessarily have been appraised by the cognitive system. Despite the apparent circularity of this position, it is perhaps more attractive than a theory in which cognition and affect are so vaguely defined that it is sometimes difficult to say whether either has occurred. Zajonc's theory tends towards this latter problem. For example, although he seems to be trying to make a general point about emotion, most of the examples cited relate to preferences and evaluative judgments. Of course this kind of response sometimes depends on emotion, but equally clearly, it does not always do so. It is a far less controversial statement that individuals decide early on in the processing sequence whether an event is good or bad (Weiner, 1985) than that emotion can occur without cognition. It is of obvious advantage to the individual to decide quickly about the pleasantness of an occurrence. Even here, however, it might well be contended that some cognitive processing is necessary before this kind of judgement can be made with any accuracy.

Much of Lazarus's (1982) rebuttal of the affective primacy position depends on his argument that the states Zajonc mentions are not actually emotional. For example, the contention that startle occurs automatically without any obvious cognitive involvement is countered by the claim that startle is not in fact an emotion. A similar conclusion was reached by Ekman, Friesen and Simons (1985), who found that the startle reaction has certain characteristics which distinguish it from the category of emotions. Startle occurs automatically in all subjects in response to the same stimuli (for example, a sudden loud gunshot), whereas the whole history of psychology of emotion attests to the fact that there is no known stimulus that will reliably produce the same emotion in all subjects. Similarly, Ekman, Friesen and Simons showed that unlike most emotions, startle cannot effectively be suppressed or simulated, is basically unaffected by anticipation, and so on. The affective primacy controversy has been useful in that it has encouraged theorists to be more precise in their specification of what it means to call a phenomenon an emotion.

It seems that the affective primacy controversy is really a dispute about definitions rather than about empirical matters. 'Cognition' is a term that has been used in many senses, two of which are relevant to the current issue. On the one hand, 'cognitive' processes are those that underlie a circumscribed set of phenomena, such as memory, attention, attribution, comparative judgement and so on. The present chapter has examined the role of some of these processes in 'emotion', and considered theories of emotion which rely on these processes to a greater or lesser extent. Some theorists argue that for a response to be emotional it must include special non-cognitive processes, and others make no such assumption. In this view of 'cognition', the debate hinges on the existence of these special processes and their causal role in the generation of emotional experience. I have suggested that the main purpose of proposing such variables is simply to distinguish emotion from other categories of human function. It is interesting to note, in this connection, that cognitive theorists often take the complementary stance of specifically excluding affective phenomena from their concept of cognition, almost as if psychologists working in the areas of emotion and cognition are jealously (or perhaps sensibly) guarding their own territories, and artificially preserving a distinction between the two sets of processes.

The second idea of 'cognition' allows a simpler resolution of the affective primacy issue. In this view, 'cognition' is defined in terms of an *approach* to psychology, rather than being a label for a restricted class of processes. Any of the explanatory concepts used within the confines of this approach come under the heading of cognition. In this second sense, the cognitive approach depends on a loose metaphor which treats the human subject as an information processing device such as a computer. The model succeeds or fails to the extent that the focus of analysis can be usefully simulated in terms of transformations of data inputs. Of course, the model is never completely realistic because human action is not only a question of processing information. However, the metaphor may be adequate for certain limited purposes. Whether it is the *best* or *most useful* approach to the phenomenon of emotion is another question. Mandler (1984) attempted to explain emotion using this second cognitive approach, and his theory offers a reasonably successful account of affective phenomena as part of a more general psychological theory.

This chapter has focused on evidence demonstrating that emotion and cognition interact with one another in a reasonably intimate manner, and suggests that they may be accommodated under the same set of explanatory principles. Whether these principles will resemble existing cognitive models remains to be seen. Recent developments in social cognition are relevant to this question. Abelson (1963) set the trend for the new approach with his attempt to simulate 'hot' (that is affect-laden) cognitions on a computer. The importance of such an approach is that it serves as a reminder that the cognitive system has to deal with information that carries personal relevance as well as with cold facts. Even where these cold facts are concerned, the cognitive system may produce solutions that are less than perfect (Kahneman and Tversky, 1982). Nisbett and Ross (1980) have discussed everyday situations in which logical inferential processes apparently fail not because of the influence of irrational emotional impulses, or motivational concerns, but simply because the cognitive system necessarily takes short cuts in interpreting data. There is never enough time to thoroughly weigh up all the available evidence, so humans utilize a number of heuristic strategies for dealing with information and solving problems.

Thus, the attempt by psychologists to apply cognitive principles to real-life social situations has revealed that humans frequently use suboptimal processing strategies. This research has led to softer and indeed warmer theories of cognition, which employ concepts such as heuristics (Kahneman and Tversky, 1982), scripts (Schank and Abelson, 1977) and prototypes (Rosch, 1978). Previously, cognitive research tended to focus on artificial and simplified laboratory situations, such as the learning of words from a list, and its explanatory principles were correspondingly cold and logical. Moving out into the real world is beginning to change that. One consequence of the introduction of these softer explanatory principles has been that social psychologists have begun to find cognitive principles more appropriate to the problem areas they explore. A case in point is emotion theory, as revealed in this chapter. However, in the final section, I suggest that the cognitive approach needs to be further broadended to incorporate affect, and to allow a general theory of human behaviour. More accurately, it needs to be socialized.

SOCIAL CONSTRUCTION OF EMOTION

In this chapter, I have considered various ideas about the relationships and interactions of the cognitive and affective systems: some theorists consider the two systems to be independent, others assume limited interrelations between them, some assume that they operate in parallel, while others assume that the same general principles may be used to explain both sets of phenomena. It is with these last theorists that my sympathies lie. Like Mandler (1984), I want to argue that 'emotion' does not necessarily refer to a precisely defined existent entity, but instead is a common sense category of phenomena which tend to cluster together. In this case, it is not psychology's job to explain emotion as such, but to specify the processes which generate the phenomena that are usually described as emotional. What kind of explanatory principles are required for such an enterprise?

As demonstrated in much of what has been said, cognitive principles, especially the newer, softer cognitive principles, have been relatively successful in accounting for some aspects of emotion. But I think a more radical development is needed. Cognitive principles, as they stand, are often specifically designed to exclude affect. Thus, to the extent that the cognitive approach is invading emotional territory, the phenomenon of emotion is rapidly shrinking. I would argue that cognitive principles, however soft they may get, are essentially inappropriate for the general theory of human action (including both reason and emotion). Their weakness is that they cannot represent any cultural, collective or, more broadly, social causation as anything beyond its impact on what goes on inside one person's head. Computers do not have their own culture. To close this chapter, I discuss a theory which is sensitive to the essentially social basis of human action and emotion.

Averill (1982, 1985) presents emotion as a social construction. Although he admits that the responses that make up an emotional reaction may be genetically programmed, the way these are organized and interpreted by the individual transcends any physiological analysis. Emotions, in Averill's (1985) view, are 'socially constituted syndromes (transitory social roles) that include a person's appraisal of the situation and that are interpreted as passions rather than actions' (p.98). They are passions rather than actions because subjects *interpret* them as things that happen to them rather than as things they do. However, this experience of passivity is a function of social demands rather than an actual reflection of reality. In fact, emotions are actions for which a person does not take responsibility, because they conflict with social norms; for example, anger goes against the norm of not harming or even wanting to harm someone. On the other hand, the same action may be consistent with another set of norms; for example, anger may be initiated by the norm of standing up for one's own rights. In other words, emotion represents a means of overcoming conflicting societal norms.

In situations in which this kind of conflict arises, there are social roles available which allow the individual to perform the proscribed action without accepting the responsibility for doing so. Such transitory roles are emotions. The way these roles are acted out depends upon cultural conventions, but is likely to include sophisticated signalling channels (for example facial expressions) designed to communicate the fact that the individual is not be sanctioned for his actions. Also, it is likely that these occasions will be accompanied by arousal, since they reflect a disruption of normal functioning and so on. At first blush, Averill's analysis seems to apply only to cases of negative emotion, but his discussion of love (usually considered to be positive) helps to correct this impression. Averill (1985) argues that love arises as a function of society's simultaneous respect for, and neglect of, the individual. Part of the core of the meaning of love is an idealization of the loved one and reciprocally of oneself; this provides a means of preserving self-worth (as demanded by society) within a system which has little time or money for the individual's needs.

So where does all this leave the cognitive approach to emotion? If, as Averill argues, emotion is *essentially* a social construction, it is hard to imagine how it could be programmed into a computer. The information processing view seems able to answer only limited questions about emotion, dealing with the conditions of onset and the interpretation of an emotional state. For example, the processes whereby subjects appraise an event as requiring an emotional response are still amenable to cognitive interpretation. Second, consideration of emotion as a transitory role allows us to predict that the presence of factors indicating emotion will tend to lead to the acting out of that emotion (to extent that this will serve the social needs of the subject), so that each of the factors of emotion may play a causal or symptomatic role by recruiting other factors. This kind of effect is psychologically interesting, but it leads to further, more fundamental questions about why action is organized emotionally in the first place. Faced with these problems, the cognitive approach may require social support.

ACKNOWLEDGEMENT

The author is currently supported by the Economic and Social Research Council under its Postdoctoral Research Fellowship Scheme. The contents of the chapter are the responsibility of the author and do not necessarily reflect with the views of the ESRC.

REFERENCES

Abelson, R.P. (1963) Computer simulation of 'hot' cognition. In S.S. Tomkins and S. Messick (eds) *Computer Simulation of Personality*. New York: John Wiley.
Abramson, L.Y. and Martin, D.J. (1981) Depression and the causal inference process. In J.H. Harvey, W.J. Ickes and R.F. Kidd (eds) *New Directions in Attribution Research, Volume 3*. Hillsdale, N.J.: Lawrence Erlbaum Associates.
Averill, J.R. (1980) An analysis of psychophysiological symbolism and its influence on theories of emotion. *Journal for the Theory of Social Behavior*, 4, 147–189.
Averill, J.R. (1982) *Anger and Aggression*. New York: Springer-Verlag.
Averill, J.R. (1985) The social construction of emotion: With special reference to love. In K.J. Gergen and K.E. Davis (eds) *The Social Construction of the Person*. New York: Springer-Verlag.
Bower, G.H. (1981) Mood and memory. *American Psychologist*, 36, 129–148.
Cannon, W.B. (1927) The James – Lange theory of emotions: A critical examination and an alternative theory. *American Journal of Psychology*, 39, 106–124.
Ekman, P. and Friesen, W.V. (1975) *Unmasking the Face*. Englewood Cliffs, N.J.: Prentice-Hall.
Ekman, P., Friesen, W.V. and Simons, R.C. (1985) Is the startle reaction an emotion? *Journal of Personality and Social Psychology*, 49, 1416–1426.
Ekman, P., Sorensen, E.R. and Friesen, W.V. (1969) Pan-cultural elements in facial displays of emotion. *Science*, 164, 86–88.
Fehr, B. and Russell, J.A. (1984) Concept of emotion viewed from a prototype perspective. *Journal of Experimental Psychology: General*, 113, 464–486.
Isen, A.M. (1984) Toward understanding the role of affect in cognition. In R.S. Wyer and T.K. Srull (eds) *Handbook of Social Cognition, Volume 3*. Hillsdale, N.J.: Lawrence Erlbaum Associates.
Izard, C.E. (1979) Emotions as motivations: An evolutionary – developmental perspective. In R. Dienstbier (ed) *Nebraska Symposium on Motivation, Volume 27*. Lincoln, Nebraska: University of Nebraska Press:
James, W. (1884) What is an emotion? *Mind*, 9, 188–205.
Johnson, E. and Tversky, A. (1983) Affect, generalization and the perception of risk. *Journal of Personality and Social Psychology*, 45, 20–31.
Kahneman, D. and Tversky, A. (1982) *Judgment under Uncertainty: Heuristics and Biases*. New YorK: Cambridge University Press.
Kleinginna, P.R., Jr and Kleinginna, A.M. (1981) A categorized list of emotion definitions, with suggestions for a consensual definition. *Motivation and Emotion*, 5, 345–379.
Laird, J.D. (1974) Self-attribution of emotion: The effects of facial expression on the quality of emotional experience. *Journal of Personality and Social Psychology*, 29, 475–486.
Laird, J.D. (1984) The real role of facial response in the experience of emotion: A reply to Tourangeau and Ellsworth and others. *Journal of Personality and Social Psychology*, 47, 909–917.
Lanzetta, J.T., Cartwright-Smith, J. and Kleck, R.E. (1976) Effects of nonverbal dissimulation on emotional experience and autonomic arousal. *Journal of Personality and Social Psychology*, 33 354–370.
Lazarus, R.S. (1968) Emotions and adaptation: Conceptual and empirical relations. In W.J. Arnold (ed) *Nebraska Symposium on Motivation 1968*. Lincoln: University of Nebraska Press.

Lazarus, R.S. (1982) Thoughts on the relations between emotion and cognition. *American Psychologist*, 37, 1019–1024.
Lazarus, R.S., Kanner, A.D. and Folkman, S. (1980) Emotions: A cognitive-phenomenonological analysis. In R. Plutchik and H. Kellerman (ed.) *Emotion: Theory, Research, and Experience, Volume 1*. New York: Academic Press.
Leventhal, H. (1980) Toward a comprehensive theory of emotion. *Advances in Experimental Social Psychology*, 13, 139–207.
Leventhal, H. (1984) A perceptual – motor theory of emotion. *Advances in Experimental Social Psychology*, 17, 117–182.
Mandler, G. (1984) *Mind and Body: The Psychology of Emotion and Stress*. New York: Norton.
Nisbett, R.E. and Ross, L. (1980) *Human Inference: Strategies and Shortcomings of Social Judgment*. Englewood Cliffs, N.J.: Prentice-Hall.
Parkinson, B. (1985) Emotional effects of false autonomic feedback. *Psychological Bulletin*, 98, 471–494.
Rosch, E. (1978) Principles of categorization. In E. Rosch and B.B. Lloyd (eds) *Cognition and Categorization*. Hillsdale, N.J.: Lawrence Erlbaum Associates.
Schachter, S. (1964) The interaction of cognitive and physiological determinants of emotional state. *Advances in Experimental Social Psychology*, 1, 49–80.
Schank, R. and Abelson, R. (1977) *Scripts, Plans, Goals and Understanding*. Hillsdale, N.J.: Lawrence Erlbaum Associates.
Seligman, M.E.P. (1975) *Helplessness: On Depression, Development, and Death*. San Francisco: Freeman.
Strongman, K.T. (1978) *The Psychology of Emotion*, 2nd ed. New York: Wiley.
Tomkins, S.S. (1962) *Affect, Imagery, Consciousness*. New York: Springer-Verlag.
Tomkins, S.S. (1981) The role of facial response in the experience of emotion: A reply to Tourangeau and Ellsworth. *Journal of Personality and Social Psychology*, 40, 355–357.
Tourangeau, R. and Ellsworth, P.C. (1979) The role of facial response in the experience of emotion. *Journal of Personality and Social Psychology*, 37, 1519–1531.
Valins, S. (1966) Cognitive effects of false heart-rate feedback. *Journal of Personality and Social Psychology*, 4, 400–408.
Weiner, B. (1985) An attributional theory of achievement motivation and emotion. *Psychological Review*, 92, 548–573.
Wittgenstein, L. (1953) *Philosophical Investigations*. Oxford: Oxford University Press.
Zajonc, R.B. (1980) Feeling and thinking: Preferences need no inferences. *American Psychologist*, 35, 151–175.
Zillmann, D. (1978) Attribution and misattribution of excitatory reactions. In J.H. Harvey, W.J. Ickes and R.F. Kidd (eds) *New Directions in Attribution Theory, Volume 2*. Hillsdale, N.J.: Lawrence Erlbaum Associates.

REASONING
Jonathan St B.T. Evans

Reasoning – the process of drawing inferences – is fundamental in human cognition. Almost all cognitive activity involves deductions, predictions or guesses that involve going beyond the information given. Many of these inferences, for example those involved in comprehending language, are *implicit*, that is made rapidly and without conscious awareness. There has, however, been considerable psychological study of *explicit* reasoning, which is the focus of interest in this chapter. In these studies experimental subjects are given certain information and asked to state explicitly what inferences may be drawn, or to evaluate the soundness of stated conclusions.

Explicit inference tasks fall into two broad categories, deductive and inductive. Deductive reasoning normally involves the presentation of verbal propositions or *premises*, from which a conclusion may be drawn. The conclusion is said to be *valid* if its truth is necessarily entailed by the premises. Consider, for example, the following argument:

All dogs are carnivorous.
All dogs are animals.
Therefore, some animals are carnivorous.

This argument is, in fact, valid because if the premises are true the conclusion necessarily follows. To put it another way, there is no model of the world consistent with the premises in which the conclusion is not also true. If, however, we replaced the conclusion with the assertion 'Therefore, all animals are carnivorous', it would no longer be valid. Such a conclusion is consistent with the premises, but not necessitated by them.

The ancient discipline of logic – a branch of philosophy – is concerned with specifying rules of 'correct' deductive reasoning. There are various types of logic dealing with problems of different structure, such as classical syllogistic logic (dating back to Aristotle). A more powerful and modern system, that of propositional logic, has provided the basis of much recent psychological work on reasoning, though studies of syllogistic reasoning are still popular. There has, in fact, been extensive psychological study of people's abilities to make deductive inferences (see Evans, 1982a, 1983).

Deductive inferences – if valid – are drawn with certainty. Much reasoning in real life, however, involves inductive or probabilistic reasoning. Such inferences normally involve attempts to infer general consequences from specific examples. We all 'induce' general rules from our specific experiences, which we then apply to predict and understand new situations. Such inferences cannot, however, be logical. They carry no deductive certainty.

Inductive reasoning has interested psychologists in three main areas. The first is in the area of scientific reasoning (see Tweney, Doherty and Mynatt, 1981), in which scientists might be seen as attempting to induce the laws of nature. Whilst the philosopher Karl Popper (for example 1959, 1962) maintains that science should proceed by attempts to falsify theories – by empirical testing of their deductive consequences – much of the psychological literature on scientific reasoning has, in fact, revolved around the contention that people behave in a contrary manner, exhibiting a 'confirmation bias'.

The second area in which inductive reasoning has been studied is in the field of intuitive statistical judgement (see Kahneman, Slovic and Tversky, 1982). Experiments in this area involve presenting subjects with statistical evidence and asking them to express confidence in or judge probabilities of certain hypotheses. Just as logic provides a normative or prescriptive theory of deductive reasoning, so statistical theory provides formal procedures for computing 'correct' probabilistic inferences, against which the accuracy of subjects' inferences are often judged. The third area of interest, which relates closely to the second, lies in the field of social inference (see Nisbett and Ross, 1980). Our views about groups, for example, may be formed by inductive inferences from observations of individuals. Studying the nature of such inferences could help us to understand phenomena such as stereotypes and prejudice.

A characteristic feature of research on reasoning is the availability of a normative logical or statistical theory which prescribes 'correct' answers to problems. On the basis of experimental findings, much evidence of errors and biases in reasoning has been claimed. Others have argued, however, on a variety of grounds, that these findings provide a highly misleading picture of people's competence in reasoning (see, for example, Cohen, 1981). The view taken here is that interest should be focused not on the question of how 'good' or 'bad' people's reasoning is, but, rather, on the nature of the psychological mechanisms and processes involved.

In the next section, four major theoretical approaches to the explanation of human reasoning are considered. In the following section a case study of empirical research on a particular reasoning problem, the Wason selection task, is presented, followed by an assessment of the ability of each of the four approaches to explain the results of these studies.

THEORETICAL APPROACHES

In this section I consider four theoretical approaches to the explanation of human reasoning: (i) inference rules, (ii) heuristics and biases, (iii) schemas and (iv) mental models. Those favouring a rational view of man's reasoning have tended to propose that people possess internalized logical systems which provide rather general rules for reasoning. Protaganists of what Cohen (1981) labels the 'pessimistic' school, on the other hand, have emphasized the existence of errors and biases, and proposed that people use 'heuristics' – rather unreliable short-cut strategies – rather than logical rules.

There is, however, a respect in which these first two approaches are similar and contrast with the last two. These approaches might be labelled *syntactic*, in that they tend to focus on the logical structure of problems without too much regard to their particular context or meaning. Both rule and heuristic-based theories have tended to propose very general mechanisms for reasoning, which people apply in many contexts. Schema and mental model theories, however, both emphasize the role of people's knowledge of the particular content and context in which problems appear and are thus essentially *semantic* in nature. I now examine each approach in detail.

(i) Inference rules

The notion that people reason by application of inference rules is closely associated with the 'rationalist' school, since it involves the notion that people possess and use internalized logics. Propositional logic, for example, contains a number of rules which can be used to determine the validity of deductive inferences. An example is the rule known as *modus tollens*:

$$\text{If } p \text{ then } q, \text{ not-}q, \text{ therefore not-}p.$$

This rule is considered valid no matter what particular propositions are substituted for the letters p and q. A real-life example of *modus tollens* reasoning might be: 'My flat is cold so the heating must be switched off' – an inference drawn from the implicit conditional, 'If the heating is switched on then my flat is warm'.

Formal logics provide sets of inference rules, such as *modus tollens*, which can be combined to derive conclusions from premisses or to test the validity of any given argument. Note that in standard logic only the structure of the statements is considered and the meaning of the propositions ignored – hence the approach is entirely syntactic rather than semantic. The simplest psychological theory of reasoning based upon inference rules takes the form of proposing that the 'standard' logics of philosophy not only prescribe correct reasoning, but also describe people's actual reasoning. For example, Henle (1962) in an influential paper, explained the frequent observation of logical errors on the assumption that whilst the process of reasoning was logical, people often understood the problems in a different way from how the experimenter intended. Hence, she argued, subjects' answers often followed logically from their *personalized* representation of the problem (see Evans, 1982a, for a detailed critique of this paper).

Henle's theory depends upon a distinction of fundamental importance in cognitive psychology, that between *representation* and *process*. Clearly, in order to explain reasoning we need to know both how the information in the problem is mentally represented by the subject and what sort of processes are applied to these representations in order to draw inferences. The difficulty of distinguishing between representational and process sources of error in reasoning should not be underestimated, however. For example, psychological models of syllogistic reasoning have been proposed both which attribute all mistakes to faulty representations rather than inferential errors (Revlis, 1975a,b) and which make precisely the reverse assumption (Guyote and Sternberg, 1981). In each case the authors claim good fits to experimental data.

A number of psychologists who posit the use of inference rules as an explanation of deductive reasoning have, however, been dissatisfied with the correspondence of standard formal logic to natural language and have proposed alternative 'natural logics' with modified sets of rules (for example Osherson, 1975; Johnson-Laird, 1975; Braine, 1978). Rips (1983), in the most recent and perhaps most ambitious attempt to explain reasoning in this way, has provided a computer model called ANDS implemented in the LISP programming language. ANDS contains a set of inference rules together with strategies for applying the rules to solve problems in deductive logic. The performance of the program is compared with protocols of human subjects attempting the same problems. This approach to psychological validation of the model is reminiscent of that of Newell and Simon's (1972) classic attempt to establish their computer program GPS (General Problem Solver) as a psychological theory of human problem solving. Like GPS, ANDS is open to criticism that the representations with which it reasons are provided by the human programmer, who has hence extracted the logical structure in advance. Proponents of the semantic approaches to reasoning might argue that (a) representation of problem content is a complex process which requires modelling in its own right, and that (b) representing problems in terms of their syntactic structure begs the essential question.

Close parallels to the inference rule approach can be found in the study of statistical reasoning. For example, in the 1960s, man was generally regarded as a good 'intuitive statistician', conforming, for example, to a Bayesian model of statistical inference (cf. Peterson and Beach, 1967). This view has been strongly challenged by the subsequent development of the 'heuristics and biases' approach, discussed below, although there is still argument as to whether subjects engage normative rules as well as heuristics (see Kahneman and Tversky, 1982*a*, Evans, 1982*b*, Kahneman and Tversky, 1982*b*) as well as attempts to refute claims for any irrational reasoning mechanism (cf. Cohen, 1979, 1981, 1982).

In summary, then, proponents of inference rules argue that subjects decode the information present in particular problems into a general abstract structure and then apply a set of general purpose rules in order to draw inferences. 'Mistakes' in reasoning are accounted for by different authors in different ways, but include the following: (i) errors of representation, (ii) errors in the process of applying inference rules (for example due to limited working memory capacity) and (iii) deviations of natural inference rules from those of the normative logic used to assess the accuracy of reasoning.

(ii) Heuristics and biases

The term 'heuristic' is normally used to mean a rule of thumb or short-cut strategy. Whilst heuristics are often seen as a sign of intelligence in solving complex problems (cf. Newell and Simon, 1972), in the field of human reasoning the term seems to have acquired a pejorative sense, perhaps because of its almost invariant usage in studies which focus on the explanation of errors and biases.

The 'heuristics and biases' approach to human inference is particularly associated with a series of highly influential papers by Amos Tversky and Daniel Kahneman. While the approach is generally associated with statistical inference and judgements under uncertainty (cf. Kahneman, Slovic and Tversky, 1982), it has also been applied to deductive reasoning, as I show later. The most famous of the heuristics proposed to explain judgements of probability are *availability* and *representativeness*, each of which is now briefly described.

Tversky and Kahneman (1973) state that 'A person is said to employ the availability heuristic whenever he estimates frequency or probability by the ease with which instances or associations could be brought to mind.' In other words, we judge events to be probable if we can think of many examples of them occurring and improbable if we can imagine few such examples. In many cases this heuristic might provide a reliable basis for probabilisitic judgements – for example, an experienced GP might reasonably base an estimate of the likelihood of symptoms indicating one disease rather than another on his or her recollection of previous cases.

Judgements by availability might, however, lead to biases in one of two ways. Firstly, the ability to call examples to mind may be biased by the organization of human memory. Tversky and Kahneman (1973) illustrate this in several ingenious experiments. In one experiment subjects were asked to judge whether the letter 'r' more commonly occurred as the first or third letter of a word in the English language. Subjects predominantly judged it more likely as an initial letter despite the fact that this is objectively the wrong answer – the finding was replicated for other letters which also occur more frequently as the third letter of a word. The explanation is that our memories are organized in such a way that word examples can more easily be generated by their initial letters. Hence, the use of the availability heuristic leads to a bias.

It is also possible that even when recalled examples do match people's experience, that experience itself may be biased. In a study by Lichtenstein *et al.* (1978) subjects were asked to estimate the relative likelihood of dying from a variety of causes. The general finding was that people considerably overestimated the likelihood of dying from accidents and underestimated the probability of dying from illnesses. The availability explanation is that spectacular causes of death, such as aeroplane crashes, receive disproportionate media coverage compared with mundane, but common causes such as strokes and heart attacks. It is the media coverage, rather than the actuarial statistics, which will determine the examples which a person can easily bring to mind.

The representativeness heuristic is used to judge the conditional probability of an event or a sample in relation to a particular population. Samples are seen to be representative when they are similar to the population in essential properties (Kahneman and Tversky, 1972). The psychologically essential properties need not include those which are relevant in normative statistical theory, however. For example, a sample from a binomial population will appear representative (and probable) if its proportion of events is similar to that in the population. Hence, people will expect the proportion of boys and girls in a small sample of children to be about 50:50. Like availability, the representativeness heuristic seems reasonable to a point but can lead to biases. For example, Kahneman and Tversky (1972) showed in several experiments that subjects will frequently ignore statistically crucial information about the size of a sample when judging certain probabilities. Subsequent research has shown that subjects do have some sensitivity to sample size, though it is often underweighted (see Pollard and Evans, 1983).

A considerable amount of research has been generated by interest in the representativeness heuristic, much of which is reviewed by Bar-Hillel (1984) and Pollard and Evans (1983). Without necessarily providing strong evidence for the theory, this has led to investigation of some very interesting phenomena, including the 'base-rate fallacy' (introduced by Kahneman and Tversky, 1973) and the so-called 'conjunction fallacy' (Tversky and Kahneman, 1983). The latter involves the curious demonstration that people will sometimes judge that the conjunction of two events is more probable than the unconditional occurrence of either.

There have been many claims of biases in the deductive reasoning literature for which explanations might also be offered in terms of 'heuristics'. Pollard (1982) presents a lengthy discussion of reasoning phenomena which he claims to be explainable in terms of the operation of the availability heuristic. Evans (1984) uses the term in a slightly different sense when arguing for a distinction between 'heuristic' and 'analytic' processes in the explanation of human reasoning. The argument here is that reasoning reflects two stages: a heuristic stage in which information is selected as 'relevant', and an analytic stage in which inferences are drawn from information encoded in this way. The difference is that Evans is associating heuristic processes with the selective representation of problem information, rather than with the drawing of inferences as such.

(iii) Schemas

Schemas (or schemata, as some authors prefer) have been proposed by a number of psychologists to explain the active role of memory in human cognition. The general notion is that knowledge is organized in units – the schemas – which include procedures for action. The application to reasoning theory lies in the possibility that inferences are the result of applying procedures embedded within schemas. The particular schema applied will have been elicited from the subjects' long-term memory according to the content and context of the problem. Hence, the notion of schemas provides a possible semantic theory of reasoning which can better explain the effects of context and content on inferences than can the assumption of general purpose inference rules or heuristics.

The notion of 'schemas' in cognitive psychology dates from the classic work of Bartlett (1932) on long-term memory and has been applied in various ways by subsequent authors, for example Neisser (1976) in his theory of perception. Also relevant are theories based on 'frames' (Minsky, 1977) and 'scripts' (Schank and Abelson, 1977). A particular formulation of schema theory which has been applied to deductive reasoning (among other things) is that of Rumelhart (1980). He proposes six main features of schemas:

1. Schemas have variables.
2. Schemas can embed, one within another.
3. Schemas represent knowledge at all levels of abstracion.
4. Schemas represent knowledge rather than definitions.
5. Schemas are active processes.
6. Schemas are recognition devices whose processing is aimed at evaluation of their goodness of fit to the data being processed.

Although Rumelhart proposes a hierarchical organization of embedded schemas, at all levels of abstraction, it is useful for our purposes to consider schemas at intermediate levels of abstraction. The knowledge contained is neither totally specific to the problem content, nor highly abstracted, as with inference rules. Such schemas can be used to explain how people can use experience to solve novel problems, for example by utilizing analogous experiences with other problems of similar structure (see, for example, Gick and Holyoak, 1983).

Rumelhart himself discusses a schema of this sort which people might use when purchasing some object. The variables in such a schema would include PURCHASER, SELLER, MERCHANDISE, MONEY and so on. The point here is that the experience one gains from purchasing objects can be applied quite widely to a variety of situations by developing and applying an appropriate schema. In application the variables are replaced by the particular content of the problem, but the procedures for action are based upon their structural relationships and are provided by the schema. Whether one is purchasing a new pen or a new car, a lot of common actions are involved, such as (i) check what items are available at what cost, (ii) decide how much you can afford to spend, (iii) assess value for money of each item, and so on.

Schemas of this sort must obviously be built up and modified with experience. Applications to reasoning theory, however, normally assume that schemas pre-exist and are elicited from long-term memory and applied to the problem in hand. Whereas inference rule theorists normally try to explain effects of problem content by changes in representation of the premises, schema theory can claim that different procedures for reasoning may be applied according to which schema is elicited. The inferences embedded in schemas are not logical rules, but appropriate procedures based on experience of domains to which the schema can be applied. Hence, reasoning may appear to be 'logical' only if the schema applied by the subject contains rules which correspond to logic in their effect (see Cheng and Holyoak, in press). In contexts where logic provides a poor model for real-world reasoning, alternative types of rules will be developed.

(iv) Mental models

An increasingly popular notion in cognitive science is that of 'mental models', though the term itself remains rather ill defined. The general notion is that many cognitive activities, such as language comprehension, pattern recognition, problem solving and decision making, involve the construction and manipulation of internal models of objects and situations in the real world. Like all models, mental models need not try to capture all properties of the thing being modelled, only those which are salient to the problem in hand. Like schema theory, mental models involve a notion of representation which is both semantic (domain dependent) and active. Both approaches assume a dynamic and fluid interaction of mental representations and cognitive processes, as opposed to the clearly separated stages required by theories of inference rules.

The term 'mental model' does, however, seem to be used in two rather different senses (cf. Rips, in press). The first involves the notion of a mental *simulation*. An obvious example lies in forecasting. Computer simulation models are used to generate forecasts of a variety of things, including weather patterns and economic developments. Such programs embody theoretical assumptions about the processes involved and are also fed appropriate data about the state of the world at the time of prediction. The notion that people may engage in 'mental modelling' of this sort in order to predict the likelihood of future events has been proposed, for example by Kahneman and Tversky (1982c). They suggest that people use a 'simulation heuristic' to generate such forecasts, which involves the construction of possible scenarios by which future events could come about.

Johnson-Laird (1983), who argues for wide application of the notion of 'mental models' in the study of language comprehension and thinking, uses the term in a slightly different sense. In his theory, the models constitute semantic representations of possible situations described by verbal statements. These representations are analogues of the situations in the world which they represent (as opposed, for example, to descriptive representations such as propositions) and are thus akin to what some authors claim for mental images (see, for example, Kosslyn, 1980). However, Johnson-Laird considers mental models to be a broader concept and treats images as corresponding to one category of mental models.

Johnson-Laird has applied the theory of mental models specifically to the explanation of deductive reasoning and is highly critical of the inference rule approach, which he labels the 'doctrine of mental logic'. The theory has been worked out in detailed application to the explanation of people's reasoning with classic syllogisms (see also Johnson-Laird and Steadman, 1978; Johnson-Laird and Bara, 1984). It is sufficient for present purposes, however, to consider the general mechanism of reasoning which he proposes.

Johnson-Laird argues that the implicit inferences involved in language comprehension involve construction of a single mental model which is the most plausible in the given context. If subsequent information invalidates this model then it is revised. For example, if I said to you 'I live with Sarah. She likes to crunch bones under the table', you might well form a mental model of Sarah on hearing the first sentence which you would have to revise after hearing the second. When explicit inferences – the subject of this chapter – are required, however, Johnson-Laird proposes that subjects attempt to construct an exhaustive set of possible models which are compatible with the premises. A conclusion will be inferred as valid only if it holds true in all possible models.

This theory of deductive reasoning assumes that people may be capable of drawing logically valid inferences, but not by a process of logical reasoning – in the sense of possessing and applying inference rules. What they need is (a) to understand the *truth conditions* of logical connectives such as 'If . . . then . . .' in order to correctly construct models compatible with premises and (b) to understand that arguments are valid only if their conclusions hold in all possible models. The theory can also explain fallacious reasoning by at least two devices. One is the supposition that people have limited working memory capacity, and so may have difficulty in considering more numerous or more complex mental models. Johnson-Laird and Bara (1984) have successfully predicted the relative difficulty of syllogisms by this principle. (They do not, however, demonstrate that their predictions diverge from a number of alternative theories of syllogistic reasoning published in recent years.)

A second principle is that subjects' prior knowledge of the context may affect the nature of models they construct and, in consequence, the nature of the inferences which they draw. For example, Oakhill and Johnson-Laird (1985) have argued that reasoning by mental models can explain 'belief bias' effects in deductive reasoning, that is the tendency to accept arguments whose conclusions you agree with regardless of their logical validity. They suggest that subjects may accept believable conclusions uncritically, that is without searching for models of the premises which could provide counter-examples. Arguments with unbelievable conclusions will, however, be more thoroughly analysed. This hypothesis is consistent with the findings of Evans, Barston and Pollard (1983) that belief bias effects are more marked in invalid than valid syllogisms.

THE WASON SELECTION TASK: CASE STUDY OF A REASONING PROBLEM

A very large number of experiments on human reasoning have been reported in the psychological literature. The most important general findings that require explanation by the various types of theory considered are (a) that people make many apparent mistakes and (b) that inferences made depend strongly upon the content and context of problems as well as upon their logical structure. In view of the limited space available in this chapter, I now consider illustrative research on a particular reasoning problem known as the Wason selection task. This problem has been the focus of considerable research interest in the field of deductive reasoning over the past 20 years and has led to demonstrations of both biases and content effects.

(i) Experimental findings

The basic problem was introduced originally by Wason (1966). Early work on the problem is described by Wason and Johnson-Laird (1972) and more recent detailed reviews are given by Evans (1982a, Chapter 9), Griggs (1983) and Wason (1983). The task is deceptively simple, for in its standard form the great majority of subjects fail to give the correct solution. In a typical version, the subject will be told that the problem concerns cards which have capital letters on one side and single figure numbers on the other. Sometimes subjects are given a pack of such cards to inspect. They are then shown four cards lying on a table and showing two letters and two numbers, for example A,D,3 and 7. The subject is then told that the experimenter has the following rule in mind, which applies to these four cards and may be true or false:

If there is an A on one side of the card, then there is a 3 on the other side of the card.

The problem is to decide which cards would, logically, need to be turned over in order to find out whether the rule is true or false. Most subjects tested say either that the A card would be sufficient or else that the A and the 3 need to be turned over. Neither answer is correct: one should turn over the A and the 7. The key to this problem lies in the realization that that the rule could only be shown to be false if a card were found which had an A on one side and did *not* have a 3 on the other. A and 7 (that is not-3) are the only choices which could lead to discovery of this falisifying combination. For example, if one turned over the 3 and found an A on the back this would prove nothing – any letter on the back of the 3 would be consistent with the rule. The interesting question, however, is why most people omit to choose the 7 card.

Wason's (1966) original explanation was that subjects were exhibiting a confimation bias, in that they were seeking the verifying combination of A and 3 rather than the falsifying combination A and not-3 (see also Johnson-Laird and Wason, 1970). Evans and Lynch (1973), however, produced evidence for an alternative explanation, namely that subjects' choices reflected a 'matching bias'. It appeared that subjects focused their attention on information which matched that actually given in the sentence. Hence, the tendency to choose A and 3 when testing the above rule could be due simply to the fact that the A and 3 are the cards referred to in the rule. Evans and Lynch separated matching from verification by introducing negative components into the rules and found, overall, that subjects' choices conformed with the matching rather than confirmation bias hypothesis. This finding has been replicated (Wason and Evans, 1975; Manktelow and Evans, 1979) although some authors have claimed evidence for both matching *and* verification biases in selection task data (Krauth, 1982; Reich and Ruth, 1982).

The early studies of the selection task, including those cited above, mostly used artificial or 'abstract' problem content. However, the main interest in the selection task in more recent work has concerned the claim that people reason more logically when the problem content is concrete and realistic, rather than abstract and artificial in nature. This idea dates back to Wilkins (1928) and gained widespread popularity following the publication of a book on reasoning by Wason and Johnson-Laird (1972). Two early studies on the Wason selection task which were cited in the book appeared to support the 'facilitation by realism' hypothesis.

Wason and Shapiro (1971) introduced the first of a series of 'realistic' problem contents investigated in the Wason selection task, which can be described as 'Towns and Transport'. In the thematic group, subjects were told that each card represented a different journey made by the experimenter, with the destination written on one side and the means of transport shown on the other. When subjects were asked to investigate the truth of the claim that 'Every time I go to Manchester I travel by car', significantly more selected the correct cards ('Manchester' and 'train') than in the abstract control group.

More spectacular results were, however, found in the study by Johnson-Laird, Legrenzi and Legrenzi (1972). Their subjects were instructed to play the role of postal workers and were asked to check whether the following rule was being enforced: 'If a letter is sealed then it has a 50 lire stamp on it.' Instead of cards they were asked which of four envelopes they would have to turn over in order find out whether the rule had been violated. Almost all subjects correctly chose to examine sealed envelopes and those with *low* value (40 lire) stamps.

A number of papers appeared to provide supporting evidence for these early experiments (see Evans, 1982a; Griggs, 1983). However, Manktelow and Evans (1979) failed to find any evidence of a thematic facilitation effect, even in an experiment which directly replicated that of Wason and Shapiro (1971). Furthermore they suggested that the facilitation reported by Johnson-Laird and his collaborators (1972) was not due to reasoning but to retrieval of answers from memory. At that time a postal rule was in operation in the United Kingdom to the effect that sealed letters must carry a higher rate of postage. Surely, subjects knew from experience that only an understamped, sealed envelope could break the law, and this knowledge – rather than a process of reasoning – was responsible for the facilitation in performance.

Further evidence for this 'memory cue' hypothesis has been found in that the envelope problem has not been shown to facilitate performance in American subjects who have never used such a rule in real life (Griggs and Cox, 1982; Yachanin and Tweney, 1982) nor in British subjects who are too young to remember it (Golding, 1981). Positive confirmation has also been provided by Griggs and Cox (1982), who found very high levels of correct selections when the problem content was modelled on the drinking age law in the state of Florida, with which their student subjects were highly familiar. The rule given was 'If a person is drinking beer, then the person must be over 19 years of age'. The cards represented four people with their age on one side and beverage drunk on the other, with the exposed surfaces showing: 'beer' (p), 'coke' (not-p), '22 years of age' (q) and '16 years of age' (not-q). Most subjects correctly chose to investigate beer drinkers and those under age.

It should not, however, be inferred that selection task performance is only facilitated by direct retrieval of the correct answer from memory. It appears that subjects can also make use of analogous experiences. For example, Cox and Griggs (1982) demonstrated transfer from solution of the drinking age problem to a structurally similar but arbitrary clothing age rule, while D'Andrade (described by Rumelhart, 1980) has also shown facilitation in a context in which subjects could draw only upon analogous rather than direct experience.

In summary, work on the selection task has shown that most subjects fail to solve what appears, on the surface, to be a quite simple logical task. This has led to claims of 'confirmation' and 'matching' bias on abstract versions of the task. The use of realistic materials appeared to facilitate reasoning on the task, though this conclusion has been revised in the light of more recent evidence. It now seems that subjects must have some prior knowledge relating to the problem content, which can be used either directly, or by analogy, to assist them in making the logically correct choices. The implications of these findings for the four theoretical approaches to reasoning discussed earlier are now considered.

(ii) Theoretical explanations

Research on the Wason selection task shows up a clear limitation in the inference rule approach. Most of the experiments have used the same basic problem, whose logical structure is unaltered, and have manipulated either the conditions of testing or the problem content. Hence, most of the findings cannot be explained by reference to rules based on the syntactic structure of the problem. If one assumes that inference rules provide the 'competence' system for reasoning, then almost all the findings on this task would have to be explained by reference to 'performance' factors.

If the effects of realistic content were simply to facilitate reasoning, as was once thought, then this might be reconciled with an inference rule approach (cf. Cohen, 1981) by arguing that the artificial nature of the problem content was preventing subjects from demonstrating their true logical competence. However, as Griggs (1983) points out, the recent work on content effects in the selection task does not support the view that facilitation of logical *reasoning* as opposed to *performance* is occurring. Performance seems too closely related to the knowledge of the particular problem domain to support the notion of reasoning by general inference rules.

Performance on the abstract version of the selection task, at least, does seem explicable by some form of heuristic reasoning. Pollard (1982) suggests that matching bias reflects the operation of an availability effect. That is, the mention of the cards in the rule makes them available and thus more likely to be chosen. This explanation does not suppose that subjects are engaged in any process of logical reasoning at all when deciding which cards to select. Nor does the explanation offered by Evans (1984), though it differs from Pollard's in certain details.

Evans' explanation of performance on the abstract selection task is that subjects do not analyse the consequence of turning the cards over, but instead choose to investigate those which appear *relevant*. Relevance is determined by heuristic processes which, in this case, are linguistic in origin. Matching bias results from the fact that negation does not alter the linguistic topic of the sentence. For example, the rule, 'If the letter is A then the number is not 3' is *about* the A and the 3 even though the latter is negated in the sentence.

It is less clear that the heuristic approach can explain the content effects observed on the selection task, though Pollard (1982) again emphasizes the role of availability – this time based on prior knowledge retrieved from memory. Perhaps the best evidence derives from demonstrations that performance is facilitated when the subject has a prior belief that the rule is *false* (see Van Duyne, 1976; Pollard and Evans, 1981, 1983) and hence can easily retrieve the *counter-example*; p and not-q will be available from long-term memory. However, recognizing the relevance of a counter-example goes beyond availability and involves the use of 'analytic' as well as 'heuristic' processes (cf. Evans, 1984).

Schema theory provides a promising approach to the explanation of content effects on the selection task, as several authors (including Rumelhart, 1980) have observed. It is particularly suited to explaining the evidence of reasoning by analogy, as for example suggested by the results of Cox and Griggs (1982). The fact that the drinking age rule transferred to an arbitrary but *structurally similar* clothing age rule can be explained by the assumption that a schema evoked by the former content was applied to the latter.

Cheng and Holyoak (in press) have argued that facilitating contents on the selection task tend to invoke a *permission schema*. For example, a postage stamp of adequate value permits sealing of an envelope and people of sufficient age are permitted to drink in bars. When a permission schema is evoked, Cheng and Holyoak contend that it contains a set of production rules, such as 'If the precondition is not satisfied, then the action must not be taken', which map directly onto the logically correct choices. For example, on the drinking age problem, the precondition rule above would lead you to check underage drinkers (precondition not satisfied) to make sure that the action (drinking beer) was not taken – and hence to choose the not-q card. In their experiments, Cheng and Holyoak demonstrate that the provision of a rationale or instructional set which evokes a permission schema will facilitate performance on problems for which subjects lack the relevant prior experience, or even those which are entirely abstract and arbitrary in nature.

The theory of reasoning by mental models does not seem to fit too well with selection task data. According to Johnson-Laird (1983) subjects reason by constructing mental models of possible situations and searching actively for counter-examples. This is precisely what is required on the selection task – constructing models by projecting possible values onto hidden sides of the cards, and checking for counter-examples to the rule. However, subjects notoriously fail to solve the selection task in most forms of presentation, and provide little evidence that they think about values on the hidden sides at all, as the analyses of Pollard (1982) and Evans (1984) demonstrate. Why does subjects' 'mental modelling' capacity fail them so badly on this particular task?

Johnson-Laird (1983) does, in fact, provide a brief discussion of research on the selection task, though mostly with reference to the problems it causes for theories of inference rules. He is unable to explain the poor performance on abstract forms of the task, but offers the following comments with reference to content effects:

> If subjects already possess a mental model of the relation expressed in the general rule, or a model that can be readily related to the rule, they are more likely to have insight into the task . . . The subjects . . . do, indeed, search for counter-examples, but their search is only comprehensive for realistic materials that relate to an existing mental model.

This account is somewhat unsatisfactory since Johnson-Laird's demonstration of mental models on syllogistic reasoning tasks (for example Johnson-Laird and Bara, 1984) involves the assumption that subjects' models are formulated purely on the basis of the connectives such as *all* and *some*, on problems where they cannot normally apply prior knowledge of the content. Nor is it apparent how the theory of mental models can explain the much poorer performance on the Wason selection task than on other problems testing people's understanding of the logic of conditional statements (see Evans, 1982*a*).

This account has favoured heuristics as an explanation of performance on the abstract form of the Wason selection task and schemas as an explanation of content effects. In fairness, however, one must point out that the selection task has special features which may not make it fully representative of reasoning problems in general. In particular, the standard task induces exceptionally poor logical performance which is hard for both inference rules and mental model theorists to explain.

Authors favouring these latter approaches would, of course, prefer their theories to be assessed with reference to the sorts of experiments highlighted in their own publications.

CONCLUSIONS

Human reasoning is a very large field of study in psychology, to which full justice obviously cannot be done in a chapter of this length. In particular, whilst the main current theoretical approaches have been covered, it has been necessary to focus the empirical review on a particular reasoning problem, the Wason selection task. Research on this problem has produced some very interesting findings, especially with reference to content and context effects. It would, however, be unwise to infer too many general conclusions from work on a single paradigm.

It is most encouraging that work on human reasoning appears to be developing away from its earlier main concern with logicality and normative theory and towards a debate between alternative descriptive theories. Whilst the relative merits of inference rules, heuristics, schemas and mental models cannot be clearly decided on the available evidence, the debate is providing a most healthy impetus to research in the field. The import of this research will not be limited to psychology alone. Understanding of the representations and processes underlying human reasoning is of utmost importance in the theory of cognitive science as a whole and has potential practical application in many fields of human endeavour.

REFERENCES

Adams, M.J. (1980) Inductive deductions and deductive inductions. In R.S. Nickerson (ed.) *Attention and Performance VIII*. Hillsdale, N.J.: Lawrence Erlbaum Associates.
Bar-Hillel, M. (1984) Representativeness and fallacies of probability judgment. *Acta Psychologica*, 55, 91–107.
Bartlett, F.C. (1932) *Remembering*. Cambridge: Cambridge University Press.
Braine, M.D.S. (1978) On the relation between the natural logic of reasoning and standard logic. *Psychological Review*, 85, 1–21.
Cheng, P.W. and Holyoak, K.J. (in press) Pragmatic reasoning schemas. *Cognitive Psychology*.
Cohen, L.J. (1979) On the psychology of prediction: Whose is the fallacy? *Cognition*, 7, 385–407.
Cohen, L.J. (1981) Can human irrationality be experimentally demonstrated? *The Behavioral and Brain Sciences*, 4, 317–370.

Cohen, L.J. (1982) Are people programmed to commit fallacies? Further thought about the interpretation of data on judgement. *Journal for the Theory of Social Behaviour*, 12, 251–247.
Cox, J.R. and Griggs, R.A. (1982) The effects of experience on performance in Wason's selection task. *Memory and Cognition*, 10, 496–502.
Evans, J. St B.T. (1977) Linguistic factors in reasoning. *Quarterly Journal of Experimental Psychology*, 29, 297–306.
Evans, J. St B.T. (1982a) *The Psychology of Deductive Reasoning*. London: Routledge & Kegan Paul.
Evans, J. St B.T. (1982b) On statistical intuitions and inferential rules: A discussion of Kahneman and Tversky. *Cognition*, 12, 319–324.
Evans, J. St B.T. (ed.) (1983) *Thinking and Reasoning: Psychological Approaches*. London: Routledge & Kegan Paul.
Evans, J. St B.T. (1984) Heuristic and analytic processes in reasoning. *British Journal of Psychology*, 75, 451–468.
Evans, J. St B.T., Barston, J.L. and Pollard, P. (1983) On the conflict between logic and belief in syllogistic reasoning. *Memory and Cognition*, 11, 295–306.
Evans, J. St B.T. and Lynch, J.S. (1973) Matching bias in the selection task. *British Journal of Psychology*, 64, 391–397.
Gick and Holyoak (1983) Schema induction and analogical transfer. *Cognitive Psychology*, 15, 1–38.
Golding, E. (1981) The effect of past experience on problem solving. Paper presented to The British Psychological Society at Surrey University.
Griggs, R.A. (1983) The role of problem content in the selection task and in the THOG problem. In J. St B.T. Evans (ed.) *Thinking and Reasoning: Psychological Approaches*. London: Routledge & Kegan Paul.
Griggs, R.A. and Cox, J.R. (1982) The elusive thematic materials effect in the Wason selection task. *British Journal of Psychology*, 73, 407–420.
Guyote, M.J. and Sternberg, R.J. (1981) A transitive chain theory of syllogistic reasoning. *Cognitive Psychology*, 13, 461–525.
Henle, M. (1962) On the relation between logic and thinking. *Psychological Review*, 69, 366–378.
Henle, M. (1971) Of the scholler of nature. *Social Research*, 38, 93–107.
Johnson-Laird, P.N. (1975) Models of deduction. In R.J. Falmagne (ed.) *Reasoning: Representation and Process*. Hillsdale, N.J.: Lawrence Erlbaum Associates.
Johnson-Laird, P.N. (1983) *Mental Models*. Cambridge: Cambridge University Press.
Johnson-Laird, P.N. and Bara, B.G. (1984) Syllogistic inference. *Cognition*, 16, 1–62.
Johnson-Laird, P.N., Legrenzi, P. and Legrenzi, M.S. (1972) Reasoning and a sense of reality. *British Journal of Psychology*, 63, 395–400.
Johnson-Laird, P.N. and Steadman, M.J. (1978) The psychology of syllogisms. *Cognitive Psychology*, 10, 64–99.
Johnson-Laird, P.N. and Wason, P.C. (1970) A theoretical analysis of insight into a reasoning task. *Cognitive Psychology*, 1, 134–148.
Kahneman, D., Slovic, P. and Tversky, A. (1982) *Judgment under Uncertainty: Heuristics and Biases*. Cambridge: Cambridge University Press.
Kahneman, D. and Tversky, A. (1972) Subjective probability: A judgment of representativeness. *Cognitive Psychology*, 3, 430–454.
Kahneman, D. and Tversky, A. (1973). On the psychology of prediction. *Psychological Review*, 80, 237–251.

Kahneman, D. and Tversky, A. (1982a). On the study of statistical intuition. *Cognition*, 12, 325–326.
Kahneman, D. and Tversky, A. (1982b) A reply to Evans. *Cognition*, 12, 325–326.
Kahneman, D. and Tversky, A. (1982c) The simulation heuristic. In D. Kahneman, P. Slovic and A. Tversky (eds) *Judgment under Uncertainty: Heuristics and Biases*. Cambridge: Cambridge University Press.
Kosslyn, S.M. (1980) *Image and Mind*. Cambridge, Mass.: Harvard University Press.
Krauth, J. (1982) Formulation and experimental verification of models in propositional reasoning. *Quarterly Journal of Experimental Psychology*, 34A, 285–298.
Lichtenstein, S., Slovic, P., Fischhoff, B., Layman, M. and Coombs, B. (1978) Judged frequency of lethal events. *Journal of Experimental Psychology: Human Learning and Memory*, 1978, 4, 551–578.
Manktelow, K.I. and Evans, J. St B.T. (1979) Facilitation of reasoning by realism: Effect or non-effect? *British Journal of Psychology*, 70, 477–488.
Minsky, M.L. (1977) Frame system theory. In P.N. Johnson-Laird and P.C. Wason (eds) *Thinking: Readings in Cognitive Science*. Cambridge: Cambridge University Press.
Neisser, U. (1976) *Cognition and Reality*. San Francisco: Freeman.
Newell, A. and Simon, H.A. (1972) *Human Problem Solving*. Englewood Cliffs, N.J.: Prentice-Hall.
Nisbett, R. and Ross, L. (1980) *Human Inference: Strategies and Shortcomings of Social Judgement*. Englewood Cliffs. N.J.: Prentice-Hall.
Oakhill, J.V. and Johnson-Laird, P.N. (1985) The effect of belief on the spontaneous production of syllogistic conclusions. *Quarterly Journal of Experimental Psychology*, 37A, 553–570.
Osherson, D. (1975) Logic and models of logical thinking. In R.J. Falmagne (ed.) *Reasoning: Representation and Process*. Hillsdale, N.J.: Lawrence Erlbaum Associates.
Peterson, C.R. and Beach, L.R. (1967) Man as an intuitive statistician. *Psychological Bulletin*, 68, 29–46.
Pollard, P. (1982) Human reasoning: Some possible effects of availability. *Cognition*, 12, 65–96.
Pollard, P. and Evans, J. St B.T. (1981) The effect of prior beliefs in reasoning: An associational interpretation. *British Journal of Psychology*, 72, 73–82.
Pollard, P. and Evans, J. St B.T. (1983) The role of representativeness in statistical inference: A critical appraisal. In J. St B.T. Evans (ed.) *Thinking and Reasoning: Psychological Approaches*. London: Routledge & Kegan Paul.
Popper, K.R. (1959) *The Logic of Scientific Discovery*. London: Hutchinson.
Popper, K.R. (1962) *Conjectures and Refutations*. London: Hutchinson.
Reich, S.S. and Ruth, P. (1982) Reasoning: Verification, falsification and matching. *British Journal of Psychology*, 73, 395–406.
Revlis, R. (1975a) Two models of syllogistic inference: Feature Selection and Conversion. *Journal of Verbal Learning and Verbal Behavior*, 14, 180–195.
Revlis, R. (1975b) Syllogistic reasoning: Logical decisions from a complex data base. In R.J. Falmagne (ed.) *Reasoning: Representation and Process*. New York: Wiley.
Rips, L.J. (1983) Cognitive processes in propositional reasoning. *Psychological Review*, 90, 38–71.

Rips, L.J. (in press) Mental muddles. In M. Brand and R.M. Harnish (eds) *Problems in the Representation of Knowledge and Belief.* Tucson: University of Arizona Press.
Rumelhart, D.E. (1980) Schemata: The building blocks of cognition. In R.J. Spiro, B.C. Bruce and W.F. Brewer (eds) *Theoretical Issues in Reading Comprehension.* Hillsdale, N.J.: Lawrence Erlbaum Associates.
Schank, R.C. and Abelson, R.P. (1977) *Scripts, Plans, Goals and Understanding.* Hillsdale, N.J.: Lawrence Erlbaum Associates.
Tversky, A. and Kahneman, D. (1973) Availability: A heuristic for judging frequency and probability. *Cognitive Psychology, 5,* 207–232.
Tversky, A. and Kahneman, D. (1983) Extensional vs intuitive reasoning: The conjunction fallacy in probability judgment. *Psychological Review, 90,* 293–315.
Tweney, R.D., Doherty, M.E. and Mynatt, C.R. (1981) *On Scientific Thinking.* New York: Columbia University Press.
Van Duyne, P.C. (1976) Necessity and contingency in reasoning. *Acta Psychologica, 40,* 85–101.
Wason, P.C. (1966) Reasoning. In B.M. Foss (ed.) *New Horizons in Psychology I.* Harmondsworth: Penguin.
Wason, P.C. (1983) Realism and rationality in the selection task. In J. St B.T. Evans (ed.) *Thinking and Reasoning: Psychological Approaches.* London: Routledge & Kegan Paul.
Wason, P.C. and Evans, J. St B.T. (1975) Dual processes in reasoning? *Cognition, 3,* 141–154.
Wason, P.C. and Johnson-Laird, P.N. (1972) *Psychology of Reasoning: Structure and Content.* London: Batsford.
Wason, P.C. and Shapiro, D. (1971) Natural and contrived experience in a reasoning problem. *Quarterly Journal of Experimental Psychology, 23,* 63–71.
Wilkins, M.C. (1928) The effect of changed material on the ability to do formal syllogistic reasoning. *Archives of Psychology, New York, No 102.*
Yachanin, S.A. and Tweney, R.D. (1982) The effect of thematic content on cognitive strategies in the four-card selection task. *Bulletin of the Psychonomic Society, 19,* 87–90.

IDENTITY
Glynis M. Breakwell

This chapter examines the concept of identity from a social psychological perspective. It discusses the structure and processes of identity and the methods which have been evolved to access identity structure and function. Embarking upon this exercise from an explicitly social psychological viewpoint means that the wealth of literature from clinical and humanistic psychology will be largely omitted and the contribution of personality and psychometric models will remain mostly unexplored. Also, since the focus is upon the structure and processes of identity in the broad sense, there will be little emphasis upon the dynamics of specific aspects of identity, for instance gender or ethnicity, except where they shed light upon general principles. Readers seeking concrete examples of the way these processes are experienced subjectively and influence subjective social behaviour might refer to Breakwell (1986) and Gergen and Davis (1985).

Gecas (1982) commented that 'The self-concept is undergoing something of a renaissance in contemporary social psychology.' To prove his point he listed areas in both sociological and psychological social psychology where there has been a burgeoning interest in the self-concept. In the former, from the symbolic interactionist and the structuralist (Turner, 1976; Kohn, 1969; Rosenberg, 1979), and the historical materialist (Leonard, 1984) schools there has been growing concern to model the relationship of social structure to personality, and this has been facilitated by developments in role theory (Turner, 1978; Biddle, 1979; Gordon, 1976) and made salient by attempts to reconceptualize methods of empirical research (Alexander and Knight, 1971; Alexander and Wiley, 1981). In psychological social psychology, the revival has had more diverse impacts but largely trails in the wake of the 'cognitive revolution' and, in some cases, has hastened the departure of behaviourist preconceptions. For instance, through Bandura's (1977) notion of self-efficacy it has penetrated social learning theory, while Bem's (1972) well-known work on self-attribution has modified behaviourist models.

But most notable is the concept's influence upon attribution theory (Epstein, 1973; Bowerman, 1978) and upon theories of attitude change (for example, Aronson's, 1968, self-enhancement reformulation of dissonance theory) and value formation (Rokeach, 1973). Indeed, Wegner and Vallacher (1980) virtually go so far as to view all social psychology through the prism of the self.

Where the self goes, identity is sure to follow. This is evident in that in parallel with the increasing use of models of the self-concept, both to explain the impact of society upon the individual and to explain the individual's actions, there has been a growing fascination for the notion of identity. Sociologists use identities as building-blocks in their topographical descriptions of the self-concept (Stryker, 1980; McCall and Simmons, 1978; Hofman, 1983). Psychologists often, though not exclusively, use identity as a motivational variable: an organizing network of self-referent memories which directs action. The precise theoretical role of the concept and its consequent operational definition varies. For instance, Harré (1983) from an ethogenic viewpoint, argues that people are perpetually guided in their actions, which are purposive, by identity projects that are similar to strategic plans intended to result in the realization of a particular self-concept. The identity project both guides and acts as an interim motive force, not determined externally to the person (see also Secord, 1977).

Tajfel (1978, 1982), within a completely different theoretical framework, also claims that identity requirements are strong determinants of action. In this case, the need for a positive social identity (which is said to be derived from the satisfaction gained from group memberships) is hypothesized to motivate intergroup conflict and discrimination (Turner and Giles, 1981). Both Harré and Tajfel emphasize how psychologists tend to treat identity as the origin of action. Sociologists, in contrast, tend to see identity as the outcome of interaction within a particular social context (characterized in terms of role and status relationships). Irrespective of their differences in emphasis, both traditions in social psychology are now approaching the concept of identity with a growing conviction that it will yield theoretical and pragmatic developments. This is particularly so, since some (for example, Ashmore and Del Boca, 1986) regard it as a central pillar in any integrative theoretical framework for social psychology.

DIFFERENTIATING BETWEEN IDENTITY AND SELF-CONCEPT

Despite recent recognition that the very concept of the 'self' is temporally relative (Verhave and van Hoorn, 1984) there is a tradition of treating identity and the self-concept as distinct, separable entities with different theoretical roles. Gecas (1982) suggests that a number of dichotomies are useful in representing their relationship. First, there is the distinction between 'self' and the 'self-concept'. According to Gecas (p.3), self 'refers to a *process*, the process of reflexivity which emanates from the dialectic between the "I" and "Me".' The self-concept is the product of this process. Rosenberg (1979) claims that the self-concept is the 'totality of an individual's thoughts and feelings having reference to himself as an object' (p. 7). Similarly, Gergen (1971, p. 23) states that the structure of the self is 'the system of concepts available to the person in attempting to define himself'.

The search for a more precise description of the self-concept leads to the second dichotomy. This is between self-conception and self-evaluation. Self-conception is concerned with the meaning of the characteristics associated with the individual. It is a compilation of the individual's experiences: a product of social interaction and social position. Typically, the self-conception is said to be comprised of identities. Self-evaluation is concerned with the subjective value placed upon the self-conception: the overall sense of self-esteem. But self-esteem itself is no longer treated as unidimensional. Various aspects are plucked out: positive and negative self-esteem, inner and outer self-esteem (Franks and Marolla, 1976), competence and worth (Smith, 1978), power and worth (Gecas, 1971), and competence and morality (Vallacher, 1980). This gives rise to a third dichotomy between self-esteem based on efficacy and that founded on worth. Efficacy based self-esteem is dependent upon competent performance (Bandura, 1978; 1982). Self-worth is founded upon gaining social approval not just in relation to direct feedback from other people (cf. the looking-glass self, Cooley, 1902) but, more abstractly, in relation to social norms or values.

These distinctions can be represented diagrammatically:

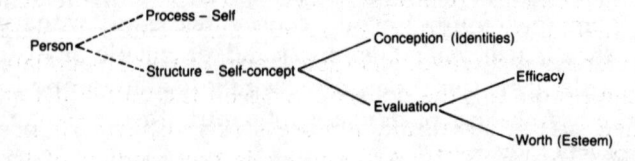

```
                    ,--Process - Self
        Person <---<                        ,--Conception (Identities)
                    `--Structure - Self-concept <---<                ,--Efficacy
                                             `--Evaluation <---<
                                                                 `--Worth (Esteem)
```

It is immediately obvious from the diagram that effort has apparently been concentrated upon the structural features, not the processual domain. The literature is redolent with an implicit notion that structure can be tapped or accessed (whether qualitatively or quantitatively), whereas process can only be inferred. The modelling of structure has proceeded but the modelling of process has not.

Even the modelling of structure has considerable weaknesses. Clearly, the dichotomies are heuristic devices. Evaluation and conception are not divisible in practice. Conceptions derived from social interaction and social position carry socially-determined values intrinsic to their defining properties. Of course, they may be subjectively re-evaluated but then the question becomes: how? This is a process question and has not been satisfactorily answered. The closest answer arises from those who suggest (Leonard, 1984) that the power of subjective re-evaluation hails from the fact that rarely is there total social consensus about the value of any particular property. Freedom for individual self-evaluation rests in the interstices of social disagreement. This is to echo Hegel (1807) in saying that it is in contradiction that intentionality can arise. There is strong evidence that people are creative in interpreting social information (Kahneman, Slovic and Tversky, 1982; Nisbett and Ross, 1980). Even assuming this power of subjective re-evaluation, it is in any case inappropriate to separate evaluation and conception so finally. Across time, one would expect conceptions of past self-concepts to motivate the evaluation of current and future self-conceptions. Time is important to a valid modelling of the self and self-concept (Luckmann, 1983) but is rarely actually considered as anything more than a cipher.

Just as evaluation and conception are indivisible, self-worth and self-efficacy are minimally distinguishable, particularly empirically (Covington and Beery, 1976).

In a very real sense, the problems associated with modelling the structure of self-conception arise because they are not accompanied by the modelling of the processes of the self. The queries revolve around the relationships between the components of the structure and their dynamics; these would be directly addressed in a model looking at process.

Leaving aside for the moment the modelling of process, the proposed structural sub-divisions allocate to the identity concept varying definitions. There are two dominant variants, coming respectively from the processual interactionists (Chicago school) and structural interactionists (Iowa school). Blumer (1969), representing processual interactionism, argues that identity is situated, emergent, reciprocal and negotiated. An identity is the product of the dialectic between the individual and the society reified in the socialization process (Openshaw, Thomas and Rollins, 1983; Denzin, 1977). An identity is the product of labelling processes (Ball, 1983). Labelling theory in relation to deviance originates in this perspective (Wells, 1978). An identity is 'situated' (Alexander and Lauderdale, 1977), that is, attributions are made about a person and by a person in accordance with the behaviour he or she exhibits in particular situations. Processual interactionists focus upon the active construction of identity within each spatial, temporal and social context.

In contrast, for structural symbolic interactionism the key to identity is found in the notion of roles. Identities are internalized 'roles', where roles represent the matrix of behavioural and conative performances expected of the occupant of a social position (Stryker, 1979). The structure of the self-concept is then seen as the product of the way in which these numerous role-identities are hierarchically organized (McCall and Simmons, 1978). The hierarchy can be described in terms of the salience of its various constituent identities, where salience is related to the degree of commitment to a role-position (Turner, 1978) and to its connectedness with others (Stryker, 1980).

This distinction between conceptualizations of identity by the processual and structural interactionists has some resemblance to the distinction made by psychological social psychologists between personal identity and social identity (Weinreich, 1983; Zavalloni, 1983). Personal identity is seen as that part of the self-concept which is largely independent of social determination: a creative product of purposive action and intentional judgement. Social identity, in contrast, is dictated by group and category memberships. However, it has been argued that this strict division is misleading, an artefact of modelling the structure of self-concept at only one moment in time (Breakwell, 1983) and ignoring the processes whereby identities are formed (Breakwell, 1986). Given these structural considerations, it is time to return to the initial question: what distinguishes between the self-concept and identity? There seem to be two dimensions of difference, both of which are questionable.

1. *There is one self-concept but many identities.* The self-concept is seen as a single framework which houses any number of identities. Indeed, there is some evidence (Thoits, 1983) that the quantity of social identities possessed is a vital determiner of psychological well-being. Thoits found that the more identities possessed by an actor, the less distress, anxiety or disordered conduct he or she exhibited.

However, the simple generalization that theorists conceive of one self-concept but many identities ignores a number of current theorists who postulate there can be numerous selves. Turner (1976) argues that people experience both real and unreal (or institutionalized) selves. Turner suggests that actions which feel authentic, accountable and responsible originate in and define the real self; actions constrained by situation or involuntary impulse give rise to the experience of unreal selves. This is reminiscent both of the personal–social identity divide and of Kuhn and McPartland's (1954) distinction between 'consensual' and 'subconsensual' identities. It also has echoes of Fenigstein, Scheier and Buss's (1975) notions of the private and public selves. Zurcher (1977) in proposing the 'mutability of self' also presages the notion of multiple selves. Zurcher suggested that in a multiplex society, subject to increasingly rapid social change, where uncertainty and marginality predominate, serial self-concept changes should be expected. The self-concept should be seen as rapidly changing to reconcile the individual to rapid societal change. Again, the notion of the singular enduring self-concept seems to be challenged. The distinction between identity and self-concept starts to waver.

2. *The self-concept encompasses an evaluative dimension whereas identities do not.* This seems to be a particularly untenable assumption: identities are subject to evaluation, socially and subjectively. The value of the components of an identity is an intrinsic part of the defining characteristics of an identity. It would be just as feasible to talk about identity-esteem and identity-efficacy as self-esteem or self-efficacy. This is particularly evident when the literature on specific identities is examined. Esteem and efficacy evaluations are intrinsic to definitions of gender (Katz, 1986; Steiner, 1985) and ethnic (Grossman, Wirt and Davids, 1985; Aboud and Skerry, 1983) identity. Moreover, this evaluative dimension of identities is not simply socially determined. It is open to subjective revision and individual action. The sources of identities can be manipulated in order to modify perceived efficacy and worth. This is at the heart of the social identity model of intergroup relations (Tajfel, 1978) and has received considerable empirical support (Tajfel, 1982).

All of the recent work on identity emphasizes that instead of treating an identity as unidimensional it should be accepted to be multidimensional. Whether the identity is derived from a particular group or category membership or from a specific pattern of interpersonal interaction, it will constitute many interrelated pieces of information about the individual (expectations of behaviour, values, worth-assessments, history, acquired skills, etc.). Bem (1981), discussing gender identity, suggests these components coalesce into an identity schema which is a discrete conceptual entity. The schema encompasses an evaluative dimension. In fact, Winters and Neale (1985) have shown that schema suffused with low esteem are associated with depressives and mania bi-polars.

The fact that self-evaluation or identity-evaluation can be seen to be an active process of negotiation and intervention which brings about change in a desirable direction introduces another question about the structure of self-concept schema often proposed. It is difficult to understand why self-evaluation is seen solely as a structural component. It could alternatively be conceived of as an active process and as such part of the self, not the self-conception (in Gecas' terms). In reality, it would seem sensible to admit to the model evaluation, which is a constituent of the self, as a process, and evaluations, which are constituents of the structure of self-conception, as a product of that process.

Given the conceptual confusion surrounding the distinction between the self-concept and identity, it is hardly surprising that their usage is inconsistent across theorists. With models of identity becoming ever more complex and all-encompassing, there is some doubt as to the actual value of maintaining the distinction. Even if it is maintained, there is a need to examine further the structure and processes of identity in the light of recent work.

THE STRUCTURAL PROPERTIES OF IDENTITY

In what follows it is assumed that the structure of identity is a dynamic product of the interaction of the capacities for memory, consciousness and organized construal which are characteristic of the biological organism within the physical and societal structures and influence processes which constitute the social context (Breakwell, 1986). Yet the identity resides in psychological processes but is manifested through thought, action and affect. Therefore, identity should be described both in terms of its structure and in terms of process.

As intimated earlier, identity structure can be envisaged along two planes: the content and the value dimensions. The content dimension comprises characteristics which define identity: the properties (personal, such as values, attitudes, or style, and social, such as group memberships or interpersonal networks) which, taken as a constellation, mark the person as unique. The content is organized and its organization has been characterized in terms of:

- degree of centrality
- the hierarchical arrangement of elements
- the relative salience of components (Kelly, 1955; Zavalloni, 1983; Liebkind, 1984.

The actual organization is not envisaged to be static by any of these theorists. It is responsive to inputs and demands from the identity processes and the social context. For instance, salience is highly situation-specific as Waddell and Cairns (1986) have shown with respect to religious components of identity.

Each element in the content dimension has a temporally-specific value appended to it; taken together these values can be said to constitute the value dimension of identity. The value dimension is constantly subject to revision as might be expected since changes in the social value systems or modifications in the individual's position relative to those systems will generate re-evaluations of the value of particular elements in identity. Moreover, changes of evaluation can be purposive, motivated by the requirements of the identity principles described below.

PROCESSES OF IDENTITY

It is time to turn from looking at identity as a structure whose parts can be dismantled and examined in terms of form and component materials. It is necessary also to look at identity as a set of processes operating in a principled manner. Most models of identity leave its processes to be inferred or, if these are specified, the principles dictating their operation are not described. Two processes are at least implicit, sometimes explicit, in these models: assimilation–accommodation and evaluation.

Assimilation–accommodation are treated as components of a single process even though they are formally distinct. Assimilation refers to the absorption of new components into the indentity structure; accommodation refers to the adjustment which occurs in the existing structure in order to find a place (metaphorically, of course) for the new elements. Assimilation–accommodation could be conceptualized as a memory system.

Kihlstrom and Cantor (1984) discuss the way in which the self may be regarded as a memory system. As such, the self-concept is simply a mental representation of a particular person – oneself – and is therefore just a part of the individual's total knowledge of the social world. This social knowledge is a segment of the entire memory system. They argue that this memory is comprised, on the one hand, of declarative knowledge and procedural knowledge and, on the other, of episodic memory and semantic memory.

Declarative knowledge consists of facts and information; procedural knowledge consists of the rules for manipulating those facts in a manner consistent with logic and socially-established codes of judgement. Procedural knowledge includes strategies for acquiring, storing and retrieving memories and motor skills.

Episodic memory comprises recollections of personal experiences within their spatial and temporal frame of reference. Semantic memory contains the person's mental lexicon, categorial information stored without reference to the context of its acquisition or its personal meaning.

There is a suggestion that, in addition to this memory system in its quadruped form, there may also be what it called a metamemory: the awareness of what facts are available in the main frame storage and what procedures may be used to access them. In their conceptualization, the components of identity would be a subset of declarative knowledge and the principles of identity an element in procedural knowledge. Memories about identity can, of course, fall into both episodic and semantic memories.

Kihlstrom and Cantor are basically treating the self-concept as the product of an information-processing system which can actively reconstruct and order inputs shaped by social experiences. This is essentially what the assimilation–accommodation process does.

In contrast, the process of evaluation, initially, seems to lie outside of the information-processing model domain. The process of evaluation entails the allocation of meaning and value to identity contents, new and old. It may be that the evaluative process is largely founded upon a system of ordered comparisons in which identity components are compared against social and objective criteria to assess their worth. This would clearly tie into the propositions of social comparison theory (Festinger, 1954) which has received so much recent attention (Suls and Miller, 1977). Yet this would, of course, be fixed within a network of rules for drawing evaluative inferences (evaluative algorithms) which would ultimately rest within an information-processing system that will depend upon memory. It seems that if the processes of identity are pushed to their sources, it will be the biochemistry of memory which will be the target for exploration.

It is worth saying that, as a memory system, the self-concept has peculiarities: it has a larger store, which can be accessed more speedily and more flexibly than most memory systems. Furthermore, there are extensive documented biases in the ways memories are encoded. Greenwald (1980) outlined three such biases:

☐ Memory is best for information highly relevant to the self. This is tied to the fact that recall of material learnt actively is better than that received passively.
☐ People readily see themselves as responsible for positive outcomes of their action but deny responsibility for negative outcomes (beneffectance).
☐ People seek information which accords with their existing self-concept and autobiographical memories are retrospectively revised to comply with the current self-concept.

These are fundamentally biases in the information-processing system which evidently has self-interest rather than accuracy of inferential logic as its prime directive.

THE PRINCIPLES GUIDING IDENTITY PROCESSES

The two processes of identity interact over time to determine the changing content and value of identity, with changing patterns of assimilation, partly driven by a changing social context, requiring changes in evaluation, and vice versa. The operation of these processes is not chaotic. It is guided by certain rules or principles which define what endstates are deemed desirable for the structure of identity. In so far as they specify endstates for identity they establish preferred goals for objectives to which changes in identity will be directed.

There is considerable evidence that three principles are particularly powerful motivators: the desire for self-esteem, continuity in self-conception and distinctiveness.

The self-esteem principle has been claimed to be universal (Rosenberg, 1979; Rokeach, 1978). Virtually every theory of identity posits some variant of this principle (Wells and Marwell, 1976). It has been shown to direct attitude change (Greenwald and Ronis, 1978). The desire to achieve self-enchancement or even simply to maintain the status quo has been shown to channel value formation (Rokeach, 1973); to modify the focus of attention in self-awareness (Duval and Wicklund, 1972); to create self-serving biases in the attribution process (Arkin, Appelman and Burger, 1980); and to induce strategies of selective perception and social comparison (Rosenberg, 1979).

The self-esteem principle is in some quarters (for example Franks and Marolla, 1976; Bandura, 1981) considered in tandem with the desire for self-efficacy. Basically, the argument is that people wish to feel that they are competent and in control of their own fate. Feelings of self-efficacy are tied to self-esteem. The absence of efficacy is associated with feelings of futility, alienation, and 'helplessness' (Seligman, 1975). Loss of efficacy is also related to health deficits (O'Leary, 1985). There seems to be little doubt that the self-esteem directive, perhaps qualified by the self-efficacy motive, will guide what is assimilated into the identity structure, how it is accommodated (in terms of salience, centrality, etc.) and how it is attributed value.

The evidence regarding the continuity principle is less unambiguous. Of course, some theorists treat continuity as an a priori defining property of identity. Erikson (1980) defined personal identity as 'persistent sameness within oneself'. There does, however, seem to be some confusion of terms in the literature, with continuity being treated as interchangeable with consistency. This is clearly an error: continuity and consistency are not the same. At the level of identity structure, continuity does not require that there is consistency amongst elements at any one time nor does it demand consistency over time. Continuity can be associated with growth and change, involving inconsistencies between the past and present components of identity, so long as the person perceives these changes to be congruent with the development of identity.

The evidence for consistency as a principle guiding the identity processes is somewhat ambivalent. Gergen (1968) queries the force of consistency as a motive; at the evaluative level it is overwhelmed by the demand for self-esteem. Its prime function lies on the content dimension of identity, organizing information-processing to achieve *perceived* consistency (Epstein, 1973; Greenwald, 1980; Markus, 1977). It is subjective consistency, not objective consistency, which is achieved. This enables these researchers to suggest that consistency guides identity processes, but it is a form of consistency which is not easy to access or measure, especially since many of the self-serving biases in information processing which it may motivate are also predicted on the basis of self-esteem requirements.

Arguments in support of continuity as a guiding principle in identity processes stem more frequently from the phenomenological and humanistic psychological traditions than the sociological or empirical schools. Where the person is viewed as an agent, intentionally creating an identity (Shotter, 1985; Harré, 1984; Gergen and Davis, 1985) or social being through the process of social accountability, continuity of self-conception is an implicit motivator.

However, the actual evidence for continuity as a guiding principle largely comes from studies of how people respond if they face the loss of continuity. For example, modifications in social position (job loss) or interpersonal networks (bereavement) can threaten continuity. Facing such threat, people resort to a massive variety of coping strategies to retrieve continuity (Breakwell, 1986).

The role of the distinctiveness principle in the guidance of identity processes has been explored mainly by researchers concerned with aspects of identity derived from group memberships and with how identity needs motivate group action (see Tajfel, 1978, 1982). They have shown that group members seek to differentiate their group from other groups and to derive personal distinctiveness from subsequent intergroup comparisons. Of course, this process of differentiation is influenced by self-esteem requirements: the object is to differentiate one's own group from others along positively valued dimensions of comparison and to achieve a more positive image for the group. So the distinctiveness principle is almost like a corollary of the self-esteem principle. It is also worth saying that distinctiveness may guide the organization of identity content and value dimensions but it does not inevitably motivate action. Much of the work on social comparison processes (Suls and Miller, 1977) suggests that people seek to be similar to others, at least those who act as referents, in action, belief and attitude. Distinctiveness may only guide the identity processes where it supports the self-esteem principle. But this is something which requires empirical examination.

Quite apart from the above evidence for the operation of the three principles, it is interesting to note that those biases in memory encoding, discussed by Greenwald (1980) and described earlier, are precisely the ones which would be predicted if the processes of identity were indeed functioning in accordance with the principles of continuity, distinctiveness and self-esteem.

While there is considerable evidence that all three principles guide identity processes, there is little information on their interrelationships with each other. If a good theoretical model of identity processes is to be produced, their relationships must be specified. This is particularly true since there will be occasions when their demands on the identity processes conflict: distinctiveness requires one type of accommodation, continuity another, and, perhaps, self-esteem a third. The questions in such a situation of conflict are: which principle has priority; and can compromise changes be wrought? It may be that these questions can only be answered empirically on each occasion. It seems likely, indeed, given the dynamic nature of identity that there will be no constant pecking order in the status of the three principles.

At the moment, the nature of this salience hierarchy is undetermined. It may be indeterminate. The problem is that it is, in all probability, situation-specific and is certainly likely to be temporally transient. Different situations, at different times, will make differential calls upon the distinctiveness, continuity and self-esteem principles. It is already fairly well-established that the expression in action of various components of the content dimension of identity is situation-specific. For example, a number of researchers (Okamura, 1981; Waddel and Cairns, 1986) have shown that people differ across contexts in the expression of their ethnicity; by and large, it becomes a more important determinant of feeling and action where inter-ethnic contacts are demanded. Moreover, it had been shown that the salience of the desire for intergroup differentiation and intragroup similarity is also dependent upon the specific network of relations between groups which pertains at any one time (Brown, 1984; Tajfel and Turner, 1979; Deschamps and Brown, 1983). It is hardly surprising then that the principles of distinctiveness, continuity and self-esteem should be seen to vary in relative, or, indeed, absolute salience according to context.

In conducting research to establish hierarchy or changing salience it is important not to impose premature closure on the model of their relationship on the basis of too few contextual examples. The real objective should be to formulate a set of rules of transition which would specify under what circumstances the individual moves from applying one principle in operating identity processes to applying the next. Such rules of transition would be likely to be historically specific but, at least, they would say something about the relationship between the principles at one time. As long as the eras across which the hierarchies held and the transition rules operated were sufficiently long-lived to be encapsulated in research, there would be little problem.

There is another possibility. This is that rules of transition might not be available for formulation because the principles operate simultaneously or are used in very quick succession (which is the functional equivalent of simultaneity). If this is proven so, the issue of salience may be illusory.

One final point needs to be made here: in describing these three principles there is no assumption that they are the only guides to identity processes. For instance, the desire for autonomy has been suggested (Apter, 1983) to be of equal importance in directing identity work. The purpose here is not to provide an exhaustive list but to outline those where the evidence is strongest and consensus greatest.

UNIVERSALS IN PROCESS AND PRINCIPLES

The recent upsurge in concern for historical social psychology (Gergen and Gergen, 1984) has highlighted the need to build theories which take account of temporal transitions. Psychological processes are said to be shaped and controlled by the social context in which they are embedded (Vygotsky, 1978). However, it is debatable whether all psychological processes are mutable (for example memory). It may not be the process which changes so much as its rules of operation (for example in memory, permissable biases or mnemonics) or realms of operation (for example the shift from public to private details). It is also debatable whether a process which is modified in minor ways can still be regarded as the same process or needs to be considered to be new for theoretical purposes.

The debate about the universality of processes is relevant to models of identity. The processes of assimilation–accommodation and of evaluation have been assumed to be universal and not temporally relative. Since both are content-free this seems a reasonable supposition. In fact, the importance of social context is acknowledged at the level of the actual content and actual value of identity which are recognized to be the product of the interaction between identity processes and social context.

While the identity processes are treated as universals, the identity principles must be regarded as culturally- and temporally-specific. They can be regarded as reifications of what society regards as acceptable endstates for identity. They are a socially-established set of criteria against which identity is measured. Whatever is socially constructed can be reconstructed socially. It is feasible to imagine a culture, for instance, where distinctiveness is not valued and would not guide identity processes. It is less easy to conceive of cultures where continuity and self-esteem are not desirable. Though it is certainly true that in historical periods when the self was not equated with individuation (Verhave and van Hoorn, 1984) neither would have operated in the manner described earlier. The principles listed can only be said to operate in current Western industrialized cultures. It is evident that only empirical work which is diachronic and cross-cultural will be able to tap changes in the actual operation of principles.

Cultural myopia must be avoided. All of the recent literature on the self emanating from anthropologists asserts the cultural relativity of the concept. Marsella, De Vos and Hsu (1985), comparing the West with Indian and Chinese traditions, argue that cultural understandings affect and, even, determine how the self is experienced in different societies. Shweder and Bourne (1984) emphasize that the concept of the person varies cross-culturally. In some cultures, for instance in Bali and New Guinea, they claim that the individual is not acknowledged as an abstract ethical or normative category. Given such examples, it would be inappropriate to assume that the model of identity principles proposed here applies universally.

Recognition that the modelling of identity is culturally-specific points to the importance of presenting a model of the social structure and processes relevant to identity as an integral part of theories of identity function. It is impossible to do this here, given the constraints of space, but it is addressed elsewhere (Breakwell, 1986) where the effects of social change are examined.

The issue of the universality of identity processes and principles also has to be viewed in the light of what is known of the development of cognitive abilities and awareness. Most models of identity are founded upon the assumption that people are self-aware, possessing abstract self-knowledge which is reflexively monitored. The model presented here does so and it is a notion which is philosophically uncontentious (Shoemaker, 1984). But this leads to questions about the development of self-awareness. Since the cognitive system underlying identity is a product of the interaction of the maturing biological organism and evolving social processes (Serafica, 1982; Doise and Mugny, 1984; Higgins, Ruble and Hartup, 1985) identity too should be subject to developmental changes.

In fact, there is evidence of developmental changes in self-concept: there are age-related trends in increased richness, differentiation and complexity of self-conception (Flavell, 1977). This implies that the content dimension of identity is actively constructed through experience and learning from experience is controlled by the rate of the development of the cognitive information-processing system. It is clear that a developmental perspective must be integrated into any modelling of identity. But this needs to go beyond stage models of identity to show how the growing cognitive abilities are determinants of the functioning of identity processes and how they probably also have spin-off implications for the guiding principles. The empirical evidence so far supports the assertion that the principles, after infancy at least (Aboud and Ruble, 1984), are developmentally constant (Flavell and Ross, 1981) but their relative salience varies across the lifespan (Savage et al., 1977).

METHODS FOR STUDYING IDENTITY

Methods used to study identity have been diverse and have reflected the theoretical preconceptions of their originators. During the history of the endeavour to understand identity, methods have included everything from introspection, through psychoanalysis, to the behavioural record of minute action segments (Ginsberg, Brenner and von Cranach, 1985). The structural symbolic interactionists have often used the Twenty Statements Test (TST), developed by Kuhn and McPartland (1954), which simply requires respondents to give twenty answers to the question 'Who am I?'. Responses are coded within classification systems designed to assess the salience of elements of identity (for example descriptions higher on the list of answers are presumed to be more salient) (Spitzer, 1976). The TST is often seen as the precursor to the more detailed examination of those elements of identity it reveals (see Wylie, 1979, for a review of the supplementary measurement strategies). Wylie notes that most of these measurement methods are psychometrically dubious in terms of both validity and reliability. The TST has particular problems for anyone seeking to use statistical analysis. This had led recently to attempts to revise the method. Burke and Tully

(1981) proposed the use of multiple-discriminant analysis of a semantic differential scaling to establish the meaning of particular role-related elements of identity. Jackson (1981) has produced a 23-item measure of commitment to role-identities which is reliable and valid.

Whilst the sociologists move towards greater psychometric rigour, psychologists have been moving away from the use of personality trait lists to elicit a person's self-description. For instance, Weinreich (1980) has evolved a method (IDEX) using repertory grids to produce an Identity Structure Analysis (ISA) which can be used idiographically or nomothetically. Also, methods are beginning to be used in conjunction.

Methodological liberation has lain in the acceptance that it is legitimate to use different approaches in unison. Contemporary researchers are more likely to rely upon a combination of multi-dimensional scaling and longitudinal autobiography or diary records (Ericsson and Simon, 1984). They do not shun indepth interviews (Brenner, Brown and Canter, 1985) or extensive observational studies (de Waele, 1985). These methods provide simultaneously information about the content and value of the identity structure and data on its variation across social context or spatial and temporal location. They echo the changed emphasis in theorizing about identity where there has been a move from centring explanation upon psychic dynamics to focusing it upon social and interactional processes.

Social and interactional processes may only rarely be amenable to examination through the use of manipulative experimental methods. Some would argue that they never are (Gergen, 1985). Most frequently it is obvious that they require other methodologies: account gathering (Brown and Sime, 1981), textual and content analysis, ethnography (Hammersley and Atkinson, 1983) and observational techniques (Forgas, 1979). To test an integrated model of identity and social process it is necessary to employ an integrated set of methods, each method providing information at a different level of analysis. The equivalence of all data need not be assumed for all of them to contribute to an understanding of identity.

CONCLUSION

It is difficult to differentiate between the concepts of identity and the self but it is clear that both are increasingly recognized as having a role to play in most current theoretical paradigms in social psychology. Consequently, a coherent model of their functioning relative to social processes could represent a timely means of integrating a whole range of research domains in social psychology. Such a model would need to encompass both the structure and processes of identity and be able to show how these processes are regulated. Some of the potential components of such a model have been discussed here. They are compatible with existing accumulated evidence, but it is recognized that these suggestions are culturally-specific and developmentally unsophisticated. Nevertheless, taken together with the available models of social change (for example Moscovici, 1976) they yield empirically verifiable predictions (Breakwell, 1986). Moreover, current developments in methodology make not just the examination of the content of identity feasible but also the exploration of its processes.

REFERENCES

Aboud, F.E. and Ruble, D. (1984) Identity constancy in children: Developmental processes and implications. Paper read at the BPS *Self and Identify* conference, Cardiff. Available from The British Psychological Society, Leicester.
Aboud, F.E. and Skerry, S.A. (1983) Self and ethnic concepts in relation to ethnic constancy. *Canadian Journal of Behavioural Science/Review of Canadian Science: Comparative*, 15(1), 14–26.
Alexander, N.C. and Knight, G.W. (1971) Situated identities and social psychological experimentation. *Sociometry*, 34, 65–82.
Alexander, N.C. and Lauderdale, P. (1977) Situated identities and social influence. *Sociometry*, 40, 225–233.
Alexander, N.C. and Wiley, M.G. (1981) Situated activity and identity formation. In M. Rosenberg and R. Turner (eds) *Sociological Perspectives on Social Psychology*. New York: Basic Books.
Apter, M.J. (1983) Negativism and the sense of identify. In G.M. Breakwell (ed.) *Threatened Identities*. Chichester: Wiley.
Arkin, R.M., Appelman, A.J. and Burger, J.M. (1980) Social anxiety, self-preservation, and the self-serving bias in causal attribution. *Journal of Personal and Social Psychology*, 38, 23–35.
Aronson, E. (1968) Dissonance theory: Progress and problems. In R.P. Abelson et al. (eds) *Theories of Cognitive Consistency: A Sourcebook*. Chicago: Rand McNally.
Ashmore, R.D. and Del Boca, F.K. (eds) (1986) *The Social Psychology of Female–Male Relations: A Critical Analysis of Central Concepts*. London: Academic Press.
Ball, R.A. (1983) Development of basic norm violation. *Criminology*, 21(1), 75–94.
Bandura, A. (1977) Self-efficacy: Toward a unifying theory of behavioural change. *Psychological Review*, 84, 191–215.
Bandura, A. (1978) The self system in reciprocal determinism. *American Psychologist*, 33, 344–358.
Bandura, A. (1981) The self and mechanisms of agency. In J. Suls (ed.) *Social Psychological Perspectives on the Self*. Hillsdale, N.J.: Lawrence Erlbaum Associates.
Bandura, A. (1982) 'Self-efficacy mechanisms' in human agency. *American Psychologist*, 37, 122–147.

Bem, D.J. (1972) Self-perception theory, In L. Berkowitz (ed.) *Advances in Experimental Psychology, Volume 6.* New York: Academic Press.
Bem, S. (1981) Gender schema theory: A cognitive account of sextyping. *Psychological Review, 88(4),* 369–371.
Biddle, B.J. (1979) *Role Theory: Expectations, Identities and Behaviours.* New York: Academic Press.
Blumer, H. (1969) *Symbolic Interactionism: Perspective and Method.* Englewood Cliffs, N.J.: Prentice-Hall.
Bowerman, W.R. (1978) Subjective competence: The structure, process, and functioning on self-referent causal attributions. *Journal for the Theory of Social Behaviour, 8,* 45–77.
Breakwell, G.M. (ed.) (1983) *Threatened Identities.* Chichester: Wiley.
Breakwell, G.M. (1986) *Coping with Threatened Identities.* London: Methuen.
Brenner, M., Brown, J. and Canter, D. (1985) *The Research Interview: Uses and Approaches.* London: Academic Press.
Brown, J. and Sime, J. (1981) A methodology for accounts. In M. Brenner (ed.) *Social Method and Social Life.* London: Academic Press.
Brown, R.J. (1984) The effects of intergroup similarity and cooperative vs competitive orientation on intergroup discrimination. *British Journal of Social Psychology, 23(1),* 21–34.
Burke, P.J. and Tully, J. (1977) The measurement of role-identities, *Social Forces,* 55, 881–897.
Cooley, C.H. (1902) *Human Nature and the Social Order,* New York: Scribner's.
Covington, M.V. and Beery, R.G. (1976) *Self-Worth and School Learning.* New York: Holt, Rinehart and Winston.
Denzin, N.K. (1977) *Childhood Socialization: Studies in the Development of Language, Social Behaviour, and Identity.* San Francisco: Jossey-Bass.
Deschamps, J.C. and Brown, R. (1983) Superordinate goals and intergroup conflict. *British Journal of Social Psychology, 22(3),* 198–196.
de Waele, J.P. (1985) The significance of action psychology for personality research and assessment. In G.P. Ginsberg, M. Brenner and M. von Cranach (eds) *Discovery Strategies in the Psychology of Action.* London: Academic Press.
Doise, W. and Mugny, G. (1984) *The Social Development of the Intellect.* Oxford: Pergamon.
Duval, S. and Wicklund, R.A. (1972) *A Theory of Objective Self-Awareness.* New York: Academic Press.
Epstein, S. (1973) The self-concept revisited or a theory of a theory. *American Psychologist, 28,* 404–416.
Ericsson, K.A. and Simon, H.A. (1984) *Protocol Analysis: Verbal Reports as Data.* Cambridge, Mass.: MIT Press.
Erikson, E.H. (1980) *Identity and the Life Cycle.* New York: Norton.
Fenigstein, A., Scheier, M.F. and Buss, A.H. (1975) Public and private self-consciousness: Assessment and theory. *Journal of Consulting and Clinical Psychology, 43,* 522–527.
Festinger, L. (1954) A theory of social comparison. *Human Relations, 14,* 48–64.
Flavell, J.H. (1977) *Cognitive Development.* Englewood Cliffs, N.J.: Prentice-Hall.
Flavell, J.H. and Ross, L. (1981) *Social Cognitive Development: Frontiers and Possible Futures.* Cambridge: Cambridge University Press.
Forgas, J. (1979) *Social Episodes: The Study of Interaction Routines.* London: Academic Press.

Franks, D.D. and Marolla, J. (1979) Efficacious action and social approval as interacting dimensions of self-esteem: A tentative formulation through construct validation. *Sociometry, 39*, 324–341.
Gecas, V. (1971) Parental behaviour and dimensions of adolescent self-evaluation. *Sociometry, 34*, 466–482.
Gecas, V. (1982) The self-concept. *Annual Review of Sociology, 8*, 1–33.
Gergen, K.J. (1968) Personal consistency and the presentation of self. In C. Gordon and K.J. Gergen (eds) *The Self in Social Interaction, Vol. 1.* New York: Wiley.
Gergen, K.J. (1971) *The Concept of Self.* New York: Holt, Rinehart and Winston.
Gergen, K.J. (1985) The social constructionist movement in modern psychology. *American Psychologist, 40(3)*, 266–275.
Gergen, K.J. and Davies, K.E. (1985) *The Social Construction of the Person.* New York: Springer-Verlag.
Gergen, K.J. and Gergen, M.M. (eds) (1984) *Historical Social Psychology.* Hillsdale, N.J.: Lawrence Erlbaum Associates.
Ginsberg, G.R., Brenner, J. and von Cranach, M. (eds) (1985) *Discovery Strategies in the Psychology of Action.* London: Academic Press.
Gordon, C. (1976) Development of evaluated role identities. *Annual Review of Sociology, 2*, 405–433.
Greenwald, A.G. (1980) The totalitarian ego: Fabrication and revision of personal history. *American Psychologist, 35*, 603–618.
Greenwald, A.G. and Ronis, D.L. (1978) Twenty years of cognitive dissonance: Case study of the evolution of a theory. *Psychological Review, 85*, 53–57.
Grossman, B., Wirt, R. and Davids, A. (1985) Self-esteem, ethnic identity, and behavioural adjustment among Anglo and Chicano adolescents in West Texas. *Journal of Adolescence, 8*, 57–68.
Hammersley, M. and Atkinson, P. (1983) *Ethnography: Principles in Practice.* London: Tavistock.
Harré, R. (1983) Identity projects. In G.M. Breakwell (ed.) *Threatened Identities.* Chichester: Wiley.
Harré, R. (1984) *Personal Being.* Oxford: Basil Blackwell.
Hegel, G.W.F. (1807) *Phenomenology of Spirit.* A.V. Miller (trans) (1977) Oxford: Clarendon Press.
Higgins, E.T., Ruble, D.N. and Hartup, W.W. (1985) *Social Development.* Cambridge: Cambridge University Press.
Hofman, J. (1983) Social identity and intergroup conflict. Paper presented at the EAESP conference *Perspectives on Group Conflict,* Tel Aviv, Israel.
Jackson, S.E. (1981) Measurement of commitment to role identities. *Journal of Personal and Social Psychology, 40*, 138–146.
Kahneman, D., Slovic, P. and Tversky, A. (1982) *Judgement under Uncertainty: Heuristics and Biases.* New York: Cambridge University Press.
Katz, P.A. (1986) Gender identity: Development and consequences. In R.B. Ashmore and F.K. Del Boca (eds) *The Social Psychology of Female–Male Relations.* Orlando, Fl.: Academic Press.
Kelly, G.A. (1955) *The Psychology of Personal Constructs, Vols 1 and 2.* New York: Norton.
Kihlstrom, J.E. and Cantor, N. (1984) Mental representations of the self. In L. Berkowitz (ed.) *Advances in Experimental Social Psychology, Vol. 17.* New York: Academic Press.
Kohn, M.L. (1969) *Class and Conformity.* Homewood, Il.: Dorsey Press.

Kuhn, M.H. and McPartland, T.S. (1954) An empirical investigation of self attitudes. *American Sociological Review*, 19, 68–76.
Leonard, K. (1984) *Personality and Ideology: Towards a Materialist Understanding of the Individual*. London: Macmillan.
Liebkind, P. (1984) Minority identity and identification processes: A social psychological study. *Commentations Scientarium Socialum*, 22.
Luckmann, T. (1983) Remarks on personal identity: Inner, social and historical time. In A.Jacobson-Widding (ed.) *Identity: Personal and Socio-Cultural*. Uppsala: Uppsala University Press.
McCall, G.J. and Simmons, J.L. (1978) *Identities and Interactions*, rev. ed. New York: The Free Press.
Markus, H. (1977) Self-schemata and processing information about the self. *Journal of Personal and Social Psychology*, 35, 63–78.
Marsella, A.J., De Vos, G. and Hsu, F. (1985) *Culture and Self*. London: Methuen.
Moscovici, S. (1976) *Social Influence and Social Change*. London: Academic Press.
Nisbett, R. and Ross, L. (1980) *Human Inference: Strategies and Shortcomings of Social Judgement*. Englewood Cliffs, N.J.: Prentice-Hall.
Okamura, J.Y. (1981) Situational ethnicity. *Journal of Ethnic and Racial Studies*, 4, 452–465.
O'Leary, A. (1985) Self-efficacy and health. *Behaviour Research and Therapy*, 23(4), 437–451.
Openshaw, D.K., Thomas, D.L. and Rollins, B.C. (1983) Socialisation and adolescent self-esteem: Symbolic interaction and social learning explanation. *Adolescence*, 17(70), 317–329.
Rokeach, M. (1973) *The Nature of Human Values*. New York: Free Press.
Rokeach, M. (1978) *Beliefs, Attitudes and Values*. San Francisco: Jossey-Bass.
Rosenberg, M. (1979) *Conceiving the Self*. New York: Basic Books.
Savage, R.D., Gaber, L.B., Britton P.G., Bolton, N. and Cooper, A. (1977) *Personality and Adjustment in the Aged*. London: Academic Press.
Secord, P.F. (1977) Making oneself behave: A critique of the behavioural paradigm and an alternative conceptualization. In T. Mischel (ed.) *The Self*. Oxford: Basil Blackwell.
Seligman, M.E.P. (1975) *Helplessness: On Depression, Development, and Death*. San Francisco: Freeman.
Serafica, F.C. (1982) *Social-Cognitive Development in Context*. London: Methuen.
Shoemaker, S. (1984) *Identity, Cause and Mind*. Cambridge: Cambridge University Press.
Shotter, J. (1985) *Social Accountability and Selfhood*. Oxford: Basil Blackwell.
Shweder, R.A. and Bourne, E.J. (1984) Does the concept of the person vary cross-culturally? In R.W. Shweder and R.A. Le Vine (eds) *Culture Theory: Essays on Mind, Self and Society*. New York: Cambridge University Press.
Smith, M.B. (1978) Perspectives on selfhood. *American Psychologist*, 33, 1053–1063.
Spitzer, S.P. (1976) Perceived validity and assessment of the self: A decade later. *Sociological Quarterly*, 17, 236–246.
Steiner, B.W. (1985) *Gender Dysphoria*. New York: Plenum.
Stryker, S. (1979) The profession: Comments from an interactionist's perspective. *Sociological Focus*, 12, 175–186.
Stryker, S. (1980) *Symbolic Interactionism: A Social Structural Version*. Menlo Park, Ca: Benjamin/Cummings.

Suls, J.M. and Miller, R.L. (eds) (1977) *Social Comparison Processes: Theoretical and Empirical Perspectives*. Washington, DC: Halsted-Wiley.
Tajfel, H. (ed.) (1978) *Differentiation Between Social Groups*. London: Academic Press.
Tajfel, H. (ed.) (1982) *Social Identity and Intergroup Relations*. Cambridge: Cambridge University Press.
Tajfel, H. and Turner, J.C. (1979) An integrative theory of intergroup conflict. In W.G. Austin and S. Worchel (eds) *The Social Psychology of Intergroup Relations*. California: Brooks/Cole.
Thoits, P.A. (1983) Multiple identities and psychological well-being: A reformulation and test of the social isolation hypothesis. *American Sociological Review*, 48, 174–187.
Turner, J.C. and Giles, H. (eds) (1981) *Intergroup Behaviour*. Oxford: Basil Blackwell.
Turner, R.H. (1976) The real self: From institution to impulse. *American Journal of Sociology*, 81, 1–23.
Turner, R.H. (1978) The role and the person. *American Journal of Sociology*, 84, 1–23.
Vallacher, R.R. (1980) An introduction to self theory. In D.M.Wegner and R.R. Vallacher (eds) *The Self in Social Psychology*. New York: Oxford University Press.
Verhave, T. and van Hoorn, W. (1984) The temporalization of the self. In K.J. Gergen and M.M. Gergen (eds) *Historical Social Psychology*. Hillsdale, N.J.: Lawrence Erlbaum Associates.
Vygotsky, L.S. (1978) Discussion comment. In M. Cole, V. John-Steiner, S. Scribner and E. Souberman (eds) *Mind in Society*. Cambridge, Mass.: Harvard University Press.
Waddell, N. and Cairns, E. (1986) Situational perspectives on social identity in Northern Ireland. *British Journal of Social Psychology*, 25, 25–31.
Wegner, D.M. and Vallacher, R.R. (eds) (1980) *The Self in Social Psychology*. New York: Oxford University Press.
Weinreich, P. (1980) *Manual for Identity Exploration Using Personal Constructs*. London: SSRC.
Weinreich, P. (1983) Emerging from threatened identities. In G.M. Breakwell (ed.) *Threatened Identities*. Chichester: Wiley.
Wells, L.E. (1978) Theories of deviance and the self-concept. *Social Psychology*, 41, 189–204.
Wells, L.E. and Marwell, G. (1976) *Self-Esteem: Its Conceptualisation and Measurement*. Beverly Hills: Sage.
Winters, K.C. and Neale, J.M. (1985) Mania and low self-esteem. *Journal of Abnormal Psychology*, 94(3), 282–290.
Wylie, R.C. (1979) *The Self-Concept, Vol.2*. Lincoln, Ne.: University of Nebraska Press.
Zavelloni, M. (1983) Ego-ecology: The study of interaction between social and personal identities. In A. Jacobson-Widding (ed.) *Identity: Personal and Socio-Cultural*. Uppsala: Uppsala University Press.
Zurcher, L.A. Jr (1977) *The Mutable Self*. Beverly Hills: Sage.

LANGUAGE, SOCIAL IDENTITY AND HEALTH
Caroline Dryden and Howard Giles

Given our social interdependence, communication between us is essential for a whole host of reasons. Not least amongst these are an access to and or exchange of information, the discussion of ideas, negotiation of arguments and conflict, and the provision of emotional support in times of stress. A lack of satisfying and quality communications can have serious implications for our psychological well-being and physical health, and yet, until recently, the study of language and communication has been peripheral to the mainstream of social psychology. Encouragingly, this state of affairs is now starting to change (for example Robinson, 1983) with more and more studies reporting 'bad' communication as being implicated in problems such as marital dissatisfaction, loneliness and depression to name but a few (for example Kitson, Babri and Roach, 1985).

Yet the state of the art is such that we are still nowhere near providing definitive solutions and remedies to the improvement of psychological well-being and physical health. Much work has even to be started, let alone more of it done, and many new, innovative, naturalistic methodologies and analyses devised. The complexity of language and communication can only be really appreciated from the vantagepoint of the interface between a number of relevant disciplines. With that in mind, we survey other literatures for their insights into these processes; a large part of the research cited has been conducted by sociolinguists, communication scholars and sociologists. Whether these researchers are themselves utilizing so-called 'psychological methods' is a moot point, yet underlines the fact that techniques and theories are not the exclusive property of particular disciplines: the boundaries between them can be ever blurred and liable to redefinition.

Our approach has been influenced by the life and work of Henri Tajfel, who himself recognized the roles of language and communication in everyday social life. His 'social identity' theory (Tajfel, 1978; Tajfel and Turner, 1979) is a crucial component in our previous thinking on the interrelationships between language, categorization, stereotyping and identity (Giles and Johnson, 1981; Hewstone and Giles, 1986). It is to these processes that we attend in the first section of this chapter, alluding to their *functional* significance for promoting or hindering psychological and physical health, both indirectly (with particular respect to ethnic and class group relations) and more directly (by reference to doctor–patient communication).

In the second section, we examine some of the assumptions underlying so-called *intergroup theory* in the area of language and communication, calling into question the 'motivational individualism' inherent in a strictly Tajfelian approach (Condor, 1985). Paradoxically in many ways, we stress the value of invoking more of a *social dimension* (cf. Tajfel, 1984) to our understanding of intergroup relations and identity.

In the third and final section, we explore the implications of this more *social* analysis for communication and health, explicitly by recourse to an examination of health care issues in the media. To this end, we suggest that important changes currently being proposed at a micro-interpersonal level to render doctor–patient communication more effective require an appreciation of the complex macro-social forces and interests against which they are proffered. This is deemed essential if the rewards and efforts anticipated are likely to yield any lasting and widespread benefits to society. We conclude that the study of language and communication *has* indeed made some important inroads into the relationships between health and identity, yet further significant advances can only come about when more social analyses focusing upon the creation and construction of meaning are available to complement our sophistication at the level of interpersonal dynamics.

LANGUAGE: CATEGORIZATION AND STEREOTYPING

Language as a social marker

Arguably, Lambert et al.'s (1960) investigation in Montreal was something of a landmark in the serious study of language within social psychology. Adopting a procedure that became known as the 'matched-guise' technique, these authors arranged that male subjects listen to a passage of prose read by a series of different male speakers in different languages – French and English – as well as dialects of the same language, and rate each speaker on various trait attributes. In fact, and unbeknown to subjects, the French and English passages were read by one and the same speakers at different points on the stimulus tape (see Ball and Giles, 1982).

Results showed that subjects rated English speakers more favourably than French speakers. An interesting, yet worrying finding from this study was that it was not only English Canadian raters who downgraded French speakers on audiotape, the French Canadian raters not only did likewise but actually accentuated the unfavourable evaluative profile. If an individual is prepared to downgrade their own ethnolinguistic group relative to another, how is this perception likely to affect the individual's psychological health?

The Montreal study was a prelude to an outpouring of similar investigations all over the world; an area now known as 'language attitude' research (Ryan and Giles, 1982). A general finding has consistently emerged from this literature (even taking into account listener group membership and facets of context), namely, that 'standard' speakers are judged more positively on dimensions of competence (that is intelligent, educated, confident, ambitious) than non-standard speakers. In Britain, the standard speech is a 'non-localized' variety typified as that of a BBC newscaster; this is termed Received Pronunciation or RP. Interestingly enough, RP speakers are even upgraded not only over regional, urban and ethnic-accented speakers in Britain but also hold sway in terms of prestige in Australia, New Zealand and the United States (Stewart, Ryan and Giles, 1985). Standard speech is of course associated with status, the media and power, and those of the higher socio-economic bracket. Non-standard speakers, however, do in some contexts gain on occasion more favourable ratings on such characteristics as integrity and benevolence (Ryan, 1979), but in general terms, the *more* non-standard accented the speech, the less favourably rated the speaker (for example Brennan and Brennan, 1981).

Let us pause for just a moment and examine what these kinds of findings might mean. Subjects placed in an experimental situation where they listen to a speaker reading a passage of prose (that is with no contextual information; see, however, Bradac and Wisegarver, 1984) seem in general able and willing to undertake this task. Furthermore, Williams (1976) shows that they are prepared to commence rating on average 16 seconds after the speaker has started, while Edwards (1979*a*) in post-experimental interviews with teachers found that the latter reluctantly agreed that they do indeed use voice cues in the classroom just as evaluatively. Why is this? Is it really the case that one can predict another's personality profile merely by the kind of accent they have?

Actually, evidence suggests that the relationship between voice and personality is not at all strong (Brown and Bradshaw, 1985) but that raters none the less espouse a social consensus of what speakers sound like psychologically. It must be remembered that matched-guise techniques eliminate a claim to individual differences anyway by using the same bidialectal/bilingual speaker each time (usually pretested for judged authenticity of guises). Therefore, judgements must be based purely on accent differences. Let us be quite clear that it is not just a case of 'different but equal'. Standard speech is consistently related to intelligence and competence, and this may well have important implications, for example, for a non-standard speaker's intellectual development, a point we return to shortly.

Edwards (1979b) has argued that it is extremely unlikely that there are any intrinsic qualitative differences between different language varieties. Empirical studies have shown that when social connotations associated with particular language varieties cannot be accessed by listeners (as when you hear different social dialects of an unfamiliar language), then no differences in aesthetics, prestige and so forth emerge in subjects' ratings of them. What appears to be happening in language attitude studies is that different languages, dialects and accents are eliciting dispositional stereotypes in the listener's mind. Language in this context is clearly acting as some kind of social marker through which people can be categorized and judged accordingly.

The nature of these judgements has been shown to have profound implications in certain applied situations, too. For instance, in a number of studies in the United States and Britain standard speakers have been judged more suited to higher and non-standard-accented speakers to lower status jobs (Kalin, 1982) and in an Australian study, in a legally-framed context, the latter were more likely to be seen as guilty of a crime of violence than the former (Seggie, 1983). Numerous other studies have pointed to the poor scholastic prognosis associated with children possessing non-standard speech patterns (Edwards, 1979b).

But do these stereotyped judgements deriving from beliefs about language groups have any direct behavioural effects? It seems highly likely that they will, although clearly it is difficult to isolate language as a variable in most real-life interactions. However, various studies having made every attempt to do this have produced compatible effects with respect to compliance. For example, Bourhis and Giles (1976) found that theatre-goers were more likely to comply with a request on those evenings when it was voiced over the loud-speaker system in RP than various degrees of the local urban accent. In the same way, Giles, Baker and Fielding (1975) and Giles and Farrar (1979) have found that high school students and housewives provide more written information (within the range 25–44 per cent more) to a psychologist physically present when the same person requests it in RP as opposed to a regionally-accented variety. Also, Cairns and Dubiez (1976) found that children in Northern Ireland had better recall of material delivered in an RP form than in other, local guises. Evidence from these studies, then, supports the strong relationship between RP and perceived status and competence.

Effects of differential language behaviour

Whilst we might hold fixed stereotypic images of various different language groups, the fact is that for the vast majority of us our speech and accent are not constant, and we have a speech repertoire from which to select. In other words, we make inferences about people based on the ways they have opted to speak at that time and in that situation. In many countries, as in the Philippines and Wales, people often switch languages between conversations and even within utterances, whilst in monolingual communities this will be manifested by strengthening or weakening accents, changing speech rate and pitch, lexical and grammatical choices, and so forth.

In an attempt to provide an understanding of the motives underlying and consequences arising from speech style shifts, speech accommodation theory has been developed over the years (see for example, Giles, 1984). This model attempts to articulate how, when and why people shift their speech styles towards (*convergence*) or away from (*divergence*) others. Let us deal with convergence for the moment. In its simplest terms, it has been proposed that speech convergence often comes about in order to gain social approval. Indeed, recipients of optimally-converging messages evaluate very positively the accommodating speaker for his or her efforts and consideration. In reality, however, individuals will shift their language patterns towards their *perceptions* of the way others speak (Thakerar, Giles and Cheshire, 1982), with this perception often being influenced by stereotyped ideas of how socially-categorized others talk. As an illustration, Bell (1982) reveals that certain New Zealand broadcasters read the same news bulletin on different radio channels quite differently in terms of pronunciation, depending on which socio-economic group they believed their listening audiences belonged to.

Yet our categorization of others into social out-groups and the assignment of dispositional stereotypes to them can have quite serious consequences for the way we treat them. More particularly, miscarried language convergence towards members of another group can be potentially detrimental to the recipient's psychological health (and sometimes glean unfavourable reactions for the perpetrator in return). For example, Caporael, Lukaszewski and Culbertson (1983) found that nurses having unfavourable views of the elderly's functional autonomy sometimes use baby talk to the institutionalized elderly irrespective of their actual capacities; a linguistic act that seems highly aggravating to the cognitively competent elderly person. (Klemz (1977) also found similar signs of the sighted 'talking down' to blind people.

A study by Word, Zanna and Cooper (1974) can be interpreted as producing evidence to suggest that white interviewers, at least in their study, talk quite differently to interviewees of different races and in ways which induce black interviewees to converge their language in the direction of the interviewers' prejudicial expectations. It was found that interviewers were verbally and non-verbally more distant and less involved with blacks, made more speech errors and conducted shorter interviews than with whites. In a second part of this study, the authors arranged that interviews were set up so that interviewers interacted with white interviewees in the very same way as had previously been observed with black interviewees. Here, the white interviewees were perceived as being more nervous and less competent than the whites interviewed earlier. In other words, a negative stereotype on the part of the interviewers appears to have been responsible for eliciting language from the black interviewees which could confirm the former's pre-existing prejudices.

In all the above cases, there is a grave danger that negative perceptions of others which mediate language performance will have the effect of producing what is known as a 'self-fulfilling' prophecy; that is they will set the stage linguistically for their dispositional expectations to be confirmed. Rodin and Langer (1980) in a study on the institutionalized elderly have found that elderly people who were treated as though they had little functional autonomy did indeed become more depressed and less able to fend for themselves as a result. Studies of depression deriving from Seligman (1975) have noted the appearance of the phenomenon known as 'learned helplessness', which seems to develop out of just this kind of situation.

As previously stated, there is evidence that speech style alone can in some circumstances be an important cue to categorization. Seligman, Tucker and Lambert (1972) have shown that speech style can be an important cue to teachers' evaluations of pupils, even when combined with other information, such as supposed photographs of the target children and some of their work. Edwards and Giles (1984) have argued that the perception of so-called 'poor speech' characteristics of children leads teachers to more negative inferences about their personalities, social background and academic abilities and, hence, to the danger, once again, of the self-fulfilling prophecy. Even more alarmingly, perceptions of speech style themselves can be influenced greatly by beliefs about the way a stereotyped individual is likely to speak. For example, Williams (1976) has shown that a black child speaking middle-class English is likely to be perceived, nevertheless, under certain circumstances as speaking with an ethnic accent.

Communication in a medical setting

There is one particular area of communication where stereotyping can be seen to have more of a *direct* effect on health. This is in the context of doctor–patient interactions, which in many instances could be the most important, almost death-defying few minutes of interaction a person can experience. 'Good' communication is obviously vital for effective health care (Pendleton and Hasler, 1983). The physician must be able to develop good rapport with the patient and draw them out in order to gain as much information as possible to provide appropriate diagnosis and treatment. In order to do this, a doctor's best bet would seem to be to encourage the patient to open up by being a good listener (a process we might term *listening* convergence), allowing the person the ideal empathic context in which to express him or herself. Indeed, Street and Wiemann (in press) found in a study of 25 physicians and 354 patients in a large United States hospital that worried patients expressed greater satisfaction with physicians perceived as involved and expressive, and lower satisfaction with those physicians viewed as non-involved and non-expressive.

Consultations are, however, often subject to time pressures and the goal of the interaction may often be simply to get the patient to do what the doctor says as quickly as possible. Moreover, doctors *as a group* are perceived as having high status in this culture and, more often than not, regard themselves as deserving of it (in much the same way that RP speakers are considered highly prestigious, competent, and so forth). This factor appears to contribute to doctors exercising a high degree of control in consultations. In short, empirical sociolinguistic research suggests that in doctor–patient interactions it is the physician that does most of the talking, whilst generally underestimating patients' medical knowledge (Wallen, Waitzkin and Stroeckle, 1979).

It is usually the doctors who determine the length of the consultation, accomplishing this by initiating most of the questions. West (1983) found that patients on average ask only 9 per cent of the questions posed in the encounter and Frankel (1984) found that physicians initiated 99 per cent of the utterances. Heath (1985) produced evidence suggesting that doctors always propose topic completion, which in turn leads to termination of the consultation. A study by West (1984) also discovered that male doctors interrupt more than patients and Frankel

(1984) found that doctors kept asking questions before the patient had *answered* the last one. Finally, forms of address may also be used as a means of retaining control. For example, Todd (1984) found that male gynaecologists often used words like 'honey' and 'little . . .' when addressing their female patients.

For the patient's part, the tendency is to behave passively in consultation, either assuming that the doctor 'knows best' or not having the confidence to voice their contributions in the medical encounter. This conversational *imbalance* presents very real problems in terms of a doctor running the risk of 'not getting to the bottom' of the problem by neither letting the patient frame the problem in their own terms nor allowing them their own interpretation of events. In this way, much valuable information may be missed. Furthermore, Robinson and Whitfield (1985) have pointed out that a patient is more likely to forget or misunderstand advice provided by a doctor if they have not *actively* contributed in the consultation to discussion of, for example, the best times to take medication; that is, if they have not been deeply *cognitively* involved in the 'negotiation'.

Whilst it would seem that there is, in general, a power discrepancy between doctor and patient dependent in part on beliefs concerning the status of doctors *vis-à-vis* everyone else, this situation is likely to be mediated by the social group memberships of the patient. For instance, Greene et al. (1986) found in tape-recording physician–patient interviews in a medical outpatient setting that doctors were less responsive to issues that elderly patients themselves raised compared with those raised by the doctors; this difference was not found with young patients. Moreover, there was a strong tendency for doctors to raise more psychosocial issues with their young rather than their elderly patients and, overall, physicians were independently rated as significantly more egalitarian, patient, engaged and respectful with the former than the latter patients.

This is in part due to the attitudes and assumptions doctors hold concerning 'categorized' others, which are likely to influence the way they perceive their patients' conditions and hence influence the manner in which they talk to them. In this way, although Wallen, Waitzkin and Stroeckle (1979) found that male doctors underestimate patients' medical knowledge in general, they underestimate *female* patients' medical knowledge in particular. Indeed, Ehrenreich and Ehrenreich (1970) found that male doctors assumed that women were difficult, neurotic, emotional and unable to understand complex explanations.

Other researchers have pointed to the existence of discrepancies between the ways working-class and middle-class patients are treated at surgery (Pendleton and Bochner, 1980); in general, working-class patients are afforded less information. In similar vein, ethnic minority groups in Britain do not seem to fare well at the doctor's surgery. Apart from the real and widespread problem of a total language barrier between doctor and patient – and no interpreter available – doctors tend to have unfavourable attitudes towards ethnic minority patients. For example, Fenton (1985) has indicated that there is a tendency amongst doctors who treat Asian patients in Britain to feel that these patients attend the surgery unnecessarily and are inclined towards time-wasting. Fenton points out that different cultural histories and beliefs are likely to lead to different views of health and illness, and hence to possible confusion about the status of ailments such as the 'common cold' between doctor and patient in an intercultural encounter. It is also worth noting that ethnic minorities are often clustered in the lower socio-economic bracket in Western cultures, frequently poor, badly housed and unlikely to be obtaining an optimal diet. In short, many of them encounter the poor standard of health shared by others in a low income bracket and are therefore likely to have good reason to present themselves at the doctor's surgery more regularly.

The 'useful' stereotype

Throughout the foregoing we have shown that stereotypes can have potentially devastating effects. If they can be so damaging, why do they exist? What purpose do they serve? It is to these more functional concerns that we now turn briefly. Research on classification and categorization systems has a long history (Doise, 1978). The human brain classifies and categorizes events and objects within the world in an effort to bring some sense and order to life. Therefore, it might be argued that people who share speech characteristics are grouped under the same umbrella for the sake of simplifying perceptual information; for example, people speaking with a similar dialect come from a similar geographical area. However, in the material we have just been discussing, it has been shown that certain speech groups have more than simply geographical origins associated with them – they are also tarred with the same dispositional brush. Let us examine, for a moment, one of these associations, the association continually made between RP and the concept of intelligence.

The first point to note is that no satisfactory definition of 'intelligence' actually exists and the tests designed to measure what are purported to be some aspects of the phenomenon have been shown to be heavily culture-bound and sub-culture-bound, in that environmental influence is highly related to test achievement (see Rose, Kamin and Lewontin, 1984). If we are unable to satisfactorily pin down the concept, how can we say who has got more and who has got less of it? We have already reported that there appears to be no intrinsic qualitative difference between different language variations. Where, then, does this pairing of intelligence and RP originate from? It is clearly inadequate to explain such a phenomenon in terms of an individual's classification system.

One possible avenue of explanation for this type of pairing might be uncovered by looking more closely at the social function of the stereotype (Tajfel, 1981). Allport (1954) has argued that a stereotype's function is to justify (rationalize) our conduct in relation to the category it represents. In this case, then, it could be argued that the stereotype of accented speakers as less intelligent than RP speakers could serve the social function of 'explaining' why more non-standard than standard speakers are clustered in the lower socio-economic strata, that is intelligence becomes both a cause and effect. It is measured in terms of economic and social success and then success in these terms is explained as being *caused* by the phenomenon known as intelligence. This stereotype could then be said to serve a function for a certain group in this society, namely, those clustered in the upper socio-economic strata. That is, it avoids any direct challenge to their position by providing a 'reasonable' explanation for the status quo. Such stereotypes can also then be utilized by (high status) physicians with their patients in order to justify their approach, command of the situation and communicative strategies. In this sense, stereotypes can be said to have social rather than cognitive origins: the fact that the human brain might need to categorize information does not in itself explain their existence. This brings us to an important issue not explicitly raised so far, and one which we will go on to discuss: language creation and use is a *social* affair.

LANGUAGE AND SOCIAL REALITY

Language and identity

Language develops between groups of people and involves shared meanings, shared expressions and shared functions. To this end, researchers over the last 15 years have begun to realize that in order to understand language processes adequately, *group* analyses must be undertaken. Speech accommodation theory did not in the early stages of its development cater for group meanings and motives and, as such, could not provide ready explanation for the phenomenon of speech divergence, or the accentuation of linguistic differences between speakers. To this end, *ethnolinguistic identity theory* was developed in order to take into account group motives, in pursuit of an understanding of the psychological climate in which linguistic differentiation between groups occurs (Giles, Bourhis and Taylor, 1977). Moreover, this theory attempts to show how different language attitude profiles emerge and become more or less elaborated as a function of the changing relations between the groups in question (see Ryan, Giles and Hewstone, 1984). It is proposed to have relevance not only for understanding individual language strategies in the immediacy of an interethnic encounter, but also for the appreciation of the dynamics of group language maintenance and erosion.

Ethnolinguistic identity theory draws heavily on the influential theory of intergroup behaviour developed by Tajfel and his associates during the 1970s. His 'social identity' theory was a concerted attempt to move social psychology into the realms of the *social* by focusing upon the dynamics of intergroup behaviour. Ethnolinguistic identity theory was a modest attempt to take this social path further by also implicating cognitions of (a) the social structural backdrop to intergroup relations, (b) intergroup boundaries and (c) multiple group memberships and moulding them into a propositional form designed to predict linguistic differentiation between groups. Yet for our present purposes it is sufficient to focus solely upon the central tenets of this theory, namely, *social identity* principles as they relate to language behaviours.

An important slice of the social identity framework can be outlined simply as follows. We categorize the social world and hence perceive ourselves as members of various groups. Such knowledge of ourselves as group members is defined as our social identity and it may be positive or negative according to how in-groups fare in social comparison with relevant out-groups (Turner, 1982). It is argued that we strive to achieve a positive identity by seeking dimensions which afford favourable comparison with out-groups. In other words, we strive to achieve 'positive distinctiveness'.

Language comes into the picture as it may well be a dimension for comparison between different groups. Indeed, as far as ethnic groups are concerned in many parts of the world, language can often be the *prime* emotional component of their identity (Fishman, 1977). For example, 'the problem of ethnolinguistic identity maintenance . . . has become the most important socio-political goal for the majority of Armenians in different countries' (E. Nercissians, personal communication). Tajfel discusses in his work various strategies that members of oppressed groups might use to enhance their position and hence improve their self-esteem.

One strategy might be to try and assimilate into the out-group if this group is considered more prestigious. If language is a relevant dimension of comparison then individuals might choose this strategy to try and 'play down' their own speech style and adopt that of the out-group; in fact, *converge*. There might, however, be situations when an individual cannot adopt this strategy; for example, when skin colour is a salient group marker. In such situations, an alternative strategy for gaining positive esteem might involve an oppressed group coming to view their own language in a more favourable light. What was once a consensually agreed upon non-standard (or even *sub*-standard) dialect or language becomes redefined by the in-group far more positively (Bourhis, 1979). Language style in this analysis can become a symbol of group identity that can be revered by the group and accentuated accordingly (that is *divergence*). In recent years, the Welsh language has become a symbol of national pride and there have been fierce attempts to formalize its official use more widely. In other words, people may deliberately use their language or speech styles as a symbolic tactic for maintaining their identity, cultural pride and distinctiveness (Ryan, 1979) and possibly go on to accentuate the linguistic and social differences between themselves and out-group members.

Group relations envisaged from this theoretical perspective – and even when propositionally sharpened by recourse to other elements inherent in ethnolinguistic identity theory just mentioned – are likely to be in conflict because the theory starts from the premise that individuals need to compare themselves favourably against others in order to achieve positive self-esteem. And, indeed, in practice, outside the laboratory this theory has generally been applied to the relationship between groups in conflict.

Other things being equal, it might at this stage have been useful to appeal to this theory for an analysis of *intergroup relations* in the medical encounter we described previously. In other words, in order to maintain their positive professional and social distinctiveness, physicians might be interpreted as differentiating themselves from their patients by all manner of linguistically diverging control devices, thereby ensuring a positively-valued psychological barrier between them and their patients. Furthermore, one could hypothesize that the more salient the *intergroup* nature of the medical interview (for example young doctor with older professional male/highly questioning and threatening ethnic minority individual) the more the physician will differentiate in terms of medical jargon, adopt controlling communicative behaviours and assume a psychological distance from the patient. Obviously, many complex factors intervene in this process, including the nature of the complaint and any structural constraints operating, yet ethnolinguistic identity principles (perhaps better referred to now as *sociolinguistic identity principles*) seem to provide a compelling first-step analysis of a very complex communication. On the basis of this position, one might even be disposed towards thinking of infusing a *psycho-social* element into physicians' training, so that they are made aware of their stereotypes, the need for positive distinctiveness and the possibility that the clinic is a potential intergroup arena. But how useful would this analysis be? In an attempt to answer this question we are now going to take a closer look at the core element of sociolinguistic identity theory, viz., social identity principles.

Motivational individualism

The particular social identity issue that we wish now to reconsider is the assertion that individuals need to make positive comparisons with others. That is, they need to perceive themselves as *coming off best* in the comparison in order to achieve a positive identity and favourable self-esteem (cf. Williams, 1984). In the grossest of terms, social differentiation has been seen as having its origins in innate individual processes. We, in contrast, would wish to provide an alternative explanation of the origin of differentiation.

Whilst it might be a truism that human beings have to condense, categorize and classify incoming information in order to cope with their social worlds, it becomes important when we examine the process on a large scale to ask just who we mean when we say 'we' categorize our world. Social identity explanations of behaviour can at times involve very fuzzy conceptualizations of 'groups'. There appears to be a tendency to lapse into a kind of 'pluralism', where social competition has the ring of a healthy and equal fight where all competitors are equally handicapped. That this is not the case in Western stratified society has been well-documented by political sociologists (Lukes, 1983). There are obviously millions of ways in which people, objects and events within our world can be classified (Spender, 1985). Within a society where access to the means of creating ideas (for example through the media or education) is by no means an 'equal-and-open-to-all-affair', it seems logical to suggest that some people will have infinitely more power than others in deciding upon these classification systems.

Social identity theory argues that differentiation occurs because individuals need to be distinct and see themselves in a favourable light. While the second part of this proposition seems intuitively true – why should anyone want to see themselves in a *negative* light? – the first part, that individuals need to be distinct, is open to question. Evidence supporting this proposition has derived from laboratory experiments that have purportedly found individuals trying to make their own group distinct from (and better than) others even when there seems no apparent objective reason for so doing (Turner, 1981). However, recent criticisms of these 'minimal categorization' studies have pointed out that people do not enter a laboratory situation and leave their history and culture outside the door (Fraser and Foster, 1984). People are of course influenced by cultural norms (Wetherell, 1982) and will not necessarily compete in a minimal categorization situation if competition is not the accepted norm (Vickers and Abrams, 1985). These intergroup studies, then, have tended to provide non-social explanations for social phenomena.

To return for a moment to the people with power, if certain factions of society have power to decide upon categorization systems they also have considerable power to (a) assign labels to groups they care to categorize and (b) put about the idea that it is meaningful to assign dispositional labels to a collection of people categorized by their criteria (for example by appealing to the 'rigidity of human nature'). Perhaps oppressed groups who accentuate features such as language are not so much attempting to use these dimensions to create and maintain identity *per se*, but rather, having been identified by others (who possibly choose to keep a lower profile), have no option but to try to work to improve *the nature of* their visibility. It is not being argued here that self-esteem has no relevance to the struggle to improve group identity. Rather, the self-esteem hypothesis is inadequate to explain such a phenomenon as the existence of group conflict in the first place (Condor, 1985).

To explain social phenomena such as conflict between groups in terms of individual cognitions and motivations has been called 'dualistic' by theorists such as Henriques *et al.* (1984). By dualism is meant the cleaving of the individual from the social as though the two concepts were additive; that is, take off all the social bits and there you will find the *real* individual underneath. To come to terms satisfactorily with social phenomena, these authors point out, we need to work towards social explanations.

Not only is a dualistic analysis conceptually inadequate, it has implications for expectations once again in terms of potentially self-fulfilling prophecies. If conflict is seen as stemming from the *natural* urge to differentiate oneself positively from others, competition is therefore regarded as inevitable and the best that can be hoped for is a kind of uneasy complementarity; that is, two groups managing to gain positive differentiation and hence self-esteem by comparing themselves along different dimensions (Taylor and Simard, 1979). (Within a stratified society, this term 'complementarity' generally amounts to no more than another word for inequality, the people with the upper hand coming out best along dimensions of status and power.) If we return for a moment to the scenario of doctor–patient communication, we might end up feeling that the real *cause* of the problem lies in the motivations of individual doctors and patients. This might then prevent us from seeing that tackling individuals alone is not being cognizant enough of their interdependence with other interested parties at the other levels of analysis. Indeed, it may sometimes be the case that social scientists within the confines and comforts of their own disciplines are let loose by certain interested funding bodies to survey complex social issues so as to demonstrate that the powerful really are concerned. Whether their findings are put to good effect is a moot point. More likely is the fact that social scientists produce non-manageable, abstract solutions in an academic vacuum, which can be used against them and the status quo thereby reinforced.

TOWARDS A MORE SOCIAL PERSPECTIVE ON LANGUAGE, IDENTITY AND HEALTH

In this last section we return to the world of health care, and with the foregoing analysis in mind, attempt to highlight the fact that communication between doctor and patient is influenced by a wider sphere of communication. Spender (1985, p.3) has stated that:

> Language helps form the limits of our reality. It is our means of ordering, classifying and manipulating the world. It is through language that we become members of a human community, that the world becomes comprehensive and meaningful, that we bring into existence the world in which we live . . . Yet it is ironic that this faculty which helps to create our world also has the capacity to restrict our world.

Hence, in these final sections we want to take a closer look at the social construction of the meaning of the concepts 'health' and 'illness' by one very powerful channel, the media. By so doing, our analytical purpose is to highlight the 'less than balanced' access different groups of people have within our society to the means of constructing interpretations of the social reality of their lives.

Models of health

Until relatively recently, the most influential model of health was that known as the 'medical model'. This is based on what Fisher and Todd (1983) have called 'a pathological germ theory of illness'. It focuses upon tissue trauma and has a fragmented, mechanistic approach to the person, treating bits of the body where organic problems can be located. If this cannot be accomplished, the problem is assumed to be psychological and thus, for many physicians, untreatable. Given this view of illness, the emphasis is on short-term, acute care and getting well quickly. Medical health care is *curative*, treating people quickly with medicines or surgery.

More recently, there has been a growing realization within the medical world that it is vitally important to look to the nature and quality of communication between doctor and patient in the consultation setting (Pendleton and Hasler, 1983). Physicians, like patients (both social creatures), will have their own sets of values, attitudes and beliefs. We have, indeed, earlier in the chapter discussed problems with stereotyped attitudes in the medical consultation. As Frankel (1983, p.45) points out, the physician's participation in the health care encounter is not as an objective, dispassionate giver of advice but as an interactive partner, who 'actively participates in the social construction of illness, its treatment and outcome'. Not only can doctors not simply operate as objective givers of advice, but the problems of diagnosis and treatment they face involve more than simply recognizing discrete disease entities and dispensing curative medication. Doctors in this sense are not superhuman and cannot be seen as omnipotent. Even with a disease as apparently 'clear cut' as cancer, some patients may live while others will not.

Apart from difficulties of diagnosis, various environmental and social factors are now understood to play an important part in the onset and development of illness, as well as death itself. The experience of loneliness, separation and bereavement have all been implicated in this way (Laudenslager and Reite, 1984) and an increasing emphasis is being placed on the importance of quality of social support and appropriate communication for fending off depression and illness. As Kaplan, Cassel and Gore (1979, p.107) have stated, 'persons who do not receive enough support from their social environment to meet their needs will, with time, experience psychologic and physiologic strain'. Added to this, there has also been much recent evidence to indicate the vital importance of environmental factors such as a 'good diet' for our health and well-being (see Krantz, Grunberg and Baum, 1985). Also, do we smoke? How many alcoholic drinks do we have a day? Do we have a high fibre diet or do we pump ourselves full of saturated fats and highly processed sugars? In short, moves have been made within the medical profession to work towards better health education within society and the development of *preventive* as well as acute health care.

However, the medical message does not appear to have penetrated to the public at large. The British (like the Americans) are a nation of unhealthy eaters, alcoholism is a very serious problem within this society and, furthermore, about 34 per cent of adults within this country and 22 per cent of all secondary schoolchildren smoke.

The power of advertising

Although comprehensive attempts to get to the bottom of problems such as alcoholism, smoking addiction and bad diet will necessarily involve taking into account very real factors such as poverty, unemployment and other life stresses, there is more to the story than this. McKinlay (1979) points an accusing finger directly at the advertisers. Indeed, Siegel (1982, p.176) in a study of American television has stated that:

> The goal of American commercial television is to attract a large audience to view advertisements. The purpose of those advertisements, in turn, is to sell products. Specifically, advertising on television aims to enlarge the demand for a commodity and to enlarge the share of the market cornered by a particular brand.

McKinlay suggests that advertisers persuade as to do things that are 'bad' for us by:

1. 'Piggybacking' appeals on the dominant culture's existing values, beliefs and norms, for example the cultural value of winning ('If only you'd take brand X you would sleep better and win that game tomorrow').

2. By suggesting that prestigious people within the culture engage in certain at risk behaviours ('If you spend your whole time wandering around with a gin glass in your hand you too can be a star like X').

3. By manufacturing 'needs' which you *must* have in order to be a useful member of society ('Every responsible citizen should have brand X').

Gerbner, Morgan and Signorielli (1982) carried out a comprehensive review of television portrayals of health in the United States. Studies during the 1970s indicated that the average child viewer will see about 22,000 commercials, 5,000 of them for food products, over half of which are high calorie, high sugar, low nutritional items. Barcus and McLaughlin (1978) discovered that 67 per cent of Saturday morning commercials and over half of the commercials shown in children's watching-time were for sweets, chocolate or sugared cereals. This even though, as the authors point out, the 1977 US Senate Select Committee on Nutrition and Human Needs emphasized the importance of a reduction in the consumption of refined and other processed sugars. Barcus and McLaughlin report that heavy television viewing amongst children does seem to be related to complacency over health issues, and quote Jeffrey et al. (1980), concluding that:

> Television advertising researchers have developed a sophisticated technology aimed not only at selling products to children but also aimed at socializing these children to eventual consumer roles.

What about television programmes themselves? Siegel (1982, p.176) has suggested that:

> The effects of television entertainment on Americans' belief systems, values, stereotypes, and social behaviour are 'side effects' of commercial television. For the most part, they are probably 'unintended side effects'. The intended effect is on consumer behaviour and buyer attitudes.

However, it would seem that in order to influence consumer behaviour with regard to, for example, products that medical experts deem harmful, it would also be necessary to manipulate belief systems, values and stereotypes so as to define what constitutes health care and what causes illness. Maybe it might be a good idea to perpetuate and bolster the idea that as a last resort the doctor is an omnipotent curer, someone who has all the answers. Television programmes themselves, according to Gerbner and his associates, have an important role to play here. They point out that prime-time characters are usually healthy. If they are vulnerable it is usually to accidents rather than disease. Such characters are usually slim, unlikely to wear spectacles and unlikely to suffer impairment of function. Yet, prime-time television characters none the less are also frequently seen to indulge in considerable bouts of 'junk' food eating and to consume vast quantities of alcohol. Prime-time heroes are also likely to be high risk takers.

To complete the perfect picture of the hero untroubled and unconcerned with issues of bad health, if doctors are seen to be needed on television, they symbolize power, authority and knowledge and possess the almost uncanny ability to dominate and control the lives of others (McLaughlin, 1975). Yet, they are also portrayed as being honest, trustworthy and kind-hearted. Gerbner and his colleagues (p.305) conclude that:

> The cultivation of ignorance and neglect . . . coupled with an unrealistic belief in the magic of medicine, is likely to perpetuate unhealthy lifestyles, hurt patients and health professionals, and frustrate efforts at health education.

Language, Social Identity and Health / 133

This state of affairs seems conveniently useful for the people in the business of selling 'unhealthy' products! This is not to say that there are not occasionally programmes on television that attempt to redress the balance, nor that television is by any means the worst media culprit. A recent programme on British television attempted to underline the double standard attitudes within this country over cigarette smoking, created, the programme makers argued, over the phenomenal advertising campaigns that undermine health educators' attempts to get the 'danger' message across (cigarette advertising is not allowed on British television). There are nearly 27,000 deaths a week from lung cancer, and 37,000 from heart disease, and yet, worryingly, the latest figures released by the Department of Health and Social Security (from a survey conducted by the Office of Population Censuses and Surveys) indicate that smoking amongst young people is on the increase. In 1982, 15 per cent of 14–15-year-old girls and 26 per cent of 16-year-old boys smoked, whilst in 1985 the figures were 24 and 31 per cent respectively.

The first British report, undertaken over 20 years ago, by the Royal College of Physicians on smoking and heart disease reported suggestive evidence of a link. By the time of the third report, the link was absolutely clear: smoking is a major cause of heart disease. Why can't health educators get the message across? They believe the reason might be something to do with the fact that they spend two million pounds a year on anti-smoking advertising campaigns while the tobacco industry spends one hundred million (even though they have no access to television advertising). The job of the cigarette advertisers is clearly made easier if the image of a doctor is of someone who is high status, powerful, successful, honest and so forth; generally a magician. In this context, it also clearly serves the advertisers to play down ideas of monitoring and taking responsibility for one's own health. In short, to muffle attempts at health education and to undermine notions of a holistic approach to medicine.

CONCLUSION

Two important points need to be underlined. First, we have used the example of the construction of concepts such as health care and illness to highlight the power of media coverage in creating definitions of such phenomena – even when these definitions can be seen to fly in the face of medical research. Second, the foregoing strongly suggests that there are more forces at work in shaping the nature of the doctor–patient relationship than the individual doctor or patient. Definitions of what it is to be a doctor or patient in a society – and indeed what it is to be ill – will all influence the shape and form of the interaction, affecting individuals' beliefs, expectations and linguistic behaviours. As we have tried to show in this chapter, these definitions are shaped to a great extent by advertising and big business. We are not for a minute trying to detract from the value of working with the individual, for example in social skills training programmes for doctors and patient groups. Rather, we are trying to say that working towards changes from the inside will likely only yield widespread success if the images created on the outside are congruent.

If we can attempt to develop an approach that examines the micro within the context of the macro, we can start to trace the communication problems of relationships such as doctor–patient, and reach a position where we can more profitably view people as social creatures who attempt to make use of and generate social explanations and strategies in order to define (and redefine) situations within the structural constraints of communication generated on a wider social scale.

In sum, our message has been this. The social psychological study of language and communication has helped to advance our understanding of interactional problems between groups and individuals in society. Intergroup theory has contributed much to advances in this direction, and crucial health issues are beginning to be implicated and in a way that the social psychology of language has largely neglected. Research is showing that when quality communication is lacking, negative consequences for health accrue; this is especially true for the doctor–patient encounter. While prospects – empirically and theoretically – appear to blossom for a greater social psychological appreciation of the roles of language and communication in society in general and for individuals' psychological well-being and physical health in particular, we would none the less advocate a serious examination of the social nature of current theory.

More specifically, we have pointed to what we believe to be a major limitation of intergroup theory and have blue-printed a theoretical direction which takes more account of societal images than hitherto. True, we have not produced definitive solutions in the area of health, nor should we have the gall to do so on the basis of our present position. Yet what we have proposed in a more positive vein is that interpersonal communication problems will not be solved even by innovatively embracing a valued intergroup perspective, nor by invoking the important cognitive roles of stereotyping and speech accommodation, but that these problems have to be conceptualized within the wider societal interests and networks in which they are embedded. Unless this is accomplished, current attempts to transform the doctor–patient relationship from a one-sided interview to a more patient-centred negotiation will be no more effective than 'picking the heads off weeds'.

ACKNOWLEDGEMENTS

We wish to acknowledge the assistance of Mary Wiemann in directing our attention to some of the health communication sources cited and for her useful analysis of them.

REFERENCES

Allport, G. (1954) *The Nature of Prejudice*. Cambridge, Mass.: Addison-Wesley.
Ball, P. and Giles, H. (1982) Speech style and employment selection: The matched-guise technique. In G.M. Breakwell, H. Foot and R. Gilmour (eds) *Social Psychology: A Practical Manual*. Leicester: The British Psychological Society/Macmillan.
Barcus, F.E. and McLaughlin, J. (1978) *Food Advertising on Children's Television: An Analysis of Appeals and Nutritional Content*. Newtonville, Mass.: Action for Children's Television.
Bell, A. (1982) Radio: The style of news language. *Journal of Communication*, 32, 150–164.
Bourhis, R.Y. (1979) Language in ethnic interaction: A social psychological approach. In H. Giles and B. Saint-Jacques (eds) *Language and Ethnic Relations*. Oxford: Pergamon.
Bourhis, R.Y. and Giles, H. (1976) The language of cooperation in Wales: A field study. *Language Sciences*, 42, 13–16.
Bradac, J.J. and Wisegarver, R. (1984) Ascribed status, lexical diversity and accent: Determinants of perceived status, solidarity and control of speech style. *Journal of Language and Social Psychology*, 3, 239–256.
Brennan, E.M. and Brennan, J.S. (1981) Accent scaling and language attitudes: Reactions to Mexican-American English speech. *Language and Speech*, 24 207–221.
Brown, B. and Bradshaw, J.M. (1985) Towards a social psychology of voice variations. In H. Giles and R.N. St Clair (eds) *Recent Advances in Language, Communication and Social Psychology*. London: Lawrence Erlbaum.
Cairns, E. and Dubiez, B. (1976) The influence of speaker's accent on recall by Catholic and Protestant schoolchildren in Northern Ireland. *British Journal of Social and Clinical Psychology*, 15, 441–442.
Caporael, L.R., Lukaszewski, M.P. and Culbertson, G.H. (1983) Secondary baby talk: Judgements by institutionalized elderly and their caregivers. *Journal of Personality and Social Psychology*, 44, 746–754.
Condor, S. (1985) *Womanhood as an Aspect of Social Identity*. Unpublished PhD thesis, University of Bristol.
Doise, W. (1978) *Groups and Individuals: Explorations in Social Psychology*. Cambridge: Cambridge University Press.

Edwards, J.R. (1979a) Judgements and confidence in reactions to disadvantaged speech. In H. Giles and R.N. St Clair (eds) *Language and Social Psychology*. Oxford: Basil Blackwell.
Edwards, J.R. (1979b) *The Language of Disadvantage*. London: Edward Arnold.
Edwards, J.R. and Giles, H. (1984) Applications of the social psychology of language: Sociolinguistics and education. In P. Trudgill (ed.) *Applied Sociolinguistics*. London: Academic Press.
Ehrenreich, B. and Ehrenreich, J. (1970) *The American Health Empire*. New York: Vintage Books.
Fenton, S. (1985) *Race, Health and Welfare: Afro-Caribbean and South Asian People in Central Bristol*. Bristol: Health and Social Sevices, University of Bristol Press.
Fisher, S. and Todd, A.D. (eds) (1983) *The Social Organization of Doctor–Patient Communication*. Washington, DC: Centre for Applied Linguistics.
Fishman, J.A. (1977) Language and ethnicity. In H. Giles (ed.) *Language, Ethnicity and Intergroup Relations*. London: Academic Press.
Frankel, R.M. (1983) The laying on of hands: Aspects of the organization of gaze, touch and talk in a medical encounter. In S. Fisher and A. Todd (eds) *The Social Organization of Doctor–Patient Communication*. Washington, DC: Centre for Applied Linguistics.
Frankel, R.M. (1984) Physicians and patients in social interaction: Medical encounters as a discourse process. *Discourse Processes, 7*, 103–104.
Fraser, C. and Foster, D. (1984) Social groups, nonsense groups and group polarization. In H. Tajfel (ed.) *The Social Dimension, Vol. 2*. Cambridge: Cambridge University Press.
Gerbner, G., Morgan, M. and Signorielli, N. (1982) Programming health portrayals: What viewers see, say and do. In D. Pearl, L. Bouthilet and J. Lazard (eds) *Television and Behaviour, Vol. 2*. Rockville, MD: National Institute of Mental Health.
Giles, H. (ed.) (1984) The dynamics of speech accommodation. Special issue of the *International Journal of the Sociology of Language, 46*.
Giles, H., Bourhis, R.Y. and Taylor, D.M. (1977) Towards a theory of language in ethnic group relations. In H. Giles (ed.) *Language, Ethnicity and Intergroup Relations*. London: Academic Press.
Giles, H., Baker S. and Fielding, G. (1975) Communication length as a behavioural index of accent prejudice. *International Journal of the Sociology of Language, 6*, 73–81.
Giles, H. and Farrar, K. (1979) Some behavioural consequences of speech and dress style. *British Journal of Social and Clinical Psychology, 18*, 209–210.
Giles, H. and Johnson, P. (1981) The role of language in ethnic group relations. In J.C. Turner and H. Giles (eds) *Intergroup Behaviour*. Oxford: Blackwell.
Greene, M.G., Adelman, R., Charon, R. and Hoffman, S. (1986) Ageism in the medical encounter: An exploratory study of the doctor–elderly patient relationship. *Language and Communication, 6*, 113–124.
Heath, C. (1985) The consultation's end: The coordination of speech and body movement. *International Journal of the Sociology of Language, 51*, 27–42.
Henriques, J., Hollway, W., Urwin, C., Venn, C. and Walkerdine, V. (1984) *Changing the Subject: Psychology, Social Regulation and Subjectivity*. London: Methuen.
Hewstone, M. and Giles, H. (1986) Social groups and social stereotypes in intergroup communication: Review and model of intergroup communication breakdown. In W.B. Gudykunst (ed.) *Intergroup Communication*. London: Edward Arnold.

Jeffrey, D., Balfour, D.B., Lemnitze N.B., Hickey, J.S., Hess, M.J. and Stroud, J.M. (1980) *The Impact of Television Advertising on Children's Eating Behaviour.* Missoula: University of Montana Psychology Dept.
Kalin, R. (1982) The social significance of speech in medical, legal and occupational settings. In E.B. Ryan and H. Giles (eds) *Attitudes towards Language Variation: Social and Applied Contexts.* London: Academic Press.
Kaplan, B.H., Cassel, J.C. and Gore, S. (1979) Social support and health. In E.G. Jaco (ed.) *Patients, Physicians and Illness,* 3rd ed. New York: Free Press.
Kitson, G.C., Babri, K.B. and Roach, M.J. (1985) Who divorces and why: A review. *Journal of Family Issues, 6, 255–294.*
Klemz, A. (1977) *Blindness and Partial Sight.* Cambridge: Woodhead-Faulkner.
Krantz, D.S., Grunberg, N.E. and Baum, A. (1985) Health psychology. *Annual Review of Psychology, 36,* 349–384.
Lambert, W.E., Hodgson, R.C., Gardner, R.C. and Fillenbaum. S. (1960) Evaluational reactions to spoken language. *Journal of Abnormal and Social Psychology,* 60, 44–51.
Laudenslager, M.L. and Reite, M.L. (1984) Losses and separations: Immunological consequences and health implications. In P. Shaver (ed.) *Emotions, Relationships and Health: Review of Personality and Social Psychology,* 5. Beverly Hills: Sage.
Lukes, S. (1983) *Power: A Radical View.* New York: Macmillan.
McKinlay, J.B. (1979) A case for refocussing upstream: The political economy of illness. In E.G. Jaco (ed.) *Patients, Physicians and Illness,* 3rd ed. New York: Free Press.
McLaughlin, J. (1975) The doctor shows. *Journal of Communication, 25,* 182–184.
Pendleton, D. and Bochner, S. (1980) The communication of medical information in general practice consultations as a function of patients' social class. *Social Science and Medicine, 14,* 669–673.
Pendleton, D. and Hasler, J. (eds) (1983) *Doctor–Patient Communication.* London: Academic Press.
Robinson, E. and Whitfield, M.J. (1985) Improving the efficiency of patients' comprehension monitoring: A way of increasing patients' participation in general practice consultations. *Social Science and Medicine, 21,* 915–919.
Robinson, W.P. (ed.) (1983) Special issue of plenary papers at the 2nd International Conference on Social Psychology and Language. *Journal of Language and Social Psychology,* 2,2–4.
Rodin, J. and Langer, E. (1980) Aging labels: The decline of control and the fall of self-esteem. *Journal of Social Issues, 36,* 12–29.
Rose, S., Kamin, J. and Lewontin, R.C. (1984) *Not in our Genes: Biology, Ideology and Human Nature.* Harmondsworth: Penguin.
Ryan, E.B. (1979) Why do low-prestige language varieties persist? In H. Giles and R.N. St Clair (eds) *Language and Social Psychology.* Oxford: Basil Blackwell.
Ryan, E.B. and Giles, H. (eds) (1982) *Attitudes towards Language Variation: Social and Applied Contexts.* London: Edward Arnold.
Ryan, E.B. Giles, H. and Hewstone, M. (1984) Language and intergroup attitudes. In J.R. Eiser (ed.) *Attitudinal Judgement.* New York: Springer-Verlag.
Seggie, I. (1983) Attribution of guilt as a function of ethnic accent and type of crime. *Journal of Multilingual and Multicultural Development, 4,* 197–206.
Seligman, C.F., Tucker, G.R. and Lambert, W.E. (1972) The effects of speech style and other attributes on teachers' attitudes towards pupils. *Language and Society, 1,* 131–142.

Seligman, M.E.P. (1975) *Helplessness: On Depression, Development and Death.* San Francisco: Freeman.
Siegel, A.E. (1982) Introductory comments: Social beliefs and social behaviour. In D. Pearl, L. Bouthilet and J. Lazar (eds) *Television and Behaviour*, Vol. 2. Rockville, MD: National Institute of Mental Health.
Spender, D. (1985) *Man Made Language*, 2nd ed. London: Routledge and Kegan Paul.
Stewart. M.A., Ryan, E.B. and Giles, H. (1985) Accent and social class effects on status and solidarity dimensions. *Personality and Social Psychology Bulletin*, 11, 98–105.
Street, R.L. Jr and Wiemann, J. (in press) Patient satisfaction with physician interpersonal involvement, expressiveness and dominance. In M. McLaughlin (ed.) *Communication Yearbook 10.* Beverly Hills: Sage.
Tajfel, H. (ed.) (1978) *Differentiation between Social Groups.* London: Academic Press.
Tajfel, H. (1981) Social stereotypes and social groups. In J.C. Turner and H. Giles (eds) *Intergroup Behaviour.* Oxford: Basil Blackwell.
Tajfel, H. (ed.) (1984) *The Social Dimension.* Cambridge: Cambridge University Press.
Tajfel, H. and Turner, J.C. (1979) An integrative theory of intergroup conflict. In W.G. Austin and S. Worchel (eds) *The Social Psychology of Intergroup Relations.* Monterey: Brooks/Cole.
Taylor, D.M. and Simard, L. (1979) Ethnic identity and intergroup relations. In D.J. Lee (ed.) *Emerging Ethnic Boundaries.* Ottawa: University of Ottawa Press.
Thakerar, J.N., Giles, H. and Cheshire, J. (1982) Psychological and linguistic parameters of speech accommodation theory. In C. Fraser and K.R. Scherer (eds) *Advances in the Social Psychology of Language.* Cambridge: Cambridge University Press.
Todd, A.D. (1984) The prescription of contraception: Negotiations between doctors and patients. *Discourse Processes*, 7, 171–200.
Turner, J.C. (1981) The experimental social psychology of intergroup behaviour. In J.C. Turner and H. Giles (eds) *Intergroup Behaviour.* Oxford: Basil Blackwell.
Turner, J.C. (1982) Towards a cognitive redefinition of the social group. In H. Tajfel (ed.) *Social Identity and Intergroup Relations.* Cambridge: Cambridge University Press.
Vickers, A. and Abrams, D. (1985) Is there a competitive norm for intergroup behaviour? Paper presented at the Annual Social Psychology Section Conference of the British Psychological Society, Cambridge. Avilable from Psychology Department, Dundee University.
Wallen, J., Waitzkin, H.B. and Stroekle, J.D. (1979) Physicians' stereotypes about female health and illness: A study of patient's sex and the informative process during medical interviews. *Women and Health*, 4, 135–146.
West, C. (1983) 'Ask me no questions . . .': An analysis of queries and replies in physician–patient dialogues. In S. Fisher and A.D. Todd (eds) *The Social Organization of Doctor–Patient Communication.* Washington, DC.: Centre for Applied Linguistics.
West, C. (1984) When the doctor is a 'lady': Power, status and gender in physician–patient encounters. *Symbolic Interaction*, 7, 87–106.
Wetherell, M. (1982) Cross-cultural studies of minimal groups: Implications for the Social Identity Theory of intergroup relations. In H. Tajfel (ed.) *Social Identity and Intergroup Relations.* Cambridge: Cambridge University Press.

Williams, F. (1976) *Explorations in the Linguistic Attitudes of Teachers*. Rowley, Mass.: Newbury House.
Williams, J.A. (1984) Gender and intergroup behaviour. *British Journal of Social Psychology*, 23, 311–316.
Word, C.O., Zanna, M.P. and Cooper, J. (1974) The nonverbal mediation of self-fulfilling prophecies in interracial interaction. *Journal of Experimental Social Psychology*, 10, 109–120.

THE PSYCHOLOGY OF EATING AND EATING DISORDERS
P. Wright

Eating is one of life's great joys, but it has also become in the affluent West a source of much distress. Excessive fatness and excessive slimness, together with a concern for the continuous monitoring and awareness of weight have been standard topics in women's magazines for more than two decades. There is little sign that this obsession is diminishing, and the incidence of eating disorders continues to increase. This chapter outlines the attempts of experimental psychologists to understand some of the factors which influence how much we eat and why some of us seem unable to maintain our weight within acceptable limits. Whereas both obesity and, more recently, bulimia have been analysed in terms of putative underlying mechanisms, anorexia remains largely unexplored by and possibly unavailable to an experimental approach and will not be discussed here. The origin of much of this human research on eating behaviour lies in the animal literature, and it is therefore useful to note at the start some of the more significant influences.

The topic of control and regulation of food intake has been a prominent feature of the specialist journals in what used to be referred to as physiological or comparative psychology since their inception. The early work was carried out almost exclusively with animals, predominantly the rat, and concentrated on the detailed analysis of the brain mechanisms; more especially, the involvement of the hypothalamus in the expression of feeding. By 1960, the 'two-centre' theory of motivation due to Stellar (1954) was a widely accepted framework, incorporating the key idea that the organization of the feeding system involved an excitatory area for eating in the lateral hypothalamus and an inhibitory area centred on the ventromedial nucleus (VMN). Direct stimulation of the lateral hypothalamus elicited eating in satiated rats and, from the first, it was open to question whether this induced eating had anything to do with hunger. In a series of experiments, Neal Miller and colleagues demonstrated that it was indeed influenced by the same factors known to control free-feeding behaviour, and therefore it was legitimate to describe this hypothalamic area in which eating was elicited as a 'hunger centre'. Conversely, destruction of the adjacent VMN produced immediate and dramatic increases in eating, which led to two or three-fold increases in weight compared with intact control animals, this area becoming known as the 'satiety centre'. This extreme hypothalamic phrenology was to dominate the accounts of feeding for almost two decades, until it gradually became apparent that the brain organization was vastly more complex (Grossman, 1979).

Equally characteristic of this period was an almost total neglect of experimentation with human subjects, although the assumption in most of the animal models was that they were equally applicable to man, with 'higher-order variables' such as social, cognitive and learned influences being especially important. What psychologists had concentrated their efforts upon understanding were the physiological antecedants of feeding, but whereas all animals feed, it can be argued that only humans eat – if by this we accept that the act of eating in humans has acquired a ritual and cultural significance of enormous richness. It is this very aspect which has made an understanding of what and how a society eats central to social anthropology, and why this discipline is so rich in observations on eating (Farb and Armelagos, 1980).

More significant, however, was the total neglect of any ecological considerations in the animal experimentation and, in particular, the ubiquitous manipulation of food deprivation as the standard experimental paradigm. Collier and Rovee-Collier (1985) have convincingly argued that in the wild a state of physiological deprivation is a rare occurrence and that most animals, especially those with high metabolic rate (including the rat), will eat in anticipation of their requirements and so will suffer physiological depletion only when their foraging strategies fail. In concluding that homeostasis is an inadequate base on which to construct a view of the controls of feeding behaviour, Collier has made use of the traditional laboratory techniques of operant conditioning. Whereas hunger may alter such aspects of the animal's feeding behaviour as the rate of eating, the tactics and strategies of foraging are not influenced by the physiological state of depletion or repletion.

The change from a totally ratomorphic view of feeding to active and prolific research into the nature of human eating behaviour originated at a period when the fundamental nature of the electrically-elicited eating was already being questioned. The speculations of Stanley Schachter, a social psychologist, on the analogy between the VMN rat and fat people succeeded more than any previous work in providing the catalyst to bring together clinicians, experimentalists and psychologists who had a common interest in eating behaviour. So influential was this research that Rodin (1981) estimated that Schachter's externality theory of obesity now appears in every contemporary introductory psychology textbook. Schachter's work encouraged researchers to leave the confines of the laboratory. He demonstrated that experimental studies of eating need not be confined to rats but that humans were also adequate subjects, and the study of the normal eating behaviour of people in real life contexts could commence. This new collaboration between animal research and those primarily interested in experimental and clinical studies with human subjects is also reflected in the contemporary interest in the so-called 'eating disorders' of obesity, anorexia and bulimia. So much so that there are now two specialist journals entirely devoted to these topics (*International Journal of Obesity*, 1977–, and the *International Journal of Eating Disorders*, 1982–), in addition to one with more general coverage of all aspects of human and animal eating (*Appetite*, 1980–).

Because the impetus for much of the human work has been the need to understand the factors influencing meal size and eating in the overweight individual, the animal models of obesity have been particularly influential in structuring the human research, with the favoured paradigm being a comparison of eating in overweight and normal subjects. Accordingly, this review will first trace the development of theories of eating in these two groups commencing with those of Schachter, and then examine the more recent research into the role of learning in human eating behaviours, before briefly asking how useful experimental studies are in understanding the common eating disorders in man.

SCHACHTER'S EXTERNALITY THEORY OF OBESITY

Schachter, no doubt influenced by his earlier work on the cognitive interpretation of emotional states (Schachter and Singer, 1962) in which he first explored the relationship between internal cues (physiological changes in heart rate, respiration and adrenalin secretion) and the context or interpretation given to the subjects in various experimental conditions, began to examine the eating behaviour of overweight people in the late 1960s. Characteristically, the experiments involved a degree of deception to ensure that subjects were unaware that the critical dependent variable was amount of food consumed, and eating was therefore always an incidental activity.

In one such experiment (Schachter, 1967), the subjects believed that the researcher was examining the effect of stimulation in one sensory modality (tactile stimulation) on perception in another modality (taste). The crucial manipulation was, in fact, the influence of fear on stomach motility, the prediction being that the high fear condition, with its associated inhibition of gastric motility, would make no difference to the eating activity of overweight subjects. For them, such internal physiological signals are relatively unimportant in controlling amount eaten, but *would* decrease the amount eaten by normal weight subjects relative to a low fear condition. The experimental procedure was described to subjects in the low fear condition as requiring a degree of electrical stimulation of the skin so weak that it was barely detectable, whereas the high fear subjects were shown leg electrodes and asked whether they were medically fit and not liable to any adverse reaction to severe shock. The subjects were then left alone to fill in questionnaires before starting the experiment proper and told that to obtain some baseline measures of their taste perception they should taste and rate a bowl of crackers available to them. As predicted, the normal weight subjects ate significantly fewer crackers in the high compared to the low fear condition, whereas the obese subjects ate the same amount in both situations. Needless to say, at this point the experiment was terminated without any electrical stimulation!

In this and other experiments, all of which used the same measure of incidental eating, Schachter and his associates showed that the overweight subjects were relatively uninfluenced by internal physiological cues compared to those of normal weight (Nisbett, 1968; Schachter, Goldman and Gordon, 1968; Schachter, 1971). Preloading subjects beforehand with food was another example of an internal cue which reduced the subsequent eating of normal weight subjects but not the overweight. And in what must surely be one of the more bizarrely entitled experimental papers – *Yom Kippur, Air France, dormitory food and the eating behaviour of obese and normal persons* (Goldman, Jaffa and Schachter, 1968) – it was shown that overweight individuals find it easier to suffer long periods of food deprivation.

What did appear to overly influence the eating of overweight individuals were external cues such as:

1. Time of day. If led to believe that it was close to a normal mealtime (by the experimenter making the wall clock run faster) overweight subjects ate more of the sandwiches which were available than they did in another condition in which the clock was not altered. Such manipulations did not influence the eating of the normal weight subjects (Schachter and Gross, 1968).

2. The taste of food. Altering the palatability of food, usually by making it taste less pleasant, decreases food intake much more in overweight subjects than in normal weight subjects (Goldman et al., 1968; Nisbett, 1968).

Schachter was particularly impressed by two lines of clinical evidence pointing to the insensitivity of the obese to internal cues, and their contrasting hypersensitivity to external cues. These are:

(a) The observation of Stunkard (1959) that normal weight women whose gastric motility was continuously monitored by means of a stomach balloon were far more likely to report feeling hungry during contractions than during periods of no contraction, whereas obese female patients did not show this association (Stunkard and Koch, 1964).

(b) Hashim and van Itallie's (1965) report that obese patients' caloric intake of a liquified, bland-tasting 'metrecal'-type diet plummetted compared with normal weight subjects, who adjusted their intake to the same energy level as when they were provided with a conventional hospital diet – despite there being no restrictions on the availability of the diet, the food being self-served by the patients.

Schachter interpreted (a) as indicating a decreased influence of an internal signal on perceived hunger and (b) as due to the heightened ability of an external cue (bland taste) to limit food intake.

Both observations are open to the criticism that the likely response bias of the overweight patient is to deny hunger anyway, hence the low association with motility, and, in the second study, that patients are complying with the regime because it is seen as a treatment for their weight problem. Schachter and his colleagues therefore began to accumulate a body of observations on the eating characteristics of people subdivided simply on the basis of weight. Within a short period of time, they had shown, using objective measures of behaviour, that compared with normal weight subjects:

☐ Fat students were significantly more likely not to renew dormitory meal tickets (Goldman et al., 1968); the 'external' cue of low palatability of the dormitory food being the important factor.

☐ A food-related but non-consummatory behaviour, that is how much produce is bought in a supermarket, varies in normal weight housewives according to how long it is since they last ate a meal, but not in the obese. In this case an internal cue (deprivation) has increased the attractiveness of food in the normal weight individuals (Nisbett and Kanouse, 1969; Dodd et al., 1977; Tom, 1983).

☐ Overweight individuals eat fewer walnuts if they have to 'work' for the reward by removing the shells than if the nuts are unshelled (Schachter and Rodin, 1974)!

☐ The visibility of food significantly influences the amount eaten by the overweight but not those of normal weight (Schachter and Rodin, 1974).

This last example resulted from direct comparison of the behavioural similarities of overweight humans and VMN rats, which predicted how the obese rats should behave in experimental situations as a result of the observations on overweight human subjects.

The clinical evidence of insensitivity to gastric signals which suggested to Schachter that decreased responsiveness to internal cues is a general characteristic of the obese is not very strong. But it is an attractive idea and therefore continues to be cited, even though the original authors have subsequently concluded that their observations were incorrect. Using a catheter to assess motility (gastric balloons promote increased stomach motility in the fasted condition) Stunkard and Fox (1971) found there were very considerable increases in the intensity of self-reported hunger for some subjects during prolonged phases of gastric motility. But in many cases there was no relationship and the previously reported difference in obese versus normal subjects was not confirmed. They concluded that the common belief that stomach contractions play a part in the experience of hunger has a factual basis, but a weak one, and there are strong individual differences in the relationship. In the light of subsequent research on dietary restraint, it might be important to know something about the dietary history of the non-obese subjects, as restrained eaters typically provide low self-reports of hunger. The critical observation would be to find a significant proportion of obese subjects who are sensitive to gastric contractions *and* feel hungry when they occur.

In another measure of gastric perceptivity, Coddington and Bruch (1970) assessed how good subjects are at estimating the amount of food which had been directly introduced into the stomach via a tube over short periods of time. With rather small numbers of subjects, they concluded that both overweight and underweight subjects were poor at the test compared with normal weight subjects. There is no study which shows that actual intake or other hunger-related behaviours are correlated with hunger contractions. So an overemphasis has been given to a cue which does not appear to have any crucial role in the initiation of eating.

BODY-WEIGHT SET-POINTS

Nisbett (1972), in an influential and widely-cited review, brought to prominence the idea that 'body-weight set-points' were of crucial importance in the behaviour shown by obese individuals. He suggested that it was *not* their obesity *per se* which determined the different behavioural characteristics described by Schachter, but that because of dieting or similar conscious attempts to keep weight down, some individuals would actually be biologically underweight and not fat enough. These individuals would therefore be in a state of more or less continuous food-deprivation and like all deprived animals would be more responsive to external stimuli. Unfortunately, this rather begs the question of how you know when someone is at their set-point. The strongest argument for a body-weight set-point is the finding that manipulations which increase or decrease weight are rapidly counteracted when conditions become normal. Whereas the rat literature does suggest that body-weight is clearly defended, and that this is equally true of the VMN rat in the static phase of its obesity (Peck, 1980), the picture is very muddled in the case of humans.

The constancy of body-weight frequently mentioned in physiology textbooks is probably not representative of the population as a whole. Long-term epidemiological studies in the USA (Framingham) show that over an 18-year period the majority of people have large swings in body-weight of between 5 and 10 kg, and that maintaining weight within 1 to 2 kg from year to year was characteristic of less than 2 per cent of the Framingham population (RCP report, 1983).

Garrow (1974) discusses two different forms of control system – 'set-point' and 'buffer' types. A set-point system requires a sensor which accurately monitors the function which is to be regulated, and most vital physiological characteristics such as temperature and pH are of this type. A buffer system is simpler but less precise, and often found in conjunction with a set-point system. In studies of long-term overfeeding in humans for many weeks, there is invariably a discrepancy between the predicted and observed gains in body-weight, with some of the dietary excess being lost. This can be used as evidence for either system, since both will tend to oppose change away from the 'normal' setting (Sims *et al.*, 1973). But in a situation where the weight is initially well below normal, which was the case for undernourished prisoners in Germany at the end of World War II, Widdowson (1951) still found that weight gains on a very high caloric diet were less than expected, even though body-weight was moving towards a normal value, a result which argues for buffer-type control.

The importance of weight as a determinant of responsiveness to food cues was also shown by Cabanac and Duclaux (1970), who demonstrated that the pleasantness of sugar solutions (tasted but not swallowed) shifted in a negative direction after the subjects ingested a glucose meal. These shifts were not observed in overweight subjects, and, like Schachter, they interpreted this to indicate an unresponsiveness to short-term changes in nutritional state. Cabanac, Duclaux and Spector (1971) examined their own responses to sucrose following a self-imposed body-weight loss of approximately 10 per cent, and reported that during the period of loss and at the targeted low weight, glucose meals no longer changed the pleasantness of the sucrose solutions. Like Nisbett, they argued that the changed responsiveness was due to the subjects falling below their body-weight set-point, and postulated a mechanism which could detect whether the organism is at its set-point, which they called a 'ponderostat'. Apart from the obvious drawbacks involved in using your own subjective assessments to test your own hypothesis, the Cabanac method is not very reliable and other factors influence the degree of shift (Wright and Crow, 1973). It is questionable whether the shifts may not be more an artefact of the aversiveness many subjects experience in ingesting the glucose meal. In unpublished experiments, Wright and Nayar (see Figure 1) found that simply adding the juice of one lemon to the glucose drink and thereby converting it into a pleasant tasting, if syrupy, lemon-flavoured drink, compared with a sickly and cloying glucose drink, completely eliminated the shifts reported one hour later.

Further doubt about the decreased internal cue sensitivity of the obese arose when it became clear that normal weight individuals are also poor at regulation based on internal signals (Rodin, 1981). Despite animal studies suggesting accurate and prompt compensation for dietary dilution, in people the response is sluggish and incomplete and when they have information only from internal signals, then regulation is poor. Internal signals do not appropriately guide eating behaviour towards stable caloric intake for most subjects unless cognitive/external cues regarding amount are also present. However, the experimental demonstration of taste as a CS in conditioning satiety in humans leaves unanswered the question why some can and others cannot learn to make use of such cues. The second pillar of Schachter's theory, that the obese are predominantly influenced by external cues, also began to crack. Obese individuals are not invariably over-responsive to external cues and most people seem to be responsive to at least some external cues (Rodin, 1981).

DIETARY RESTRAINT

The most consistent subsequent line of research has been that first suggested by Nisbett (1972), namely the measurement of dieting behav-

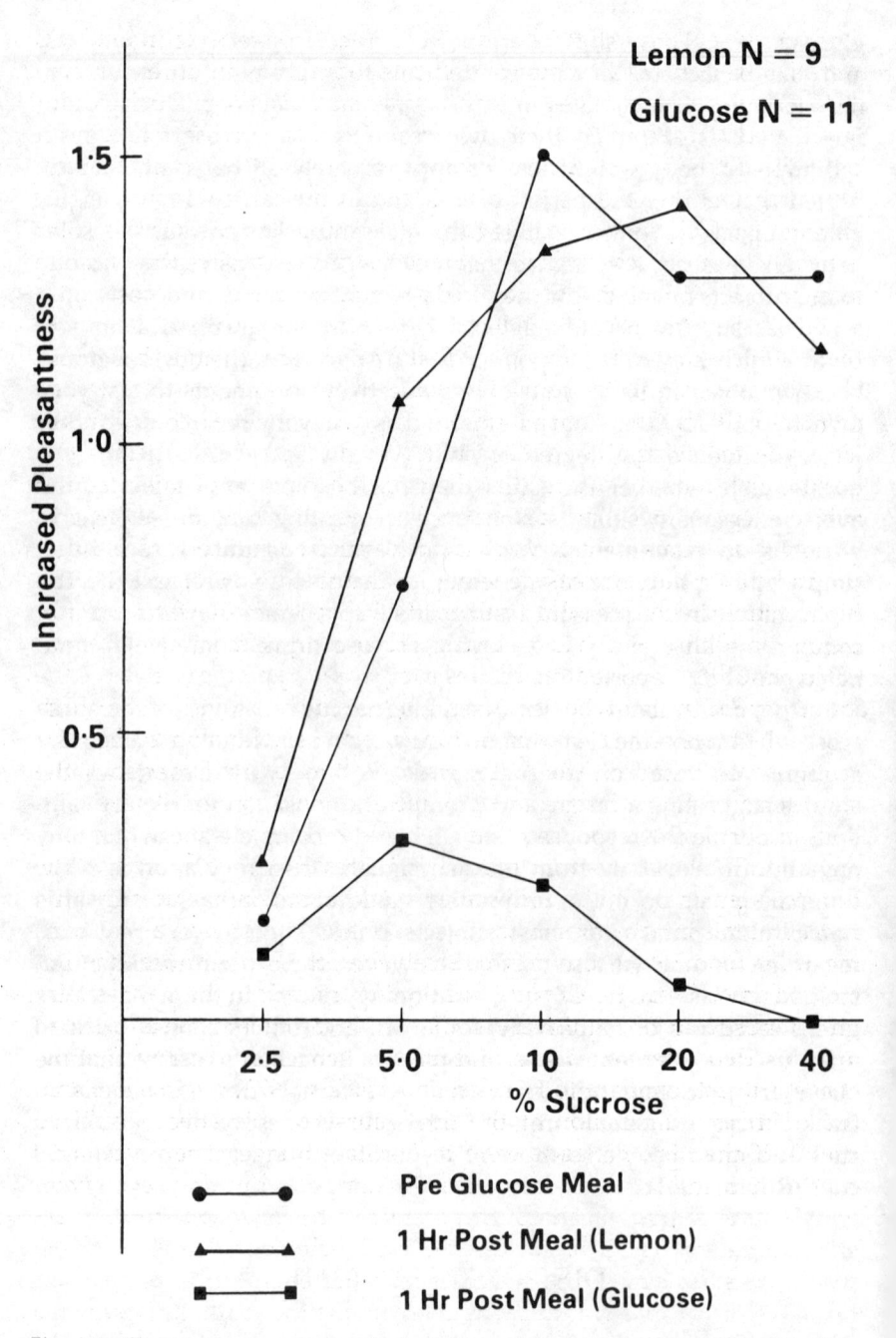

Figure 1. Changes in the ratings of pleasantness for various concentrations of sugar solution following ingestion of flavoured and unflavoured glucose meals.

iour which sets out to devise a means of assessing whether individuals were 'above' or 'below' their biological set-point (Herman and Mack, 1975). From self-report questionnaires dieters and non-dieters are differentiated on the basis of their score on a Restraint Scale which assesses concern with weight loss and its maintenance, as well as weight history. The scale provides a continuous distribution of scores, ranging at one extreme from those who never consider dieting, to those at the other extreme, who diet continuously. Nisbett's theory implies that all subjects will differ in their state of relative food deprivation (according to whether they are above or below their set-point weight). Therefore those subjects *within the normal weight range* will show eating behaviour characteristic of either a high or low score on the restraint scale. Herman and Mack (1975) found that a high restraint group ate greater amounts of ice cream following a large milkshake preload than with either a small preload or no preload, and that the eating behaviour of low restraint subjects agrees with the pattern Schachter attributed to all normal weight individuals, that is 'internal' regulation of intake with a larger preload producing decreased eating subsequently (see Figure 2). The high restraint subjects who consumed two preloads ate far more ice-cream than those who had no milkshake as a preload.

Herman and Mack contrasted this compensatory eating pattern of the low restraint group with the 'counter-regulatory' eating of the high restraint subjects, and explained the latter's behaviour in terms of a motivational collapse. The large preload, they argued, destroys the short-term cognitive restriction of intake and the dieter is left without a sufficient reason for dieting – an 'in for a penny, in for a pound' scenario. The small amount eaten by the restrained compared to the unrestrained group in the zero preload condition demonstrates that the restraint scale clearly does classify appropriately those who are restricting their food intake by cognitive self-control. Furthermore, the decreased amount eaten following one or two preloads in the low restraint group must also be cognitively mediated, as the time between preload and the dependent measure of eating is too short for any internal changes to act, contrary to Herman and Mack's (1975) original explanation. Further examination of the time-course of this effect would be useful. If the high preloads were to facilitate hunger, then we might expect their influence on ice cream consumption to decay over time, with a time-course which could potentially be estimated from unrestrained eaters. There might also be an interaction with flavour – it would be surprising if the preload facilitated eating of unpleasant or bland tasting ice cream as much as good quality ice cream. But even on a cognitive interpretation, someone whose diet has been spoiled by the experimenter's milkshakes at 1 p.m. should be no more or less ready to

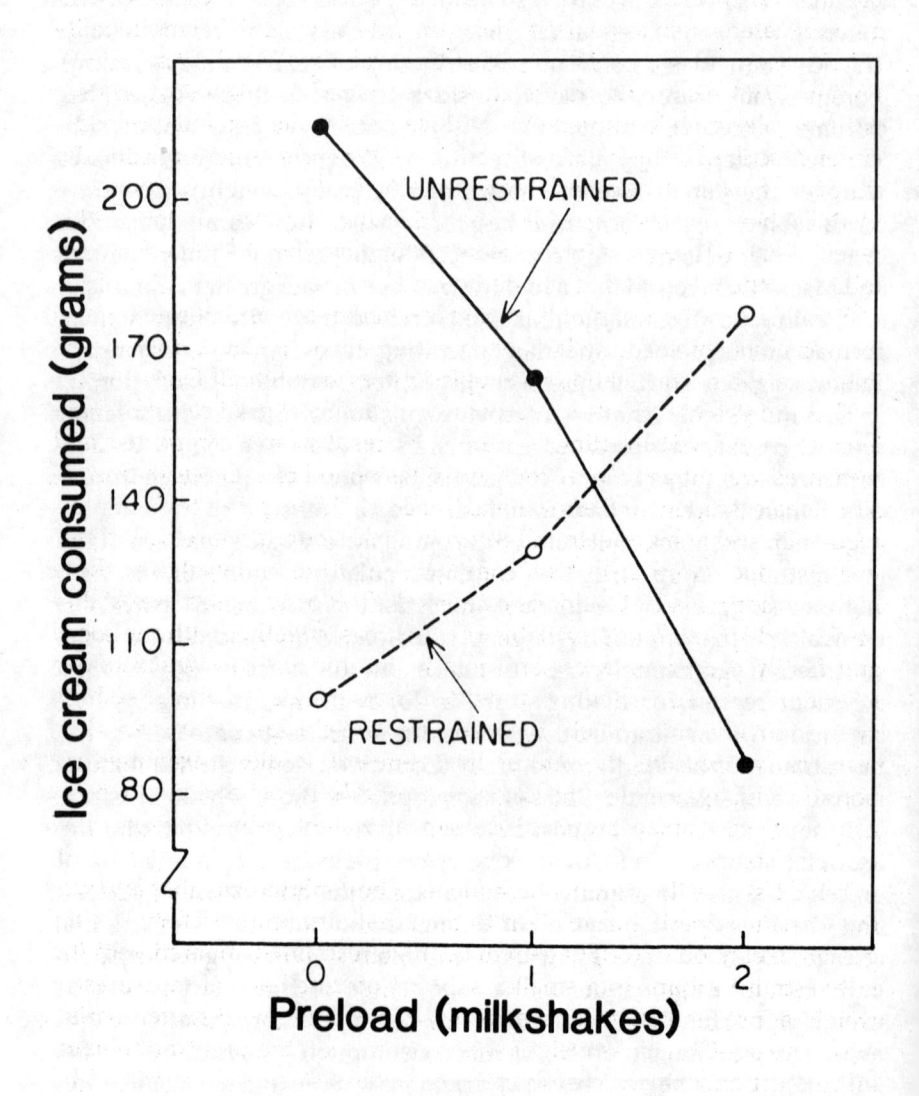

Figure 2. Response to preload in restrained and unrestrained eaters. (Reprinted with the permission of the publishers, W.B. Saunders Company, from *Obesity*, ed. A.J. Stunkard, 1980.)

eat ice cream at 1.15 p.m. rather than at 4.15 p.m., because, for the dieter, calories are counted by the day rather than by the hour.

Subsequent research has centred on the factors which influence the breakdown in restraint, that is the sudden loss of cognitive control over amount eaten, such as anxiety (Herman and Polivy, 1975), emotionality (Polivy, Herman and Warsh, 1978) and palatability (Woody et al., 1981). Polivy (1976) examined the relative importance of physiological cues (size of caloric preload) versus cognitive cues (beliefs about preload – either described as high or low in calories). Whereas larger preloads did result in greater intake in a high restraint group, if the preload was identical but subjects *believed* it to be either high or low in calories, this resulted in a three-fold increase in eating by the restrained eaters, following the alleged high caloric preload.

A problem in the restraint literature is whether the findings generalize from the incidental eating largely characteristic of the laboratory experiments to the normal eating of people in their day-to-day lives.

That the Restraint Scale can provide a meaningful predictor of behaviour in an everyday setting is shown by results on the reported and measured weight gains over the Christmas period of Edinburgh university female students. Herman and Mack (1975) explain the counter-regulation of the high restraint group in their laboratory preload experiment as due to 'collapse' as a consequence of the knowledge of these high caloric preloads. Could the combined effect of increased availability of rich and special foods available at Christmas, together with the social and family pressures to eat and join in the fun, be analogous to the laboratory preload procedure; and would those students who score high on restraint be more likely to experience weight gain than their low restraint companions, therefore? In a series of studies I examined reported weight gains over the Christmas period, the beliefs about weight gain and, in a smaller group, the actual weight gains in relation to restraint scores.

Table 1 shows the number of students who reported weight gain over the Christmas period in relation to their restraint scores. There is a far greater likelihood of weight gain in the high restraint compared with the low restraint group. In a smaller subset I obtained actual measures of weight approximately three weeks before and three weeks after Christmas. The pre-Christmas weight was measured on the pretext of obtaining weight and height distributions as a class statistical exercise. The post-Christmas measurements were taken immediately after completing a food and appetite questionnaire which included the relevant questions on the Restraint Scale. Table 2 shows the numbers who actually gained weight in this time, and again there is a significant difference, with high restrainers being more likely to gain weight. The percentages of the high

Table 1. Reported weight gain over the Christmas period

		High restraint	Low restraint
Weight gain over Christmas?	Yes	69	32
	No	38	68

$x^2 = 20.55$, df = 1, $p < .001$

Table 2. Actual weight gain over the Christmas period

		High restraint	Low restraint
Weight gain over Christmas?	Yes	18*	8*
	No	10	24

$x^2 = 7.85$, df = 1, $p < .01$

*Mean weight gain in the high restraint group = 2.27 + 1.09 kg; mean weight gain in the low restraint group = 1.07 + 0.79 kg. U = 30, p < .02, 2 tailed.

restrained groups who either reported or showed a measured weight gain over the Christmas period are virtually identical, which increases confidence in the self-report data. Finally, I compared the reported weight gain of two groups of students, separated in terms of their own view of the factors involved in weight gain at festive times. Having completed the questionnaire, the students were asked to choose which of the following two statements most closely agreed with their own beliefs:

(A) people who are not bothered about how much they weigh and who do not watch their diet will be most likely to over-eat and gain weight over the Christmas holiday period

(B) people who are weight-conscious and who carefully monitor their eating will be most likely to over-eat and gain weight over the Christmas holiday period.

Female students were marginally more likely to support statement (b) but this was not statistically significant. Of those who did believe that the weight-conscious are more at risk of weight gain (Table 3), it is the restrained eaters who were more likely to report weight gain. Those students who felt that if you were indifferent about weight gain you would gain more weight showed no differences in reported weight gain according to their scores on restraint.

Table 3. Beliefs and reported weight gain

	Belief (A)				Belief (B)	
	High	Low			High	Low
Weight gain Yes	13	16	Weight gain	Yes	29	12
No	13	15		No	14	27
$x^2 = 2.09$, N.S.					$x^2 = 9.58, p < .01$	

As dieting is such a prevalent behaviour and such a powerful influence on the eating behaviour of many women, it is important to examine its effect on some of the common experimental paradigms. The results of this survey do indicate that performance on the Restraint Scale predicts the likelihood of weight gain in certain contexts. The use of such scales together with other measures of eating attitudes is very necessary in order to obtain populations of subjects with similar beliefs about food and eating. Recent research (see final section) has begun to explore the connection between restrained eating and the development of more serious eating disorders.

LEARNING ABOUT HUNGER AND SATIETY

It was pointed out at the start of this chapter that a milestone in studies of feeding behaviour in animals was the recognition that the homeostatic viewpoint is inadequate as a basis for understanding the control of food intake, and that active learning processes must be used to explain a great deal of the normal feeding patterns in both animals and humans. Although there are physiological mechanisms which ensure that under emergency conditions eating is initiated as a consequence of metabolic deficit, under most circumstances this situation will not arise. We might expect to be able to identify examples of such learning particularly during infancy and childhood, as these will be the periods of greatest change in the acquisition of knowledge about foods and eating. Indeed, we have every reason to suppose that in man such influences would be much more obvious than in animals, if only as a result of the enormous cultural variation in feeding patterns. Humans live in a wider variety of habitats than any other well-studied mammal, and no one has attempted to look at population differences in feeding patterns in primates, for example. Within Western culture there are particular constraints on the feeding behaviour of infants, which appear very early in development, to do with the preparedness to feed ad lib; the desire to achieve early sleeping through the night; and pressures to move to a three meal a day pattern, and similar constraints in which the infant has to adapt to the desires of the mother (Wright, Macleod and Cooper, 1983).

Early infancy

Many clinicians, particularly those who deal with eating disorders, subscribe to a 'child is father to the man' notion and attribute eating problems in adulthood to early childhood experience.

Bruch (1974) in particular has stressed the importance of early learning and the need to provide opportunities for the child to develop an appropriate 'engram' of hunger. According to Bruch, hunger awareness is not innate, and she believes that the common factor in obesity and anorexia is an inability to identify hunger correctly or to distinguish it from other states of bodily need or emotional arousal. Bruch argues persuasively, and with a unique biological and psychoanalytic viewpoint, from the basis of individual case studies of patients with severe eating disorders that:

> It gradually became apparent that something had gone wrong in the experiential and interpersonal processes surrounding the satisfaction of nutritional and other bodily needs of these patients, and that incorrect and confusing early experiences had interfered with their ability to recognize hunger and satiation, and to differentiate 'hunger', the urge to eat, from other signals of discomfort that had nothing to do with 'food deprivation', and from emotional states aroused by the greatest variety of conflicts and problems (p. 45).

This distinction between the physiological state of nutritional depletion and the psychological processes involved in perceptual and conceptual awareness of nutritional state is one for which we have already seen some clinical and experimental evidence in adults (Stunkard and Koch, 1964) and which was a basis for Schachter's influential external–internal dichotomy (Schachter, 1971). Bruch maintains that such differentiation depends on 'correct' learning experiences being provided by the mother, such as offers of food in response to signals indicating hunger. More recently, Bruch (1981) has highlighted early infancy as an especially important time in this learning process:

> Behaviour, from birth on, needs to be differentiated in two forms, namely that initiated in the individual, and that in response to external stimuli. For normal development it appears to be essential that there are sufficient appropriate responses to cues originating in

the child, in addition to stimulation from the environment . . . How it operates can be observed in the feeding situation, which is also the area in which there is most interaction between mother and infant in the first year of life. When a mother offers food only in response to signals indicating nutritional need, the growing child will gradually develop a definite concept of 'hunger' as a sensation distinct from other tensions or needs. If, on the other hand, a mother's reaction is continuously inappropriate, be it neglectful, oversolicitous, inhibitory, or indiscriminately permissive, the outcome for the child will be a perplexing confusion, and he will not learn to differentiate between being hungry or sated, or whether he suffers from some other discomfort (p. 214).

Direct observational studies support the view that learning experiences have an important role in the development of feeding behaviour in human infants. From videotapes of the interactions between mothers and their infants during feeding sessions, it is possible to examine all instances of breaks in the feeding sequence – teat or nipple coming out of the mouth – and to ask whether the termination and to some extent the initiation of such sucking episodes is under the control of the mother or the baby. Wright, Fawcett and Crow (1980) observed that whereas the control of feeding in bottle-feed infants was predominantly a mother-determined activity, the situation was more fluid for the breast-feeding infants, with some mothers allowing both initiation and termination of sucking episodes to be predominantly under the control of the infant. Crying episodes in bottle-fed infants are increasingly associated with such breaks in the feed with age, but decrease with age in the breast-fed infants. As crying is invariably interpreted by the mother as indicating hunger, this reinforces the importance to the mother of ensuring that the entire bottle is consumed (Wright, 1982). The two feeding techniques therefore produce different interactions between mother and infant, which make the mother less responsive to infant cues in the bottle-feeding situation and contribute to the more commonly reported rapid weight gain in the bottle-fed infants (Crow, Fawcett and Wright, 1981).

Breast-fed infants by approximately eight weeks of age develop a pronounced diurnal pattern of meal size, with the largest meals tending to occur in the early morning and then progressively decreasing in size across the day (Wright, 1981). In older infants aged between four and six months this pattern reverses, with the largest meals now falling at the end of the day. One explanation for this change is that it results from the infant learning to anticipate periods of absence of food by taking larger meals ahead of the long night-time fast. As it is possible to obtain similar changes in meal size in a bottle-fed infant, this strengthens the evidence that the explanation involves active learning on the part of the infant, since it allows us to eliminate restriction in the availability of supply or variation in milk composition across the day as potential cues (Wright, 1986).

There is no experimental evidence to link directly poor ability to learn in some individuals with later eating disorders, but there have been some attempts to relate early infant feeding experience to rapid weight gain and obesity in later infancy. Ainsworth and Bell (1969) observed the interaction between mother and baby during feeds in the first year of life and concluded that growth was related to the sensitivity with which the mother responded to the baby's signals. In the few overweight infants they ascribed the over-feeding to treating too broad a spectrum of cries as signals indicating hunger. But Dubois, Hill and Beaton (1979), who questioned mothers (admittedly retrospectively) of normal weight and obese six-month-old infants, found no evidence that maternal disregard for infant hunger and satiety signals or maternal use of food in response to signals of non-nutritional needs had contributed to the obesity.

In a recent investigation of how good breast-feeding mothers are at estimating their infants' intensity of hunger in relation to amount taken at a feed, there does appear to be considerable scope for errors of interpretation, with some 30 per cent of mothers not performing very well at the task (Wright, 1986). One difficulty is the wide range of behaviours and attributions which the mothers put forward as indicating hunger. Particularly striking is the sex difference in reported awareness of variations in hunger across the day. At two months all but one of the mothers of female infants stated there was a particular time of day when they felt their baby was more hungry than any other time. If the infant was male then approximately 30 per cent of the mothers reported that they were unaware of any differences in hunger across the day – often saying he was either revenous all the time or not especially interested in any feed. This sex difference is also apparent at four months of age (see Figure 3). Female infants are more expressive than males in communicating their hunger needs and yet still almost one third of their mothers are not good at matching hunger with intake. If learning about hunger at this age is important for later eating behaviour, this might suggest a greater likelihood of problems with females than with males.

Learning about foods and eating rules in childhood

Interest by psychologists in how children acquire food preferences is of recent origin, but with the conflicting advice on what is a nutritionally

2 months

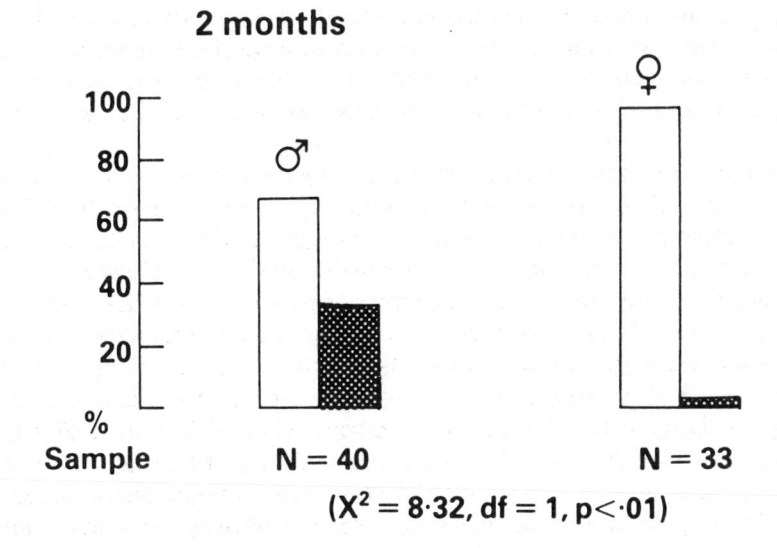

[Bar chart showing % Sample for males (N = 40) and females (N = 33), with Yes/No responses to Hunger Variation]

($X^2 = 8.32$, df = 1, p<.01)

4 months

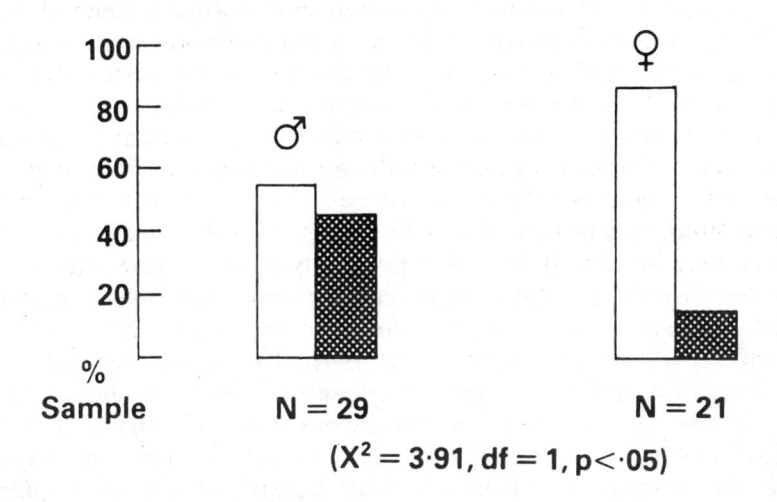

[Bar chart showing % Sample for males (N = 29) and females (N = 21), with Yes/No responses to Hunger Variation]

($X^2 = 3.91$, df = 1, p<.05)

Hunger Variation?

☐ Yes

▨ No

Figure 3. Awareness of variation in hunger across the day in mothers of two-and four-month-old infants.

adequate diet more attention to this problem is likely. Rozin (1982) has emphasized the continuity between some of the basic biological rules which govern food selection both in rats and in humans. Prominent here is the powerful long-delay learning first described by Garcia and Koelling (1966), which accounts for the connection between the delayed internal adverse metabolic consequences and the eating of a distinctive tasting food an hour or more previously. We find it easier to associate stomachaches with tastes than with lights or sounds, and, characteristically, many food dislikes in humans seem to be acquired as a result of a single experience and, moreover, often stem from childhood. This may be related to the fact that gastrointestinal upsets are relatively common in the early years (Garb and Stunkard, 1974).

A second important influence is likely to be the degree of neophobia in food selection, that is the fear and active avoidance of new foods because ingestion of a novel substance is potentially dangerous. Successive exposures to the new substance with no unpleasant consequences reduce the negative affect, resulting in enhanced liking (Rozin, 1976). Minimal neophobia for foods is likely to be adaptive during the post-weaning period, when the child is introduced to a variety of new foods and when acceptance is essential to growth and health. The relatively high incidence of accidental poisoning among preschool children provides some support for minimal neophobia among this age group. Birch (1986) suggests that whereas for three-year-olds familiarity is the most important determinant of food preference, children probably become less susceptible to exposure effects as they near the end of the preschool period.

In childhood, foods are the focus of a great deal of interaction with caretakers and a common source of difficulty between child and parent, and there have been recent attempts to describe the stages at which children acquire ideas of disgust and contamination with respect to foodstuffs (Fallon, Rozin and Pliner, 1984). For most parents of small children, the British cartoonist Posy Simmonds says it all with her spot-on caricature of typical mealtime experiences (see Figure 4).

In a series of studies, Birch and colleagues have devised a number of clear experimental situations which illuminate some of the conflicts present in these early experiences with food. Parents have strong views on what is good nutritionally for their children and frequently resort to a variety of control techniques in an attempt to regulate the child's intake. If they underestimate the adequacy of the diet or are concerned with food wastage, they require the child to eat all the food at that particular mealtime, and often use various contingencies to increase consumption; 'Eat up your cabbage and then you can . . . do something nice, such as have some ice cream, watch TV, play outside', etc. Birch, Marlin and

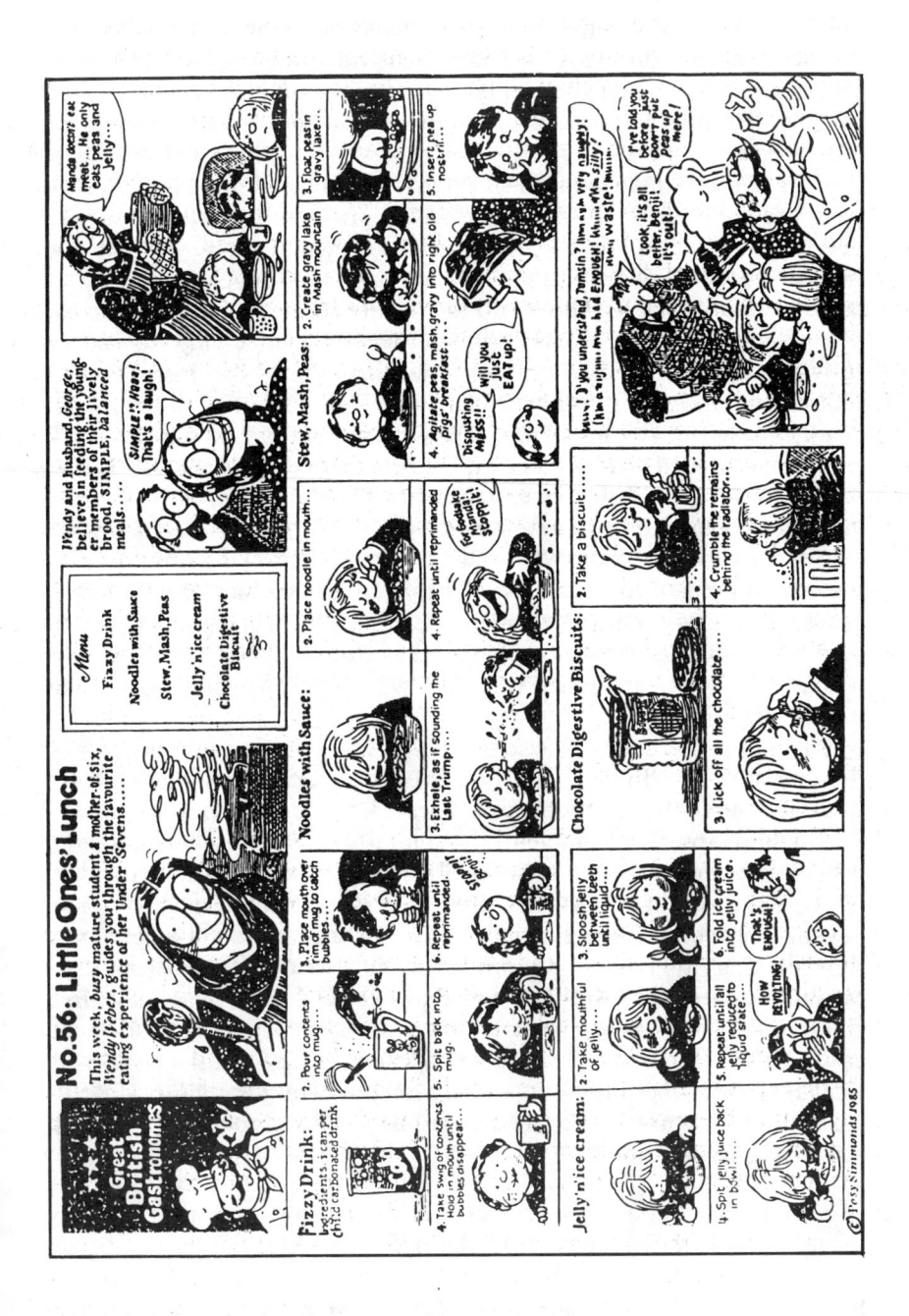

The Psychology of Eating and Eating Disorders / 159

Figure 4. Reprinted with the artist's kind permission.

Rotter (1984) asked whether the use of such contingencies had effects on the acceptability of foods consumed instrumentally. The children's preferences were initially found for a variety of fruit juices and an equal number of play activities in the nursery school, both before and following a series of contingency schedules in which the children drank juice in order to gain access to the play activity. The children actually *decreased* their preferences for the instrumentally consumed juice, that is repeated association of a food with the instrumental eating context decreases the food's acceptability, and such parental strategies are likely to be counter-productive. There is direct evidence that children see such instrumental eating negatively – when told stories involving the eating of two imaginary foods, in which one food was in the instrumental component and the other in the reward component of a mealtime contingency, the children indicated that they would prefer the food used as a reward to the food eaten instrumentally (Lepper et al., 1982). Although this is unlikely to mean that requiring children to eat ice cream in order to obtain cabbage as a reward would be a successful strategy in improving cabbage consumption, Birch's data indicate that increases in acceptability result from the use of foods as rewards and instrumental eating results in reduced acceptability. She feels that parental use of such contingencies implicitly denies that the child has the ability to regulate intake adequately in response to internal physiological cues of hunger and satiety.

Finally, it is perhaps no accident that in the Posy Simmonds cartoon the accent is on 'British'. The perceived high degree of faddishness, pernicketiness and anxiety towards particular foods may be a peculiarly British (and American) problem. In examining the history of eating and taste in England and France, Mennell (1985) puts forward the view that whereas the idea of a special children's food – a nursery food syndrome – seems to have been especially prominent in England, there is very little sign of this in France. Commencing in the nineteenth century, Mennell suggests that the widespread anxiety and concern about giving children only very plain, simply cooked, weakly flavoured food must easily have communicated itself to children and led some of them to remain anxious about food as adults; a very different tradition from the gastronomic culture in France, which has always emphasized food as something to be enjoyed.

CONDITIONED SATIETY IN ADULTS

Because bouts of eating come to an end long before the various digestive and absorptive processes have had time to take effect, it has been suggested by Stunkard (1975) that satiety must be a conditioned response to a familiar food, with the conditioning resulting from the delayed after-effects of eating that food on earlier occasions. The first clear demonstration of satiety conditioning was by Booth (1972), who showed that if rats are fed weak or strong carbohydrate solutions on alternate days, each marked with a distinct odour, after several weeks' training, if the rats are presented with an intermediate strength carbohydrate drink, they will drink more of it if it is paired with the 'weak-solution' odour cue than with the 'rich-solution' odour cue.

Subsequently Booth, Lee and McAleavey (1976) demonstrated a similar acquired sensory control of satiation in man. In the training phase, 65 per cent starch was given before lunches which included a yoghurt-based dessert of one flavour and 5 per cent starch was given before another flavour. Subjects who initially ate lunches of similar size following the drinks began after several pairings to take larger lunches following dilute starch than following concentrated starch. In extinction tests, in which identical 35 per cent starch drinks were given before lunches including desserts of both flavours, lunches which included the flavour previously paired with dilute starch remained larger than lunches including the other flavour. As the starch drinks are difficult to disguise and therefore subjects may have explicit cues at the start of the meal rather than consequent on later absorption, in other experiments a design with greater ecological validity was employed, the varying starch levels now disguised in hot soups served at the beginning of meals (Booth, Mather and Fuller, 1982).

The learning about foods that Booth and his colleagues have demonstrated is important, but it is unclear how efficient such learning would be in a less optimal environment than that provided in the laboratory. We do not usually eat identical meals over several consecutive days, and it would be useful to know the limits of such learning – can it occur for example with several days of uncontrolled meals between the learning trials? How much individual variation is there in this kind of learning and is it related to previous eating history? Booth (1981) speculates that over-reacting in the Schachter sense to the most obvious sensory characteristics of a food will distract from or swamp reaction to its presumably less obvious post-ingestional effects and interfere with or block the learning of associations between predictive sensory cues and post-ingestional effects.

Birch (1986) describes similar experiments with preschool children, designed to see whether they can learn about the nutrient consequences of eating by associating distinctive food cues with the distinctive physiological consequences of consuming those foods. She finds that provided the children have repeated experience of eating the foods, they do learn to associate flavour cues with the consequences of ingestion. She suggests that the contingencies employed by parents and described in the previous section may create an eating environment which is not optimal for the child to learn about the nutrient consequences of eating foods and to regulate consumption in response to any such internal cues that are perceived.

DIETING AND EATING DISORDERS

Bouts of excessive and uncontrolled eating which abruptly terminate dieting are characteristic of many overweight patients (Stunkard, 1980), and have also been described in anorexia (Garfinkel et al., 1980). Only recently has it been recognized that many women who are well within the normal weight range for their age indulge in equally bizarre eating episodes, so much so that this has acquired the status of a distinct eating disorder with episodes of binge eating as its chief characteristic. The condition was first described by Russell (1979) and given the name bulimia nervosa. It achieved a high media profile in the UK following the innovative use by Fairburn and Cooper (1982) of the women's magazine *Cosmopolitan* to identify sufferers by means of self-report questionnaires. The diagnostic criteria for bulimia nervosa (Cooper, 1985) are:

- patients suffer from powerful and intractable urges to over-eat
- they seek to avoid the fattening effects of food by inducing vomiting or abusing purgatives, or both
- they have a morbid fear of becoming fat.

Restraint in eating is characteristic of female compared with male students (Hibscher and Herman, 1977) and Starkey (1983), working with university students, found that high scores on the Restraint Scale are associated with a greater degree of overweight than are low scores, confirming the interaction of weight and restraint suggested by Ruderman and Wilson (1979). Similarly, binge eating is most prevalent in young females who have a tendency to be at least slightly overweight (Halmi et al., 1981; Fairburn and Cooper, 1982; Beaumont, 1982).

Further similarities between restrained eaters and binge eaters were apparent in Starkey's 1983 study: restrained subjects were more preoccupied with their weight; showed greater dissatisfaction and self-consciousness about their body; were more likely to over-eat when depressed and had more frequent urges to over-eat; and more frequently felt out of control of their eating – all characteristics which have been reported in binge eaters (Russell, 1979; Orbach, 1978). In her population of university students, Starkey also noted features which contrasted with the clinical evidence for binge eaters, for example restrained eaters did not exhibit the distorted perception of how much they were overweight which is characteristic of binge eaters (Halmi *et al.*, 1981), nor did they have a significantly lower self-esteem than unrestrained subjects, unlike binge eaters, who are consistently reported to feel inadequate, depressed and longing for the approval of others (Dunn and Onderin, 1981; Orbach, 1978). Restrained eaters did not report the abnormal, chaotic pattern of meals and snacks common in binge eaters (Palmer, 1979).

It is likely that these differences merely reflect a difference in degree of severity of the problem between normal individuals exercising restraint who binge occasionally and those eventually coming to clinical attention. This connection between restraint and binging has recently been made by Wooley and Wooley (1984), by Rodin, Silberstein and Stiegel-Moore (1984) and most forcibly by Polivy and Herman (1985), who propose that dieting *causes* binging by promoting the adoption of a cognitively regulated eating style, which is necessary if the physiological defence of body-weight is to be overcome. They argue from clinical case studies of anorexia nervosa that signs of bulimia do not usually appear until after the patients have established significant weight loss as a result of severe dieting. From case studies of long-standing bulimic patients, the Wooleys found that the first episode of vomiting usually followed a severe dietary lapse when celebrating or on holiday. Further sequences of binging and purging would then occur for some time before the advent of planned binges, so what has begun as a way of undoing a lapse in otherwise tight dietary control eventually allows the regular abandonment of control.

Many other studies in the USA (reviewed in Rodin *et al.*, 1984) support the view that increased concern to diet and obsession with thinness contribute to the increased incidence of eating disorders. A distinct socio-cultural climate encouraging the propagation of thinness as a way of life is now so prevalent among women in the USA that Schwartz, Thompson and Johnson (1982) found that a college student who practises purging almost always knows another who purges, whilst a woman who does not purge rarely knows someone who does. Indeed, as bulimia is a more effective method of weight control than any medically recommended therapeutic regime, the Wooleys (1982) comment that it is hardly surprising that intelligent young women gratefully practise it. In the USA one of the most popular best-selling diet books (Mazel, 1981) actually advocates a form of bulimia in which dieters are advised to counteract an eating binge by consuming large amounts of raw fruit in order to produce diarrhoea.

As the claim that dieting causes binging is based on the notion that the resultant depression of body-weight below a set-point results in heightened internal pressures to eat such as increased hunger and increased appetite, via enhanced palatability of foods, it is important to find a means of independently assessing hunger or appetite in order to investigate such claims.

Wooley and Wooley (1973) contend that we can objectively assess hunger and appetite using salivation as a measure, and they describe easy and non-intrusive measures in human subjects. They report (Wooley et al., 1975) elevated salivation in obese subjects when presented with palatable foods especially when this follows a high calorie meal. But salivation turns out to be a troublesome measure (see Sahakian, 1981) with conflicting results. The Wooleys (1981) remain strong advocates of its usefulness as a measure of appetite and interest in food and speculate that salivation probably parallels secretions of insulin and gastric acid, and may even serve as a rough index of the magnitude of these and other functions.

One example of the marked contradictions obtained using the salivary response measure is their claim that prolonged dieting suppresses both baseline measures of resting salivation and the response to food, which they argue is consistent with reports that severe deprivation is often accompanied by loss of appetite (Keys et al., 1950). Conversely, Herman et al. (1981) report that dieters over-salivate to palatable foods and, furthermore, if their data is graded according to whether subjects were within a normal weight range or classified as overweight, then dieting, not weight, was the important determinant of the salivary response, and this they maintain is due to the greater feelings of hunger in the dietary population.

Such discrepancies are avoided by Herman and Polivy (1985), who relegate the physiological changes consequent on food deprivation to a metabolic rather than behavioural role, by claiming that the deprivation-induced hormonal adjustments are attempts to provide optimal adaptations to the prevailing conditions of scarcity. They adopt an evolutionary argument, relying heavily on the observation by Coscina and Dixon (1983) that food deprivation in young female rats leads to increased efficiency of food utilization once access to food is restored, with a switch to a more thrifty metabolism. Furthermore, the same rats, under conditions where they are provided with an excess of highly palatable foods, gain weight at a faster rate than controls, the previously acquired physiological conservational mechanisms now resulting in behavioural strategies that protect them against future starvation.

Polivy and Herman (1985) maintain that successful dieters must ignore the normal body-weight regulatory pressures as represented in the experiences of hunger and satiety and must replace physiological controls, which by themselves are conducive to a 'desirable' weight level, with cognitive controls designed to achieve a lower weight in line with their personal goals. It is therefore not surprising that therapists find the need for cognitive change as essential to the successful treatment of bulimia nervosa (Cooper, 1985; Fairburn, 1984).

The concept of restrained eating has therefore been useful both in research and in the explanations it generates to understand bulimia. Its origins, as a means of accounting for the discrepant behaviour of some overweight subjects in terms of Schachter's externality theory, also highlight how unproductive it is to compare the obese and the normal weight and hope to find consistent differences in behaviour. Explanations for obesity are legion, encompassing genetic, metabolic, endocrine and learning processes, with the clear implication that treatment must be appropriate for the different causes. There is not one kind of obesity but many different kinds. A greater understanding of the processes involved in learning about foods and the bodily sensations accompanying eating at different developmental life-stages – infancy, childhood, adolescence and adulthood – is clearly needed to account for the prevalence of eating disorders in particular social and age groups and, predominantly, in women. This will require less adherence to medical and biological models and an increased understanding of family transactions around food before there can be a comprehensive psychology of human eating.

REFERENCES

Ainsworth, M.S. and Bell, S.M. (1969) Some contemporary patterns of mother-infant interaction in the feeding situation. In A. Ambrose (ed.) *Stimulation in Early Infancy*. New York: Academic Press.
Beaumont, P. (1982) How patients describe bulimia or binge-eating. *Psychological Medicine*, 12, 625–628.
Birch, L.L. (1986) The acquisition of food acceptance patterns in children. In R.A. Boakes, M.J. Burton and D.A. Popplewell (eds) *Eating Habits*. Chichester. John Wiley and Sons:
Birch, L.L., Marlin, D. and Rotter, J. (1984) Eating as the 'means' activity in a contingency: Effects on young children's food preference. *Child Development*, 55, 431–439.
Booth, D.A. (1972) Conditioned satiety in the rat. *Journal of Comparative and Physiological Psychology*, 81, 457–471.
Booth, D.A. (1981) Hunger and satiety as conditioned reflexes. In H. Weiner, M.A. Hofer and A.J. Stunkard (eds) *Brain, Behaviour and Bodily Disease*. New York: Raven Press.
Booth, D.A., Lee, M. and McAleavey, C. (1976). Acquired sensory control of satiation in man. *British Journal of Psychology*, 67, 137–147.

Booth, D.A., Mather, P. and Fuller, J. (1982) Starch content of ordinary foods associatively conditions human appetite and satiation, indexed by intake and eating pleasantness of starch-paired flavours. *Appetite*, 3, 163–184.
Bruch, H. (1974) *Eating Disorders, Obesity, Anorexia Nervosa and the Person Within*. London: Routledge and Kegan Paul Ltd.
Bruch, H. (1981) Developmental considerations of anorexia nervosa and obesity. *Can. J. Psychiatry*, 26, 212–217.
Cabanac, M. and Duclaux, R. (1970) Obesity: Absence of satiety aversion to sucrose. *Science*, 168, 496–497.
Cabanac, Duclaux, N.H. and Spector, R. (1971) Sensory feedback regulation of body weight: Is there a ponderostat? *Nature*, 229, 125–127.
Coddington, R.D. and Bruch, H. (1970) Gastric perceptivity in normal, obese and schizophrenic subjects. *Psychosomatics*, 11, 571–579.
Collier, G.H. and Rovee-Collier, C.K. (1983) An ecological perspective of reinforcement and motivation. In E. Satinoff and P. Teitelbaum (eds) *Handbook of Neurobiology, 6. Motivation*. New York: Plenum Press.
Cooper, P.J. (1985) Eating disorders. In F.N. Watts (ed.) *New Developments in Clinical Psychology*. Leicester: The British Psychological Society.
Coscina, D.V. and Dixon, L.M. (1983) Bodyweight regulation in anorexia nervosa: Insights from an animal model. In P.L. Darby, P.E. Garfinkel, D.M. Garner and D.V. Coscina (eds) *Anorexia Nervosa: Recent Developments in Research*. New York: Allan R. Liss.
Crow, R.A., Fawcett, J.N. and Wright, P. (1980) Maternal behaviour during breast and bottle-feeding. *Journal of Behavioural Medicine*, 3, 259–277.
Dodd, D.K., Stalling, R.B. and Bedell, J. (1977) Grocery purchases as a function of obesity and assumed food deprivation. *International Journal of Obesity*, 1, 43–47.
Dubois, S., Hill, D.E. and Beaton, G.H. (1979) An examination of factors believed to be associated with infantile obesity. *American Journal of Clinical Nutrition*, 32, 1997–2004.
Dunn, P. and Onderin, A. (1981) Personality variables related to compulsive eating in college women. *Journal of Clinical Psychology*, 37, 43–47.
Fairburn, C.G. (1984) Bulimia: Its epidemiology and management. In A.J. Stunkard and E. Steller (eds). *Eating and its Disorders*. New York: Raven Press.
Fairburn, C. and Cooper, P.J. (1982) Self-induced vomiting and bulimia nervosa – an undetected problem. *British Medical Journal*, 284, 1153–55.
Fallon, A.E., Rozin, P. and Pliner, P. (1984) The child's conception of food: The development of food rejections with special reference to disgust and contamination sensitivity. *Child Development*, 55, 566–575.
Farb, P. and G. Armelagos (1980) *Consuming Passions: The Anthropology of Eating*. New York: Washington Square Press.
Garb, J.L. and Stunkard, A.J. (1974) Taste aversions in man. *American Journal of Psychiatry*, 131, 1204–1207.
Garcia, J. and Koelling, R.A. (1966) Relation of cue to consequences in avoidance learning. *Psychonomic Science*, 4, 123–124.
Garfinkel, P.E., Moldofsky, H. and Garner, D.M. (1980) The heterogeneity of anorexia nervosa: Bulimia as a distinct subgroup. *Archives of General Psychiatry*, 37, 1036–1040.
Garrow, J.S. (1974) *Energy, Balance and Obesity in Man*. Amsterdam: Elsevier.
Goldman, R., Jaffa, M. and Schachter, S. (1968) Yom Kippur, Air France, dormitory food and the eating behaviour of obese and normal persons. *Journal of Personality and Social Psychology*, 10, 117–123.

Grossman, S.P. (1979) The biology of motivation. *Annual Review of Psychology*, 30, 209–242.
Halmi, K.A., Falk, J.R. and Schwartz, E. (1981) Binge eating and vomiting: A survey of a college population. *Psychological Medicine*, 11, 697–706.
Hashim, S.A. and von Itallie, T.B. (1965) Studies in normal and obese subjects with a monitored food dispensing service. *Annals of the New York Academy of Sciences*, 131, 654–61.
Herman, C.P. and Mack, D. (1975) Restrained and unrestrained eating. *Journal of Personality*, 43, 647–660.
Herman, C.P. and Polivy, J. (1975) Anxiety, restraint and eating behaviour. *Journal of Abnormal Psychology*, 84, 666–672.
Herman, C.P., Polivy, J., Klajner, F. and Esses, V.M. (1981) Salivation in dieters and non-dieters. *Appetite*, 2, 356–361.
Hibscher, J.A. and Herman, C.P. (1977) Obesity, dieting and the expression of 'obese' characteristics. *Journal of Comparative Physiology and Psychology*, 91, 374–380.
Keys, A., Brozek, J., Henschel, A., Micheksen, O. and Taylor, H.L (1950) *The Biology of Human Starvation*. Minneapolis: University of Minnesota Press.
Lepper, M., Sagotsky, G., Dafoe, J.L. and Greene, D. (1982) Consequences of superfluous social constraints: Effects on young children's social influences and subsequent intrinsic interest. *Journal of Personality and Social Psychology*, 42, 51–65.
Mazel, J. (1981) *The Beverley Hills Diet*. New York: Macmillan Publishing Co. Inc.
Mennell, S. (1985) *All Manners of Food*. Oxford: Basil Blackwell.
Nisbett, R.E. (1968) Taste, deprivation and weight determinants of eating behaviour. *Journal of Personal and Social Psychology*, 10, 107–116.
Nisbett, R.E. (1972) Hunger, obesity and the ventromedial hypothalamus. *Psychological Review*, 79, 433–453.
Nisbett, R.E. and Kanouse, D.E. (1969) Obesity, food deprivation and supermarket shopping behaviour. *Journal of Personal and Social Psychology*, 12, 289–294.
Orbach, S. (1978) *Fat is a Feminist Issue*. London: Paddington Press Ltd.
Palmer, R.L. (1979) The dietary chaos syndrome: A useful new term? *British Journal of Medical Psychology*, 52, 187–190.
Peck, J.W. (1980) Homeostatic analyses and relations between nutrition and ecology. In F.M. Toates and T.R. Halliday (eds) *Analysis of Motivational Processes*. Academic Press.
Polivy, J. (1976) Perception of calories and regulation of intake in restrained and unrestrained subjects. *Addictive Behaviour*, 1, 237–243.
Polivy, J. and Herman, C.P. (1985) Dieting and binging. *American Psychologist*, 40, 193–201.
Polivy, J., Herman, C.P. and Warsh, S. (1978). Internal and external components of emotionality in restrained eaters. *Journal of Abnormal Psychology*, 87: 497–504.
Rodin, J. (1975) The effects of obesity and set points on taste responsiveness and intake in humans. *Journal of Comparative and Physiological Psychology*, 89: 1003–1009.
Rodin, J. (1981) Current solutions of the internal–external hypothesis for obesity. *American Psychologist*, 36, 361–372.
Rodin, J., Silberstein, L. and Stiegel-Moore, R. (1984) Women and weight: A normative discontent. In T.B. Sonderegger (ed.) *Nebraska Symposium on Motivation*, 32, 267–307.

Rodin, J. and Slachwer, J. (1967). Externality in the non-obese: The effects of environmental responsiveness on weight. *Journal of Personal and Social Psychology*, 29: 557–565.
Royal College of Physicians (1983) Report on Obesity. *Journal of the Royal College of Physicians*, 17, 5–65.
Rozin, P. (1976) The selection of foods by rats, humans and other animals. In J.S. Rosenblatt, R.A. Hinde, E. Shaw and C. Beer (eds) *Advances in the Study of Behaviour*.
Rozin, P. (1982) Human food selection: The interaction of biology, culture, and individual experience. In L.M. Barker (ed.) *Psychobiology of Human Food Selection*. Westport, C.T.: AVI, 225–254.
Ruderman, A. and Wilson, G.T. (1979) Weight restraint, cognitions and counter-regulation. *Behaviour Therapy and Research*, 17, 581–590.
Russell, G.F.M. (1979) Bulimia nervosa: An ominous variant of anorexia nervosa. *Psychological Medicine*, 9, 429–448.
Sahakian, B.J. (ed.) (1981) Forum on salivation in response to food-related stimuli. *Appetite*, 2, 331–392.
Schachter, S. (1967) Cognitive effects on bodily functioning: Studies of obesity and eating. In D. Glass (ed.) *Neurophysiology and Emotion*. New York: Rockefeller Press:
Schachter, S. (1971) *Emotion, Obesity and Crime*. New York: Academic Press.
Schachter, S., Goldman, R. and Gordon, A. (1968) The effects of fear, food deprivation and obesity on eating. *Journal of Personality and Social Psychology*, 10, 91–97.
Schachter, S. and Gross, L.P. (1968) Manipulated taste and eating behaviour. *Journal of Personality and Social Psychology*, 10, 98–106.
Schachter, S. and Rodin, J. (1974) *Obese Humans and Rats*. Potomac, USA: Lawrence Erlbaum.
Schachter, S. and Singer, J.E. (1962) Cognitive, serial and situational determinants of emotional state. *Psychological Review*, 69, 379–99.
Schwartz, D.M., Thompson, M.G. and Johnson, C.L. (1982) Anorexia nervosa and bulimia: The social-cultlural context. *International Journal of Eating Disorders*, 1, 20–36.
Sims, E.A.H., Danforth, E., Horton, E.S., Bray, E.A., Glennon, J.A. and Salans, L.B. (1973) Endocrine and metabolic effects of experimental obesity in man. *Recent Progress in Hormone Research*, 29, 457–496.
Starkey, H.E. (1983) Restraint and binge-eating – is there a link? Unpublished BSc honours thesis, University of Edinburgh.
Stellar, E. (1954) The physiology of motivation. *Psychological Review*, 61, 5–22.
Stunkard, A.J. (1959) Obesity and the denial of hunger. *Psychosomatic Medicine* 21, 281–289.
Stunkard, A.J. (1975) Satiety is a conditioned reflex. *Psychosomatic Medicine*, 37, 383–387.
Stunkard, A.J. (1980) Psychoanalysis and psychotherapy. In A.J. Stunkard (ed.) *Obesity*. Philadelphia: W.B. Saunders Company.
Stunkard, A.J. and Fox, S. (1971) The relationship of gastric motility and hunger. *Psychosomatics*, 11, 571–579.
Stunkard, A.J. and Koch, C. (1964) The interpretation of gastric motility: I – Apparent bias in the reports of hunger by obese persons. *Archives of General Psychiatry*, 11, 74–82.

Tom, G. (1983) Effect of deprivation on the grocery shopping behaviours of obese and non-obese consumers. *International Journal of Obesity,* 7, 307–311.
Widdowson, E.M. (1951) The response to unlimited food. In *Studies in Undernutrition, Wuppertal, 1946–49.* (Special Report of the Medical Research Council, no 375.) London: MRC.
Woody, E.Z., Constanzo, P.R., Liefer, H. and Conger, J. (1981) The effects of taste and caloric perceptions on the eating behaviour of restrained and unrestrained subjects. *Cognitive Research and Therapy,* 5, 381–390.
Wooley, O.W. and Wooley, S.C. (1981) Relationship of salivation in humans to deprivation, inhibition and the encephalization of hunger. *Appetite,* 2, 331–350.
Wooley, O.W. and Wooley, S.C. (1982) The Beverly Hills eating disorder: The new marketing of anorexia nervosa. *International Journal of Eating Disorders,* 1, 57–69.
Wooley, O.W., Wooley, S.C. and Woods, W.A. (1975) Effects of calories on appetite for palatable food in obese and non-obese humans. *Journal of Comparative and Physiological Psychology,* 89, 619–625.
Wooley, S.C. and Wooley, O.W. (1973) Salivation to the sight and the thought of food: A new measure of appetite. *Appetite,* 35, 136–142.
Wooley, S.C. and Wooley, O.W. (1984) Should obesity be treated at all? In A.J. Stunkard and E. Stellar (eds) *Eating and its Disorders.* New York: Raven Press.
Wright, P. (1981) Development of feeding behaviour in early infancy: implications for obesity. *Health Bulletin,* 39, 197–206.
Wright, P. (1982) Nutrition and feeding. In P. Stratton (ed.) *Psychobiology of the Human Newborn.* Chichester: John Wiley and Sons Ltd.
Wright, P. (1986) Hunger, satiety and feeding behaviour in early infancy. In R.A. Boakes, M.J. Burton and D.A. Popplewell (eds) *Eating Habits.* Chichester: John Wiley and Sons Ltd.
Wright, P. and Crow, R.A. (1973) Menstrual cycle: Effect on sweetness preferences in women. *Hormones and Behaviours,* 4, 387–391.
Wright, P., Fawcett, J.A. and Crow, R.A. (1980) The development of differences in the feeding behaviour of bottle and breast-fed human infants. *Behavioural Processes,* 5, 1–20.
Wright, P., Macleod, H.A. and Cooper, M.J. (1983) Waking at night: The effect of early feeding experiences. *Child: Care, Health and Development,* 9, 309–319.

HUMAN ORGANIC MEMORY DISORDERS
Andrew Mayes

There is preliminary evidence for the existence of five major groups of relatively independent organic memory disorders.

☐ The first group comprises short-term memory deficits caused by neocortical lesions.
☐ The second group comprises disturbances of previously very well-established semantic information again caused by neocortical lesions, particularly of the posterior association areas.
☐ The third group comprises memory failures that seem, in the main, to be secondary to deficits in planning ability, which are caused by lesions of the prefrontal neocortex.
☐ The fourth group is that of the organic amnesias, which are caused by lesions in the limbic system of the medial temporal lobe, or of certain diencephalic structures, or possibly of connected frontal lobe structures.
☐ Very little work has been done on the fifth potential group of disorders – those in which memory for skills or conditioning is selectively affected – but animal studies suggest that selective deficits for certain kinds of classical conditioning can be caused by lesions in the cerebellum (Lincoln, McCormick and Thompson, 1982).

Each of these groups of memory deficit almost certainly divides into related subgroups of disorders, which are each caused by distinct lesions, although this last claim is less well established. This further subdivision is based, first, on the kind of information for which memory is affected, and, secondly, on whether the disturbance is caused by encoding, storage or retrieval failures. Analyses of such disorders lie at the heart of neuropsychological research on memory. Their current status is outlined, bearing in mind the implications of such analyses for our knowledge both of normal memory and of how specific brain regions mediate different kinds of memory.

SHORT-TERM MEMORY DISORDERS

Apparently selective short-term memory disorders for several different kinds of information have been reported, in accordance with the view that short-term or working memory comprises several distinct storage systems. Thus, some patients show an impairment in auditory-verbal short-term memory (see Shallice and Warrington, 1977); some show selective reduction in visual short-term memory for verbal and non-verbal material (Warrington and Rabin, 1971; Samuels, Butters and Fedio, 1972) after posterior neocortical lesions; some show selective reduction in visuospatial short-term memory (De Renzi and Nichelli, 1975); and one patient has been reported who, it is argued, has a short-term memory deficit that is selective for colour information (Davidoff and Ostergaard, 1984). In all these cases a memory impairment is apparent immediately after the target stimuli are removed.

Several important questions apply to each proposed impairment. First, is the deficit really specific to just one kind of information, for example colour? Second, is only short-term memory for this kind of information affected or is longer-term memory also bad? The answer to this question is salient to the issue of whether information is passed serially from short-term into long-term storage or whether there is parallel processing direct into both stores. This issue is also addressed by a third question. Is the poor immediate memory caused by a storage deficit, or by an encoding or related kind of processing deficit? This question is logically prior to the second because it is necessary to postulate a separate short-term store only if the immediate memory failure is caused by storage deficit. Processing deficits might be expected to cause immediate memory failures even if there is only one kind of storage and not distinct short and long-term stores.

The only short-term memory disorder that has been intensively investigated is the reported deficit in auditory-verbal short-term memory, so this is discussed in the context of the three questions previously listed. With respect to the first question, it has been shown that the ability to recall or recognize spoken inputs may be impaired in certain patients, who are usually conduction aphasics in whom poor ability to repeat what is spoken is associated with relatively preserved speech and comprehension. Such patients show digit spans of one or two digits, a reduced recency effect in the free recall of a list of spoken words and faster forgetting of a single item in the Brown–Peterson task, in which item presentation is followed by a distractor task to prevent rehearsal before recall is allowed (see Shallice and Warrington, 1979). Poor performance is unlikely to be caused either by bad comprehension, as this is usually good, or by speech output problems, as recognition, which does not require speech, has also been shown to be poor. Despite this, span for visually presented words is good and immediate memory for non-verbal sounds (like jangling keys) is unaffected if subjects are prevented from using verbal labelling strategies. The deficit therefore seems to be specific.

With respect to the second question, Shallice (1979) has shown that these patients can learn paired associates or lists of unrelated words normally over several trials. But does this indicate normal long-term memory for the kind of information for which these patients have poor short-term memory? There is good evidence that they can usually retain the *gist* of spoken sentences, but cannot give verbatim recall (Shallice, 1979). This accords with the widely held view that they have a selective memory deficit for phonological inputs, but in spite of this they are quite good at deciphering what spoken utterances mean and storing these meanings (or gists). If this view is correct, then determining whether the memory loss is selective for short-term memory will require tests that use phonological inputs that are meaningless, for example spoken nonsense syllables or words. Both short and long-term memory would probably be impaired if such tests were given.

The third question can be approached by seeing whether the failure of immediate memory is associated with deficits in processing phonological inputs, and if it is not, arguing by process of elimination that a storage deficit is involved. It is plausible to suggest that normal immediate memory depends on the appropriate encoding of phonological forms, their maintenance in a limited capacity, fast decaying short-term store, and their periodic refreshment through a process of rehearsal. This rehearsal process seems to be important in the digit span task, where getting subjects to make simple, repetitive articulations when the digits are presented impairs performance, but not with the recency effect, which is not affected by such articulations when the digits are presented (Baddeley, 1983). Two kinds of processing deficit have, in fact, been reported in patients with short-term memory deficits for phonological inputs. The first is an encoding deficit (Allport, 1984) and the second corresponds to a rehearsal deficit (Kinsbourne, 1972). Allport (1984) has reported that one patient with poor phonological short-term memory also performed badly on a 'same–different' judgement task with successively presented spoken syllables, which strongly suggested she had difficulty in discriminating and hence encoding phonemes, a problem that could have caused or contributed to her memory deficit.

Vallar and Baddeley's (1984) patient P.V., however, has been reported to perform normally on this kind of task despite having a short-term memory deficit. Although she may have a subtler encoding deficiency (such as poor discrimination of voice onset time) it seems unlikely that her memory deficit can be explained completely as an encoding failure of this kind.

Kinsbourne (1972) argued that poor ability to repeat spoken utterances is caused by a disconnection between the system that makes and stores phonological analyses and the system that articulates these phonological forms. Such a deficit should cause a reduction in the rehearsal of items that are phonologically represented, which studies of normal people show can cause a reduction in digit span (Vallar and Baddeley, 1984). Although rehearsal is not involved in the recency effect a disconnection deficit should increase the time it takes to articulate the last items heard in a word list, that is the ones involved in the recency effect. The extra delay might be sufficient to cause more forgetting and the reduced recency effect shown by some patients. Indeed, it might be argued that even recognition of recently spoken words may depend on covert articulation, which would be slow and impaired in these patients. What is the evidence that patients with poor phonological short-term memories have a deficit which reduces rehearsal and slows articulatory retrieval?

First, Vallar and Baddeley's (1984) patient did not appear to rehearse in a task of sequential word recall, but this lack of rehearsal could have been a strategic decision (because her storage was poor) rather than an absolute deficiency. A second source of evidence is merely suggestive, but is more direct. In normal people, repetition seems to be a privileged route relative to associative naming (for example, giving an associate to the word 'cat') in so far as it is achieved more quickly and with much less effort. Although normal people's repetition is not impaired by the simultaneous performance of an unrelated task, Friedrich, Glenn and Marin (1984) found that this was not so in a short-term memory deficient patient, which suggests that this privileged route was impaired. There have been no studies that have compared patients' and controls' reaction times to produce articulated repetitions to individual spoken words. If patients' reaction times are prolonged an attempt could be made to simulate their reduced recency effect in normal people by preventing them from producing responses or rehearsing for times comparable to those of the patients.

At present, we cannot say whether there are any acoustic verbal short-term memory patients whose deficit is one of storage rather than of phonological processing or of articulating recently heard phonology. Future research may reveal that short-term memory deficits, such as that for phonological information, may arise from several functional failures, including subtle processing problems, disconnection and rehearsal problems and storage failures. Unless storage deficits are found there will be no unequivocal proof for the existence of distinct short and long-term stores for any kind of information. Normal performance by organic amnesics (who are bad at long-term memory tasks) on tests of short-term memory might simply mean that certain kinds of processing are operating normally in them.

DISORDERS OF PREVIOUSLY WELL-ESTABLISHED MEMORY

There are certain kinds of thing that people learn very thoroughly and practise frequently over long periods of time. Some of these things are verbal, such as our knowledge of word meanings and usages; others involve our knowledge about the properties of objects that we perceive through our various senses; and there are yet other kinds of memory, required for the performance of other skilled operations, such as doing mental arithmetic. It has long been known that brain lesions can cause selective deficits in verbal abilities (dysphasias) and deficits in the ability to identify what objects are when these are sensorily presented despite the fact that basic sensory processes seem to be intact and the instructions are understood (agnosias). Although these deficits could arise from a variety of processing failures there has been a trend in recent years to argue that they sometimes result from memory disturbances (for example, Warrington, 1975 and 1986).

There are several questions that need to be asked to clarify what is involved in these claims. First, is the disorder truly one of memory or could it arise from either a processing failure at input or disconnection between the earlier stages of processing and the intact semantic memories? The current conceptualization of the problem makes it very hard to distinguish this latter possibility from a specific deficit in retrieving certain memories. So, provided the early stages of processing are unimpaired a disconnection deficit can be regarded as a retrieval failure. A second and related question is whether the deficit is caused by a disturbance of retrieval, of storage or of both. As will be discussed later, Shallice (1986) has proposed some criteria to differentiate between storage and retrieval failures, such as consistency of retrieval successes or failures on different occasions. A third question, less fraught with interpretative problems, is how specific can the kinds of memory disturbance be in terms of the information affected? The answer to this question should give clues about the way in which the semantic memory system is organized. Fourth, as many of these disturbances are regarded as deficits specific to semantic memory, it is important to ask what are the effects on corresponding episodic memories, and the ability to acquire new semantic and episodic memories in the 'area' affected.

As research in this area is comparatively recent the above questions have been only partially addressed. Most can be said about question three – how specific can the disorders be? Deficits can be highly specific. Thus, Warrington (1982) has described an acalculic patient, whose poor ability to do mental arithmetic seemed to result from a selective memory loss for previously well-established arithmetical facts, such as '2 + 4 = 6'. There is also some evidence that there is a verbal semantic memory system distinct from semantic memory systems that are specific to each sensory modality. If this is so, it raises the interesting question of whether the same information has multiple representations in different semantic systems or whether these systems contain somewhat different information.

Warrington and Shallice (1984) investigated four patients who had made partial recoveries from encephalitis, which caused damage to their temporal lobes. These patients were impaired in their ability to identify pictures of common objects by naming or description, and at giving definitions of the object names presented auditorially. When the tests were given on separate occasions the patients performed consistently with items presented within one sensory modality, but there was no consistency in their performance on items presented to different modalities. This could mean that visual-semantic and verbal-semantic memory systems had been independently damaged. The patients also provided evidence that these systems are further subdivisible, as their ability to identify both pictures and names of common animals and foods was significantly more impaired that their ability to identify pictures and names of common inanimate objects. Although this category-specific dissociation is incomplete in that performance with inanimate objects was not normal, a converse dissociation has been reported by Warrington and McCarthy (1983), who described an aphasic patient with grossly impaired comprehension of inanimate object names and relatively preserved comprehension of animal and plant names.

Warrington and Shallice (1984) argue that these category-specific dissociations arise because knowledge of inanimate objects is largely based on their functional characteristics, whereas knowledge of animate objects depends on semantic features closely tied to sensory properties. If so, one must assume that functional and sensory semantic memories are stored in somewhat different cortical regions that only overlap to a small degree. As their four patients showed stable but poor semantic memory, with a lack of concordance between visual and auditory modalities, Warrington and Shallice also argue that there are distinct modality-specific and verbal-semantic systems, which must be divisible into functional and 'sensory' subsystems. They oppose the view that there is one semantic memory system with multiple inputs that can be selectively disrupted. The multi-system argument depends on the ability to distinguish between storage and retrieval failures of the semantic system, as will shortly be discussed. The case for subdividing the proposed semantic systems into functional and 'sensory' stores has yet to be properly assessed. Some evidence suggests the distinction is too crude. For example, Hart, Berndt and Caramazza (1985) have described a patient who is selectively unable to name common fruits and vegetables. This patient was able to name food objects provided they were not fruit or vegetables. His deficit was also specifically one of retrieving such names, as he was able to classify names into their correct semantic categories when they were given to him, despite being unable to relearn how to name fruits and vegetables. These results suggest the patient had a retrieval deficit for category-specific names which, if retrieved, would have provided access to an intact semantic system.

Other kinds of specific semantic memory impairment have been reported. Thus, one of Warrington and Shallice's (1984) patients was markedly better at identifying the meaning of abstract as opposed to concrete words. Similarly, Warrington (1975) reported a partial double dissociation in which one patient was poor at defining spoken concrete words and another was relatively poor at defining abstract words. Similarly, some dyslexics have been found to be selectively very poor at reading concrete words, whereas it is well known that deep dyslexics are specifically bad at reading abstract words (Warrington, 1981). The evidence therefore suggests that large lesions can independently (or nearly so) compromise abstract and concrete word semantic systems, and that smaller lesions can cause category-specific breakdowns within the concrete system and possibly also within the abstract one. Goodglass et al. (1966) have noted that such category specific impairments, selective to categories like colour and body part names, are quite common in dysphasics. More recently, McCarthy and Warrington (1985) have described an agrammatic patient whose problem seems to arise from a relatively selective difficulty in the comprehension of action words, such as verbs.

Multiple dissociable deficits have also been reported with visual agnosia for objects, colours, faces, topography, parts of the body, letters and numbers (see Hécaen and Albert, 1978, for a review). Although the majority of these deficits have not been analysed sufficiently to determine whether they are caused by perceptual or memory disturbances, recent work on prosopagnosia (agnosia for familiar faces) suggests that sometimes at least they are caused by specific memory impairments. Prosopagnosics fail to recognize faces to which they have been heavily exposed for years (they may fail to recognize themselves in the mirror) and yet some can match photographs of faces taken from different angles, or with different illumination or disguises, indicating that encoding of faces is reasonably intact (see De Renzi, 1982). Recently, it has been shown, in two independent studies, that although prosopagnosics fail to recognize photographs of previously familiar faces, their electrodermal responses show clear discrimination between correct and incorrect names of the faces (Bauer, 1984) or between familiar and unfamiliar faces (Tranel and Damasio, 1985).

As these studies show one measure of face memory to be normal in some prosopagnosics, it is unlikely that their deficit can be caused by degraded perceptual input to the face memory system. Rather, it looks as if either storage or retrieval of familiar faces can be selectively impaired. The impairment cannot affect all aspects of memory for familiar faces, because the patients were relatively normal at the automatic discrimination of familiar faces or their names. This could mean either that there are independent recognition and automatic discrimination memory systems for faces or that the recognition system includes the automatic one and, perhaps, also stores a set of associated contextual features that serve to identify the faces.

There is then growing evidence that well-established semantic memories can be disturbed for highly specific kinds of information. In many cases, however, much more work needs to be done before a role for serious perceptual and hence encoding problems can be excluded. Even if this can be done, arguments about the divisibility of semantic memory (for example, into verbal and modality-specific systems) depend on the ability to distinguish between storage and retrieval failures. For example, if a lesion causes unrelated impairments of verbal-semantic and visual-semantic memory, then provided the deficit is of retrieval one can argue that two independent inputs to *one* store have been disconnected. If, however, the failure is one of storage it is necessary to argue that two independent stores have been disrupted.

Shallice (1986) has proposed several criteria to identify whether a deficit is one of storage or retrieval.

☐ First, he argues that a storage deficit will lead to consistently poor, indifferent or good retrieval of particular items on separate occasions.
☐ Second, if the store is degraded, superordinate information will more likely be retrieved than subordinate information. For example, a patient would remember that a canary is a bird, but not that it is yellow.

☐ Third, it should not be possible to improve identification of items in a degraded store by priming, because a destroyed memory cannot be activated by presenting a priming picture or word.
☐ Fourth, more frequently encountered items should be more immune to storage degradation.
☐ Fifth, as suggested by Warrington and McCarthy (1983), retrieval should not improve appreciably when more time is allowed for it if the deficit is one of storage degradation. In contrast, retrieval deficits should produce inconsistent retrieval at different times, insensitivity to frequency effects and equivalent impairments in retrieving superordinate and subordinate features, positive effects of priming, and improved retrieval when more time is allowed.

Only if patients fall into either a 'storage deficit' pattern or a 'retrieval deficit' pattern on all five criteria can one place much confidence in Shallice's interpretation. The problem is basically that the criteria are not derived fron an agreed theory of how semantic storage and retrieval operates. Shallice (1986) has analysed the performance of eight semantic memory impaired patients with respect to the five criteria and argues that they clearly fall into two groups. Although consistent retrieval tended to go with sensitivity to frequency and the superordinate–subordinate distinction whereas inconsistent retrieval went with insensitivity to frequency and the superordinate–subordinate distinction, the patients were not tested on all measures, so the strength of these associations is currently difficult to appraise. Until we can confidently identify storage deficits the issue of whether there is one semantic memory system or distinct verbal and modality-specific systems is unlikely to be resolved.

Patients with semantic memory deficits may be impaired on learning much new episodic material, but can acquire some things easily, such as recognition of representational pictures (Warrington, 1975), whereas organic amnesics retain well-established semantic information, but are poor at acquiring all episodic information. This apparent double dissociation has been taken to support the view that semantic and episodic memory comprise independent systems with distinct neural underpinning. An alternative interpretation is that episodic memory depends on semantic memory and the operation of certain additional processes. If this is correct, one would predict two things. First, acquisition of new episodic memories should be impaired in semantic memory deficit patients to the extent that the new memories draw on semantic material, memory for which has been impaired. Thus, a patient with a selective deficit in remembering animate things should have greater difficulty in learning a list of animal words, but perhaps learn a list of inanimate object names normally. Second, such semantic memory patients should show retrograde amnesia even for events that occurred in childhood, provided these personal events draw on the kind of semantic information for which memory is impaired. For example, if memory is lost for animate things there should be a severe retrograde amnesia for experiences with animals, but other early experiences may be normally remembered. These predictions remain to be tested.

MEMORY DEFICITS CAUSED BY FRONTAL LOBE LESIONS

Although lesions of the posterior cortex are known to cause a variety of disorders of short-term and well-established memory, the mnemonic effects of frontal lobe lesions are more polemical. On the one hand it has been argued that frontal lesions may cause a global amnesic deficit. Thus, recognition as well as recall problems have been reported for recently experienced events in human patients (Warrington, 1985). Also, a deficit on a delayed non-matching-to-sample task has been reported in monkeys following lesions of the ventromedial prefrontal cortex (Mishkin and Bachevalier, 1983). This task is analogous to one of recognition in humans, because the monkeys performing it have to pick a novel object and reject an object that has just been shown. On the other hand, this radical view has been criticized and many researchers seem to believe that most frontal memory problems are secondary to impairments in the ability to plan complex encoding and retrieval operations. It is argued that global amnesia is only seen in humans if lesions extend beyond the frontal lobes, and that the lesioned monkeys' impairment *may not be a result of poor recognition* but is caused by a failure to relearn what the delayed non-matching task involves. Instead it has been suggested that frontal lobe lesions impair the ability to plan more elaborate encoding and retrieval strategies so that some kinds of memory are affected more than others (see Luria, 1973 and Shallice, 1982 for views of the frontal lobes as a planning system). If this second position is broadly correct, different frontal lesions may affect memory differently, as measures of cerebral metabolism indicate that there may be as many as 17 functionally distinct regions in the frontal lobes (Roland, 1984).

Most mnemonic effects of selective frontal lobe lesions are consistent with the hypothesis that the deficits are secondary to poor ability to plan elaborate encoding and retrieval. First, frontal patients are poor at unguided learning of unrelated word pairs, such as 'chicken-mountain', but approach normal levels when they are shown how to create mediating images between the words (see Signoret and Lhermitte, 1976). Controls do this spontaneously and it greatly aids recall. This is consistent with the suggestion that frontal patients cannot initiate and maintain a plan to engage in complex imagery encoding, but require guidance.

Second, frontal lesions probably impair recall of events acquired decades before, when their brains were normal: that is, they show retrograde amnesia. It has been observed that patients with the motor disorder of Huntington's chorea, in which there is frontal cortex as well as caudate atrophy, show a mild retrograde amnesia that extends back decades. Unlike global amnesics their memory for the oldest events is as impaired as memory for more recent events (Albert, Butters and Brandt, 1981). Stuss et al. (1982) found a similar impairment in leucotomized patients with more selective frontal lobe lesions although the deficit was of borderline significance. Further studies need to be done, but there is a hint that frontal lesions impair the ability to set up and maintain complex retrieval strategies necessary for the recall of memories laid down when the brain was working normally. This view is supported by the finding that frontally lesioned patients are poor at retrieving familiar items according to some rule, which suggests that they cannot initiate strategies to retrieve from semantic memory (see Miller, 1984).

Third, although frontally lesioned patients are usually found to show normal recognition of recently acquired material (Milner, 1971; Hirst, 1985) their recall is poor (Hirst, 1985). Hirst gave patients with bilateral frontal lesions a list of words to learn, and then, after a five-minute delay, gave a recall test followed by one of recognition. The patients were impaired only on the former task. Recall probably depends more than recognition on elaborative encoding and elaborative retrieval strategies and Hirst's patients were found to categorize words inefficiently.

Hirst also noted a fourth and related impairment, consistent with the patients having poor ability to engage in elaborative encoding and retrieval. They were found to have disturbed metamemory as revealed by their poor knowledge of what they would need to do if they were to remember sucessfully in different circumstances. Clearly, such poor knowledge will contribute to the inadequate memory processing strategies spontaneously displayed by patients with frontal lobe lesions.

Frontally lesioned patients are also bad at two tasks that tap relatively short-term memory. First, they are poor at recalling items after delays of a few seconds, which are filled with a distracting task involving counting backwards by threes (Stuss et al., 1982). This deficit probably occurs because a frontal planning problem prevents the two activities of rehearsal and counting from being interdigitated. Second, Moscovitch (1982) has reported that patients with unilateral frontal lobe lesions fail to show release from proactive interference. He presented five lists containing 12 words each to subjects who were asked to recall as many of the words as possible immediately after each presentation. Words from the first four lists were drawn from one semantic category and recall declined between list one and list four, an effect put down to proactive interference from the earlier lists. Words from the fifth list were drawn from a different semantic category, but whereas this shift led to an improvement in normal subjects' recall, it did not do so with the patients. This inability to shift encoding and retrieval strategies (perseveration) is a kind of planning failure often noted in frontal patients and in Moscovitch's task might be expected to be associated with inappropriate intrusions from the first four lists (see Luria, 1973). Frontal lobe lesions might therefore particularly affect retrieval when a change of mental set is required as applies in interference tasks.

Patients with frontal lobe lesions show another group of memory deficits that are harder to explain as results of poor elaborative encoding and retrieval. It has been reported that such patients are very bad at judging which of two events was most recent, despite showing normal recognition for the events (see Milner, 1971). In a second, similar study, Smith and Milner (1983) found that frontal patients are bad at making judgements about the frequency with which events occur. Third, Petrides and Milner (1982) found that frontal patients were impaired at a self-ordered pointing task, in which subjects were given stacks of cards, each having a regular array of the same stimuli, the positions of which varied from card to card. Subjects had to work through each card stack touching a different item on each card. Patients with left frontal lobe lesions were particularly impaired at this task, performing poorly with both verbal and non-verbal items.

Hasher and Zacks (1979) have argued that a variety of background contextual features are automatically encoded with minimal attentional effort. More controversially, according to Hasher and Zacks, it also means that applying effort to the encoding will not improve memory for the features. The contextual features involved include event recency and frequency, and it seems likely that encoding of recent actions may also be automatic. As frontal lesions impair the ability to make judgements of recency, frequency and self-ordered responses, it could be that the lesions impair not only effortful encoding and retrieval in several ways, but that they also impair automatic encoding processes. If this were so, however, one might expect that frontal lobe lesions would impair memory for other automatically encoded features, such as spatial location. Smith and Milner (1984) have reported, however, that frontal patients are normal on one test of spatial memory. The issue is unresolved, but it could be that all frontal memory deficits are caused by disturbances of effortful encoding and retrieval, and that the recency, frequency and self-ordered tasks require the making of difficult judgements, which involve setting up a complex retrieval plan. Whether this is so and whether frontal lobe lesions compromise the ability to set up such a plan remains to be tested.

THE ORGANIC AMNESIAS

Cases of selective organic amnesia are characterized by poor recognition and recall of semantic and episodic information acquired after the brain damage (anterograde amnesia), and by poor recognition and recall of some of the semantic and episodic information acquired before the brain damage (retrograde amnesia). At the same time, amnesics may have normal short-term memory as shown by digit span performance, and normal intelligence. This pattern of symptoms seems to be caused by lesions either in the medial temporal lobes, affecting structures such as the hippocampus and possibly the amygdala, or in the diencephalon, affecting structures such as the mammillary bodies and the dorsomedial nucleus of the thalamus. This syndrome has been the most studied of all the organic memory deficits. It is of interest for two reasons. The occurrence of drastic memory loss in the face of normal intelligence suggests that the impairment cannot result from a crude encoding and/or retrieval deficit, as this would be likely to disturb intelligence. Also, the critical lesions that cause the memory loss are not neocortical and yet it seems probable that complex information, including semantic and perhaps episodic memories, are stored in the neocortex. This suggests that the medial temporal and diencephalic structures either facilitate neocortical storage in some way or themselves store certain features, necessary for retrieving many episodic and semantic memories that are mainly stored in the neocortex (see Mayes, Meudell and Pickering, 1985).

There have been four different kinds of claim that amnesia comprises several distinct disorders of function. First, it has been argued that left and right hemisphere lesions can cause material-specific amnesias for verbal and difficult-to-verbalize material respectively (see Milner, 1971). Such amnesias probably arise because specific neocortical processing and storage regions are denied the processing facilities provided by disconnected or damaged limbic-diencephalic structures. A second, currently criticized claim, is that medial temporal (limbic) amnesia is associated with poor memory and pathologically fast forgetting (Huppert and Piercy, 1978a, 1979; Squire, 1981; Freed, Corkin and Cohen, 1984; Kopelman, 1985), whereas diencephalic amnesia is characterized by poor memory and a normal forgetting rate (see Kopelman, 1985). It has also been argued that the lesions cause different types of retrograde amnesia, but this and the previous claim lack firm support. Third, some believe that anterograde and retrograde amnesia can be found in isolation and must therefore arise from distinct functional deficits. Although convincing reports of isolated anterograde amnesia are elusive (but see Leipman in Talland, 1965 and Syz, 1937), several cases of isolated retrograde amnesia have been reported (Andrews, Kessler and Poser, 1982; Goldberg et al., 1981; Wood, Ebert and Kinsbourne, 1982.) These cases may, however, have lesions in brain regions other than those which produce the full syndrome. Fourth, on the basis of monkey models of human amnesia, Mishkin (1982) has argued that the severe form of the full syndrome is found only when there is conjoint damage to a hippocampal circuit and an amygdala one. Both circuits run from the neocortex through the limbic system to the diencephalon, then back to the neocortex, and play different functional roles (perhaps mediating different kinds of contextual memory). This view is currently well-supported by animal studies.

Whether there is a single functional deficit or several deficits underlying amnesia the main means of identifying them is through an analysis of the patterns of performance characterizing the anterograde and retrograde amnesias of patients. Most research has explored anterograde amnesia and one of its major findings has been that amnesics show normal learning and retention in several different kinds of task despite their very poor ability to recall or recognize anything to do with the task, including the fact that they learned it. Thus amnesics have been reported to show good classical conditioning despite failing to recognize what the training apparatus was (Weiskrantz and Warrington, 1979). They have also been reported to learn and retain normally motor skills, such as mirror drawing and pursuit rotor (Corkin, 1968), perceptual skills, such as reading mirror reversed words (Cohen and Squire, 1980) and perhaps even cognitive skills, such as solving the Tower of Hanoi puzzle (Cohen, 1984). Most interestingly, amnesics show normal facilitation or biasing of their processing of specific items as a result of having recently perceived them, that is they show normal priming.

Several kinds of priming have been found to be normal in amnesics. First, when subjects are shown words and are later asked to complete the opening letters of the shown words with the first word that comes to mind, amnesics show as great a tendency as controls to generate the previously presented words even though they do not recognize them (Warrington and Weiskrantz, 1974, 1978; Graf, Squire and Mandler, 1984; Mayes and Meudell, 1981). This is known as word-completion priming. Second, Jacoby and Witherspoon (1982) showed that the normal tendency to spell an orally presented homophone according to its most common variant is reversed if subjects have recently encountered its less common variant, and that this effect is as great in amnesics as their controls, despite the formers' inability to recall encountering the rarer homophonic variant. Third, amnesics have been found to 'free associate' normally to words that have either recently been encountered as the response members of related paired associates (for example 'soldier–army') or have been recently encountered alone. Subjects either free associate from the stimulus term of the recently encountered pairs or from a word that could have been a semantically related stimulus term if the target words had not been encountered alone, for example free associate from 'floor' to the target 'ceiling' which was shown alone (Shimamura and Squire, 1984; Schacter, 1985). Fourth, there is evidence that amnesics show a normal facilitation in their ability to make lexical decisions about or to name briefly exposed words that they have recently perceived (Moscovitch, 1982; Cermak et al., 1985).

All these kinds of priming, preserved in amnesics, and described so far, are compatible with the view that priming involves a 'hot-tubes' effect in which encountering certain items activates well-established perceptual and semantic representations which continue to glow for at least two hours, thus facilitating or biasing the way those items are processed. Recent evidence suggests, however, that there may also be kinds of priming, preserved in amnesics, that must involve setting up new associations between items. First, Johnson, Kim and Risse (1985) have shown that amnesics and controls show an equivalent enhancement in preference for recently heard Korean melodies (previously totally unfamiliar) despite the amnesics' poor recognition of the tunes. Second, Graf and Schacter (1985) presented amnesics and controls with unrelated word pairs (for example 'house–sheep') using an incidental learning task, and then asked for 'word completion' responses either in the context of the same stimulus words (for example 'house–she') or in the context of a different stimulus word (for example 'town–she'). Both groups performed equally well and did better when tested in context.

In a similar way, Moscovitch (1984) has shown that amnesics speed up their reading of lists of unrelated word pairs as much as their controls and this effect is not due simply to reading the individual words faster. Priming may therefore involve more than one memory system. Thus, it may comprise a way of storing new, as well as activating old, perceptual and semantic representations. The evidence suggests either that this memory system is quite independent of the conscious recollection memory system, impaired in amnesics, or that it contributes to the recollection memory system, which also requires other processes to operate, one or more of which is impaired in amnesics.

If priming does contribute to a recognition memory system impaired in amnesics, what is likely to be deficient in amnesics? There are two obvious differences between showing normal priming and recognition or recall of particular items that suggest an answer. The former involves effortless or automatic retrieval whereas the latter may require effortful retrieval, and, secondly, the former involves context-free retrieval of target items whereas the latter can only succeed if items are retrieved *as belonging in a given spatiotemporal or background context*. These two differences may be related because the need to retrieve an item's background context may require the expenditure of effort. One of the most popular explanations of amnesia has, in fact, been that it arises from a selective failure of the ability to remember the kinds of background contextual information that are normally encoded incidentally with minimal attentional effort (Hirst, 1982). This hypothesis presupposes that classical conditioning, skill memory and priming do not depend on this kind of remembering, but that recognition and recall of target material is critically dependent on the initial retrieval of background contextual features. Furthermore, it postulates that acquisition of episodic *and* semantic memories requires the storage and retrieval of background context.

One expectation of the hypothesis is that amnesics should be disproportionately bad at contextual memory. The only convincing way to show this is to match amnesics and their controls on recall or recognition of targets (usually by testing the controls at much longer delays) and see whether their memory for various aspects of context is still worse. In experiments where matches on target memory have been achieved it has been reported that alcoholic amnesics still have worse memory for temporal order (Squire, 1982; Kohl and Brandt, 1985); event frequency (Kohl and Brandt, 1985); the source from which the target information came (Schacter, Harbluk and McLachlan, 1984); the location of items (Kohl and Brandt, 1985) and the sensory modality in which items are presented (Pickering and Mayes, in press). There is also evidence that alcoholic amnesics base their judgements of item recency and frequency on how familiar a memory is rather than on specific contextual tags, unlike controls (Huppert and Piercy, 1978b). It remains to be shown, however, that these deficits are essential to the core memory deficit rather than incidental results of damage to the frontal lobes, which is common in amnesics with a history of chronic alcoholism. For example, the extent to which temporal judgements are bad and the degree of source amnesia in alcoholic amnesics has been reported to correlate with their level of disturbance on tests sensitive to frontal lobe lesions (Squire, 1982; Schacter, Harbluk and McLachlan, 1984). Amnesic context memory should correlate with their target recognition and recall if their context-memory deficit causes their global amnesia.

If the anterograde and retrograde amnesia are caused by the same functional deficit(s), the context-memory deficit hypothesis must also account for the pattern of retrograde amnesia. This is a controversial issue, but there is good evidence that many amnesics are roughly equally impaired in their ability to recall pretraumatically acquired episodic and semantic information that is likely to have been little rehearsed (see Zola-Morgan, Cohen and Squire, 1983). Most studies, using objective measures of datable public information, also support the clinical impressions that older memories are usually spared in amnesics (Cohen and Squire, 1981). One way the hypothesis might accommodate these data is by proposing that as memories age, they are recognized through periodic rehearsals, so that their retrieval ceases to depend on initially accessing contextual cues, regardless of whether these memories are nominally episodic or semantic. This *ad hoc* proposal needs to be tested, but is compatible with the view that the critical brain damage in amnesics selectively impairs the ability to encode, store and retrieve background contextual features.

To summarize our current knowledge of organic amnesia, it must be said that there is uncertainty about whether the disorder is unitary and also about the precise locations of the critical lesions which cause it. On the basis of what is known about patterns of memory apparent in anterograde and, to a less extent, retrograde amnesia, the suggestion that the deficit arises from a selective failure of memory for background contextual information has become popular. Other explanations should, however, be considered. For example, Warrington and Weiskrantz (1982) proposed that amnesia is caused by a specific failure to store and/or retrieve elaborated semantic information of the kind which is processed by the frontal lobes. Although there is evidence that amnesic memory benefits as much as normal memory from the encoding of elaborated semantic information (Meudell, Mayes and Neary, 1980) and also that frontal lobe lesions do not cause severe amnesia, this interesting hypothesis deserves further investigation. Knowledge of hippocampal anatomy and physiology also suggests a third hypothesis according to which amnesics cannot store or retrieve and may be not even encode an integrated or associated representation of complex information unless that representation has been very well-established pretraumatically. Thus, episodic encounters with previously well-integrated words would not be remembered because amnesics cannot store word–context associations, and similarly, new facts are forgotten because amnesics cannot store the links between the components of the facts. This hypothesis clearly has some conceptual links with the other two.

CONCLUSIONS

Very little is known about the fifth group of disorders, described in the introduction, although Martone et al. (1984) have reported that patients with Huntington's chorea showed normal verbal recognition, but were very poor at learning how to read mirror-reversed words. This is interesting because these patients suffer from caudate nucleus atrophy and Mishkin and Petri (1984) have argued that habits (equivalent to skills) are stored in a cortico-striatal system that includes the caudate. The effect of striatal lesions on skill acquisition and memory requires more research.

The picture that emerges from the evidence about these five groups of memory disorders is that the brain comprises many modules, which process particular kinds of information in particular ways. In some cases, these modules may also store the processed information. So, in the neocortex, there will be modules that store particular kinds of semantic and episodic information for long periods. Activation of these modules enables new inputs to be interpreted, although elaborating the meaning of the input will also involve frontal cortex modules that coordinate activity in the more posterior complex memory modules. There may also be auxiliary modules that keep the 'mainstream' modules active for a brief time so that more information can be related. New information will only be remembered if the neocortical storage modules interact with limbic-diencephalic modules that perhaps store contextual or 'integrating' information. Finally, neocortical inputs to the striatum may be integrated with motor outputs so that skills may be developed and stored in striatal processing and storage modules. Future research will either refine this broad picture or show it to be basically flawed.

REFERENCES

Albert, M.S., Butters, N. and Brandt, J. (1981) Patterns of remote memory in amnesic and demented patients. *Archives of Neurology, 38,* 495–500.

Allport, D.A. (1984) Auditory verbal short-term memory and conduction aphasia. In H. Bouma and D.G. Bouwhuis (eds) *Attention and Performance, X.* London: Lawrence Erlbaum.

Andrews, E., Kessler, M. and Poser, E. (1982) Retrograde amnesia for forty years. *Cortex, 18,* 441–458.

Baddeley, A.D. (1983) Working memory. *Philosophical Transactions of the Royal Society, London: Series B, 302,* 311–324.

Bauer, R.M. (1984) Autonomic recognition of names and faces in prosopagnosia: Neuropsychological application of the guilty knowledge test. *Neuropsychologia, 22,* 457–469.

Cermak, L.S., Talbot, N., Chandler, K. and Wolbarst, L.R. (1985) The perceptual priming phenomenon in amnesia. *Neuropsychologia, 23,* 615–622.

Cohen, N.J. (1984) Preserved learning capacity in amnesia: Evidence for multiple memory systems. In L.R. Squire and N. Butters (eds) *Neuropsychology of Memory.* New York: Guilford.

Cohen, N.J. and Squire, L.R. (1980) Preserved learning and retention of pattern-analyzing skill in amnesia: Dissociation of knowing that. *Science, 210,* 207–210.

Cohen, N.J. and Squire, L.R. (1981) Retrograde amnesia and remote memory impairment. *Neuropsychologia, 19,* 337–356.

Corkin, S. (1968) Acquisition of motor skill after bilateral medial temporal-lobe excision. *Neuropsychologia, 6,* 225–265.

Davidoff, J.B. and Ostergaard, A.L. (1984) Colour anomia resulting from weakened short-term memory: A case study. *Brain, 107,* 415–430.

De Renzi, E. (1982) Memory disorders following focal neocortical damage. *Philosophical Transactions of the Royal Society, London: Series B, 298,* 73–83.

De Renzi, E. and Nichelli, P. (1975) Verbal and non-verbal short-term memory impairment following hemispheric damage. *Cortex, 11,* 341–353.

Freed, D.M., Corkin, S. and Cohen, N.J. (1984) Rate of forgetting in H.M.: A reanalysis. *Society for Neuroscience Abstracts, 10,* 383.

Friedrich, F.J., Glenn, C.G. and Marin, O.S.M. (1984) Interruption of phonological coding in conduction aphasia. *Brain and Language, 22,* 288–291.

Goldberg, E., Antin, E. Jr, Bilder, S.P., Gerstman, L.H., Hughes, J.E.O. and Mattis, S. (1984) Retrograde amnesia: Possible role of mesencephalic reticular activation system in long-term memory. *Science, 213,* 1392–1394.

Goodglass, H., Klein, B., Carey, P. and Jones, K. (1966) Specific semantic word categories in aphasia. *Cortex, 2,* 74–89.

Graf, P. and Schacter, D.L. (1985) Implicit and explicit memory for new associations in normal and amnesic subjects. *Journal of Experimental Psychology: Learning, Memory and Cognition, 11,* 501–508.

Graf, P., Squire, L.R. and Mandler, G. (1984) The information that amnesic patients do not forget. *Journal of Experimental Psychology: Learning, Memory and Cognition, 10,* 164–178.

Hart, J., Berndt, R.S. and Caramazza, A. (1985) Category-specific naming deficit following cerebral infarction. *Nature, 316,* 439–440.

Hasher, L. and Zacks, R.T. (1979) Automatic and effortful processes in memory. *Journal of Experimental Psychology: General, 108,* 356–388.

Hécaen, H. and Albert, M.L. (1978) *Human Neuropsychology.* New York: John Wiley.

Hirst, W. (1982) The amnesic syndrome: Descriptions and explanations. *Psychological Bulletin, 9,* 435–460.

Hirst, W. (1985) Use of mnemonic in patients with frontal lobe damage. *Journal of Clinical and Experimental Neuropsychology, 7,* 175.

Hitch, G. (1983) Short-term memory processes in humans and animals. In A.R. Mayes (ed.) *Memory in Animals and Humans.* Wokingham: Van Nostrand.

Huppert, F.A. and Piercy, M. (1978a) Dissociation between learning and remembering in organic amnesia. *Nature, 275,* 317–318.

Huppert, F.A. and Piercy, M. (1978b) The role of trace strength in recency and frequency judgements by amnesic and control subjects. *Quarterly Journal of Experimental Psychology, 30,* 346–354.

Huppert, F.A. and Piercy, M. (1979) Normal and abnormal forgetting in organic amnesia: Effect of locus of lesion. *Cortex, 15,* 385–390.

Jacoby, J.L. and Witherspoon, D. (1982) Remembering without awareness. *Canadian Journal of Psychology, 36,* 300–324.

Johnson, M.K., Kim, J.K. and Risse, G. (1985) Do alcoholic Korsakoff's syndrome patients acquire affective reactions? *Memory and Cognition, 11,* 22–36.

Kinsbourne, M. (1972) Behavioural analysis of the repetition deficit in conduction aphasia. *Neurology, 22,* 1126–1132.

Kohl, D. and Brandt, J. (1985) An automatic encoding deficit in the amnesia of Korsakoff's syndrome. *Annals of the New York Academy of Sciences, 444,* 460–462.

Kopelman, M.D. (1985) Rates of forgetting in Alzheimer-type dementia and Korsakoff's syndrome. *Neuropsychologia, 23,* 623–638.

Lincoln, J.S., McCormick, D.A. and Thompson, R.F. (1982) Ipsilateral cerebellar lesions prevent learning of classically conditioned nictitating membrane/ eyelid responses. *Brain Research, 242,* 190–193.

Luria, A.R. (1973) *The Working Brain.* Harmondsworth: Penguin.

McCarthy, R. and Warrington, E.K. (1985) Category specificity in an agrammatic patient: The relative impairment of verb retrieval and comprehension. *Neuropsychologia, 23,* 709–728.

Martone, M., Butters, N., Payne, M., Becker, J.T. and Sax, D.S. (1984) Dissociations between skill learning and verbal recognition in amnesia and dementia. *Archives of Neurology, 41,* 965–970.

Mayes, A.R. and Meudell, P. (1981) How similar is immediate memory in amnesic patients to delayed memory in normal subjects? A replication, extension and reassessment of the amnesic cueing effect. *Neuropsychologia, 19,* 647–654.

Mayes, A.R., Meudell, P.R. and Pickering, A. (1985) Is organic amnesia caused by a selective deficit in remembering contextual information? *Cortex, 21,* 167–202.

Meudell, P., Mayes, A.R. and Neary, D. (1980) Orienting task effects on the recognition of humorous pictures in amnesic and normal subjects. *Journal of Clinical Neuropsychology, 2,* 75–88.

Miller, E. (1984) Verbal fluency as a function of a measure of verbal intelligence and in relation to different types of cerebral pathology. *British Journal of Clinical Psychology, 23,* 53–57.

Milner, B. (1971) Interhemispheric differences in the location of psychological processes in man. *British Medical Bulletin, 27,* 272–277.

Mishkin, M. (1982) A memory system in the monkey. *Philosophical Transactions of the Royal Society, 298,* 85–95.

Mishkin, M. (1985) A neural hierarchy of memory: Recognition, recency and recall. Thirteenth Sir Frederick Bartlett Lecture given at the January meeting of the Experimental Psychology Society, University College, London.

Mishkin, M. and Bachevalier, J. (1984) Object recognition impaired by ventromedial but not dorsolateral prefrontal cortical lesions in monkeys. *Society for Neuroscience Abstracts, 10.*

Mishkin, M. and Petri, H.L. (1984) Memories and habits: Some implications for the analysis of learning and retention. In L.R. Squire and N. Butters (eds) *Neuropsychology of Memory.* New York: Guilford.

Moscovitch, M. (1982) Multiple dissociations of functions in amnesia. In L.S. Cermak (ed.) *Human Memory and Amnesia.* Hillsdale, N.J.: Lawrence Erlbaum Associates.

Moscovitch, M. (1984) The sufficient conditions for demonstrating preserved memory in amnesia: A task analysis. In L.R. Squire and N. Butters (eds) *The Neuropsychology of Learning*. New York: Guilford Press.

Petrides. M. and Milner, B. (1982) Deficits in subject-ordered tasks after frontal- and temporal-lobe lesions in man. *Neuropsychologia*, 20, 249–262.

Pickering, A. and Mayes, A.R. (in preparation) Evidence for a disproportionately poor memory for the sensory modality in which items are presented in alcoholic amnesics.

Roland, P.E. (1984) Metabolic measurements of the working frontal cortex in man. *Trends in Neurosciences*, 7, 430–435.

Samuels, I., Butters, N. and Fedio, P. (1972) Short-term memory disorders following temporal lobe removals in humans. *Cortex*, 9, 283–298.

Schacter, D.L. (1985) Priming of old and new knowledge in amnesic patients and normal subjects. *Annals of the New York Academy of Sciences*, 444, 41–53.

Schacter, D.L., Harbluk, J.L. and McLachlan, D.R. (1984) Retrieval without recollection: An experimental analysis of source amnesia. *Journal of Verbal Learning and Verbal Behaviour*, 23, 592–611.

Shallice, T. (1979) Case study approach in neuropsychological research. *Journal of Clinical Neuropsychology*, 1, 183–211.

Shallice, T. (1982) Specific impairments of planning. *Philosophical Transactions of the Royal Society*, 298, 199–209.

Shallice, T. (1986) Impairments of semantic processing: Multiple dissociations. In M. Coltheart, R. Job and G. Sartori (eds) *The Cognitive Neuropsychology of Language*. Hillsdale, N.J.: Lawrence Erlbaum Associates.

Shallice, T. and Warrington, E.K. (1979) Auditory-verbal short-term memory impairment and conduction aphasia. *Brain and Language*, 4, 479–491.

Shimamura, A.P. and Squire, L.R. (1984) Paired-associate learning and priming effects in amnesia: A neuropsychological study. *Journal of Experimental Psychology: General*, 113, 556–570.

Signoret, J.L. Lhermitte, F. (1976) The amnesic syndromes and the encoding process. In M.R. Rosenzweig and E.L. Bennet (eds) *Neural Mechanisms of Learning and Memory*. Cambridge, Mass.: MIT Press.

Smith, M.L. and Milner, B. (1983) Effect of focal brain lesions on sensitivity to frequency of occurrence. *Society for Neuroscience Abstracts*, 9.

Smith, M.L. and Milner, B. (1984) Differential effects of frontal lobe lesions on cognitive estimation and spatial memory. *Neuropsychologia*, 22, 697–705.

Squire, L.R. (1981) Two forms of human amnesia: An analysis of forgetting. *Journal of Neuroscience*, 1, 635–640.

Squire, L.R. (1982) Comparison between forms of amnesia: Some deficits are unique to Korsakoff's syndrome. *Journal of Experimental Psychology: Learning, Memory and Cognition*, 8, 560–571.

Stuss, D.T., Benson, E.F., Weir, W.S., Chiulli, S. and Sarazin, F.F. (1982) Evidence for the involvement of the orbitofrontal cortex in memory functions: An interference effect. *Journal of Comparative and Physiological Psychology*, 96, 913–925.

Syz, H. (1937) Recovery from loss of mnemic retention after head trauma. *Journal of General Psychology*, 17, 355–387.

Talland, G. (1965) *Deranged Memory*. New York: Academic Press.

Tranel, D. and Damasio, A.R. (1985) Knowledge without awareness: An autonomic index of facial recognition. *Science*, 288, 1453–1454.

Tulving, E. (1983) *Elements of Episodic Memory*. Oxford: Oxford University Press.
Tulving, E., Schacter, D. and Startk, H.A. (1982) Priming effects in word-fragment completion are independent of recognition memory. *Journal of Experimental Psychology: Learning, Memory and Cognition*, 8, 352–373.
Vallar, G. and Baddeley, A.D. (1984) Fractionation of working memory: Neuropsychological evidence for a phonological short-term store. *Journal of Verbal Learning and Verbal Behaviour*, 23, 151–161.
Warrington, E.K. (1975) The selective impairment of semantic memory. *Quarterly Journal of Experimental Psychology*, 24, 30–40.
Warrington, E.K. (1981) Concrete word dyslexia. *British Journal of Psychology*, 72, 175–196.
Warrington, E.K. (1982) The fractionation of arithmetical skills: A single case study. *Quarterly Journal of Experimental Psychology*, 34A, 31–52.
Warrington, E.K. (1985) A disconnection analysis of amnesia. *Annals of the New York Academy of Sciences*, 444, 72–77.
Warrington, E.K. (1986) Memory for facts and memory for events. *British Journal of Clinical Psychology*, 25, 1–12.
Warrington, E.K. and McCarthy, R. (1983) Category specific access dysphasia. *Brain*, 106, 859–878.
Warrington, E.K. and Rabin, P. (1971) Visual span of apprehension in patients with unilateral cerebral lesions. *Quarterly Journal of Experimental Psychology*, 23, 423–431.
Warrington, E.K. and Shallice, T. (1984) Category specific semantic impairments. *Brain*, 107, 829–854.
Warrington, E.K. and Weiskrantz, L. (1968) New method of testing long-term retention with special reference to amnesic patients. *Nature*, 217, 972–974.
Warrington, E.K. and Weiskrantz, L. (1974) The effect of prior learning on subsequent retention in amnesic patients. *Neuropsychologia*, 419, 419–428.
Warrington, E.K. and Weiskrantz, L. (1978) Further analysis of the prior learning effect in amnesic patients. *Neuropsychologia*, 16, 169–177.
Warrington, E.K. and Weiskrantz, L. (1982) A disconnection syndrome? *Neuropsychologia*, 20, 233–248.
Weiskrantz, L. and Warrington, E.K. (1979) Conditioning in amnesic patients. *Neuropsychologia*, 17, 187–194.
Wood, F., Ebert, V. and Kinsbourne, M. (1982) The episodic–semantic memory distinction in memory and amnesia: Clinical and experimental observations. In L.S. Cermak (ed.) *Human Memory and Amnesia*. Hillsdale, N.J.: Lawrence Erlbaum Associates.
Zola-Morgan, S., Cohen, N.J. and Squire, L.R. (1983) Recall of remote episodic memory in amnesia. *Neuropsychologia*, 21, 487–500.
Zola-Morgan, S., Squire, L.R. and Amaral, D.G. (1985) Human amnesia and the medial temporal region: Memory impairment following a bilateral lesion to the CAI field of the hippocampus. *Society for Neuroscience Abstracts*, 11(459).

THE CONCEPTS OF SOCIOBIOLOGY
John Lazarus

Our understanding of how the social behaviour of animals evolves has increased immeasurably over the last two decades as a result of important new concepts and theories. These new ideas form the foundations of sociobiology, which can be defined as the study of the functions and evolution of social behaviour.

My intention in this chapter is to describe the major evolutionary problems posed by social behaviour and to show how these new ideas have helped to solve them. General principles are dealt with first and are followed by the particular problems raised by different forms of social behaviour. I shall not say much about the evidence that relates to these problems but instead point the reader to other sources for this. My reason for concentrating on theory to the neglect of data is the belief that the concepts and theories of sociobiology are often subtle and easily misunderstood, and that their comprehension should be the first task for those new to the subject. I must also confess a certain missionary zeal; I find these ideas both elegant and intellectually challenging and hope to persuade you to a similar view.

The sociobiology of human behaviour is a sub-discipline of the subject with its own concepts and problems. It is the subject of a chapter in a recent *Psychology Survey* (Smith, 1983) and will not be dealt with here.

FOUNDATION PRINCIPLES

Natural selection

Darwin's (1859) theory of natural selection (Figure 1) forms the starting point for all further theorizing. It provides a mechanism for evolutionary change that leads us to predict that behaviour will be adaptive – that it will increase *fitness*. An individual's fitness is a measure of the number

The Concepts of Sociobiology / 193

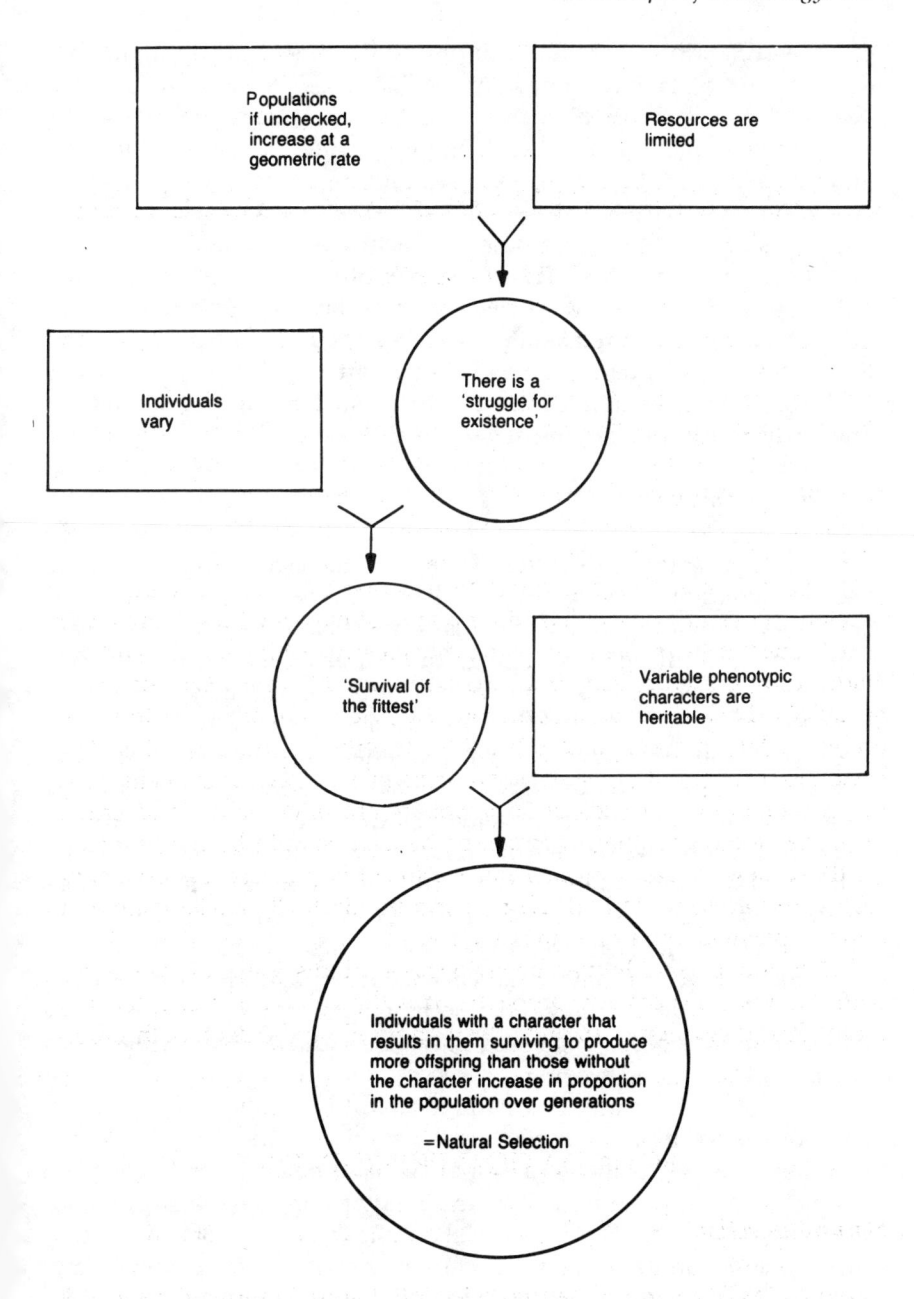

Figure 1. The structure of Darwin's theory of natural selection. Observations known to Darwin are shown in rectangles and Darwin's inferences in circles (see Flew, 1959).

of viable offspring it produces during its lifetime and, by definition, natural selection favours behaviour that increases fitness, or *reproductive success*. The task of sociobiology is to discover how social behaviour has been moulded by natural selection in the past and how it is maintained in its present form by present-day selection pressures. A *selection pressure* is simply a particular action of natural selection – a feature of the environment that influences fitness by acting on particular features of the phenotype. Predators, for example, represent a selection pressure on the behaviour of prey species that may favour cryptic behaviour, distraction displays or retaliation in the face of attack. The predators and food of a species represent the most important selection pressures on its social behaviour; escaping from the first and locating the second are obviously crucial to any animal's survival.

Genetic determinism?

It is a mistake sometimes made to imagine that sociobiological theories necessarily assume a very simple relationship between genotype and behaviour, in which a single gene is responsible for a complex behaviour, such as altruistic food sharing, for example. There are actually two possible confusions here. First, a behaviour pattern may well be influenced by many genes; all that the sociobiologist needs to assume is that a mutation in one or more of these genes will influence behaviour. Interest then centres on the *difference* in behaviour between individuals with and without the mutation and the difference in fitness that results (Dawkins, 1979). In fact, when we say that natural selection favours genes that increase fitness this is actually a shorthand for the more correct statement that natural selection favours a gene that results in *greater* fitness for its bearer than alternative genes at the same locus (that is position) on the chromosome. Given this exclusive interest in *differences* in behaviour we need know nothing about the way in which the information in genes is expressed in the individual, which brings us to the second misunderstanding.

For a behaviour pattern to be amenable to evolutionary enquiry it must obviously be influenced by the genotype. This does not mean, however, that sociobiology assumes 'genetic determinism', the view that behaviour is 'determined' by the genotype and resistant to modification by experience. This is a view about the *development* of behaviour in the individual and not about the causes of evolutionary change (Bateson, 1982). Behaviour moulded by natural selection may develop in a variety of ways within the individual, some very resistant to environmental influence and some not. To take one example, the choice of a suitable mate in terms of species and sex is a highly adaptive ability moulded by natural selection; in birds it is very sensitive to early experience but in insects the opposite is the case.

Adaptation, optimization and modelling

One of the major advances of the subject has been the development of theoretical models that go beyond proposing *how* selection pressures are acting, to predict precise quantitative values for behaviour (Krebs and McCleery, 1984). Such models test the hypothesis that natural selection has, given certain assumptions, produced the best possible solution to some behavioural problem; that is, the solution that produces the greatest increase in fitness. In practice, fitness can be difficult to measure, so that many models predict a solution that maximizes some other criterion that *can* be measured and that is assumed to be maximized when fitness is maximized. For example, a model may predict how long a male insect will copulate with a female on the assumption that he is selected to maximize the number of eggs fertilized in a given period. The model would have to balance the cost to the male of lost mating opportunities with new females while he is copulating, against the advantage of fertilizing more eggs the longer he copulates with the present female. Parker (1978) has developed just such a model for the dung fly, *Scatophaga stercoraria*, and found quite a good agreement between predicted (41.4 min) and observed (35.5 min) copulation time, which supports the hypothesis that natural selection has optimized copulation time in this species. Note that the quantity assumed to be maximized in this model is not *lifetime* reproductive success (that is fitness) but fertilization rate during some short period, and that the two quantities may not be optimized by the same behavioural option. This is because the short-term measure ignores costs borne later, which *will* influence the lifetime optimal value. For example, copulation may expose a male to injury by competitors or predators, which reduces its chances of future copulations.

What would we have concluded if the data had *not* fitted the prediction? We could infer either that male copulation time is not optimized or that one or more of the assumptions of the model are incorrect. If the latter were thought to be the case then different assumptions might be sought. Sociobiologists have been criticized for being all too ready to alter their models rather than accept the conclusion that behaviour might not be optimally designed, or even adaptive (Gould and Lewontin, 1979), and there is some truth in this claim. However, the problem of when to modify a model or hypothesis and when to throw it overboard, is not unique to sociobiology; it is a problem for the progress of all sciences.

Suppose we concluded that male copulation time was not optimal. How damaging would that be for the more general belief in the adaptiveness of behaviour that underpins sociobiology? First, it might be the case that optimality in copulation had been sacrificed in order to accommodate a competing demand, such as hiding from predators. This would mean that the wrong criterion for optimality had been chosen, since it might be the *joint* allocation of time devoted to copulation and hiding that had been the focus of selection. This example raises the general point that behavioural decisions have both benefits and costs in terms of fitness and that consequently we should not expect a single outcome of behaviour to determine its response to natural selection. We expect, instead, that natural selection will tend to *maximize the net benefit of behaviour*; that is the sum of all benefits minus all costs. If either the benefits of the behaviour increase, or its costs diminish, then the optimal level of investment in the behaviour – in terms of time, for example – increases (Figure 2).

Second, there might be some *constraint* which prevents an optimal solution being reached. In the present example it might be a constraint on the ability of the nervous system to tune behaviour as finely as required for the optimal solution, or on the ability of the male to control the behaviour of the female. Lastly, the behaviour might be suboptimal even though there are no constraints or competing demands. Environmental factors influencing the optimum might have changed too recently or be fluctuating too fast to have been tracked by selection, for example, or genes deleterious to the behaviour in question might have escaped the action of natural selection by chance.

None of these possibilities constitutes a serious threat to the theory of natural selection, although those in the previous paragraph show the weakness of the extreme view that *all* behaviour is adaptive. This discussion shows, also, that optimization is not a *necessary* consequence of the theory of natural selection; Darwin (1859) himself was clear on that point. The merit of optimization models, however, is that they provide precise and testable predictions and a sensible starting point for the investigation of adaptation. Where they fail, a study of the possibilities outlined above leads to a fuller understanding. Quite often, however, such models are vindicated by the data; often enough for us to realize now that animals have a quite astonishing ability – either through innate mechanisms or by flexible learning programmes – to achieve optimal solutions to complex problems.

Evolutionary stability

The optimal value for, say, the time to be devoted to grooming by a

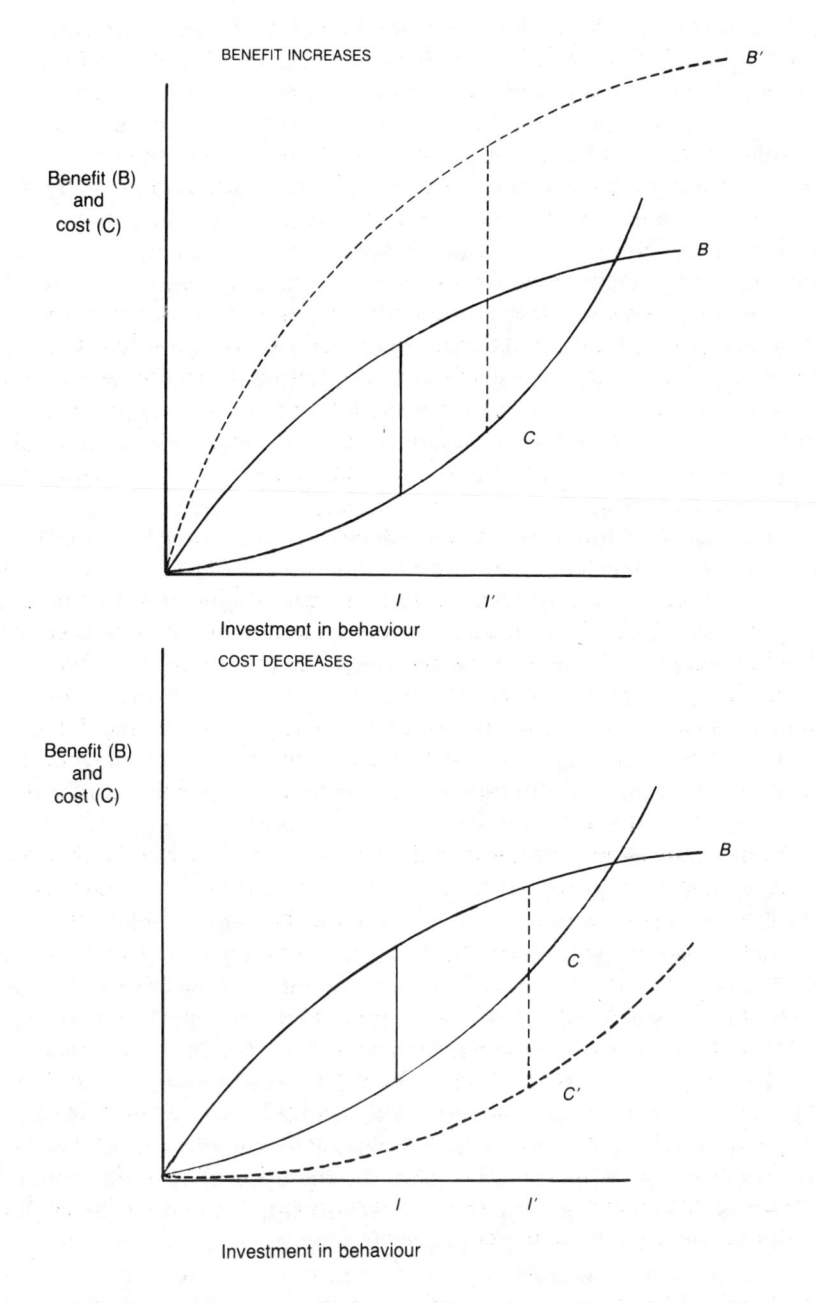

Figure 2. The optimal level of investment in behaviour is the point *I*, at which the net benefit (= benefit − cost) of the investment is greatest. This optimal level increases (to *I'*) if either the benefit increases (from *B* to *B'*) or the cost decreases (from *C* to *C'*).

mouse will be influenced by many factors, but it is unlikely to be affected by the grooming times of others in the population. There will be some optimal value and we expect grooming time to approximate that value, taking into account constraints and trade-offs with other adaptations. *Social* behaviour, however, is different in a crucially important way. The fitness consequences of a social action depend on the response to that action by others, and its fate under natural selection will therefore depend upon the relative frequency with which it meets with different responses. Selection is then said to be *frequency-dependent*. Imagine, for example, two methods, or 'strategies', for competition over a resource. The first is to fight for it viciously, the second to threaten the opponent but to withdraw if things get nasty. If most of the population threaten, a rare fighter will do very well, since it will beat every threatener it meets, and most of its opponents will be threateners. Natural selection therefore favours fighters and they increase in frequency. As they do so, however, they meet each other more often as opponents and now lose some encounters, often sustaining injury. The success of fighting therefore depends crucially on its frequency in the population.

The important evolutionary question now centres on the eventual fate of fighters and threateners. Will fighters take over the entire population or will they wipe each other out, leaving only the more peaceful threateners? Could both strategies coexist in the population at stable frequencies, or might the evolutionary outcome be an endless cycle of fluctuating frequencies? More generally, we wish to know if there is a *stable* outcome to the evolutionary history of some social action and, if so, what it will be. In fact we can now see that stability is a more important concept for social evolution than optimality (Dawkins, 1980; Parker, 1984), an insight that we owe to the work of Maynard Smith (1982). If, in our example, fighters became fixed in the population (that is all individuals were fighters) and threateners could not get a foothold in such a population, then fighting would be both optimal and stable. But suppose the stable outcome were a mix of the two strategies; what is optimal in the stable population? There is now no single best strategy; both are equally optimal, since they both promote fitness equally. If they did not, the mix would not be stable. And what is optimal *before* the population reaches stability? In an unstable population either strategy can give greater fitness and therefore be the optimal one of the two; it depends on the strategy frequencies at the time. Moreover, the fitness achieved by the strategy or strategies in the stable state is unlikely to be as great as that attainable at some unstable frequencies. So, it is *stable* behavioural strategies that natural selection is expected to produce, and not necessarily optimal ones.

Maynard Smith (1972, 1976a) developed these ideas first in the context of competitive behaviour, as illustrated in the previous example, and coined the term *evolutionarily stable strategy* (ESS) for the strategy observed in the stable state. The concept of evolutionary stability is now seen to be fundamental to an understanding of the evolution of social behaviour, as becomes apparent later in this chapter. It is arguably the most important contribution to the study of behavioural evolution since Darwin's theory of natural selection.

Finally, a word about 'strategies'. A strategy is simply a behavioural option, something an animal does. It implies nothing about the mechanism responsible for the action and nothing about the cognitive powers of the species concerned. In fact sociobiologists have only recently begun to investigate the cues and 'rules of thumb' that animals actually seem to use in solving some of their more complex everyday problems (Krebs and McCleery, 1984; Shettleworth, 1984).

THE PROBLEMS OF SOCIAL BEHAVIOUR

A useful way to classify social behaviour from an evolutionary point of view is in terms of the costs and benefits to the fitness of the interactors (Hamilton, 1964). Figure 3 illustrates the four possible outcomes defined in this way. The terms used are familiar in the context of human motivation, but in sociobiology they are defined solely in terms of the *consequences* of action for fitness; they imply nothing about motives or emotions.

Although this classification might encompass all forms of social behaviour, sexual behaviour and parental care raise special evolutionary problems and so require separate treatment. In discussing the different

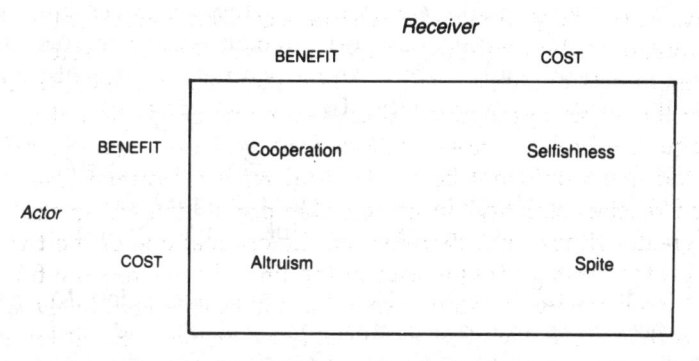

	Receiver	
	BENEFIT	COST
Actor BENEFIT	Cooperation	Selfishness
Actor COST	Altruism	Spite

Figure 3. Four categories of social behaviour defined in terms of the consequence for fitness to actor and receiver. Benefit = increment in fitness; cost = decrement in fitness.

forms of social behaviour I shall concentrate on the general evolutionary problems that they raise. How can we explain the existence of cooperation and altruism, for example, and why do the sexual strategies of males and females differ?

Selfishness: Why don't animals fight more fiercely?

Since natural selection is based on the existence of competition between individuals, the evolution of selfishness is not difficult to understand. In fact, selfish behaviour is generally synonymous with competition; a struggle for a resource at the expense of the loser. The problem is not to understand why animals are competitive but why they are not more so; why aggressive disputes are not more injurious and why they often involve display without physical contact between the opponents. The large carnivores, for example, refrain from attacking each other in the way they treat their prey; deer use their antlers for pushing but rarely for piercing; rattlesnakes wrestle but do not bite. The answer has already been hinted at in my discussion of evolutionary stability. It is, briefly, that hawkish tactics of all-out attack are often unstable, as Maynard Smith (1972, 1976a; Maynard Smith and Price, 1973) demonstrated. The essence of the argument, and of the method employed, can be appreciated by considering the very simplest of his models.

Imagine two strategies for competition, 'Hawk' and 'Dove' (Maynard Smith, 1976a) – like the fighter and threatener previously mentioned – which involve three tactics: display, escalate (with a risk of injury) and retreat. A Hawk always escalates a fight until either it is injured, and loses, or its opponent retreats. A Dove displays but if its opponent escalates it retreats before getting injured. We assume that when two Hawks meet each is equally likely to win and that winning the resource increases fitness by an amount V, whereas injury reduces it by W. Similarly, when two Doves compete each is equally likely to win, but only after a period of display which costs them both T units of fitness due to the time and energy involved. To summarize:

V (for Value) = increase in fitness for winning the resource
W (for Wound) = decrease in fitness due to injury
T (for Time) = decrease in fitness due to time spent displaying.

To analyse the evolutionary outcome for such strategies, Maynard Smith employed the methods of game theory, which already had a long history of application to human social interaction (Colman, 1982). The average change in fitness (or 'payoff') to Hawk and Dove of fighting each type of opponent is cast in a *payoff matrix* as shown in Figure 4. For example, when a Hawk meets another Hawk it wins (payoff = V) and loses (payoff = $-W$) with equal probability, giving a mean payoff of $\frac{1}{2}(V - W)$. Similarly, when a Dove meets another Dove it is equally likely to win $(V - T)$ and lose $(-T)$, resulting in a mean payoff of $\frac{1}{2}V - T$. We now ask whether there is a stable evolutinary outcome to this situation; in particular we seek an evolutionarily stable strategy, or ESS, which, if adopted by most members of a population, does not allow any other strategy (from the specified set of strategies) to spread through the population against it.

The solution depends on the relative magnitude of V and W. If $W < V$ (that is the cost of injury is outweighed by the benefit of winning) then Hawk is an ESS, since Hawks gain more when fighting Hawks than Doves do ($\frac{1}{2}(V - W) > 0$), and also gain more against Doves than Doves do against each other ($V > \frac{1}{2}V - T$). This means that Hawks will spread through the population to fixation and that Doves would not be able to spread in a population of Hawks. When a single strategy fixates in the population in this way it is termed a *pure ESS*. If $W > V$, so that the benefit of victory does *not* outweigh the cost of injury, then Hawks will successfully invade a population of Doves (since $V > \frac{1}{2}V - T$, as before) but now Doves will spread through a population of Hawks (since $0 > \frac{1}{2}(V - W)$). This means that the stable outcome is a mixture of Hawks and Doves in the population – a *mixed ESS* – with the two strategies gaining equal payoff. The stable frequencies of Hawk and Dove are maintained because an increase in either is accompanied by a decrease in its average payoff, which returns it to the stable frequency.

This very simple model shows that all-out attack is not necessarily expected to evolve, because of the injuries sustained when most individuals are hawkish. Since this pioneering development more complex models have been developed, incorporating aspects of real-life encounters. They demonstrate the evolutionary stability of more subtle non-hawkish tactics and are well supported by the evidence from empirical studies (Lazarus, 1982).

	When competing against:	
	HAWK	DOVE
Payoff to: HAWK	$\frac{1}{2}(V - W)$	V
Payoff to: DOVE	0	$\frac{1}{2}V - T$

Figure 4. Payoff matrix for competition between Hawks and Doves.

Cooperation: Why should animals benefit others?

If natural selection is based on competition, why should an individual behave so as to increase the fitness of another, even if it benefits in the process itself? It is not difficult to think of cases where cooperation seems obviously adaptive. Wolves hunting together in a coordinated pack, for example, can bring down a large animal like a moose, a task almost impossible for a single animal. However, a more subtle problem remains. Why don't animals that receive the fruits of cooperation without reciprocating replace those that give as well as receive? In other words, it is difficult at first sight to see how cooperative behaviour could be *stable*. If it did arise it should quickly be replaced by a more selfish alternative.

Axelrod and Hamilton (1981) have analysed this problem and their answer shows once more the importance of ESS thinking. They point out that if individuals meet only once, then cooperation will be less successful than a more selfish strategy which 'defects' on the system of cooperation. However, if individuals encounter each other repeatedly and can modify their behaviour as a function of past experience, then more subtle strategies can develop in which defectors can be penalized. Axelrod solicited strategies of this type from a number of social scientists and biologists and pitted them against each other using game theory methods. He found that the simplest strategy submitted, *Tit for Tat*, was a pure ESS in competition against all others, provided that the probability of individuals meeting again was high enough. *Tit for Tat* cooperates on the first encounter and then does whatever its opponent did on the previous encounter. It is therefore a strategy of cooperation based on reciprocity. Its success is dependent on three factors: it retaliates, by defecting in response to defection by the opponent; it is forgiving if a defector cooperates in the next encounter; and it is never the first to defect.

Although *Tit for Tat* can increase in frequency and become a pure ESS it has difficulty getting started in the first place in a selfish population in which individuals always defect. Axelrod and Hamilton suggest that cooperation might be initiated amongst groups of related individuals (see next section). Then, where relatedness is uncertain, the reciprocation of cooperation provides one clue that the reciprocator is related, because relatives will tend to share heritable behaviour patterns. This provides a selection pressure for being cooperative only to cooperators and selfish to others, which is the *Tit for Tat* strategy. In this way *Tit for Tat* could get a foothold, which is all it needs to spread to fixation.

As already stated, however, *Tit for Tat* is stable only if the probability of two individuals continuing to interact is high, and this, together with the reciprocal nature of the strategy, gives us a strong indication of the contexts in which we would expect to see cooperation in nature. It is not necessary for reciprocation, nor for repeated encounter, that those involved be capable of individual recognition. In interspecific mutualisms, for example, such as that between a hermit crab and the sea anemone it carries around, continuous contact provides the necessary conditions. A second mechanism is the meeting of the interactors at a fixed place, such as the cleaning station at which a cleaner fish removes and eats ectoparasites from a potential predator that even allows the cleaner inside its mouth without eating it. In the stable social groups of some birds and mammals both individual recognition and retaliation are possible and, in many primate societies, the same individuals interact repeatedly for many years. Huntingford (1982) discusses a number of examples of this kind, as well as cases of altruism, which presents evolutionary problems of even greater difficulty.

Altruism: Why should animals sacrifice themselves for others?

The suicidal sting of the honeybee; the sharing of food; the alarm call that attracts the attention of a predator: how can natural selection explain such behaviour when its mechanism is based on selfish competition, the very antithesis of altruism (Figure 3)? There are two major ways in which this might come about, the first of which has much in common with the case of cooperation just discussed.

When individuals interact repeatedly there is the opportunity for altruistic acts to be reciprocated, just as for cooperative acts. After one such act the actor has suffered a cost and the receiver a benefit and, after reciprocation, both have suffered a cost and a benefit. Now, if the benefit outweighs the cost, both individuals will have increased their fitness as a result of the pair of interactions, so that natural selection could potentially favour such acts of *reciprocal altruism* (Trivers, 1971). It will only do so, however, if non-altruists can be distinguished and penalized – by being denied the benefits of altruism in the future, for example. If this is not possible then non-altruists will be favoured in competition with reciprocal altruists, since they will receive altruistic acts but not offer them. The conditions allowing such retaliation against defectors have already been considered in the context of cooperation, with which there is a close correspondence. While *each act* here is altruistic, the *pair of acts* is cooperative; reciprocal altruism is cooperation involving a time delay.

To appreciate the second way in which altruism might evolve we have to abandon the Darwinian notion of the individual as the unit upon which natural selection acts. Whilst selection pressures act directly on the individual's phenotype, the heritable unit responsible for changes in phenotype frequencies over time is the gene. A special property of social behaviour is that it affects the fitness not only of the performer but also of the recipient of the social act. Now, *if the recipient bears the same gene or genes that were responsible for the act in the performer*, the evolutionary fate of the behaviour in question will be determined by its consequences for the fitness of *both* parties, since both bear the relevant genetic material. The behaviour pattern will be favoured by natural selection as long as it results in the genes controlling it having a greater chance of replication into the next generation. This could be the case for any combination of benefit and cost to performer and receiver as long as the summed changes in fitness of the interactors bearing the genes in question is positive. It follows that the unit upon which natural selection acts is, most generally, the gene rather than the individual (Dawkins, 1976, 1982).

When an individual acts selfishly the gene responsible for the selfish act will certainly be favoured, since it must be in the selfish actor. For altruism, however, only the cost is certain; the benefit relies on the beneficiary of the altruism bearing the altruistic gene. So our task is to identify situations in which this will be the case and to determine the conditions in which altruism will be favoured.

The commonest way in which individuals come to share the same genes is by inheriting those genes by recent common descent. A parental gene, for example, has a probability of 0.5 of appearing in any particular offspring, and full siblings have a probability of 0.5 of sharing a gene by common descent from their parents. This probability is termed the *coefficient of relatedness*, r, and the values of r for more distant relatives can be calculated from these two basic values. Now, suppose an altruistic act produces a benefit B to the recipient and a cost C to the actor and is directed to a relative with coefficient of relatedness r. Recall that it is not the benefit to the recipient as an individual that interests us but the benefit to the gene influencing the social act that the recipient might contain. This gene will only be benefitted if the relative contains it and the probability that it does so is r. So, *on average*, the benefit of such acts to the relevant genes in such relatives is equal to Br. For natural selection to favour this social act its benefit must outweigh its cost, so that the condition favouring altruism between relatives can be expressed as:

$$Br > C \qquad (1)$$

or, as it is sometimes written,

$$B/C > 1/r.$$

For altruism between full sibs ($r = 0.5$) to be favoured, for example, the benefit must be greater than twice the cost.

This gene-centred view, and the condition derived from it (1, above) for the evolution of altruism (Hamilton, 1963, 1964), has necessitated a new measure to replace the Darwinian concept of individual fitness. Hamilton (1964) introduced the concept of *inclusive fitness*, which takes into account the effects of social acts directed towards and received from relatives (Grafen, 1984), and Maynard Smith (1964) coined the term *kin selection* to describe the action of natural selection on behavioural interactions between relatives. Since altruism between relatives is common in nature these ideas have thrown light on a great variety of social actions, from parental care to alarm calls (Sherman 1977), and from cooperative breeding in birds (Emlen, 1984) to worker sterility in social insects (Wilson, 1971; Brockmann, 1984).

Although the derivation of condition (1) above has ignored the genetic details of inheritance and relatedness, the same simple condition can be derived from a genetically more realistic foundation (Grafen, 1984). However, genetic considerations do complicate the picture (see, for example, Charlesworth, 1978) and have been the source of a number of misunderstandings (Dawkins, 1979).

If altruism towards kin is to be favoured, animals must be able to distinguish kin from non-kin. As already argued for the case of cooperation, however, this need not require individual recognition. There are many correlates of relatedness that kin selection can employ (Dawkins, 1976). For an avian mother, for example, there is a high probability that the eggs or young in her nest are her own offspring, although it is precisely this fact that is exploited by the cuckoo, and sometimes by conspecifics, who dump their eggs in another's nest. For the mammalian mother it is obviously certain that the infants she gives birth to are her own offspring. For the mates of such females the probability of parentage is lower, since paternity is inherently less certain than maternity. Given the high probability with which a mother can identify her infant, there is a high probability for the infant, in turn, that the female caring for it is its mother. This knowledge will be important if the mother–infant bond is maintained into adulthood and there are opportunities for altruistic acts by the offspring. For nestlings there is a good chance that their nestmates are sibs (or half-sibs), but more mobile infants may require more indirect cues to tell who their sibs are; those being cared for by the same adult that cares for *them* would be a simple criterion. Once relatives can be discriminated in this way, individual recognition allows knowledge of relatedness to be maintained when these simple spatial and behavioural clues are no longer available.

Spite: Can behaviour evolve that benefits no one?

When an individual behaves spitefully it harms itself to harm another even more. Whilst neither party benefits, it is not impossible that natural selection might favour such behaviour, since it is always a *relative* process, selecting those that do better than others. The problem for the evolution of spite, however, is that non-spiteful individuals are also better off than the spited one but without suffering the cost of the spite. The spiteful animal effectively increases the relative fitness of most of its non-spiteful companions above its own in order to reduce the fitness of just one or a few individuals even further. Consequently, when spite is rare the *average* fitness of non-spiteful individuals will exceed that of the spiteful ones, so that it is difficult to see how spiteful behaviour could arise and flourish in a non-spiteful population.

The context in which spite has most often been discussed is that of territoriality. Verner (1977) proposed that individuals would be selected to defend a territory larger than is optimal for their own requirements, in order to reduce the resources available for others. It would be difficult to obtain unequivocal evidence for such a proposal since territories that were larger than optimal in the short term might be optimal in the longer term, when additional resources might be needed. Other territorial functions might also favour a territory larger than is optimal for short-term resource defence (Davies and Houston, 1984). In spite of the general problems already raised, however, theoretical models show that a modest degree of 'superterritoriality' can be an ESS, particularly in small populations (see, for example, Knowlton and Parker, 1979).

Sex and parental care: Why do the sexes differ?

Having completed the social quartet of selfishness, cooperation, altruism and spite, we now move on to consider the evolutionary problems raised by sexual behaviour and parental care. New concepts are necessary here, partly because the interactions involved are asymmetrical in nature. Males and females must cooperate in order to reproduce and yet they differ fundamentally in their evolutionary response to selection pressures acting on the reproductive process. In addition, sexual strategies often involve a great deal more than a single interaction. Sexual partners may remain together to raise offspring, sometimes for more than a single breeding episode, so that long-term strategies of exploitation and cooperation become possible. The parent–offspring relationship also has asymmetrical and long-term properties that require new concepts for their understanding (Trivers, 1974).

An individual can enhance its production of offspring in two ways: by increasing the number of offspring it brings into the world and by improving the survival chances of each offspring. Similarly, an individual's mating strategy can be aimed towards either or both of these same two goals. This simple starting point leads to some very general predictions about mating strategies. Taking each goal in turn, the argument – summarized in Figure 5 – runs as follows:

1. *Increasing offspring numbers.* An individual can achieve this by:
(a) taking more mates, and taking
(b) more fertile mates, that is, mates with more gametes or more viable gametes.

2. *Increasing offspring fitness.* This goal is achieved by taking:
(c) mates that increase the fitness of the offspring produced (by passing on heritable traits of high fitness value, or by providing the offspring with access to resources or with parental care).

These three tactics imply, in turn, two more general sexual strategies:

1. All three imply the possibility of *competition between members of the same sex* for: (a) more mates; (b) more fertile mates; and (c) mates producing fitter offspring. This competition leads to *intrasexual selection;* the evolution of greater competitive ability and weaponry in order to win such contests.

2. The last two imply the potential for *mate choice*: a preference for more fertile mates and mates producing fitter offspring. This, in turn, favours more obvious indicators of these attributes, since they would improve the chances of their bearers being selected as mates. The evolutionary forces responsible for these phenomena are termed *intersexual selection.*

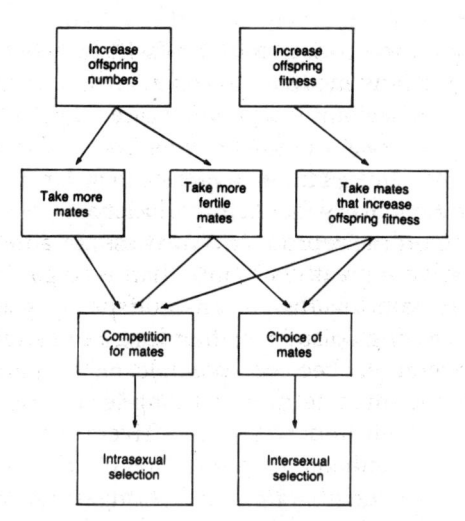

Figure 5. The relationship between strategies for increasing the production of offspring, mating strategies and sexual selection.

As Darwin (1871) realized, sexual competition and mate choice are ubiquitous in nature but do not occur equally in males and females. Although by no means a universal rule, males commonly compete amongst themselves for females, and females exercise a choice between males. Why should these phenomena be so common and why are the sex roles so often arranged in this way?

The reason stems from the fundamental difference between the sexes, which concerns the nature of the gametes they produce. Males produce a large number of very small gametes – sperms – while females produce a far smaller number of much larger, food-rich gametes – eggs. It is this difference which *defines* maleness and femaleness for both plants and animals. The gamete is the first act of *parental investment* (PI) that a parent makes in its offspring, PI being defined as any act by a parent that increases the fitness of its offspring at the cost of the parent's ability to produce other offspring in the future (Trivers, 1972). This definition puts the benefits and costs of parental care in the same currency of offspring numbers.

The sex difference in gamete size means that a male's initial PI in its offspring is less than that of the female. Since an offspring is less costly for a male to produce than for a female, it follows that the optimal total investment in offspring – and therefore the optimal total *number* of offspring – is greater for the male (Trivers, 1972). This was shown earlier for investment in general (Figure 2) and is illustrated for the present case in Figure 6, where the following argument is summarized. A greater number of offspring for the male obviously requires a greater number of matings and this is made possible by the fact that sperm are far more rapidly renewable than eggs. (Even where the cost of the ejaculate necessary to ensure fertilization exceeds that of the egg, as in mammals, the far greater renewability of sperm means that the male's optimal number of offspring still exceeds the female's *realizable* optimum since her rate of gamete production is severely constrained.)

If males were in a sufficient minority in a population they could attain their required number of matings without intermale competition by each monopolizing a number of females. For good evolutionary reasons (Fisher, 1958), however, the sex ratio in animal populations is commonly close to 1:1 so that if males attempt to obtain more matings than females some must inevitably fail. Consequently competition between males occurs, with intrasexual selection favouring greater size, strength and weaponry.

The second phenomenon to be explained, female choice of male partners, also follows directly from the inequality in optimal number of matings between the sexes. If males are selected to mate with more than one female, and the sex ratio is 1:1, then each female will be courted by

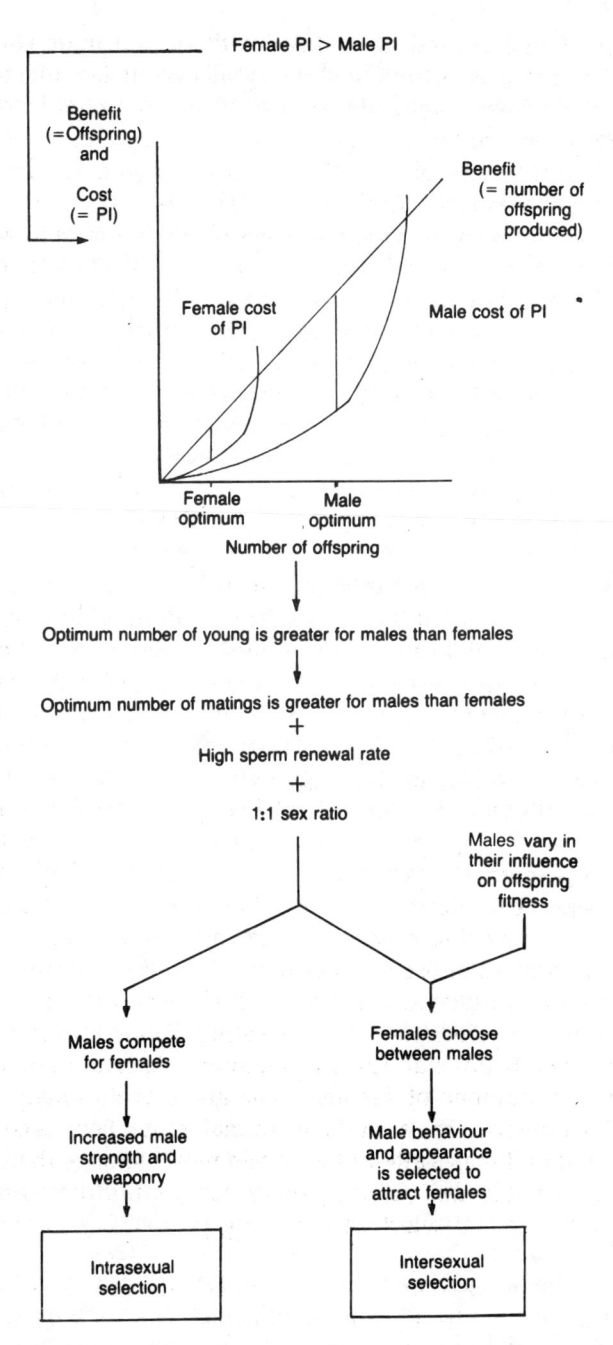

Figure 6. Deriving sexual selection from a sex difference in parental investment (PI). The common case of greater PI by the female is illustrated. The graph is adapted from Trivers, 1972.

more than one male and has the opportunity to choose between them. Natural selection will only favour choosiness, of course, if males differ in ways that affect their mates' fitness, and this they can do in the ways summarized under 2(c).

The importance of the sex difference in gamete size for the action of sexual selection was shown by Bateman (1948), but, as Trivers (1972) pointed out, the argument developed above holds, more properly, for the sex difference in the *total* amount of PI devoted to the young. This means that the relative size of eggs and sperm are not a sufficient predictor of observed sexual strategies, but that later investment must also be taken into account. It turns out, however, that total PI is often greater in females, so that the conclusion based on gamete size difference can stand. But this only raises another question: *why* do females often invest more in their offspring than males?

There are several reasons for this, but the most generally relevant is a result of the gamete size difference itself. The action of natural selection on PI determines whether a parent continues investing at any stage or deserts the young, with the possibility of finding another sexual partner and producing more offspring. If a parent invests only its gamete before deserting, a female will, as for its first offspring, have to invest more in any future offspring than a male. This makes the production of further offspring, following desertion, more costly for a female, and therefore a less favourable option than for a male. In other words an initial greater investment by the female commits her to further investment, and further investment to even more (Dawkins, 1976: Dawkins and Carlisle, 1976).

Where fertilization is internal, as in birds and mammals, there is a further reason for expecting greater PI by the female. In these circumstances the male can desert his mate immediately after copulation, so that if one parent is required to raise the young it will inevitably be the female. In fish, where eggs are generally fertilized in the water, both parents are free to desert and male parental care is far more common (Breder and Rosen, 1966).

A final reason for greater female PI is the slower rate of replenishment of eggs compared to sperm. This means that a deserting female would have to wait longer than a male before she could mate again and might therefore fit fewer mating attempts into a breeding season, in the extreme being able to breed only once each season. In these circumstances desertion would be less beneficial for the female.

Since it is the sex difference in *total* PI that predicts the direction of sexual selection, we should expect species in which the male bears the greater burden of PI to show reversal of sexual roles, with females competing amongst themselves to court the males. This prediction is a strong test of the theory and is broadly supported by the evidence. In the phalaropes (small wading birds), for example, males incubate the eggs and care for the young, while females – which have the brighter plumage – compete for, and court, the males.

To summarize the conclusions of this section, we expect to find in nature a correspondence between parental investment and sexual behaviour such that the sex investing less in the offspring will compete for mates and the sex investing more will exercise mate choice. We also predict that the female will often be the sex investing more. These predictions fit the facts well and illustrate the interdependence between mating strategies and parental care. However, we are left with the problem of understanding the great variety of parental care patterns observed in nature. In particular, why do males sometimes play an equal or major part in parental care?

In order to explain why *some* species act in a particular way, very general evolutionary principles will clearly not suffice. There must be something about the species' biology, ecology or evolutionary history that imposes *particular* demands or constraints on its behaviour. Nevertheless, we can still seek general rules for understanding how these particular demands will act. In the present case we need to understand the selection pressures favouring PI on the one hand and desertion on the other. One general rule that can be stated is that the demands of PI will be strongly determined by the requirements of the young. For birds that feed their young in the nest, for example, two parents will be able to raise about twice as many young as one, and this may be a sufficient explanation for the common occurrence of monogamy in such birds, with both parents caring for the young until they fledge (Lack, 1968). In this case a male may produce more offspring in a season in a monogamous relationship than by attempting to fertilize a number of females but assisting none of them. In mammals, on the other hand, in which female lactation largely frees the male from parental duties, monogamy is rare and males are commonly polygynous or mate promiscuously and provide no PI at all.

This kind of cost-benefit analysis does not provide the whole answer, however. Male strategies of PI may be constrained as a result of female choice. If females reject the advances of a male who is obviously already mated, because of the disadvantage of sharing his parental duties with another female, then monogamy may be imposed on the male population. However, a female may accept an already mated male if he can offer her offspring better resources – such as a territory containing food – than an unmated male, and there is now evidence that female birds make such judgements (Orians, 1969; Pleszczynska, 1978; Vehrencamp and Bradbury, 1984). Of course, a female cannot prevent her mate from deserting but, if females are available synchronously, or if they are widely spaced in the habitat, then the deserting male may find no new mates available. The general point here is that environmental factors can have a profound influence on sexual and parental behaviour; the distribution of food, for example, will influence the distribution of females which, in turn, might constrain the male's power to monopolize sexual access to a number of females (Emlen and Oring, 1977).

The existence of this kind of interaction between male and female shows that an ESS (evolutionary stability) type of analysis is required for a full understanding of the evolution of sexual and parental behaviour, since the success of one strategy depends on what other strategies exist in the population. In fact, the evolution of sexual and parental strategies represents one of the most complex problems in sociobiology, since the success of a strategy depends not only on the strategies of other members of the same sex but also on those of the opposite sex. What we are seeking is a stable set of male strategies that can coexist in stable equilibrium with a stable set of female strategies. For example, males that helped with parental care would produce more offspring than deserting males if females rejected the latter, but might not if they agreed to copulate with any male that courted them. The success of such male and female strategies will also depend on the frequencies of all strategies in the population. Some headway has been made with these problems (Dawkins, 1976; Maynard Smith, 1977; Rubenstein, 1980) but we are still some way from a full understanding.

SOCIAL ORGANIZATION

Although the evolutionary principles described here have brought order to the great diversity of social behaviour patterns seen in nature, there is also another level of phenomena to be understood. Social interactions between individuals result in *patterns of relationships*, which may not be fully explicable at the level of dyadic interactions. For example, repeated aggressive encounters between the same set of individuals generally result in a consistent set of dominance relationships which, in turn, form a *dominance hierarchy*. Individuals in such a hierarchy dominate all or most of those below them and this pattern is not always explicable solely in terms of the concepts described here for the analysis of competition (Lazarus, 1982).

Another pattern resulting from individual social actions concerns the *spatial* relationships between individuals. At one extreme, individuals form close-knit, long-term groups and at the other live solitarily, their only claim to the label 'social' being occasional interactions with members of the opposite sex in order to mate. The existence of animal groups, such as fish schools and bird flocks, raises questions about the costs and benefits of gregariousness and the optimal and stable size of such groups (Bertram, 1978; Sibly, 1983; Pulliam and Caraco, 1984).

These and many other features make up the *social organization* or *social system* of a population. Although the list of such features in Table 1 shows that social organization is a multidimensional concept, animal societies are most often characterized by their dispersion pattern (for example, gregarious or territorial) and mating system (see Crook, Ellis and Goss-Custard, 1976, on mammals, for example).

It is important not to be misled by the existence of such group phenomena into believing that there must be evolutionary forces acting directly at the group level. Group phenomena are the consequence of individual actions moulded by selection pressures acting on individuals. There are in any case severe problems with the notion of the group as a unit on which natural selection acts (Maynard Smith, 1976b; Grafen, 1984).

Table 1. Features of social organization (some general references are given)

---

1. Group dispersion
    - random, regular or clumped distribution of individuals
    - size of home range
    - exclusivity of range from other groups
    - defence of range (= territoriality)? (Davies and Houston, 1984)
2. Group size (Bertram, 1978; Pulliam and Caraco, 1984)
3. Group composition
    - number of group types
    - sex and age structure
    - differentiation of behavioural roles (Wilson, 1975. chapter 14)
4. Movement patterns
    - movement within group: e.g. nomadic, refuging (i.e. return to central place such as a roost)
    - natal dispersal
    - movement between groups: voluntary or forced? sex difference?
    - migration patterns
5. Mating and parental care
    - mating system: monogamy, polygyny, polyandry, promiscuity (Vehrencamp and Bradbury, 1984)
    - duration of male–female bonds
    - parental care by male, female, neither or both
    - duration of parental care
    - life history features: e.g. age of first breeding; frequency of breeding; clutch/litter size
6. Changes in social organization over time
    - changes between breeding and non-breeding seasons
    - growth and division of groups

FURTHER READING

The best introduction to sociobiology is Richard Dawkins' (1976) *The Selfish Gene*. I'll stick my neck out and say that if you don't enjoy it then sociobiology is probably not for you. Krebs and Davies (1981) have written an excellent introduction to this area and have edited two books (Krebs and Davies 1978, 1984) which go deeper into various aspects of the subject. Their 1981 book describes the methods used by sociobiologists to test their hypotheses, an issue not dealt with here. Wilson (1975) and Wittenberger (1981) provide more detailed texts, Wilson's being an important early synthesis of theory and data, and particularly useful for its coverage of related issues in population biology and genetics. The importance of Maynard Smith's ESS concept can be appreciated by reading his own book on the subject (Maynard Smith, 1982) or the article by Dawkins (1980). Finally, Krebs and Dawkins (1984) examine animal communication in sociobiological terms.

There are excellent and extensive field studies on individual species, which show how many of the principles described here interact in nature in particular cases. Clutton-Brock, Guinness and Albon (1982) describe a long-term study of the red deer, *Cervus elaphus*, and, in a series of papers, Davies (Davies, 1983, 1985, 1986; Davies and Houston, 1986; Davies and Lundberg, 1984, 1985; Houston and Davies, 1985) uncovers the extraordinary sex life of the hedge sparrow, *Prunella modularis*.

ACKNOWLEDGEMENTS

My thanks to Helen Frankenberg, Peter Garson, Sue Larminie and Dennis Lendrem for their critical reading of this chapter.

REFERENCES

Axelrod, R. and Hamilton. W.D. (1981) The evolution of cooperation. *Science*, 211, 1390–1396.
Bateman, A.J. (1948) Intra-sexual selection in *Drosophila*. *Heredity*, 2, 349–368.
Bateson, P.P.G. (1982) Behavioural development and evolutionary processes. In King's College Sociobiology Group (eds) *Current Problems in Sociobiology*. Cambridge: Cambridge University Press.
Bertram, B.C.R. (1978) Living in groups: Predators and prey. In J.R. Krebs and N.B. Davies (eds) *Behavioural Ecology: An Evolutionary Approach*. Oxford: Basil Blackwell.
Breder, C.M. Jr and Rosen, D.E. (1966) *Modes of Reproduction in Fishes*. Neptune City, New Jersey: T.F.H. Publications.

Brockmann, H.J. (1984) The evolution of social behaviour in insects. In J.R. Krebs and N.B. Davies (eds) *Behavioural Ecology: An Evolutionary Approach*, 2nd ed. Oxford: Basil Blackwell.
Charlesworth, B. (1978) Some models of the evolution of altruistic behaviour between siblings. *Journal of Theoretical Biology*, 72, 297–319.
Clutton-Brock, T.H., Guinness, F.E. and Albon, S.D. (1982) *Red Deer: The Behavior and Ecology of Two Sexes*. Chicago: Chicago University Press.
Colman, A.M. (1982) Experimental games. In A.M. Colman (ed.) *Cooperation and Competition in Humans and Animals*. Wokingham: Van Nostrand Reinhold.
Crook, J.H., Ellis J.E. and Goss-Custard, J.D. (1976) Mammalian social systems: Structure and function. *Animal Behaviour*, 24, 261–274.
Darwin, C. (1859) *The Origin of Species by Means of Natural Selection, or the Preservation of Favoured Races in the Struggle for Life*. London: John Murray.
Darwin, C. (1871) *The Descent of Man, and Selection in Relation to Sex*. London: John Murray.
Davies, N.B. (1983) Polyandry, cloaca-pecking and sperm competition in dunnocks. *Nature, London*, 302, 334–336.
Davies, N.B. (1985) Cooperation and conflict among dunnocks, *Prunella modularis*, in a variable mating system. *Animal Behaviour*, 33, 628–648.
Davies, N.B. (1986) Reproductive success of dunnocks, *Prunella modularis*, in a variable mating system. I. Factors influencing provisioning rate, nestling weight and fledging success. *Journal of Animal Ecology*, 55, 123–138.
Davies, N.B. and Houston, A.I. (1984) Territory economics. In J.R. Krebs and N.B. Davies (eds) *Behavioural Ecology: An Evolutionary Approach*, 2nd ed. Oxford: Basil Blackwell.
Davies, N.B. and Houston, A.I. (1986) Reproductive success of dunnocks, *Prunella modularis*, in a variable mating system. II. Conflicts of interest among breeding adults. *Journal of Animal Ecology*, 55, 139–154.
Davies, N.B. and Lundberg, A. (1984) Food distribution and a variable mating system in the dunnock, *Prunella modularis*. *Journal of Animal Ecology*, 53, 895–912.
Davies, N.B. and Lundberg, A. (1985) The influence of food on time budgets and timing of breeding of the dunnock, *Prunella modularis*. *Ibis*, 127, 100–110.
Dawkins, R. (1976) *The Selfish Gene*. Oxford: Oxford University Press.
Dawkins, R. (1979) Twelve misunderstandings of kin selection. *Zietschrift für Tierpsychologie*, 51, 184–200.
Dawkins, R. (1980) Good strategy or evolutionarily stable strategy? In G.W. Barlow and J. Silverberg (eds) *Sociobiology: Beyond Nature/Nurture? Reports, Definitions and Debate*. (AAAS Selected Symposium 35.) Boulder, Co.: Westview.
Dawkins, R. (1982) Replicators and vehicles. In King's College Sociobiology Group (eds) *Current Problems in Sociobiology*. Cambridge: Cambridge University Press.
Dawkins, R. and Carlisle, T.R. (1976) Parental investment, mate desertion, and a fallacy. *Nature, London*, 262, 131–133.
Emlen, S.T. (1984) Cooperative breeding in birds and mammals. In J.R. Krebs and N.B. Davies (eds) *Behavioural Ecology: An Evolutionary Approach*, 2nd ed. Oxford: Basil Blackwell.
Emlen, S.T. and Oring, L.W. (1977) Ecology, sexual selection and the evolution of mating systems. *Science*, 197, 215–223.
Fisher, R.A. (1958) *The Genetical Theory of Natural Selection*, 2nd ed. New York: Dover.

Flew, A.G.N. (1959) The structure of Darwinism. *Penguin New Biology*, 28, 25–44.
Gould, S.J. and Lewontin, R.C. (1979) The spandrels of San Marco and the Panglossian paradigm: A critique of the adaptationist programme. *Proceedings of the Royal Society of London, Series B*, 205, 581–598.
Grafen, A. (1984) Natural selection, kin selection and group selection. In J.R. Krebs and N.B. Davies (eds) *Behavioural Ecology: An Evolutionary Approach*, 2nd ed. Oxford: Basil Blackwell.
Hamilton, W.D. (1963) The evolution of altruistic behaviour. *American Naturalist*, 97, 354–356.
Hamilton, W.D. (1964) The genetical evolution of social behaviour. I and II. *Journal of Theoretical Biology*, 7, 1–16, 17–52.
Houston, A.I. and Davies, N.B. (1985) The evolution of cooperation and life history in the dunnock, *Prunella modularis*. In R.M. Sibly and R.H. Smith (eds) *Behavioural Ecology: Ecological Consequences of Adaptive Behaviour*. (25th Symposium of the British Ecological Society, Reading, 1984.) Oxford: Basil Blackwell.
Huntingford, F. (1982) The evolution of cooperation and altruism. In A.M. Colman (ed.) *Cooperation and Competition in Humans and Animals*. Wokingham: Van Nostrand Reinhold.
Knowlton, N. and Parker, G.A. (1979) An evolutionarily stable strategy approach to indiscriminate spite. *Nature, London*, 279, 419–421.
Krebs, J.R. and Davies, N.B. (eds) (1978) *Behavioural Ecology: An Evolutionary Approach*. Oxford: Basil Blackwell.
Krebs, J.R. and Davies, N.B. (1981) *An Introduction to Behavioural Ecology*. Oxford: Basil Blackwell.
Krebs, J.R. and Davies, N.B. (eds) (1984) *Behavioural Ecology: An Evolutionary Approach*, 2nd ed. Oxford: Basil Blackwell.
Krebs, J.R. and Dawkins, R. (1984) Animal signals: Mind-reading and manipulation. In J.R. Krebs and N.B. Davies (eds) *Behavioural Ecology: An Evolutionary Approach*, 2nd ed. Oxford: Basil Blackwell.
Krebs, J.R. and McCleery, R.H. (1984) Optimization in behavioural ecology. In J.R. Krebs and N.B. Davies (eds) *Behavioural Ecology: An Evolutionary Approach*, 2nd ed. Oxford: Basil Blackwell.
Lack, D. (1968) *Ecological Adaptations for Breeding in Birds*. London: Methuen.
Lazarus, J. (1982) Competition and conflict in animals. In A.M. Colman (ed.) *Cooperation and Competition in Humans and Animals*. Wokingham: Van Nostrand Reinhold.
Maynard Smith, J. (1964) Group selection and kin selection. *Nature, London*, 201, 1145–1147.
Maynard Smith, J. (1972) *On Evolution*. Edinburgh: Edinburgh University Press.
Maynard Smith, J. (1976a) Evolution and the theory of games. *American Scientist*, 64, 41–45.
Maynard Smith, J. (1976b) Group selection. *Quarterly Review of Biology*, 51, 277–283.
Maynard Smith, J. (1977) Parental investment: A prospective analysis. *Animal Behaviour*, 25, 1–9.
Maynard Smith, J. (1982) *Evolution and the Theory of Games*. Cambridge: Cambridge University Press.
Maynard Smith, J. and Price, G.R. (1973) The logic of animal conflict. *Nature, London*, 246, 15–18.
Orians, G.H. (1969) On the evolution of mating systems in birds and mammals. *American Naturalist*, 103, 589–603.

Parker, G.A. (1978) Searching for mates. In J.R. Krebs and N.B. Davies (eds) *Behavioural Ecology: An Evolutionary Approach*. Oxford: Basil Blackwell.

Parker, G.A. (1984) Evolutionarily stable strategies. In J.R. Krebs and N.B. Davies (eds) *Behavioural Ecology: An Evolutionary Approach*, 2nd ed. Oxford: Basil Blackwell.

Pleszczynska, W.K. (1978) Microgeographic prediction of polygyny in the lark bunting. *Science, 201,* 935–937.

Pulliam, H.R. and Caraco, T. (1984) Living in groups: Is there an optimal group size? In J.R. Krebs and N.B. Davies (eds) *Behavioural Ecology: An Evolutionary Approach*, 2nd ed. Oxford: Basil Blackwell.

Rubenstein, D.I. (1980) On the evolution of alternative mating strategies. In J.R. Staddon (ed.) *Limits to Action: The Allocation of Individual Behavior*. New York: Academic Press.

Sherman, P.W. (1977) Nepotism and the evolution of alarm calls. *Science, 197,* 1246–1253.

Shettleworth, S.J. (1984) Learning and behavioural ecology. In J.R. Krebs and N.B. Davies (eds) *Behavioural Ecology: An Evolutionary Approach*, 2nd ed. Oxford: Basil Blackwell.

Sibly, R.M. (1983) Optimal group size is unstable. *Animal Behaviour, 31,* 947–948.

Smith, P.K. (1983) Human sociobiology. In J. Nicholson and B. Foss (eds) *Psychology Survey 4*. Leicester: The British Psychological Society.

Trivers, R.L. (1971) The evolution of reciprocal altruism. *Quarterly Review of Biology, 46,* 35–57.

Trivers, R.L. (1972) Parental investment and sexual selection. In B. Campbell (ed.) *Sexual Selection and the Descent of Man 1871–1971*. Chicago: Aldine.

Trivers, R.L. (1974) Parent–offspring conflict. *American Zoologist, 14,* 249–264.

Vehrencamp, S.L. and Bradbury, J.W. (1984) Mating systems and ecology. In J.R. Krebs and N.B. Davies (eds) *Behavioural Ecology: An Evolutionary Approach*, 2nd ed. Oxford: Basil Blackwell.

Verner, J. (1977) On the adaptive significance of territoriality. *American Naturalist, 111,* 769–775.

Wilson, E.O. (1971) *The Insect Societies*. Cambridge, Mass.: Belknap Press of Harvard University Press.

Wilson, E.O. (1975) *Sociobiology: The New Synthesis*. Cambridge, Mass.: Belknap Press of Harvard University Press.

Wittenberger, J.F. (1981) *Animal Social Behavior*. Boston: Duxbury.

THE ETHICS AND POLITICS OF ANIMAL EXPERIMENTATION
Jeffrey A. Gray

The case made against psychological experiments with animals by the 'animal liberationists' is false at almost every point; worse, it is deliberately so.

I start by asking why the liberationists have specially targeted psychological experiments (the British Union for the Abolition of Vivisection or BUAV aims to have had such experiments banned by the end of 1986). Is this because psychological experiments inflict particularly severe suffering upon their subjects? This is certainly not so, a point I take up later; nor does the BUAV claim this as the reason for their particular animus against psychology. On the contrary, their campaign literature is disarmingly frank on the subject: their reason for focusing on psychological experiments is that psychologists are a soft target.

There are several reasons for the peculiarly exposed position we occupy.

- First, we are not seen as contributing to medicine (as are, say, physiologists); though in fact, the contributions we have made and can make towards the treatment and prevention of mental illness are many, substantial and varied (see below).
- Second, we cannot count on the support of the more prestigious biological disciplines if the wolves come running for us. Indeed, certain defenders of animal experiments have been known to mutter, as a sop to their opponents, 'Of course, I would not wish to defend the things the *psychologists* get up to.'
- Third, the aims, methods and findings of animal psychology are still little understood outside the profession, so that the slanders of the liberationists are all too easily believed.
- Fourth, and not least important, there has been a substantial infiltration by the liberationists of the ranks of psychologists themselves.

This infiltration is made easier by the ideological split between those psychologists who recognize our close relationship to other animal species, and therefore the relevance of animal research to human psychology, and those who cling to the belief that human beings have some unique essence setting them quite apart from the rest of evolution, so lending colour to the liberationist claim that research with animals is not only morally wrong, but also of no practical value for people.

It is with deliberation that I employed, in the preceding paragraph, the politically loaded term 'infiltration'. The liberationist literature is that of a political, not an ethical movement; and the chief concern of its leaders is with effective propoganda, not the suffering of the animals they purport to defend. However, before documenting these assertions, let me take the liberationists seriously and consider the ethical issues which one might expect to underlie their political campaign.

No 'ought' can be derived from an 'is'. The only source of ethical authority is the assent of the individual conscience. In arguments concerning moral doctrines one may rationally analyse the coherence or logical interrelations between different components of an ethical code; but the choice between rival doctrines is in the end an act of arbitrary (though not unmotivated) preference (Warnock, 1986). Unfortunately, however, there appears to be an almost irresistible tendency to impose one's own moral code on everyone else. And, since there is no rational way of deciding between rival codes, this tendency can lead to strife, mayhem or the coercion of a minority by a majority holding different beliefs. As a way out of this dilemma, the liberal democracies have evolved a set of politico-legal rules that attempt to enforce only such ethical constraints as receive widespread consent. In the best circumstances, such consent is reached after wide-ranging, informed and honest public discussion. We are now witnessing just such a discussion as society grapples with the new issues raised by advances in reproductive biology that allow human embryos to be kept alive outside the womb or implanted into a surrogate mother (Warnock, 1984).

Against this background, we may legitimately ask of the animal liberationists two questions:

- Do they have a coherent case?
- In putting it, do they abide by the rules of democratic debate?

I am in no doubt that there *is* a coherent case that can be put against the use of animals in experiments (which is not to say that this case should be preferred to all others). Such a case would not abscribe to animals 'rights', since rights may belong only to members of a moral community able to press them by appropriate argument. But we might choose to accept *duties*; and these might include the duty not to experiment with animals. Indeed, in the UK, we have recognized a form of this duty since the 1876 Cruelty to Animals Act forbade such experiments except with the consent of the Home Secretary – consent that is granted only if the Home Secretary, upon the advice of suitably qualified scientists and professors of medicine, believes that the gain to the community justifies the experiments. But animal liberationists claim that no such justification can ever be provided: there should be an absolute duty upon us never to use animals in experiments.

Now, in considering this claim, bear in mind that people use animals for other ends than experimentation: for food, clothing, as a means of travel or as pets. Should we then pick out *experiments* with animals as peculiarly vicious, so that this way of using them is morally wrong, whereas all these other ways are acceptable? That would imply that the need for food, clothing, etc. is in some way of greater worth (whether utilitarian or moral) than the need for scientific understanding and/or medical care which animal experiments satisfy. The ranking of needs of these diverse kinds is as arbitrary as the choice between ethical codes; but I doubt that the proposition that food is of greater intrinsic value than health would gain much approval in a Gallup poll. And, for my own part, I give scant respect to the opinion that food is more worthy of pursuit than an understanding of the biological world of which we form part. Thus the only *coherent* claim that might lead to the imposition of an absolute duty not to experiment with animals must be the claim that *it is wrong to use animals for any purpose at all* (Singer, 1976).

Now, while this proposition is coherent, it is not self-evident. Consider the man who keeps a dog as a pet, the farmer milking a cow, or the rider on a horse. I find it hard to whip up moral indignation at these images. I suspect that the same failure afflicts many who put money into liberationist collecting boxes, yet suffer no moral qualms about the pets they keep at home. However, some liberationists do adopt this coherent position, becoming in consequence vegetarians and eschewing the keeping of pets. But notice that, when they do take up such a coherent position, the liberationists keep the matter to themselves: we do not often see marches in our streets demanding that we should forthwith give up eating meat and set our pets free.

The first question asked above was 'Do the liberationists have a coherent moral case?' We now see the answer to this question: if the liberationists have a coherent case, they keep it well hidden. Let us turn then to the second question: in putting their case, do the liberationists keep to the rules of democratic debate? There are two closely related reasons for answering this question with a firm 'no': the liberationists' resort to violence and their use of lies.

The first rule of democratic debate is that one must rely upon argument and discussion to convince one's opponent. The resort to violence at once puts its user beyond the pale of the democratic community. But it is well known that some liberationists have resorted, and continue to resort, to acts of violence ranging from the destruction of property, through arson and physical attack, to the final terrorist acts of the parcel and car bomb (see, among many examples, the *Daily Telegraph*, 7 January, 1985, and the *Oxford Mail*, 8 January, 1986). This catalogue of crime is alleged to spring from the humane impulse to minimize the suffering of animals; but I doubt the humane impulse, seeing instead the all-too-*human* instinct to impose one's own ethical code on everyone else, Ayatollah-style.

This instinct towards moral tyranny is buttressed by perfectly rational political considerations. To begin with, the liberationists are surely aware of the value of violence in keeping their cause in the public eye. They are also perhaps comforted by that all-too-common public response to acts of political violence, that those who perpetrate them must have strong reasons to behave as they do. So, from the fact that a scientist is singled out for a bomb attack it is inferred that he must inflict particular cruelty upon the animals in his charge. In fact, the distinctive characteristic of those singled out for liberationist terror is not that they do particular violence to animals, but that they speak out against liberationists. So, for example, Professor Roy Calne and Dr Brian Meldrum were targets of bomb attacks shortly after each had publicly defended scientists who work with animals, the one in a letter to *The Times*, the other in a television broadcast. The most parsimonious explanation of this pattern of events is that liberationists use violence, not out of deep moral outrage, but as a calculated political act.

To be sure, the use of violence makes the more moderate members of the animal liberation movement uneasy. Like their counterparts in more frankly political movements, they are inclined to deplore it, but rarely condemn it outright without exculpation. However, should they ever need fully to dissociate themselves from the extremists, they now have a ready-made alibi. For the police report that the Animal Liberation Front has been joined by a number of anarchists, who have no doubt spotted suitably high moral ground from which to 'smash the system'. But it would be naïve to blame a handful of anarchists for the excesses of the animal liberation movement. On the contrary, the fact that the movement is seen as a suitable home for men of violence is testimony to the atmosphere of hatred that reigns there; and for this it is the writings of the *moderates* that are to blame.

From the argument so far, it can be seen that a coherent moral case for banning all animal experiments can be made only if one is willing to proscribe most, if not all, other uses of animals; and while some liberationists are willing to go this far, society as a whole is not. It is necessary, therefore, for the liberationists to retreat to a weaker position. Now, one first posits a duty to minimize animal suffering. This is a claim which meets widespread acceptance in all walks of life, certainly including the scientists who actually work with animals. Indeed, it is a claim already embodied in the 1876 Act governing the conduct of animal experiments. But it is not easy to deduce from it (as the liberationists wish) that experiments with animals ought to be banned.

There are essentially two ways in which such an argument might be made out.

The first interprets the duty to minimize animal suffering as requiring us to abandon *any* activity which entails *any* degree of animal suffering, no matter how slight. This position, if accepted, might indeed require us to abandon experiments with animals. But it would also (if applied coherently) require us to give up most of the other activities we pursue with animals, and so would be politically ineffective.

The second interprets the duty to minimize animal suffering more flexibly, allowing for the imposition upon animals of some degree of suffering depending upon the consequent benefit to mankind, but not for the imposition of unnecessary suffering. This is probably the position that most humane people (scientists included) in fact adopt. But can it lead to the moral requirement specifically to ban experiments with animals? Only if one were to show (1) that suffering in experiments is excessive relative to suffering when animals are used as a source of food, clothing, etc; or (2) that the benefits claimed for mankind from animal experiments are illusory. It is in their attempts to substantiate these two claims that the liberationists have lied (Coile and Miller, 1984); and it is these lies that have created the climate of opinion in which it is possible for letter bombs and car bombs to be aimed at scientists who work with animals.

The ground where we now find ourselves is the central ground on which the battle between liberationists and research workers is usually fought. The score is measured in units of cost (to the animals) and benefit (to mankind) (Dawkins, 1980; Bateson, 1986). Liberationists aim to magnify the costs and demean the benefits. Their propoganda has had such success that the battle is usually fought on their terms, the poor scientists trying desperately to justify the 'torture' they are deemed to inflict upon the animals in their charge. These are terms that must be rejected from the outset: the overwhelming majority of scientists working with animals have no need to justify causing excessive suffering to animals *because they do not cause them such a suffering*. Yet many people believe otherwise. Why? First, and most important, because the liberationists have grossly distorted what goes on in animal laboratories. Second, because scientists have for the most part ignored these attacks, finding it hard to believe that they would gain credit with ordinary people. Alas, they underestimated the power of systematic, ruthless propaganda.

I have accused the liberationists of lies and distortion. It is time to put flesh upon this accusation. Since this chapter is addressed to psychologists, and since psychological experiments are in any case the ones I know best, I shall confine my examples to this type of research.

Most psychological experiments are performed with rats. Other commonly used species are mice and pigeons. Cats and dogs are rarely used in behavioural research in this country, though sometimes elsewhere. This does not stop liberationists decorating their pamphlets with pictures of cats and dogs, made to look suitably wretched. Morally, of course, the issue is identical whether the experiments are done with rats or cats (given that these species appear to be of an equivalent level of psychological complexity). But once more the liberationists act politically: laypeople are not much affected by the suffering of a rat, but cats and dogs tug at the heart-strings.

A few experiments are done with primates, usually macaques or marmosets. Such experiments are kept to a minimum, since they are expensive and confined to a few chosen centres. In consequence they typically address questions that cannot be tackled at other phylogenetic levels. A further motive for using primates arises when it is intended to apply a new technique in human medicine, and it is therefore vital to test the technique in a species closely related to our own. The new legislation (May, 1986) for the further regulation of animal experiments formalizes the requirement that primates should be used only if other species are not suitable.

The typical psychological experiment, then, uses rats, as any undergraduate rapidly learns. These are not your ordinary rats, captured on a garbage heap and deprived of their freedom to roam the city streets. On the contrary, they have been bred over generations for laboratory life, achieving the same kind of symbiosis with human purpose as the cattle of the field. Where would they be if they were not in the laboratory? Nowhere at all, for they would not have been born. Are they happy with their lot? Would they prefer to be with their wild cousins, or even never to have been born? It is hard enough to get answers to questions like these from human beings, let alone from a rat. The best we can do is to let the animals vote with their feet, and they often do. It is common in even the best run laboratory for a rat to escape from its cage. Finding the escapee is not difficult: it is usually sitting two or three feet from the cage. The security that surrounds animal laboratories is to keep liberationists out, not rats in.

So far, I have considered the plight of the laboratory animal before it enters an experiment. At this point, it is alleged, animals undergo every kind of imaginable torture. The choice of the word 'torture' (as common in the sober tracts of the 'moderates' as in the pamphlets of the 'extremists') is itself a political act (Gallup and Suarez, 1985). It aligns liberationists with humanitarian organizations like Amnesty International, almost guaranteeing the adherence of the liberal and the left. More ominously, conversion of scientists into 'torturers' starts the process of public alienation that terminates with bombs. The technique is familiar to radical political movements of left and right. It should have been equally familiar to those social scientists who, alas, figure in the so-called moderate wing of the liberationist movement; I trust therefore that they will one day own up to their share of responsibility for the acts of violence perpetrated by their more extreme colleagues.

To describe experiments with animals as 'torture' carries several implications:

- that the pain or suffering is extreme
- that it is gratuitous
- that the experimenter derives pleasure from it.

All these implications are made explicit in one or other of the writings of liberationists. We need, therefore, to examine and refute them one by one.

The accusations levelled at psychologist include the following (see Sharpe, 1985; and the reply by the Experimental Psychology Society, 1986).

First, we are accused of 'starving' our animals. It is of course true that in many experiments it is necessary to motivate the animal by rewarding it with food and correspondingly to deprive it of food prior to experimental sessions. The most common procedure is to feed the rat once a day, after experiments are completed. An alternative procedure is to maintain the animal's weight at some fixed percentage (typically, about 85 per cent) of its free-feeding value (allowing for normal weight gain at the appropriate age). In my own laboratory we use the former procedure and have never needed to go beyond this level of food deprivation (nor do we have permission from the Home Office to do so). Does this constitute extreme suffering? Does it constitute suffering at all? If it does, then many pet owners (who need no Home Office licence before they decide how frequently to feed *their* animals) are equally at fault, since it is a widespread practice to feed pets only once a day. More objectively, we may enquire whether rats thrive under this kind of feeding regime. Indeed they do: a number of experiments have shown that, when feeding is restricted in this or a comparable manner, animals are healthier and live longer than when allowed food ad lib (for example Berg and Simms, 1960). This observation will come as no surprise to anyone familiar with the statistics on overeating and health in our own species; but it provides a conclusive rebuttal to the charge that the food deprivation employed in psychological experiments is a source of suffering.

Second, we are accused of inflicting extreme pain upon our animals when they are trained with electric shock as a punishment or a negative reinforcer. Before we consider the substance of this charge, it is worth saying a word about electric shock. This has become the standard way of delivering punishment in the animal laboratory for a number of technical reasons: it is easy to control, measure and standardize, it is easily programmed with electronically operated apparatus, the timing of its delivery is precise, etc. But, had the founders of current laboratory methodology been granted precognition of the animal liberation movement, they might have chosen differently. For 'electric shock' is almost as emotive a phrase as 'torture': it conjures up visions of Nazi guards brandishing bared wires near the genitals. No better weapon could have been placed in the hands of the hostile propagandist.

But what of the reality? Do the shocks used in psychological experiments cause great pain? Certainly, they cause *some* pain, otherwise they could not serve as punishments. But, equally certainly, they do not normally cause extreme pain. I can make this assertion with confidence for several reasons. First, the permitted levels of shock are closely controlled by the Home Office. One of the liberationists claims is that the Home Office Inspectors fail in their duty to exercise such control. This, too, is a lie: the Inspector responsible for my own laboratory has frequently and carefully observed the reactions of our animals to the shocks we employ. Second, these reactions are a clear sign that the *rat* does not regard the shock as inflicting extreme pain. For, in many of the experiments we carry out, the animal has a choice: it may, for example, press a bar now, take a shock, and get a food reward; or wait a few minutes, then press the bar, take no shock, but still receive a food reward. The levels of shock that we employ typically act as a sufficient deterrent so that the rat reduces its rate of barpressing by about half when shock is threatened, but does not give up pressing entirely. The rat, then, shows by its behaviour that the shock we use is painful, but *not* excessively so.

It is notoriously difficult to compare the intensity of pain of different kinds. But, given these behavioural observations, we believe that we inflict upon our rats about the same level of pain as the dog-owner who uses a mild blow in the pet's training. Indeed, so certain am I that we do not inflict extreme pain upon our rats that I once demonstrated on national television ('Man Alive', BBC, 1980) their reaction to the shocks we use. The programme was seen by many viewers. There were no horrified letters from the public – not surprisingly, since the animal could be seen barely to flinch when the shock occurred. This demonstration could have come from any British laboratory, since the permitted levels of shock are much the same throughout the country. Indeed, the average level of shock used in behavioural experiments with rats in the UK between 1980 and 1985 has been estimated as 0.68 mA for an average duration of 0.57 seconds; such shocks produce an unpleasant tickling sensation when applied to human beings (Experimental Psychology Society, 1986).

So psychologists do not inflict extreme pain upon animals. But why inflict any pain at all? Indeed, if the aim of the experiment is to study, say, learning and it is possible to do so using either food or shock avoidance as the reinforcer, then there is a clear obligation to choose food. However, the use of a painful stimulus may be essential for the experiment; one may, for example, be studying the mechanisms of perception of pain itself, or the anxiety evoked by conditioned stimuli associated with pain – both matters of great clinical, as well as scientific, importance.

Even in this type of case, ingenuity can sometimes avoid the use of painful stimuli. There is, for example, much evidence that the omission of anticipated reward ('nonreward') has the same emotional properties as a painful stimulus and engages the same neurological mechanisms (Gray, 1982). In studying anxiety, therefore, one may sometimes substitute stimuli associated with nonreward for stimuli associated with pain. But note that this substitution is possible only *after* research has first established the equivalence between nonreward and the punishment upon which it is based. This is likely to be the rule: the ability to develop substitutes for existing methods invariably rests upon a solid body of prior research, research which the liberationists strive to prevent. The substitution of nonreward for pain is a minor advance of this kind, but an advance none the less.

I have discussed pain without yet mentioning surgery. But then, why should I? Surgery is invariably carried out (as legally it must be) under full anaesthesia, just as in human medicine. The animal liberationists are well aware of this, yet they harp upon the various operations that psychologists perform. No doubt they hope that the public, unfamiliar with the details of experiments and the law that governs them, will suppose that these operations are carried out on conscious animals. Nor do they miss any opportunity to mislead people into this belief. At one time, for example, the local campaign literature in Oxford pilloried Alan Cowey (who would no more operate upon a conscious rat than upon a conscious baby) for operating upon 'unanaesthetized' rat pups. Now, it is true that the pups had not been given a *chemical* anaesthetic in these experiments. But that was because there was no need for one: at the time of surgery the animals could feel no pain, since they had been rapidly cooled until their hearts were no longer beating. Another motive for the liberationist attack upon surgery is to trade upon the human revulsion for mutilation. Laypeople find the idea of a rat with part of its brain missing, or bearing implanted electrodes, deeply shocking. They do not ask whether these operations cause pain, but simply react to the idea of mutilation as such. But if one is concerned with *animal* suffering, it is pain that matters. It is improbable that animals can form the concept of mutilation or suffer from the knowledge that they have undergone brain surgery. But if animals are undisturbed by such ratiocinations, then so should we be, in so far as our concern is with *their* suffering.

What of the other side of the coin, the benefits to mankind from animal research? Here the liberationist attack is two-pronged: first, they deride the benefits claimed to be the objects of research by the experimenters themselves; second, they assert that the experimenters have in any case different and more self-seeking motives for their research than those they publicly proclaim. Let us first dispose of the second prong of this attack.

The hidden benefits said to be the *real* motives behind research with animals are variously described as the need to get a PhD; the desire for prestige; the satisfaction of 'idle curiosity'; and sadistic pleasure in the actual infliction of pain. Strictly speaking, these charges are irrelevant to the central ethical issue, which is (or should be) the suffering of animals, not the moral worth of experimenters. From the animal's point of view it is of no consequence whether experimenters enjoy the pain they are inflicting or are busy thinking about a PhD – the pain is the same. It *would* matter, of course, if these factors caused the experimenter to inflict more pain than required by the scientific purpose of the experiment; but both the law and the general climate of opinion in British laboratories strongly militate against this possibility. So, once again, we must seek elsewhere than in the liberationists' concern for animal welfare if we wish to enquire about their reasons for making these allegations. And, once made, the answer to this enquiry is clear: the allegations are made so as to whip up hatred for the scientist, another small step on the road to the parcel bomb.

None the less, let us consider these charges a little more closely. We start with the charge of sadism. A priori I know no reason to suppose that psychologists interact any more sadistically with animals than do animal liberationists with psychologists. Empirically, the accusation of sadism (taking pleasure from the infliction of pain) is not easy to refute without a survey of the personalities and motivation of the scientists concerned. If some social psychologist ever conducts this survey, I have little doubt of the outcome: I have never met an animal psychologist who appears to derive any pleasure from the pain that experimental animals sometimes suffer.

The charge that scientists are motivated to obtain higher degrees or professional prestige is neither refutable nor worth refuting, since there is nothing disreputable *per se* in these motives. As with sadism, they would matter only if they distorted the nature of experiments ostensibly performed for scientific reasons. But this is precisely the charge that the liberationists make. They allege that many experiments are scientifically worthless and/or mere repetitions of established phenomena, conducted solely for the purpose of obtaining a degree or a publication. *This* charge is serious; but it can be made only by someone who has little knowledge of contemporary scientific research, or little honesty in the use made of that knowledge. There may have been a time when research was the business of gentlemen, funded from their own pockets. If so, that time is long past. Nowadays virtually all research is conducted with public or charitable support, obtained after fierce competition. Only the cheapest of research can be carried out with the surplus funds available in the universities. Research with animals is not cheap. Within psychology it is far and away the most expensive type of research. In consequence, it is conducted in only a minority of departments of psychology, and university appointments in this field are in short supply. So any psychologist aiming to climb up the university ladder as rapidly as possible is ill-advised to choose research with animals.

But let us come to the kernel of the 'prestige' accusation: namely, that much research with animals is done purely to gain a degree or a publication, with the consequence that it is scientifically poor and (a charge repeated *ad nauseam* in the liberationist literature) mere repetition of established facts. That research in animal psychology is done *inter alia* to gain degrees or publications is beyond dispute, just as in other fields of science. But this in no way implies that the research so conducted is of poor quality. On the contrary, the method by which animal research is funded virtually guarantees that it is both of high quality and innovative. For, as noted above, without funds there can be no research, and funds are not easily obtained. The peer review system ruthlessly weeds out research that is of little scientific value or unlikely to yield new insights; and it takes no cognizance of the scientist's desire for fame, PhDs or publications. So while scientists may have, and indeed satisfy, these legitimate desires, this does not materially affect the nature of the research they are empowered to carry out. If, none the less, they obtained funds that permitted them merely to repeat established facts, they would find their desire for personal advancement little satisfied by doing so. For they must then face a second scrutiny before such work is published, and this uses the same criteria as before – scientific quality and the establishment of *new* facts. As for the PhD, it is normally a *requirement* for this degree that the candidate has demonstrated new facts.

Given the implausibility of the charge that scientists repeatedly observe established facts, how can the liberationist keep making it? The answer is that they deliberately confuse mere repetition with the important scientific tool of public replication. 'Established facts' in science are facts that are demonstrable in more than one laboratory; this rule eliminates false trails and provides an empirical means for deciding between rival claims to the truth. When new findings are reported that are of great theoretical significance they are treated with caution until they have been replicated elsewhere. This type of repetition of facts, far from being in any way disreputable, is an essential part of scientific procedure. Thus the typical scientific paper will contain statements to the effect that 'We replicated the so-and-so effect of x upon y, confirming the previous report by Jones, and showed *in addition* that this effect is due to z (or related to w, enhanced by v, etc).' The liberationists cling to statements of this kind like leeches, spattering their campaign literature with quotations which, taken out of context, imply that modern biology has no other aim to confirm Jones (for some specific examples, see Experimental Psychology Society, 1986).

We turn finally to the other prong of the liberationist attack on animal research, namely, the allegation that its results are 'irrelevant'. The first thing to do, faced with this allegation, is to ask: 'irrelevant to what?'. There are two types of objective at which animal research is aimed, both enshrined in the 1876 Act as legitimate purposes for the licensing of experiments: the pursuit of scientific knowledge and the advancement of medicine. Correspondingly, there are two kinds of relevance which animal experiments might be found to lack. But just how might such experiments be irrelevant to the pursuit of scientific knowledge? Science is concerned with understanding the whole of our universe, and the behaviour of animals is as legitimate an object of this understanding as any other part of the natural world. It needs no further justification in terms of relevance to human beings, medical or otherwise, any more than does the study of astronomy or fundamental particles. This is perhaps the attitude scorned as 'idle curiosity'. If so, Galileo was motivated in the same way. And, in his day as in ours, there were those who would keep one from the tree of knowledge. To liberationists, this tree is of no value: the relevance they trouble to deny to animal psychology is the medical kind. They judge that the public cares little for scientific knowledge in its own right; but people might think twice before banning animal experiments if they believed them to contribute to the elimination of disease or the promotion of better medical care. So the liberationist is at pains to deny to animal experiments any such benefits.

Let me stress that liberationists deny medical benefits to animal experiments across the whole range of biology, not just in psychology. It is not our business to point out the falsity of these allegations in so far as general medical advances are concerned (see Calne, 1984; Vane, 1985). Rather, I shall confine myself to a few examples that directly relate to psychology. And even in this connection I shall be brief, since the job has been done before, and superlatively well (Miller, 1985a).

Much psychological research with animals is concerned with learning. This research has been especially influential in the development of behavioural methods for the treatment of neurotic conditions, such as agoraphobia and obsessive-compulsive neurosis. These conditions may be so severe as completely to distort the patient's normal life, and they frequently last for a decade or more. Until the development of behavioural methods there was no effective treatment of any kind. Nowadays, success rates of about 90 per cent are achieved speedily and reliably (for example Mathews, Gelder and Johnston, 1981). A number of different methods are in use, each of which has undergone modification in the light of clinical experience. None the less, the starting point for the development of these methods has in each case been part of the literature on animal learning.

Consider, for example, systematic desensitization (Wolpe, 1958). This technique gave rise to the first major progress in the treatment of neurotic fears by behavioural methods. The therapist establishes conditions in which the patient can form an association between a phobic stimulus and a relaxation response which is intended to overcome the initial association between the stimulus and the neurotic fear that it evokes. Wolpe (1958) developed this approach on the basis of observations of the effectiveness of different methods for the elimination of avoidance behaviour in laboratory animals. Subsequent research has required revision of Wolpe's particular theory of the mode of action of systematic disensitization; but there are today many thousands of patients who owe their recovery to the therapy that he pioneered. Some of the animal experiments (Gray, in press) that have led to these revisions have shown that simple extinction (that is repeated presentation of a fear stimulus) is as effective in eliminating avoidance behaviour as pairing the fear stimulus with food (theoretically, the equivalent of the relaxation used in disensitization therapy). These experiments then provided part of the rationale for the introduction of a new technique, 'flooding' (Levis and Hare, 1977), as a behavioural treatment for neurotic fears. This method depends upon simple exposure to the phobic object or situation until the patient's fears subside. As well as being effective, flooding is speedy and therefore cheap.

A further example concerns obsessive-compulsive neurosis. This is a particularly mysterious type of behaviour: the patient feels compelled to repeat some apparently meaningless ritual (washing of already clean hands is a common example). On one theoretical analysis, such rituals are a form of active avoidance behaviour (Gray, 1971). Given this analysis, it is relevant that, in animal experiments, one can eliminate active avoidance by temporarily preventing the animal from making the avoidance response. On this basis Rachman and Hodgson (1979) developed response prevention clinically. This treatment has greatly improved the prospects for patients suffering from this disorder.

These are but three examples (systematic disensitization, flooding and response prevention) of the application of behavioural principles taken from the animal laboratory to the treatment of psychiatric disorders. Other examples can easily be given. At an early age, the most effective method for the treatment of nocturnal enuresis is a device developed by Mowrer and Mowrer (1938) which applies the principles of classical conditioning first established by Pavlov in his studies of dogs. In a different area of psychiatric disorder, Oatley (this volume) describes the influence of Seligman's (1975) studies of 'learned helplessness' in dogs upon the analysis and treatment – again, *effective* treatment – of human depression in cognitive terms. Still further examples can be drawn from the newer field of behavioural medicine. Dworkin (1982) has described the application of the principles of instrumental learning, as first established in Skinner's studies of pigeons and rats, in the construction of a device for treating scoliosis, a disfiguring and dangerous S-shaped curvature of the spine that is otherwise treatable only by encasing the patient in a heavy brace.

Each of these transfers of technology from the animal laboratory to the human clinic depends upon the generality of the laws of learning (Razran, 1971). But learning is by no means the only area of psychology in which advances in the animal laboratory have had direct consequences for the treatment of human ills. Many more examples come to hand if we expand our horizon from purely behavioural experiments to include those that also involve the brain. Behavioural methods have played a vital role, for example, in developing drugs used clinically to control anxiety (Gray, 1982) and schizophrenia (Miller, 1985*b*). Conversely, studies of the action of these drugs in the brains of animals has brought about a deeper understanding of the nature of the conditions they are used to treat. In the case of anxiety, for example, research on the brain sites at which benzodiazepines affect behaviour has strongly implicated a particular set of neural structures (Gray, 1982). The relevance of this research to the human case was dramatically demonstrated when the technique of postron-emission tomography was first used to study the brains of patients with spontaneous panic attacks (Reiman et al., 1984): the only brain region which differentiated the patients from controls turned out to contain just those structures already picked out by the animal experiments.

These advances have already been made; but it is the advances that are to come that are threatened by the liberationists. Take Alzheimer's disease. This is the commonest form of senile and pre-senile dementia, affecting 5 per cent of people over the age of 65. The disease is thought to be due in part to degeneration in a set of cholinergic neurons that innervate wide regions of the forebrain. The best hopes for treating this disease (one of the greatest medical problems of our time) lie in the development either of pharmacological means of boosting cholinergic function or of brain tissue transplant surgery (Björklund et al., 1983). In either of these endeavours, behavioural studies of learning, memory and cognition in animals will play a vital role, and indeed already are. Let me therefore close by repeating a plea I have made before (Gray, 1985); don't let the lies, the propaganda, the false moral claims or the violence of the liberationists stop us from making the contributions that, as psychologists, we *can* and *should* make to the elimination of this and other diseases of the mind.

REFERENCES

Bateson, P. (1986) When to experiment on animals. *New Scientist*, 109 (1496), 30–32.
Berg, B.N. and Simms, H.S. (1960) Nutrition and longevity in the rat. II Longevity and onset of disease with different levels of food intake. *Journal of Nutrition*, 71, 255–265.
Björklund, A. et al. mult. (1983) Intracerebral grafting of neuronal cell suspensions. *Acta Physiologica Scandinavica*, Suppl. 522, 1–75.
Calne, R. (1984) Can medicine advance without experiments on animals? *Conquest*, 173, 1–4.
Coile, D.C. and Miller, N.E. (1984) How radical animal activists try to mislead humane people. *American Psychologist*, 39, 700–701.
Dawkins, M.S. (1980) *Animal Suffering*. London: Chapman & Hall.
Dworkin, B.R. (1982) Instrumental learning for the treatment of disease. *Health Psychology*, 1, 45–59.

Experimental Psychology Society (1986) The use of animals for research by psychologists. Published by the Experimental Psychology Society.

Gallup, G.G. and Suarez, S.D. (1985) Animal research versus the care and maintenance of pets: The names have been changed but the results remain the same. *American Psychologist, 40,* 968.

Gray, J.A. (1971). *The Psychology of Fear and Stress.* London: Weidenfeld & Nicolson.

Gray, J.A. (1982). *The Neuropsychology of Anxiety: An Enquiry into the Functions of the Septo-Hippocampal System.* Oxford: Oxford University Press.

Gray, J.A. (1985). A whole and its parts; Behaviour, the brain, cognition and emotion. *Bulletin of The British Psychological Society, 38,* 99–112.

Gray, J.A. (in press) *The Psychology of Fear and Stress,* 2nd ed. Cambridge: Cambridge University Press.

Levis D.J. and Hare, N.P. (1977) A review of the theoretical rationale and empirical support for the extinction approach of implosive (flooding) therapy. In M. Hersen, R.M. Eisler and P.M. Moller (eds) *Progress in Behavior Modification, Vol. 4.* New York: Academic Press.

Mathews, A.M., Gelder, M.G. and Johnston, D.W. (1981) *Agoraphobia: Nature and Treatment.* New York: Guilford Press.

Miller, N.E. (1985a) The value of behavioral research on animals. *American Psychologist, 40,* 423–440.

Miller, N.E. (1985b) Prologue. In P.G. Zimbardo (ed.) *Psychology and Life,* 11th ed. Glenview, Illinois: Scott, Foresman.

Mowrer, O.H. and Mowrer, W.M. (1938) Enuresis – a method for its study and treatment. *American Journal of Orthopsychiatry, 8,* 436–459.

Oatley, K. (this volume) Experiments and experience: Usefulness and insight in psychology.

Rachman, S. and Hodgson, R. (1979) *Obsessions and Compulsions.* New York: Prentice-Hall.

Razran, G. (1971) *Mind in Evolution.* Boston: Houghton Mifflin.

Reiman, E.M., Raichle, M.E., Butler, F.K., Hersovich, P. and Robins, E. (1984) A focal brain abnormality in panic disorder, a severe form of anxiety. *Nature, 310,* 683–685.

Seligman, M.E.P. (1975) *Helplessness.* San Francisco: Freeman.

Sharpe, R. (1985) Psychological and behavioural research. Published by 'Mobilization for Laboratory Animals against the Government's Proposals', 51 Harley Street, London.

Singer, P. (1976) *Animal Liberation.* London: Cape.

Vane, J. (1985) How animals discover drugs. *Conquest, 174,* 1–12.

Warnock, M. (Chairman) (1984) Report of the Committee of Inquiry into Human Fertilisation and Embryology. London: Her Majesty's Stationery Office.

Warnock, M. (1986) Law and the pursuit of knowledge. *Conquest, 175,* 1–7.

Wolpe, J. (1958) *Psychotherapy by Reciprocal Inhibition.* Stanford: Stanford University Press.

HYPNOSIS
Graham F. Wagstaff

Since the early days of hypnosis in the late eighteenth century a controversy has existed between two opposing schools of thought. At one extreme is the traditional 'state' or 'special process' view. According to this position hypnotic phenomena come about because individuals enter a special altered state of consciousness, or 'trance'. Opposing this view is the 'non-state' position, sometimes called the social psychological view, which argues that it is not necessary to put forward a special process or an altered state to explain hypnotic phenomena, instead a number of other, more mundane, 'normal' psychological factors may be responsible: conformity, obedience, attitudes, expectancies, imagination and relaxation. This controversy has generated a considerable amount of research, especially over the last two or three decades, and in this chapter I attempt to bring you up to date with this research and indicate whether we are any closer to answering the question 'what is hypnosis?'

THE 'STATE' OR 'SPECIAL PROCESS' VIEW

Although it was once thought that hypnosis was a special sort of sleep (the word hypnosis actually derives from the Greek word *hypnos*, sleep), certainly not all modern state theorists subscribe to a relationship between hypnosis and sleep. However, state theorists continue to see hypnosis as an altered state of consciousness with various depths, the assumption being that the deeper into hypnosis one goes, the more likely one is to manifest hypnotic phenomena (Hilgard, 1978; Bowers, 1983). According to this view, the state of trance, which is allegedly qualitatively different from a normal waking state, may occur spontaneously, but usually it is brought about through induction procedures, which commonly include eye fixation and vocal suggestions for sleep and relaxation. In order to quantify and measure hypnotic susceptibility and hypnotic depth, a variety of standardized scales have been developed. Amongst those most frequently used in hypnosis research are the Stanford Hypnotic Susceptibility Scale (forms A, B and C) and the Harvard Group Scale of Hypnotic Susceptibility. These scales typically start off with a reassuring preamble stressing how interesting hypnosis is, followed by an induction procedure with instructions for relaxation and suggestions for sleep. Following the induction are suggestions for items such as hand lowering ('your hand is heavy and falling'), arm rigidity ('you cannot bend your arm'), amnesia ('you will find it difficult to remember') and sometimes an hallucination ('there is a fly buzzing round your head'). It should be noted that implicit in these suggestions is the notion that the response should be automatic. Thus an essential characteristic of the state view of hypnosis is that subjects experience their responses as something 'happening to them' (Bowers, 1983).

Another feature of the traditional state view is that subjects will be able to do things whilst under hypnosis of which they would be incapable in a waking state; or at least their performance would be inferior in the waking state. The range of phenomena alleged to demonstrate this pattern of hypnosis is enormous, and the degree to which state theorists accept such claims is variable. Most state theorists accept that 'hypnotized' subjects possess a special capacity to control pain (Hilgard and Hilgard, 1984) and distinct abilities in displays of amnesia and hallucinations (Orne, 1979; Kihlstrom, 1980; Bowers, 1983). At the other extreme, most academic state theorists do not appear to accept claims that 'hypnotized' people can actually be regressed back before birth to appear in Roman Britain or medieval York.

One of the most appealing characteristics of the 'state' or 'special process' approach is the sheer range of phenomena that a theory of hypnosis must encompass. 'Hypnotized' individuals can apparently turn on hallucinations at will, do amazing impressions of sailors, dancers and zombies, regress back to childhood with great accuracy, lose warts, be cured of phobias, become deaf, blind and amnesic, survive pins, ice cold water and the surgeon's knife without flinching, lift extremely heavy weights, show improved eyesight, show 'automatic' writing and talking (that is write and talk whilst being unaware that they are doing so) and so on. We cannot simply dismiss all these demonstrations, as many appear to have considerable support from controlled experiments, so the idea that they must be due to a rather unique psychological process is very attractive. There is also support, however, for an alternative explanation of these phenomena.

THE NON-STATE APPROACH

The main challenge to the state view of hypnosis has come from a group of psychologists who stress that the hypnotic phenomena may be seen in terms of normal psychological processes, particularly from the areas of social psychology and cognitive psychology (Sarbin and Coe, 1972, 1979; Barber and Wilson, 1977; Wagstaff, 1981a; Sarbin, 1982; Spanos, 1982). According to this view the hypnotic situation is primarily a social psychological interaction, that is the hypnotist and the subject act out social roles. The role of the subject is to present him or herself as a 'hypnotized' subject according to previous expectations and to cues given by the hypnotist. The subject may thus try very hard to act *as if* 'hypnotized'. It is important to stress, however, that this view does not mean that all hypnotic behaviour is faked or sham (though some may be). People may become very involved in this role, and use a number of techniques or strategies to bring about suggested effects. Some of these may be implied in the suggestion itself, such as trying hard to imagine one's arm is heavy; or the subject may invent them, as when, in response to a suggestion to feel no pain, he or she may try distraction, or imagining a pleasant scene. In fact Wagstaff (1983) has speculated that hypnotic responding may involve three stages. First the subject figures out what is expected on the basis of previous experience and the hypnotist's instructions. Second the subject employs imaginative or other deliberate strategies to try to bring about the suggested effects, and third, if the strategies fail, or are judged to be inappropriate, the subject either gives up or reverts to behavioural compliance or shamming.

The idea that subjects should start acting out the role, and then, in some instances, actually fake effects may seem ridiculous, but there is an impressive literature which indicates that subjects who enter experiments and comparable situations have a strong desire to please the experimenter and 'look good'. As Milgram (1974) and others have pointed out, the desire not to commit a social impropriety and not to ruin an experiment is extremely powerful: often more powerful than we realize. So powerful is this effect that investigators found that a large proportion of ordinary people were prepared to give high doses of *real* electric shocks to a *real* innocent victim, a puppy (Sheridan and King, 1972).

Orne (1962) has also stressed how easy it is to get subjects to agree to ridiculous requests if the context is appropriate. In one example subjects were required to perform additions on sheets filled with random digits; this required 224 additions per sheet, and subjects were given 2,000 sheets to complete. The subjects were told by the experimenter, 'Continue to work: I will return eventually'. The result was that, 'Five and a half hours later, the experimenter gave up'! In other words it appeared that the subjects were quite willing to go on for hours and hours rather than let the experimenter down.

Such examples indicate that it is very likely that similar pressures will apply in the hypnotic situation, and people may feel strongly obliged not to disobey and embarrass the hypnotist. The desire to obey may also come from subjects' genuine curiosity and their attempts to try and experience hypnosis. Having started, they may find it difficult to back out; having finished, they may find it difficult to understand why they did it.

EXPERIMENTAL APPROACHES

It is important to stress that state theorists do not reject social psychological factors in influencing responses to hypnotic suggestions. Indeed Orne (1959, 1966, 1970, 1979), himself a state theorist, has been in the forefront of attempts to tease out the effects of simple compliance or sham behaviour, to see what is left. However, non-state theorists argue that it is unnecessary to put forward any unique or special hypnotic process in addition to compliance and the use of imagination, relaxation and other normal processes to explain hypnotic phenomena.

Most experiments in hypnosis have therefore compared groups of hypnotic subjects (that is subjects who have been given a hypnotic induction procedure) with various control groups set up to test alternative, non-state, explanations. One of the most frequently used control groups is the simulating group (Orne, 1959, 1979). These are subjects told to fake hypnosis, but they are not told how to do it. Other control groups include 'task-motivated' groups, instructed, for example, to try hard to imagine and experience suggestions, but they are not given formal hypnotic induction procedures (Barber, 1969). The logic behind this approach is that if hypnotic subjects respond no differently from non-hypnotic control simulating or task-motivated subjects, then there is no necessity to postulate a special state or trance to explain the behaviour of the hypnotic subjects. If, on the other hand, simulating the task-motivated groups cannot reproduce the behaviours of hypnotic subjects, then one may suggest that hypnosis does involve an additional, unique element.

At this point, in order to avoid confusion it may be useful to define some terms as they will be used in this chapter. So as not to assume what is not yet established, terms will be used operationally to define procedures and situations; it will not be assumed that they refer to 'state' or 'trance' processes. For example, a 'hypnotic' or 'hypnosis' situation is simply one in which a hypnotic induction procedure has been applied. 'Hypnotic' subjects are those who have been given a hypnotic induction procedure, 'non-hypnotic' or 'waking' subjects are those who have *not* been given a hypnotic induction procedure. 'Hypnotized' or 'hypnotically susceptible' subjects are those who tend to respond positively to suggestions in a hypnotic context; 'insusceptible' subjects do not.

THE PHYSIOLOGY OF THE HYPNOTIC STATE

It is well known that sleep is accompanied by a number of physiological changes, especially changes in EEG brain-wave measures. It would be very useful for the state position if it could be shown that 'hypnotized' subjects showed similar responses to those of people asleep, or at least that they show a number of physiological changes not shown by subjects in non-hypnotic control groups. However, the search for unique physiological changes accompanying hypnotic induction has not been successful. A large number of measures have been applied, including EEG, blood pressure, blood clotting time, breathing rate, skin temperature and oral temperature, but none consistently differentiates between hypnotic and control subjects. These responses can *change* when a person is given hypnotic induction, but equivalent changes can be shown by other subjects given other instructions, for example, to close their eyes, relax and imagine various effects. Neither are the hypnotic physiological changes equivalent to those shown by people asleep or sleepwalking (Sarbin and Slagle, 1972; Wagstaff, 1981a; Spanos, 1982).

The failure to find a physiological measure of the hypnotic trance does not, of course, mean that one does not exist, and the search continues. However, this finding is certainly in line with the non-state approach.

EXTRAORDINARY FEATS

Since the beginnings of hypnosis claims have been made that 'hypnotized' individuals can transcend their normal capacities. It was once believed that hypnotic subjects could see with the back of their heads, see through the skin to the internal organs of others and communicate with the dead (Spanos, 1982). Such claims are rarely made nowadays, and indeed many state theorists say they have rejected the idea that hypnotic subjects can transcend normal capacities. Nevertheless, claims continue to be made and tested.

The testing of such claims has taught us a lot about how and how not to conduct hypnosis research. For example, it is of little use comparing the performance of the *same* subjects when they are not 'hyphotized' and when they are 'hypnotized'; what seems to happen in such cases is that subjects do not try as hard in the non-hypnotic control situation, so they will look better in the hypnotic or 'hypnotized' situation. Most early research was confounded by this problem (Wagstaff, 1981a). When more appropriate experimental controls are applied, such as the use of the independent groups of simulating or task-motivated subjects, there is no conclusive evidence that hypnotic subjects are superior on a variety of tasks, including appearing deaf, blind, colour blind, acting like a child and recalling events from childhood, producing perceptual effects whilst 'hallucinating' (such as changing eye movements), producing 'hypnotic dreams', lifting weights, improving eyesight, and learning and remembering, provided the non-hypnotic control subjects are motivated to try hard and to take the task seriously (Barber, 1969, 1972; Wagstaff, 1981a, 1982b,c, 1984).

Some of these studies have produced some striking results, especially those comparing 'simulators' (people faking hypnosis) with 'hypnotized' individuals. Very often simulators overplay their role and outperform the hypnotic groups! Simulators have been shown to pick up a poisonous snake, throw acid at the experimenter (both actually tricks, of course!), peddle heroin, mutilate the Bible, and commit slanders, among other things (Wagstaff, 1981a, 1982b). However, if, as Milgram (1974) showed, people are prepared, in experimental situations, to deliver high doses of shock to an innocent victim, it is not surprising that both hypnotic and simulating subjects (or at least equivalent numbers of each) will be prepared to do the above. Sometimes 'hypnotized' subjects have produced unusual, childlike responses such as supposedly age-specific reflexes. In one case three 'deep trance' subjects when regressed back to the age of four months showed a Babinski reflex (the large toe reflexively moves backwards and the other toes spread out), but subsequently it was announced that four-month-old infants do *not* show this response (Barber, 1969). It seems that these three subjects must have gathered this incorrect information prior to the experiment.

More recent studies allegedly showing that hypnotic procedures can reinstate perceptual abilities characteristic of childhood, like eidetic imagery, or photographic memory, and differential responding to visual illusions, have not been replicated in further investigations (Spanos, 1982; Wagstaff, 1981a, 1984). Though it has been assumed that hypnosis may be especially useful in helping people to remember details of crimes, most current research suggests that hypnosis does not increase memory any more than other procedures such as instructing people to relax and vividly imagine events (Wagstaff, 1984).

In the context of this research the apparently extraordinary activities of performers in stage hypnosis demonstrations appear somewhat less spectacular. There is nothing unusual about people being able to dance, sing, fall over, eat raw onions whilst pretending they are apples, kiss one another, pretend that they have forgotten something, and so on. Even one of the most dramatic phenomena, the human plank feat, whereby an individual is suspended between two chairs and others sit on him or her, is readily achieved by 'unhypnotized' people, if they are motivated to try in the first place (Barber, 1969). Although studies of pain will be considered later, it should be noted that simulators are just as able as 'hypnotized' subjects to give the impression that painful stimuli do not hurt (Hilgard et al.,1978).

What conclusion can be drawn from all this? As most state theorists now admit, there is no conclusive evidence that hypnosis enables people to transcend their normal capacities. This is, of course, exactly what would be predicted by a non-state theory. Evidence indicating that people are even willing to cheat to fulfil the expectations of the hypnotist (Wagstaff, 1981a) further reinforces the non-state case. The results of these studies appear to support the non-state view, but if there are real differences between behaviours in the 'hypnotized' and 'unhypnotized' states, perhaps they can be tapped by some rather more subtle measures.

SUBTLE MEASURES OF HYPNOTIC RESPONDING

There have been a number of attempts to isolate possible differences between 'hypnotized' and simulating (or faking) subjects using measures which do not simply look at the hypnotic transcendence of normal capacities.

Probably the most significant demonstration of a difference between hypnotic and simulating behaviour concerns a phenomenon called 'trance-logic' (Orne, 1959, 1979). If it is suggested to 'hypnotized' subjects that they cannot see an object which is actually before them, for example a chair, then though some subjects will assert they cannot see the chair, they will still walk round it rather than bump into it. On the other hand, simulators will tend to bump into the chair whilst asserting they cannot see it. Also, if, for example, 'hypnotized' subjects are shown a chair and asked to hallucinate a man sitting in it, they will tend to report the image of the hallucinated man as transparent, that is they can still see the chair through the man. Simulators, however, tend to report the image as opaque, that is as not transparent, so that they cannot see the back of the chair. According to the state view these demonstrations show that 'hypnotized' subjects appear to have little need for logical consistency, and can tolerate illogical responses; this is 'trance-logic'. This idea has been extended to other phenomena. For example, some 'hypnotized' subjects, when regressed back to childhood, will correctly write a complex sentence (something a child should not be able to do) and will report that they felt like a child only some of the time. However, simulators tend to write the sentence incorrectly (as a child would) and report that they felt like a child *all* the time (Nogrady et al., 1983; Spanos, in press).

Recent research indicates that not all these examples can be reliably repeated, though some are quite robust, such as transparent hallucinations and incongruous writing (Spanos, in press). There is, however, a non-state explanation for these phenomena but, in order to understand this alternative interpretation, we need to look in more detail at the experimental design which compares 'hypnotized' subjects with simulators, often referred to as the 'real-simulator' design. In this design simulating subjects are instructed to fake 'hypnosis', but they are not told how to do it. Subjects chosen to be simulators have usually previously been selected out as *not* hypnotically susceptible. This is so that they do not accidentally fall into a 'trance' during the hypnosis session (this somewhat begs the question, since only to state supporters is this condition important). Also, simulators are instructed to behave like excellent hypnotic subjects. We can thus see that the two groups are not really comparable. Hypnotic subjects are not under instructions to behave like excellent subjects, they can behave as they wish, depending on their expectations and how they interpret the situation.

Furthermore, there may be differences in the characteristics of subjects who respond and those who do not respond to hypnotic suggestions. For example, insusceptible subjects may have exaggerated ideas about how a 'hypnotized' person may behave, and this is why they do *not* usually respond to hypnotic suggestions (Wagstaff, 1981b, 1985b). Thus, when playing the role of the 'hypnotized' subject the insusceptible simulators may play it differently (that is in a more extreme way). Given these basic differences between the two groups, a non-state interpretation would be as follows. Taking hypnotic hallucinations first, in order to fulfil the requirement of excellent hypnotic subjects, insusceptible simulators feel that they have to report complete, opaque hallucinations. However, when Johnson, Maher and Barber (1972) instructed *non-hypnotic* subjects to *imagine* an object, they found that these subjects tended to report the same transparent images as 'hypnotized' individuals. Thus it could be argued that when so called 'trance-logical' hypnotic subjects report that they have 'seen' a transparent hallucinated object, what they really mean is they have *imagined* an object (Wagstaff, 1981a,b).

The idea that transparency in 'hallucinations' is due to the simple use of imagination and not a form of special trance-logic is supported by further evidence. Thus if hypnotically susceptible subjects are tested without 'hypnosis' (that is given non-hypnotic or 'waking' suggestions) they still report transparent hallucinations, and *if given the option* subjects prefer to say that the suggested hallucinations were imagined rather than seen. Also, though a few subjects report that they have seen rather than imagined suggested hallucinations, these occur as often in non-hypnotic task-motivated conditions as in hypnotic ones (Spanos, 1982). A similar analysis can be applied to incongruous writing and 'duality' (that is feeling like an adult as well as a child) during regression. The non-state interpretation would argue that if you try hard to *imagine* you are a child you will still write a sentence correctly, and you are likely to feel like a child only some of the time. So this is what 'hypnotized' subjects tend to do. On the other hand, simulators, trying to act like excellent hypnotic subjects, will write the sentence incorrectly (like a child) and report they felt like a child *all* the time. In line with this interpretation Spanos and his associates found that if hypnotically susceptible subjects were given suggestions *without* hypnosis (that is were not given hypnotic induction) they were just as likely to display incongruous writing and say they felt like a children only some of the time as susceptible subjects tested *with* hypnotic induction, thus being 'hypnotized' was irrelevant (Spanos, in press).

Another phenomenon put forward by some state theorists as differentiating between 'hypnotized' and simulating subjects is 'source amnesia'. In a typical demonstration hypnotic subjects are asked questions such as 'What is the diameter of the earth?' As they usually do not know they are told the answers. They are then 'woken up' and the questions are asked again. If a subject answers a question correctly he or she is then asked, 'How did you know that?' If the subject claims he or she cannot recall how the answer was learned, then 'source amnesia' has occurred, that is the subject remembers the answers, but has amnesia for the source. According to some investigators simulators tend not to show this response (Evans, 1979). This again has been interpreted by some state theorists as evidence for a special kind of responding which occurs during 'hypnosis'. However, non-state theorists have suggested an alternative explanation. Because simulators play excellent hypnotic subjects they tend to report *complete* amnesia. As they do not know the answer, they are never asked the critical question about the source, so they *cannot* display source amnesia (Wagstaff, 1981a,b). In other words, simulators do not report source amnesia, because, on average, they are better at playing amnesic than the 'hypnotized' subjects!

What can we conclude from this research? First, as state theorists would predict, if we employ some rather subtle measures, simulators *do* sometimes behave differently from highly susceptible individuals given hypnotic suggestions. However, non-state theorists have argued that because simulators come from a different subject population, and because they operate under different instructions and play a more extreme role, the differences are not necessarily due to the existence of a special altered state of consciousness in 'hypnotized' subjects. Second, nevertheless, non-state theorists would also conclude that hypnotic subjects are not necessarily lying or faking when they report certain experiences; their reports, or at least many of them, may reflect genuine attempts to experience suggestions, for example, by trying to imagine what is suggested to them.

But what of the state view? It is all very well saying that trance-logic and source amnesia are features of a hypnotic state, but why should the hypnotic state produce these effects? In order to explore the state interpretation we need to examine developments in the state view of hypnosis.

NEO-DISSOCIATION THEORY

The most popular contemporary state or special process theory of hypnosis is 'neo-dissociation theory' (Hilgard, 1974, 1977, 1978, 1979; Bowers, 1983). This theory, based on some early ideas by writers such as Prince and Janet, proposes that we have multiple systems of control which are not all conscious at the same time, but can be brought into consciousness 'under hypnosis.' The principle is best illustrated by Hilgard's demonstration of the 'hidden-observer' phenomenon. In order to demonstrate this, Hilgard 'hypnotizes' subjects and gives them the following instruction:

> When I place my hand on your shoulder, I shall be able to talk to a hidden part of you that knows things are going on in your body, things that are unknown to the part of you to which I am now talking. The part to which I am now talking will not know what you are telling me or even that you are talking. . . You will remember that there is a part of you that knows many things that are going on that may be hidden from either your normal consciousness or the hypnotised part of you (Knox, Morgan and Hilgard, 1974, p.842).

By doing this Hilgard and his associates argue that one can contact another system of control, or 'part' of you, which will then speak, unaware of the normal 'waking part', or the 'hypnotized part'.

It was originally proposed by Prince and Janet that if two tasks were performed simultaneously 'under hypnosis' then the dissociation between the tasks would be reduced and the tasks would be performed better than in the 'waking state'. However, Hilgard (1974) reports that no such reduction in interference is evident . He has thus amended 'dissociation theory' to '*neo*-dissociation theory'. If we look at trance-logic and source amnesia in terms of neo-dissociation theory then the explanation is that the elements of incongruity reside in dissociated 'parts'. For example, the 'part' which sees an hallucinated object is dissociated from the 'part' which does not see it; thus the 'part' which does not see the chair is dissociated from the 'part' which knows it is there, and walks round it. Also the 'part' which sees the man in the chair is dissociated from the 'part' which does not see the hallucination, and both the man and the back of the chair are reported at once. Similarly, the 'part' which feels like a child is dissociated from the 'part' which knows it is an adult, and writes like an adult, and the 'part' which remembers the answer to a question is dissociated from the 'part' which was 'hypnotized' and remembers the source.

Hilgard argues that these 'parts' are not aware of each other because they are separated by 'amnesic barriers' but they can break through simultaneously, so that the subject reports incongruities. Hilgard suggests that hypnotic dissociation can even be performed post-hypnotically. After 'waking up', the subject may respond to a suggestion given previously 'under hypnosis' to perform a task without being aware of it. For example, a subject's hand can write away, hidden inside a box, without the subject being aware of it (Hilgard, 1974, 1978).

The impact of neo-dissociation theory on contemporary hypnosis has been considerable. One element in its appeal has been its ability to reinterpret some results which otherwise would appear to support the non-state view. For example, it has been noted that if hypnotic subjects are given suggestions for deafness and the hypnotist then asks 'Can you hear me?' some subjects will answer, 'No, I can't hear you' (Barber, Spanos and Chaves, 1974). From the non-state view, these subjects have fallen for a simple trick: for neo-dissociation theorists, the 'part' which answers, 'No, I can't hear you', is dissociated from the 'part' which cannot hear (though perhaps it would make more sense if the 'hidden-part' said 'I *can* hear you').

There is no conclusive evidence for either the state or non-state explanations of trance-logic and source amnesia. Ultimately, it boils down to a question of parsimony, that is, is it *necessary* to postulate dissociative processes and amnesic barriers when more 'normal' factors such as imagination, attitudes and expectations will do the job? As we shall see, the same conclusion could be applied to some other well-known hypnotic phenomena.

HYPNOTIC AMNESIA

To demonstrate hypnotic amnesia a subject is given a hypnotic induction procedure, followed by suggestions, and is then told that he or she will forget what has happened until the hypnotist gives a signal such as 'Now you can remember'. The subject is then challenged to remember. If the subject does not recall part or all of what has happened, but subsequently *can* recall the 'missing' information when the 'release' signal is given, it is said that hypnotic amnesia has occurred. The information to be 'forgotten' and then remembered does not have to be a series of suggestions, it can be lists of words, or single items such as the subject's own name.

It is well known from work on memory that if you give a person a list of items to remember and then a second similar list to remember, it will be more difficult to learn and remember the second list, because the first list will interfere with it. A good test of whether hypnotic amnesia is equivalent to actual forgetting is, therefore, to get 'hypnotized' subjects to learn two lists, and then to instruct them to forget one of the lists. If the 'forgetting' is effective, there should be a reduction in the amount of interference between the two lists. However, this is not the case; hypnotic amnesia does not reduce interference, thus the list is not actually 'forgotten' (Wagstaff, 1981a).

Neo-dissociation theory copes with this finding by arguing that the memories of the amnesic subject are still there, but they are dissociated from conscious control, and cannot be accessed voluntarily. Thus although hypnotic subjects may try very hard to remember, they find it difficult and sometimes impossible to do so (Bowers, 1983; Hilgard, 1977).

As an alternative, the non-state view argues that hypnotic subjects interpret an amnesia suggestion as an instruction to *try not to remember*. In order to do this they may try do adopt strategies so that they cannot remember; for example, by thinking about something else, by making no effort to think back over the material or, if necessary, deliberately withholding material (Wagstaff, 1981a; Spanos, 1982). Indeed, Spanos and his associates found that if subjects were instructed to interpret the amnesia suggestion as a request to attend away (or not attend to) the target material, amnesia was significantly increased. Amnesia decreased, however, when the challenge to remember was to be interpreted as a challenge to focus attention and actively recall (Spanos, 1982, in press).

Recently there has been quite a battle between these two points of view. In support of the state view Kihlstrom et al. (1980) found that some highly susceptible subjects continued to show amnesia in spite of explicit instructions to actively try to remember, and to be honest. Indeed, it seems that for some subjects hypnotic amnesia is extremely difficult to 'breach'. In reply to this, non-state theorists argue that the few subjects involved have such an investment in the role of appearing hypnotically amnesic that they do not wish to discredit themselves by showing themselves not to be amnesic. Therefore, to 'breach' or eliminate amnesia in these subjects one needs a special instruction or situation which will overcome this investment. Spanos, Radtke and Bertrand (1985) found that if subjects were told that the 'forgotten' material was located in 'hidden parts' of the mind, then amnesia could be breached, even in these subjects. All one needs to do is contact the 'hidden parts' using the hidden-observer technique. Of course state theorists could argue that the material really was 'hidden' in the mind. However, Wagstaff (1977a) found that amnesia could be eliminated completely, if subjects were given an opportunity to say they were 'role-playing' rather than in a hypnotic 'trance'.

A variety of other amnesia effects have been investigated. For example, Kihlstrom (1980), for the state view, found that hypnotic amnesia only affected episodic memory (memory for episodes or contexts) but not semantic memory (memory independent of context or situations in which facts are learned). However, Spanos and his associates (Spanos, in press) found that this effect disappeared if it was subtly implied to subjects that amnesia would occur on the semantic task; that is Kihlstrom's (1980) instructions did not imply that amnesia should occur on the semantic task.

For the state position, it has also been argued that if we select hypnotic subjects who remember a few items (partial amnesics) and look at the way they recall the few items they do remember, they will tend to recall them in a disorganized fashion (not in serial order, and not in semantic 'clusters'). This is unlike recall in 'normal' memory (Kihlstrom and Wilson, 1984). However, for the non-state position, Wagstaff (1977b, 1981a, 1982a) and Spanos and his associates (Spanos 1982, in press) have found that the same responses can be elicited from subjects instructed to 'pretend to forget', or given instructions to 'attend away' (for example, by performing other mental activities). Also some of the disorganization findings are not very robust and cannot easily be repeated (Spanos, 1982).

The debate on hypnotic amnesia will no doubt continue and become even more complicated! So let us now turn to what is, in many respects, the 'pièce de résistance' of hypnosis, hypnotic analgesia, or the elimination of pain through hypnosis.

HYPNOSIS AND PAIN

On first consideration, the fact that hypnosis can be used to reduce or sometimes eliminate pain of various kinds, especially surgical and post-surgical pain, would seem to invalidate the 'role-play' view. It does seem very unlikely that people would 'pretend' that they were not feeling pain in clinical situations, and the fact that techniques labelled as hypnotic can be useful in the alleviation of clinical pain seems well-documented and undeniable (Wadden and Anderton, 1982; Hilgard and Hilgard, 1984). However, it should be remembered that non-state theorists do not argue that all hypnotic phenomena are 'faked'. Instead, they argue that one does not need to put forward a 'special process' as an explanation; hypnotic pain relief could occur because of a variety of factors which may be potent pain relievers, but are not particularly unusual. To this end non-state theorists have drawn attention to the following points (for reviews see Barber, Spanos and Chaves, 1974; Chaves and Barber, 1976; Wagstaff, 1981a).

First, clinical cases are very carefully selected; surgery with 'hypnosis' is still comparatively rare. Second, many surgical procedures are less painful than might be commonly predicted. Many of the internal organs of the body are actually insensitive to incision. It should be noted here that most of us can tolerate injections without collapsing with pain, people seem to be able to have their ears pierced, and 'punks' tolerate safety pins in the most unlikely places, all without an anaesthetic. It is not therefore surprising that people can tolerate having needles stuck into them when 'hypnotized'. It is *not* the case that the 'deeper' you cut into the body the more it hurts, though pulling and stretching of damaged tissues is painful. Furthermore, some people seem to be able to tolerate surgery with little or no sign of pain, without anaesthetics or 'hypnosis'. Third, pain is a complex psychological experience and can be reduced through the alleviation of anxiety, and the use of relaxation and distraction. These factors alone rather than 'hypnosis' may be responsible for hypnotic pain relief.

Because of the problems involved in assessing factors such as the placebo effect ('believing' in the treatment), the role of anxiety, fear, distraction, coping instructions without 'hypnosis' and so on, psychologists have turned to the investigation of pain in the laboratory, where such factors can be systematically controlled, to see if there is an extra 'hypnotic' element operating. Of course in the laboratory one cannot ethically operate on people, but a variety of unpleasant, painful techniques have been applied. The most frequently used is the cold-pressor test where the subject's arm is plunged into ice-cold water. This is extremely painful but produces no lasting damage.

For the 'state' position it has been argued that suggestions for analgesia are more effective if given in the 'hypnotic' state rather than the 'waking' state (Hilgard, 1977). However, the state position has leaned heavily on the 'same-subjects' design, that is looking at the responses of the *same* subjects before and during 'hypnosis'. As was pointed out earlier, such studies are difficult to interpret because subjects may not try very hard in the 'awake' condition (for example, they may not try 'coping' strategies such as relaxation or distraction). Against the state view, a number of studies have shown that suggestions for analgesia given without 'hypnosis' are as effective as instructions given with 'hypnosis', if the *different* subjects are used in the hypnotic and non-hypnotic conditions (Spanos, 1982). Moreover, Stam and Spanos (1980), using the same-subjects design, found that hypnotic analgesia was as effective as, less effective than, and more effective than the same suggestions given without 'hypnosis', depending upon the order in which the treatments were presented; if subjects thought that hypnotic analgesia was to follow they performed less than optimally in the 'waking' situation.

A most important recent controversy has concerned the application of the 'hidden-observer' technique to hypnotic analgesia. According to Hilgard (1977, 1979), whilst the conscious 'hypnotized' part seems unaware of pain, the 'hidden-observer' (contacted by placing a hand on the subject's shoulder) reports high levels of pain only slightly less than the pain reported in the normal 'waking' state. This has led Hilgard to speculate that pain *is* occurring during hypnotic analgesia but it is dissociated from awareness by an 'amnesic barrier'. However, non-state theorists have argued that the pain reports of the 'hidden-observer' occur because this is what the 'hypnotized' subject thinks he or she is *expected* to say, that is it is part of the required role (Wagstaff, 1981a; Spanos, 1982, in press). In support of the non-state explanation Spanos and Hewitt (1980) found that the 'hidden-observer' could be made to report greater, the same, or less pain than the ordinary 'hypnotized' part, if the instructions implied that greater, the same, or less pain should be reported.

It should be emphasized yet again that the non-state view does not argue that all reports of hypnotic analgesia are faked. Indeed coping instructions for dealing with pain, such as relaxation, distraction and inattention can be very effective. Rather, non-state theorists argue that hypnotic subjects tend to selectively apply these coping skills in accordance with how they think they are expected to behave.

There is some evidence from experimental studies that subjects judged to be highly hypnotically susceptible appear to tolerate and report less pain than subjects who are insusceptible. State theorists have interpreted this finding as indicating that only highly susceptible subjects can achieve the depth of trance, or the degree of dissociation, necessary to reduce pain. However, non-state theorists argue that the difference occurs because insusceptible subjects do not think the hypnosis situation is one in which they should exercise deliberate coping strategies. In line with the non-state explanation, Spanos, Kennedy and Gwynn (1984) found that, outside the hypnosis situation, low susceptibles are as successful as high susceptibles at reducing pain, but the performance of the low susceptibles deteriorates during 'hypnosis', whereas that of the high susceptibles does not.

The state and non-state views thus diverge widely on how we interpret reports of hypnotic analgesia, the choice boils down to dissociated cognitive subsystems with amnesic barriers, or the selective use of cognitive strategies or coping skills. Research continues.

CLINICAL HYPNOSIS

As the reader will no doubt be aware, hypnotic techniques have a much wider clinical application than that of the alleviation of pain. It seems that hypnosis has been effectively applied to the treatment of problems such as insomnia, obesity, mild phobias, smoking, dental stress and alcoholism. However, little can be concluded about the state versus non-state controversy as regards these phenomena, because treatment success seems largely attributable to factors which are not unique to hypnosis, but are employed in hypnotic treatments, such as social support, relaxation and covert modelling (Wadden and Anderton, 1982; Wagstaff, 1981a). Although the evidence is not conclusive, there are some studies which indicate that 'hypnosis' may be especially useful in the treatment of skin diseases, such as warts, and also asthma (Wadden and Anderton, 1982; Bowers and Kelly, 1979).

Whilst this could be viewed as support for a 'state' view, non-state theorists have argued that such a conclusion would be premature until the effects of suggestions without hypnosis, and possible placebo components have been fully isolated. Barber (1983), for example, has presented a number of phenomena achieved, *without* 'hypnosis', in predisposed individuals. These include suggested bruising, dermatitis and an increase in breast size! Barber argues that in order to achieve such effects subjects must be able and willing to feel, imagine and think with the suggestions and *believe* they will work, and it is these factors which are responsible, not a special hypnotic process. This suggests that it is not only the techniques used by hypnotists that are important in eliciting the effects, but that characteristics of the subjects are also important: they must be willing to engage in the imaginative activities and 'think along with' the suggestions. So is there a particular kind of person who is more likely to respond to hypnotic suggestions?

HYPNOTIC SUSCEPTIBILITY

There is some evidence to suggest that hypnotic susceptibility may to a small extent relate to conformity (Graham and Green, 1981; Shames, 1981). However, it has been argued that certain skills may also be involved, in particular acting and drama skills (Sarbin and Coe, 1972) and a willingness to become absorbed in imaginings. That the willingness to become imaginatively involved is an important characteristic of hypnotic susceptibility is agreed upon by both state and non-state theorists. Barber and his associates have suggested that there may actually be a 'fantasy-prone personality' who is particularly susceptible to hypnotic, and also non-hypnotic, suggestions (Wilson and Barber, 1983).

Nevertheless, state theorists believe that there is something else beyond a willingness to become imaginatively involved, and this is the ability to 'dissociate' (Bowers, 1983). To bolster this position state theorists point to research which indicates that hypnotically susceptible subjects may have very good attention skills, and may be able to attend better than insusceptible subjects to more than one stimulus. However, attempts to relate hypnotic susceptibility to attention skills have been difficult to replicate (Spanos, 1982) or leave significant numbers of subjects low in the skills still able to perform well on scales of hypnotic susceptibility (Wagstaff, 1985a). Attempts to relate hypnotic susceptibility to a variety of other measures, including EEG activity, right brain hemisphere processing, eye-rolling (the ability to roll one's eyes up into one's head) and responding to stimuli during sleep, have proved inconclusive (Spanos, 1982). On the other hand, relationships have been found between hypnotic susceptibility and attitudes and expectations toward hypnosis; if attitudes are negative, subjects are less likely to respond (Spanos, 1982).

The overwhelming picture which seems to emerge is that someone who responds to hypnotic suggestions has no single hypnotic skill, instead the person who is judged to be hypnotically susceptible is someone who has positive attitudes to the situation, and particularly a willingness to become imaginatively involved in the hypnotic situation. Possibly, some attention skills might be involved but these are by no means essential. However, when these factors are combined, performance on scales of hypnotic susceptibility can be remarkably stable (Bowers, 1983).

CONCLUSIONS

I have been able to sketch only the briefest outline of research into the topic of hypnosis; but as you will have seen the controversy surrounding the subject is still very much alive. But as in any scientific debate there is no absolute answer. We cannot conclusively say whether or not the hypnotic 'trance' or 'state' exists; non-state theorists cannot prove that the trance does not exist any more than one can prove that unicorns do not exist. But perhaps we are at the stage of arguing that it is not *necessary* to put forward the notion of a special hypnotic process to explain hypnotic phenomena. The onus now must surely be on the state theorists to show that non-state explanations are inadequate, rather than vice versa.

REFERENCES

Barber, T.X. (1969) *Hypnosis: A Scientific Approach*. New York: Van Nostrand.
Barber, T.X. (1972) Suggested ('Hypnotic') behaviour: The trance paradigm versus an alternative paradigm. In E. Fromm and R.E. Shor (eds) *Hypnosis: Research Developments and Perspectives*. Chicago: Aldine-Atherton.
Barber, T.X. (1983) Changing 'unchangeable' bodily processes by (hypnotic) suggestions: A new look at hypnosis, cognitions, imagining and the mind – body problem. In A.A. Sheikh (ed.) *Imagination and Healing*. New York: Baywood.
Barber, T.X., Spanos, N.P. and Chaves, J.F. (1974) *Hypnotism: Imagination and Human Potentialities*. New York: Pergamon.
Barber, T.X. and Wilson, S.C. (1977) Hypnosis, suggestions and altered states of consciousness: Experimental evaluation of the new cognitive-behavioural theory and the traditional trance-state theory of 'hypnosis'. *Annals of the New York Academy of Sciences, 296*, 34–47.
Bowers, K.S. (1983) *Hypnosis for the Seriously Curious*. New York: W.W. Norton.
Bowers, K.S. and Kelly, P. (1979) Stress, disease, psychotheraphy and hypnosis. *Journal of Abnormal Psychology, 88*, 490–505.
Chaves, J.F. and Barber, T.X. (1976) Hypnotic procedures and surgery: A critical analysis with applications to 'acupuncture analgesia'. *American Journal of Clinical Hypnosis, 18*, 217–236.
Evans, F.J. (1979) Contextual forgetting: Posthypnotic source amnesia. *Journal of Abnormal Psychology, 88*, 556–563.

Graham, K.R. and Green, L.D. (1981) Hypnotic susceptibility related to an independent measure of compliance-alumni annual giving: A brief communication. *International Journal of Clinical and Experimental Hypnosis*,29, 351–354.

Hilgard, E.R. (1974) Toward a neo-dissociation theory: Multiple cognitive controls in human functioning. *Perspectives in Biology and Medicine*, 17,, 301–316.

Hilgard, E.R. (1977) *Divided Consciousness: Multiple Controls in Human Thought and Action.* New York: Wiley.

Hilgard, E.R. (1978) States of consciousness in hypnosis: Divisions or levels? In F.H. Frankel and H.S. Zamansky (eds) *Hypnosis at Its Bicentennial: Selected Papers.* New York: Plenum.

Hilgard, E.R. (1979) Divided consciousness in hypnosis: The implications of the hidden observer. In E. Fromm and R.E. Shor (eds) *Hypnosis: Developments in Research and New Perspectives*, 2nd ed. New York: Aldine.

Hilgard, E.R. and Hilgard, J.R. (1984) *Hypnosis in the Relief of Pain.* New York: W. Kaufmann.

Hilgard, E.R., Hilgard, J.R., Macdonald, H., Morgan, A.H. and Johnson, L.S. (1978) Covert pain in hypnotic analgesia: Its reality as tested by the real-simulator. *Journal of Abnormal Psychology*, 87, 655–663.

Johnson, R.F., Maher, B.A. and Barber, T.X. (1972) Artifact in the 'essence of hypnosis': An evaluation of trance logic. *Journal of Abnormal Psychology*, 79, 212–220.

Kihlstrom, J.F. (1980) Posthypnotic amnesia for recently learned material: Interactions with 'episodic' and 'semantic' memory. *Cognitive Psychology*, 12, 227–251.

Kihlstrom, J.F., Evans, F.J., Orne, E.C. and Orne, M.T. (1980) Attempting to breach posthypnotic amnesia. *Journal of Abnormal Psychology*, 89, 603–616.

Kihlstrom, J.F. and Wilson, L. (1984) Temporal organization of recall during posthypnotic amnesia. *Journal of Abnormal Psychology*, 93, 200–208.

Knox, J.V., Morgan, A.H. and Hilgard, E.R. (1974) Pain and suffering in ischemia: The paradox of hypnotically suggested anaesthesia as contradicted by reports from the 'hidden'observer'. *Archives of General Psychiatry*, 30, 840–847.

Milgram, S. (1974) *Obedience to Authority.* London: Tavistock.

Nogrady, H., McConkey, K.M., Laurence, J.R. and Perry, C. (1983) Dissociation' duality and demand characteristics in hypnosis. *Journal of Abnormal Psychology*, 92, 223–235.

Orne, M.T. (1959) The nature of hypnosis: Artifact and essence. *Journal of Abnormal and Social Psychology*, 58, 277–299.

Orne, M.T. (1962) On the social psychology of he psychological experiment: With particular reference to demand characteristics and their implications. *American Psychologist*, 17, 276–783.

Orne, M.T. (1966) Hypnosis, motivation and compliance. *American Journal of Psychiatry*, 122, 721–726.

Orne, M.T. (1970) Hypnosis: motivation and the ecological validity of the psychological experiment. In W.J. Arnold and M.M. Page (eds) *Nebraska Symposium on Motivation.* Lincoln, Nebraska: University of Nebraska Press.

Orne, M.T. (1979) On the simulating subject as quasi-control group in hypnosis research: What, why, and how? In E. Fromm and R.E. Shor (eds) *Hypnosis: Research Developments and Perspectives*, 2nd ed. New York: Aldine.

Sarbin, T.R. (1982) Hypnosis: The dramaturgical perspective. In V.L. Allen and K.E. Scheib (eds) *The Social Context of Conduct: Psychological Writings of Theodore Sarbin.* New York: Praeger.

Sarbin, T.R. and Coe, W.C. (1972) *Hypnosis: a Social Psychological Analysis of Influence Communication* New York: Holt, Rinehart and Winston.

Sarbin, T.R. and Coe, W.C (1979) Hypnosis and psychopathology: Replacing old myths with fresh metaphors. *Journal of Abnormal Psychology, 88,* 506–526.

Sarbin, T.R. and Slagle, R.W. (1972) Hypnosis and psychophysiological outcomes. In E. Fromm and R.E. Shor (eds) *Hypnosis: Research Developments and Perspectives.* Chicago: Aldine-Atherton.

Shames, M.L. (1981) Hypnotic susceptibility and conformity: On the mediational mechanism of suggestibility. *Psychological Reports, 49,* 563–565.

Sheridan, C.L. and King, R.G. (1972) Obedience to authority with an authentic victim. Proceedings, Eightieth Annual Convention, American Psychological Association. Washington, D. C.: American Psychological Association.

Spanos, N.P. (1982) A social psychological approach to hypnotic behaviour. In G. Weary and H.L. Mirels (eds) *Integrations of Clinical and Social Psychology.* New York: Oxford University Press.

Spanos, N.P. (in press) Hypnotic behaviour: A social psychological interpretation of amnesia, analgesia and 'trance logic'. *The Behavioural and Brain Sciences.*

Spanos, N.P. and Hewitt, E.C. (1980) The hidden observer in hypnotic analgesia: Discovery or experimental creation? *Journal of Personality and Social Psychology, 39,* 1201–1214.

Spanos, N.P., Kennedy, S.K. and Gwynn, M.I. (1984) Moderating effects of contextual variables on the relationship between hypnotic susceptibility and suggested analgesia. *Journal of Abnormal Pschology, 93,* 3, 285–294.

Spanos, N.P., Radtke, L. and Bertrand, L.D. (1985) Hypnotic amnesia as a strategic enactment: Breaching amnesia in highly susceptible subjects. *Journal of Personality and Social Psychology, 47,* 1155–1169.

Stam, H.J. and Spanos, N.P. (1980) Experimental designs, expectancy effects and hypnotic analgesia. *Journal of Abnormal Psychology, 89,* 751–762.

Wadden, T. and Anderton, C.H. (1982) The clinical use of hypnosis. *Psychological Bulletin, 91,* 215–243.

Wagstaff, G.F. (1977a) An experimental study of compliance and posthypnotic amnesia. *British Journal of Social and Clinical Psychology, 16,* 225–228.

Wagstaff, G.F. (1977b) Post-hypnotic amnesia as disrupted retrieval: A role-playing paradigm. *Quarterly Journal of Experimental Psychology, 29,* 499–504.

Wagstaff, G.F. (1981a) *Hypnosis, Compliance and Belief.* Brighton: Harvester and New York: St Martin's Press.

Wagstaff, G.F. (1981b) Source amnesia and trance logic: Artifacts in the essence of hypnosis? *Bulletin of the British Society of Experimental and Clinical Hypnosis, 4,* 3–5.

Wagstaff, G.F. (1982a) Disorganized recall, suggested amnesia and compliance. *Psychological Reports, 51,* 1255–1258.

Wagstaff, G.F. (1982b) Hypnosis and witness recall: A discussion paper. *Journal of the Royal Society of Medicine, 75,* 793–798.

Wagstaff, G.F. (1982c) Recall of witnesses under hypnosis. *Journal of the Forensic Science Society, 22,* 33–39.

Wagstaff, G.F. (1983) A comment on McConkey's 'Challenging hypnotic effects?: The impact of conflicting influences on response to hypnotic suggestion. *British Journal of Experimental and Clinical Hypnosis*, 1, 11–15.

Wagstaff, G.F. (1984) The enhancement of witness memory by 'hypnosis': A review and methodological critique of the experimental literature. *British Journal of Experimental and Clinical Hypnosis*, 2, 3–12.

Wagstaff, G.F. (1985a) A comment on 'Attentional concomitants of hypnotic susceptibility' by A. Sigman, K.C. Phillipps and B. Clifford. *British Journal of Experimental and Clinical Hypnosis*, 2, 2, 76–80.

Wagstaff, G.F. (1985b) Discussion commentary on Gibson's 'Experiencing hypnosis versus pretending to be hypnotized'. Observations on hypnosis training workshops. *British Journal of Experimental and Clinical Hypnosis*, 2, 2, 114–117.

Wilson, S.C. and Barber, T.X. (1983) The fantasy-prone personality: Implications for understanding imagery, hypnosis and parapsychological phenomena. In A. Sheikh (ed.) *Imagery: Current Theory, Research and Application*. New York: Wiley.

PSYCHOLOGY AND COMPUTER DESIGN
David J. Oborne

Like it or not we are in the information age – the age of the computer. These information-processing machines are becoming increasingly more powerful, smaller, transportable, omniscient and omnipresent. They range from the very expensive mainframe affairs used by large organizations and governments to control and to predict events, through rather smaller (but often nearly as powerful) mini and self-contained desk-top computers – systems which are capable of transmitting data via a number of electronic systems such as telephone lines or radio transmitters, to small, sometimes pocket-sized, computers that can perform fast, reliable calculations that would have shortened World War II considerably had they been available only 40 or 50 years ago. The information revolution is certainly with us.

Unfortunately, this information technology explosion has happened too fast and we are unready for it. Individuals are often slow to adapt to new concepts and the concept of information manipulation, with its associated jargon and implications for living and for employment, has often been hard to grasp. In some ways it is as if history is repeating itself. During World War II, for example, technology developed so fast that machines were designed that required social, cognitive and motor skills quite outside the capabilities of those who were to operate them. The result was often operator failure, sometimes of a dramatic kind. Only when psychologists combined their skills with those of other practitioners to investigate the working environment and the interaction between people and their machines – when the discipline of *ergonomics* was born – was it possible to design systems that were within the capabilities of the operators. The repetition of history is that psychologists are again being called on to use their knowledge to help develop computing systems that fit the behaviour of the operator.

This chapter approaches the problem of ensuring that computers operate in a way that fits the user from two directions. First it considers the hardware associated with computers. It is a truism that, presently at least, computers can operate only on the information provided by the operator, and this must somehow be entered – often through a keyboard but increasingly through other types of device. Similarly, the information presented – the type and the quality – will be related to what the operator 'perceives' from the machine; from the screen, for example. Psychologists, with their knowledge of perceptual–motor skilled behaviour and of perception in its widest sense, have provided a great deal of information to help in the design of such features.

Second, the software aspects are discussed – the 'brain' of the machine. The analogy with human cognition is ideal in this respect since to be operated usefully the machine's behaviour needs to match the operator's. Compatibility with memory, cognitive style and schema, structure, expectations, etc. all play important roles.

HARDWARE ASPECTS

The hardware aspects of computers comprise, essentially, features such as keyboards that enable information to be passed from the operator to the machine, and features such as screens which allow information to be transmitted back from the machine to the operator. Both types of hardware need to act as efficient extensions of the operator's own mechanisms – motor and perceptual. For both aspects, knowledge of behavioural processes can suggest features of their design.

Input hardware

The main ways in which information is generally passed (input) to the computer is via one of three of the operator's effector systems: limb movement and touch (usually using the hands or fingers), speech, and even eye movement. A number of possible devices can be conceived, although unfortunately there have been very few comparative studies to investigate which is the best type of control for particular circumstances. Those that have been reported have generally been restricted in their application and have considered simply the relative efficiencies of different controls for the simple task of selecting an item from a screen. Furthermore, no study has been reported that has considered operator preference. The work that has been done, however, has consistently indicated keyboard controls to take longer and to be more prone to errors (Earl and Goff, 1965; Goodwin, 1975). For inputting discrete pieces of information, continuous positioning devices such as lightpens are the most efficient (Card, English and Burr, 1978).

Keyboards

(This overview of research on keyboard design and input devices also appears in 'Information Technology and People: Designing for the Future', edited by F. Blackler and D.J. Oborne, published by The British Psychological Society, 1987.)

Aphabetic keyboards. The normal QWERTY typewriter keyboard has been in existence since before the beginning of this century and was designed to conform to the mechanical constraints of contemporary typewriters. Since typists were able to press keys at faster rates than the machines could respond without jamming, the apparent haphazard arrangement of letters was developed to *slow down* typists by ensuring that the letter most likely to be typed next was obscured by the operator's hand. Despite the arrangement, however, the QWERTY keyboard does distribute evenly the workload assigned to each hand and thus may reduce fatigue. Noyes (1983a), for example, argues that common letter sequences typed on the QWERTY board involve either alternate hands being used, the whole hand being moved over the keyboard or non-adjacent fingers being moved sequentially.

A number of alternative keyboard arrangements have subsequently been proposed. All are based on the frequencies with which letters and letter pairs occur in the English language. The two which have captured most experimental time are the Dvorak and the alphabetic board.

The Dvorak board (patented by A. Dvorak in 1932) was produced as a result of a decade of physiological and language research. The essential feature of the key arrangement is that all vowels and the most used consonants are on the second (or 'home') row, so that something like 70 per cent of common words are typed on this row alone. Generally, the arrangement means that vowels are typed with the left hand and frequent (home row) consonants with the right hand, producing, it is argued, a more even distribution of finger movements and a bias towards the right hand. It also reduces the between-rows movement by 90 per cent.

Controversy exists as to the relative merits of the QWERTY and the Dvorak boards. For example, a United States government-sponsored study in 1956 demonstrated little difference between the arrangements (Alden, Daniels and Kanarick, 1976). Martin (1972), however, discusses (unreported) novice training experiments carried out in Great Britain which demonstrated a 10 per cent saving in training time using the

Dvorak board. Furthermore, Dunn (1971) argues that the Dvorak board is superior in terms of ease of learning, reduced likelihood of error and fatigue and increased speed of entry.

On the alphabetic board, keys are arranged as the name suggests: from A to Z. The argument behind the use of this arrangement is, quite simply, that an alphabetical ordering of the keys makes logical sense, particularly to inexperienced typists, who need to spend considerable time learning the QWERTY arrangement.

Despite the apparent logic of using an alphabetically arranged board, Norman and Fisher (1982) point out that the available studies do not support the view that inexperienced typists find the alphabetic board easier to use. Indeed both Hirsch (1970) and Michaelis (1971) have shown that for semi-skilled typists, keying rates and error correction are better using the QWERTY board, and performance on the two boards is essentially the same for novices. Norman and Fisher suggest two reasons for these findings. First, an experimental one: it is difficult to find subjects who have not had some exposure to the QWERTY arrangement. Second, the alphabetic keyboard, although logically superior, still requires considerable visual search and mental processing (to remember, for example, that 'M' appears after 'K'). At the novice stage at least, therefore, all keyboard layouts are roughly equivalent. Once the skill has been learned visual feedback gives way to kinaesthetic feedback, so that the different board arrangements are likely to be equally efficient.

Numeric keyboards. Fewer studies have been performed to determine the optimum arrangement of the numeric keys (0–9) than the alphabetic keys – possibly because, with only 10 keys, there are fewer sensible arrangements that can be accommodated. A number of these arrangements were investigated by Deininger (1960) in a study of pushbutton telephone sets. Four designs were shown to be roughly equally acceptable on criteria such as keying time, errors, and 'votes' for and against. For engineering reasons, however, Deininger suggested an arrangement of a 3+3+3+1 matrix starting with 1,2,3 on the top row and ending with 0 below the third row. Indeed, the standard telephone keypad has this arrangement.

Although this arrangement has become standard for telephone keypads, it is not currently used for numerical input on keyboards such as calculators. This is normally the reverse of the telephone arrangement, the keys on the 3+3+3+1 matrix having the order, 7,8,9; 4,5,6; 1,2,3; and 0. Conrad and Hull (1968) compared the keying efficiency of these two types of arrangement. No significant differences were obtained in terms of the speed of data entry but they did find that significantly fewer errors were made using the telephone keypad (1,2,3; 4,5,6; etc.) than with the calculator pad arrangement (7,8,9; 4,5,6; etc.) (6.4 per cent versus 8.2 per cent).

Chord keyboards. In the search for improved ways of keying data, particularly alphabetic data, the possibility of reducing the number of keys by requiring the operator to press more than one key at a time has often been suggested. Such key arrangements are called *chord keyboards* and they appear in many different forms. (Litterick, 1981, describes some of these boards, and Noyes, 1983b, describes the history and development of chord keying.) The efficiency of such boards, of course, is determined by the combinations of keys used to produce particular letters – from the viewpoint both of the operator's ability to use various finger combinations and to learn and remember key sets (see Seibel, 1964).

Very few experiments have been performed to compare directly keying performance using a typewriter and a chord keyboard. Again, this is probably because of difficulties in obtaining matched groups of subjects and being able to train them for very long periods of time using the same instructor. Nevertheless, the comparative studies that are available have demonstrated a chord keyboard performance superiority (Bowen and Guiness, 1965) and reduced training time (Conrad and Longman, 1965).

Other types of input device

Touch displays. These allow the user to input information to the machine simply by touching an appropriate part of the screen or some representation of the screen. Since the computer screen both presents information to and receives information from the operator, it combines the functions of keyboard and display. Both Hopkin (1971) and McEwing (1977) discuss the advantages of screen-based displays, which can be summarized thus: they are easy and fast to use, training time is reduced (Usher, 1982), they minimize errors, they are flexible and operator reaction is generally favourable. Against these advantages, however, Pfauth and Priest (1981) suggest a number of disadvantages: an initial high cost for the system, increased programmer time, reduced flexibility for some types of input, possible screen glare, physical fatigue from reaching to the screen, and the finger and hand blocking the operator's line of sight to important areas of the screen.

Lightpens. Like touch displays, light pens are fully interactive control devices. They can be used effectively to position the cursor on the screen or to select responses from a 'menu' displayed to the operator. Unfortunately, little research appears to have been carried out to investigate either the design or the efficiency of this type of control, although Oborne (1985) discusses various features that should be important.

Bar code scanners. These are devices which both look and operate very much like lightpens, but they are not used interactively with the computer screen; rather they are passed over alternate black and white bars, the composition of which contains the information to be input. They have a major advantage in that their operating postures are not constrained by the computer system itself, so that the arm and hand do not need to be maintained under static load to enable the pen to touch the screen. However, Wilson and Grey (1983) point out that the fixed pen system of scanners, in which the material to be read is passed over the scanner, can create postural difficulties for the operator.

Levers and joysticks. The difference between a lever and a joystick is simply that joysticks operate in two dimensions whereas levers only operate in one. For this reason, joysticks are used more often for cursor positioning. Because they are used in situations in which precision adjustments are made, it is desirable that only the hand and fingers are used, since these muscles are more densely supplied with nerves than, for example, the arm. For this reason joysticks are generally smaller than levers. To aid precision they should have resistance in all directions with, perhaps, a return to centre position if the hand is moved. Morgan *et al.* (1963) further suggest that the joystick should be designed to enable the operator to rest the wrist while making the movements, and that the pivot point should be positioned under the point at which the wrist is rested.

The roller ball and mouse. As their name suggests, roller balls are spherically-shaped objects which the operator can rotate in any direction. Their distinctive characteristic is that they rotate within a socket in fixed pieces of equipment. The mouse, on the other hand, operates in a similar fashion to the roller ball but it is not fixed; the ball is on the underside of the device which the operator moves around, much like a pen is moved around paper to form characters. Card, English and Burr (1978) have demonstrated the superiority of these input devices over the conventional keyboard when used to move the cursor around the screen.

Speech input

Speech might appear to be the most obvious way of communicating with computers. Historically, it has dominated the human scene as a basis for immediate, person-to-person communication; communicating through the written word is generally used only when a permanent record is required or when communicating over long distances. Neither of these two conditions applies to human–computer interaction. The advantages and disadvantages of speech input have been summarized by Hill (1977). However, its primary value is that it is natural, convenient and immediate. It enables ideas to be transmitted and received with less effort and with greater efficiency than other forms of communication such as writing.

The effect of these points was demonstrated well in a simple experiment by Ochsman and Chapanis (1974). They asked pairs of subjects to solve 'credible real-life problems' using one of 10 communication modes: typewriters only, handwriting only, handwriting and video, voice and handwriting, etc. Subjects who included a voice channel solved their problems consistently faster than those who were forced to use only the written word. Interestingly, there was no evidence to suggest that the addition of a video channel had any significant effects on communication times. Conclusions of this nature have been supported by Gould (1982): composing spoken letters took only 35–75 per cent of the time that writing did.

A further analysis of these data, reported by Chapanis et al. (1977), suggests additional, more qualitative differences between the behaviours of subjects using the different modes. Thus, although oral modes were faster, the messages sent were more wordy with more unique words being used. Whether these alterations are good or bad is a matter which can only be assessed with regard to specific situations.

OUTPUT HARDWARE

Psychologists have provided a considerable amount of information to enable appropriate visual display units (VDUs) to be designed. These aspects include contrast, luminance levels and the type and shape of the characters displayed. Oborne (1985) has discussed them in detail.

Possible health hazards from visual display units

In recent years, with the increased use of computer-controlled displays in industry, offices and the home, fears have arisen concerning possible risks to health from continued use of VDUs. As Oborne (1985) argues, however, fears of direct health hazards are groundless – although a very small proportion of the community may suffer from epileptic seizures as a result of flickering screens. Any other hazards to health that can be linked to computer terminal use arise not from the terminal itself but from poor interactions between its facilities and the user's requirements – for example, poor environmental design, poor seating, posture, social interaction, etc. (See also Sauter *et al* 1983.)

Visual strain and fatigue

Dainoff (1982) presented a comprehensive and recent review of studies investigating the effects of both short and prolonged use of VDUs on visual fatigue. All studies report significant fatiguing effects, although it should be pointed out that many of the earlier studies lacked good control groups against which the results should be compared (groups of equivalent workers who did *not* use VDUs), and some of the more recent studies simply asked operators what effects they *felt* VDUs had (this is not the same as asking what effects they actually had).

Regarding the nature of the complaint Läubli, Hünting and Grandjean (1981) asked a number of VDU operators to provide details of the visual impairments that they felt were caused by VDU operation. From the responses they were able to extract two eye impairment factors: the major group is composed of a 'discomfort' dimension, whereas the minor group of factors comprises, essentially, a visual impairment dimension.

As far as the effects of the task are concernced, Dainoff (1982) describes studies by Coe *et al.* (1980) who sampled nearly 400 employees from 19 different firms. Significant differences were obtained between the VDU users and the controls (50 per cent vs 33 per cent) but only for the *fatigue-like* symptoms. Creative workers (for example, programmers) reported fewer symptoms than workers doing any other type of task. Furthermore, full-time operators were significantly more likely to report asthenopic complaints (both fatigue and irritation) than were part-time operators.

A task duration effect has also been reported by other investigators. For example, Rey and Meyer (1980) found that VDU operators who worked six to nine hours per day at their terminals were significantly more likely to have visual complaints (73 per cent) than those who used their terminals for less than four hours per day. These patterns of complaints appeared to be the same for young and old operators. Ghiringhelli (1980) also found that complaints of eye irritations increased for workers who used terminals for more than three hours per day, and they were significantly greater than for control (clerical) workers.

Finally, Läubli, Hünting and Grandjean (1981) investigated how different aspects of the display affected these complaints. With regard to contrast between the screen and surround, their data suggest that it is the high contrast displays which cause more eye complaints. In addition, the extent of reflections off the screen correlated well with operator annoyance, although there was no relationship between measured reflection luminances and actual eye complaints. Regarding the characters themselves, the authors demonstrated that complaints of eye irritations and red eyes were more frequent from operators who had used displays with strongly oscillating luminances. Character luminance oscillation was also related to performance – with high oscillation leading to reduced visual acuity.

Speech output

Just as it is difficult to produce a speech decoding system that can accept natural speech for input so, too, are speech output devices limited (presently to vocabularies of around 200 words). Although this is certainly not enough to allow the machine either to carry out 'intelligent' conversations or even to generate unique sentences directed to specific actions, the lack of a comprehensive vocabulary does not necessarily present a major obstacle when using speech for output. As Kelly and Chapanis (1977) and Michaelis et al. (1977) have demonstrated, even highly restricted vocabularies, *if properly chosen*, can be just as efficient as unrestricted vocabularies. Michaelis (1980) further suggests that there is some evidence that, when compared with unrestricted dialogue, a well-chosen restricted vocabulary can actually improve user efficiency.

Although a restricted vocabulary can be used effectively, synthesized speech is still not natural speech and lacks many of the cues from which we extract much of the meaning – such as stress, intonation, accent. With regard to intonation, however, Michaelis (1980) reports that by varying the length of time between words he was able to 'convey enough of a hint of inflection for your ears to fill in the rest' (p.293). Although this report was not supported by any statement of the success of the approach, the conclusions might have been expected, given an interaction between timing and intonation in natural speech (Pike, 1972).

Whereas some form of communication may be possible using synthesized speech, evidence does exist to suggest that recognition and memory for the spoken messages is lower than with natural speech (Pisoni, 1981; Pisoni and Hunnicutt, 1980). Luce, Feustel and Pisoni (1983) suggest that many of these difficulties arise as a result of the synthesized speech placing increased processing demands on our short-term memory capacities.

Finally, the message itself obviously needs to be considered – in terms both of the speed of presentation and the words that it contains. With regard to speed of presentation, Cox (1982) reports studies which suggest that memory performance could be improved considerably by increasing the duration of pauses between sub-groups of digits within the string. He suggests that pauses of about one second should suffice.

With regard to the message content Simpson and Hart (1977) have shown that, for two-word warning messages, response time to messages was shorter, and intelligibility higher, when additional (redundant) words were included in the message to enhance contextual meaning. These findings were replicated by Simpson and Williams (1980).

SOFTWARE ASPECTS

If a system's hardware can be considered to be related to the operator's effector mechanisms, the software is very much analogous to cognition. It represents the 'brains' of the system, and allows it to perceive the input, decide on actions and present an output. However, in reality the software takes two forms. First, there is the set of rules provided by programmers to make the machine work – to receive, to decide and to present. Secondly there are the protocols used by the programmer to allow the machine to receive and present information – the display and the ways in which it is displayed. To work properly, both of these aspects need to be compatible with the user's cognitive capabilities. The first part of this section deals with programmers and their abilities; the second with presenting the information to users.

PROGRAMMING BEHAVIOUR

Learning

When learning programs and program structures, it appears that it is important to have some concrete model of the proposed outcome. Thus, in a series of experiments Mayer (1975, 1979a, 1981) investigated the factors that a novice has to learn when learning how to program a computer (in BASIC). He suggests (1981) that to learn effectively, students need to be able to liken their actions to some physical or mechanical models, from which they can abstract the programming syntax. In a series of investigations, Mayer (1975, 1976) investigated the efficiency of such concrete models for learning BASIC. Although the non-model group learned their material quicker, those provided with a concrete model performed better when the test material required the subjects to go beyond what was in the manual – that is, they had learned the syntax better.

Mayer (1976) also considered when in the learning process the model should be presented. Interestingly the results demonstrated qualitative differences in performance between the two groups. The 'after' group excelled on problems which required some degree of retention of the material, whereas the group which was given the model before learning the material performed better on problems which required creative transfer to new situations.

Memory

The presence and use of a complex human memory system forms the basis for the most models of computer programming behaviour that have been advanced (for example, Brooks, 1977, or Shneiderman and Mayer, 1979). The little empirical work that has been performed to investigate its role in programming behaviour has considered the problem primarily from the viewpoint of attempting to increase the memorability of program structures through the use of both appropriate file and variable names and of concrete models. The practical application of this work has been to aid the programmer when the program has been written – that is, to help in the elimination of errors from the program. This process is called 'debugging'.

The role of memory in programming ability was investigated by Shneiderman (1976) who asked a variety of subjects (from non-programmers to expert programmers) to memorize two identical FORTRAN computer programs. Although the first was printed as a complete and working program, the second was a jumbled version of the first. His results suggested that experience had no effect on the ability to recall accurately the 'shuffled' version of the program, although performance increased with programming ability for the complete and working program listing. Shneiderman attributes these results to an increased ability to recognize program sub-structures with experience and to apply this knowledge to the problem in hand.

Shneiderman (1980) later took the argument further to suggest that research performed on the memorization of English sentences can be used to imply that programmers store the semantics rather than the syntax of computer statements (that is the meaning rather than the rules.) They then use the semantic information and recode groups of statements into higher-level semantic structures which can represent the operation of a group of statements.

A similar technique to using concrete models to improve the memorability of program structures has been proposed in a different context by Ausubel (1968), who has argued that learning new technical prose may be enhanced by providing an *advance organizer*. This normally takes the form of a short expository introduction, presented prior to the text. It contains no specific pieces from the text but provides the general concepts and ideas that will be used in the text. West and Fensham (1976) and Mayer (1979b) have investigated the use of such advance organizers for computer programmers and demonstrated that they have their greatest effect in situations where the material is new or difficult for the learner (for example, for 'low-ability' or inexperienced students, or where information has to be transferred from one situation to another).

DIALOGUE DESIGN

User-friendliness

As with human–human communication, the level of understanding can be affected by the type of dialogue entered into. For example, the message can often be lost or distorted if the social and cognitive abilities of the transmitter and receiver are at variance.

Morton et al. (1979) suggest that one reason why computer dialogues may *not* be user-friendly is because languages are often 'computer-centric'. The software designers have assumed either that the users share their specialist knowledge and experience, or that they will learn to adapt to it. Just as a person can be 'egocentric', therefore, a computer-centric dialogue would insist that the computer is at the 'centre of events' and that all commands and operations are performed in one direction only: for and towards the computer. This can lead to mistakes in interpreting the meaning of command words, particularly if the user neither understands nor naturally adheres to such computer-centricity. In these cases the computer commands are not compatible with the user's expectations.

Wasserman (1973) and Jones (1978) describe a number of examples of the ways in which jargon can interfere with efficient dialogue, ranging from using completely idiosyncratic terms known only to experts, to demanding that the user input information to the computer in particularly idiosyncratic ways – ways which might be logically correct and understandable by an expert but which are not immediately obvious to a naïve user.

Human–human communication, of course, consists of more than simply verbal communication. As Jones (1978) stressed when discussing computer dialogues, the importance of non-verbal signals such as voice intonation or body movements in everyday communication should not be overlooked. He argues that computer dialogues should include non-verbal signals to enrich the 'conversation'. Such signals might include bells, bleeps, 'reverse video' (that is dark characters on a light background), colour or flashing characters. Shneiderman, however, does caution against the over-use of such extra facilities – for example a bell might 'embarrass' the user – and Stewart (1976) argues that too many such signals may overload the operator.

It is important to realize that over-employment of the concept of user-friendliness has recently been criticized (Thimbleby, 1980). For example, Stevens (1983) points out that too much friendliness on the part of the dialogue can lead to a restrictive or misleading view of computer capabilites. The user might come to believe that the computer can do more than it can, in fact, do. In addition, the human–human dialogue analogue should not be forgotten: excessive friendliness in humans often leads to mistrust or exasperation.

Cognitive compatibility

The importance of ensuring cognitive compatibility in computer programs and system commands has been highlighted by workers at the Applied Psychology Unit in Cambridge (Morton *et al.*, 1979; Barnard *et al.*, 1981; Hammond *et al.*, 1981; Barnard *et al.*, 1982). Their concern was the concept of computer-centricity discussed earlier. In essence, they extract three forms of cognitive incompatibility which can occur: linguistic, memory and perceptual.

Linguistic incompatibility can occur at both a syntactic and a semantic level. It often arises at a syntactic level because the information following commands such as DELETE, MOVE, INSERT, etc., often have to be used in abbreviated forms, such as DELETE x,y. or MOVE x,y. In natural language, that is the language used by the operator, the above abbreviated commands might well be interpreted as DELETE (information x) from (file y), or MOVE (information x) to (file y). If this is how the computer programmer or system designer intended the actions to take place, then there is no syntactic incompatibility. Often, however, commands of the form DELETE x,y imply the reverse of what is expected in natural language, that is, DELETE y from file x.

Semantic linguistic incompatibility can occur in a similar way. In this case, however, the problem arises over meanings of commands – particularly when the commands are computer-centric. Examples might include the use of the terms PUT and GET or LOAD and DUMP. Both of these pairs of operators are often used to transfer information from the computer to some storage medium and vice versa. However, the *direction* of the transfer is only immediately obvious if the user has already accepted that the computer is at the centre of the operation. Carroll (1982) also discusses some of these semantic incompatibility problems.

Memory incompatibility arises because the machine's requirements of the user's memory capabilities can be incompatible with the user's actual abilities. Again, linguistically incompatible terms can increase the memory load required because they require the user to remember, for each command, the relationship between the variables x and y.

Perceptual incompatibility relates primarily to the presentation of information as displayed on the computer screen and its relationship to the operations required of the user.

DISPLAYING THE INFORMATION

The way in which the software is displayed to the operator can significantly affect whether the message will be received and understood. Considerations of how we read, search, organize and understand the material presented – whether in the form of text or pictorially – are needed in order that the displayed information can be made compatible with the user's expectations, requirements and abilities. The purpose of this section is to consider what ought to be presented, how and where. As Stewart (1980) argues 'Good formats need to be designed and tested, not left to chance or to the most junior programmer on the team' (p. 913). Oborne (1985) considers many important aspects, which space limitations must preclude from this chapter.

The size of display areas and layout

The question of the size of the text area relates to the normal reading and comprehension processes. These involve saccadic eye movements and the division of words, phrases and sentences so that they are not frequently split in places that make comprehension difficult.

With regard to saccadic eye movements each saccade encompasses about six to eight character spaces (Rayner, 1978). Furthermore, the available evidence suggests that we do not sweep our eyes over the text in a rigid left–right direction, but often make recursive movements, perhaps to correct mistakes or to aid comprehension (Bouma, 1980). Thus, although unfortunately no evidence is available to suggest the optimum width of the text area, it should be clear that it ought to be neither too small nor too large. If the width is too small, only a few saccades may be possible on any one line, thus necessitating recursions to previous lines with the attendant problems of directing the eyes to the beginning of another line. If it is too large, too many saccades may be needed to scan the line. More importantly, perhaps, it is necessary to ensure that when the eye is at the extreme right-hand end of one line it does not have too far to travel back to begin the next line (again, the optic control mechanism can lead the eye to the beginning of the wrong line). In this context, Bouma (1980) relates the length of a line of text (that is the distance between the left and the right-hand margins) to the angle over which the eye travels to reach the next line. This, he suggests, should be approximately 2° so that appropriate text lines can be calculated.

Subsumed under the topic of display width lies the question of whether text is better presented as a single block or in a column format as in newspapers and magazines. Again, this question relates to the control of eye movements between lines. With very long text lines (as would occur in a newspaper that did not use a column format) the interline spacing would have to be extremely small to retain the optimal 2° recursive movement to the beginning of the next line. By keeping the line length small, columns help to produce reasonable interline spacing.

The experimental evidence does suggest that column formats are advantageous, but only under certain circumstances. Thus, Tinker (1965) demonstrated that both speed and comprehension are superior when text is arranged in a two-column layout compared with an arrangement in which it is spread across the page. However, Kak and Knight (1980) report that this column format was beneficial only for normal reading speeds. Subjects who had been taught to 'speed-read' showed no advantage when using such a format, and even some disadvantage. It may be, of course, that the training that these subjects underwent during the speed reading course (for example, to control recursive eye movements, to scan efficiently) may have directly interfered with the eye movement patterns needed for column formats.

Colour

Possibly because the use of colour in VDU displays is quite a recent advance, little published work is presently available to suggest which colours should be used. Radl (1980) investigated operator performance and preference for different coloured phosphors and filters. His results indicate that both performance (a letter-transcribing task) and preference were maximum for the yellow phosphors. Of the yellows, the true yellow phosphor produced maximum performance and preference, although a monochrome screen with a yellow filter was nearly as good.

Radl also considered the combined effects of different coloured characters and backgrounds. Using five character colours and seven background colours he showed that the different colour combinations produced error rates which varied between 4 and 95 per cent. Not unreasonably, the maximum error rates occurred when the character and background colours had wavelengths close to each other (for example, violet on blue, yellow on green). His results also showed that *minimum* overall error was obtained when coloured characters were presented on a *grey* background.

Finally, colour appears to be the most useful technique for coding and highlighting visual information (Hitt, 1961; Smith and Thomas, 1964; Fowler and Barker, 1974). Christ (1975) has reviewed a number of similarly conducted experiments and has shown that colour is superior to size, brightness and shape coding for accuracy of identification, particularly when material has to be searched for.

Speed of presentation

Since it is usually visual information that is transmitted from the computer to the operator, and since the normal modes of presenting such information include printers and visual display units, it is appropriate to consider whether there is an optimal speed of presenting such material. Bevan (1981) considered the question from the point of view of presenting solely textual information. In terms of errors, significantly more mistakes and longer response times were made with information presented at 60 characters per second (cps) than at other presentation rates. However, when the overall time spent at the terminal was analysed ('frame-rate') subjects spent only about one half of the time with the 60 cps display than at 10 cps. Considering that a 60 cps display presents text six times (and not twice) as fast as a 10 cps display, this result suggests that more 'cognitive' time is spent at the 60 cps display.

In a second experiment, Bevan presented subjects with the same task, but included a very fast presentation rate of 480 cps (which, essentially, presents text in a page-wise fashion). Errors with this faster rate were approximately the same as at a 25 cps rate. Interestingly, the maximum number of errors was obtained at 18 cps, which suggests that whereas subjects could read and follow the text at 10 cps, at 18 cps they were forced to read faster than they could take it in. At 480 cps the frame rate, again, was only about twice the speed it was at 18 cps.

On the basis of these studies, and of subsequent interviews with the subjects, Bevan suggests an optimum rate of 10–15 cps for maximum understanding and retention of textual material.

Display and control compatibility

The concept of compatibility has already been considered. Regarding compatibility between control and display, two main considerations exist. First, *spatial compatibility* occurs when the position of items in the display suggests either the appropriate control response or the control position. Second is *movement compatibility*. In this case the movement of items in the display suggests the way in which the associated control should be operated, and vice versa. For example, most operators would expect the right-hand cursor control key to move the cursor to the right of a screen. Relationships which are expected by the majority of the population are described as population stereotypes. Oborne (1982) and Loveless (1962) provide details of these types of compatibility relationships and suggest means of predicting their direction.

With computer systems, the problems associated with ensuring movement compatibility relate also to the display, since, as well as the cursor, displayed information often also moves. Since in this case the two components, cursor and displayed text, are related in the operator's mind, it is important to ensure that their directions of movement are compatible with each other and with the control. Bury *et al.* (1982) discuss one particular movement compatibility problem that applies to apparent text movement through a word processing file.

CONCLUSION

To introduce the reader to a rapidly expanding field, this chapter has covered briefly the major topics that are important when considering the design of computers fit for human use. Since people have to operate computers – computers are nothing more than inanimate pieces of electronics and metal without people – such design must be related to human behaviour. It is through the discipline of ergonomics that psychology combines with other related subjects to become involved with designing equipment to fit the behaviour of the user. Although there are, of course, a number of other features of this area that could have been considered, from a topic-based viewpoint – artificial intelligence, image processing, medical and educational computing, etc. – the approach taken in this chapter has been to present aspects of the hardware and software features of the interaction since these underlie other areas.

From this account it is clear that psychology and computing have very much a symbiotic nature: much of what is considered to fall under the heading of present-day information technology can be conceived as being fundamental to psychology – perception, cognition, social interaction, etc. Similarly, much of psychology has relevance to information technology – display design, machine control, programming, implementation, etc. There is thus a natural symbiosis between the two areas, and it is hoped that, within a relatively narrow field, this chapter has illustrated some of the features of such a symbiotic relationship.

REFERENCES

Alden, D.G., Daniels, R.W. and Kanarick, A.F. (1972) Keyboard design and operation: A review of the major issues. *Human Factors, 14,* 275–293.

Ausubel, D.P. (1968) *Educational Psychology: A Cognitive View,* 2nd ed. New York: Holt, Rinehart and Winston.

Barnard, P.J., Hammond, N.V., Morton, J., Long, J.B. and Clarke, I.A. (1981) Consistency and compatibility in human–computer dialogue. *International Journal of Man–Machine Systems, 15,* 87–134.

Barnard, P.J., Hammond, N.V., MacLean, A., and Morton, J. (1982) *Learning and Remembering Interactive Commands.* IBM research report HF 055. Portsmouth: IBM.

Bouma, H. (1980) Visual reading processes and the quality of text displays. In E. Grandjean and E. Vigliani (eds) *Ergonomic Aspects of Visual Display Terminals.* London: Taylor and Francis.

Bowen, H.M. and Guiness, G.V. (1965) Preliminary experiments on keyboard design. *Journal of Applied Psychology, 49,* 194–198.

Brooks, R. (1977) Towards a theory of the cognitive processes in computer programming. *International Journal of Man–Machine Studies, 9,* 737–751.

Bury, K.F., Boyle, J.M., Evey, R.J. and Neal, A.S. (1982) Windowing versus scrolling on a visual display terminal. *Human Factors, 24,* 385–394.

Card, S.K., English, W.K. and Burr, B.J. (1978) Evaluation of mouse, rate-controlled isometric joystick, step keys, and text keys for selection on a CRT. *Ergonomics, 21,* 601–613.

Chapanis, A., Parrish, R.N., Ochsman, R.B. and Weeks, G.D. (1977) Studies in interactive communication. II The effects of four communication modes on the linguistic performance of teams during co-operative problem solving. *Human Factors, 19,* 101–126.

Christ, R.E. (1975) Review and analysis of colour coding research for visual displays. *Human Factors, 17,* 542–570.

Coe, J.B., Cuttle, K., McClellon, W.C., Warden, N.J. and Turner, P.J. (1980) *Visual Display Units.* Report W/1/80. Wellington: New Zealand Department of Health.

Conrad, R. and Hull, A.J. (1968) The preferred layout for data-entry keysets. *Ergonomics, 11,* 165–173.

Conrad, R. and Longman, D.J.A. (1965) Standard typewriter versus chord keyboard – an experimental comparison. *Ergonomics, 8,* 77–88.

Cox, A.C. (1982) Human factors investigations into interactions with machines by voice. IEE document No. 212.

Dainoff, M.J. (1982) Occupational stress factors in visual display terminal (VDT) operation: A review of empirical research. *Behaviour and Information Technology, 1,* 141–176.

Deininger, R.L. (1960) Human factors engineering studies of the design and use of pushbutton telephone sets. *The Bell System Technical Journal, 39,* 995–1012.

Dunn, A.G. (1971) Engineering the keyboard from the human factors viewpoint. *Computers and Automation,* February, 32–33.

Earl, W.K. and Goff, J.D. (1965) Comparison of two data entry methods. *Perceptual and Motor Skills*, 20, 369–384.
Fowler, R.L. and Barker, A.S. (1974) Effectiveness of highlighting for retention of text material. *Journal of Applied Psychology*, 63, 309–313.
Ghiringhelli, L. (1980) Collection of subjective opinions on use of VDUs. In E. Grandjean and E. Vigliani (eds) *Ergonomic Aspects of Visual Display Terminals*. London: Taylor and Francis.
Goodwin, N.C. (1975) Cursor positioning on an electronic display using lightpen, lightgun, or keyboard for three basic tasks. *Human Factors*, 17, 289–295.
Gould, J. (1982) Writing and speaking letters and messages. *International Journal of Man–Machine Studies*, 16, 147–171.
Hammond, N.V., Long, J.B., Morton, J., Barnard, P.J. and Clark, A. (1981) *Documenting Human–Computer Mismatch at the Individual and Organisational Levels*. IBM research report HF 040. Portsmouth: IBM.
Hill, D.R. (1977) Using speech to communicate with machines. In B. Shackel (ed.) *Man/Computer Communication, Volume 2*. Maidenhead: Infotech International Ltd.
Hirsch, R.S. (1970) Effects of standard versus alphabetical keyboard formats on typing performance. *Journal of Applied Psychology*, 54, 484–490.
Hitt, W.D. (1961) An evaluation of five different abstract coding methods. *Human Factors*, 3, 120–130.
Hopkin, V.D. (1971) The evaluation of touch displays for air traffic control tasks. IEE Conference on Displays: Publication no. 80.
Jones, P.F. (1978) Four principles of man–computer dialogue. *Computer Aided Design*, 10, 197–202.
Kak, A.V. and Knight, J.L. (1980) Text formatting effects in speed reading. *Proceedings of the 24th Human Factors Society Meeting, Baltimore*. Baltimore: HFS.
Kelly, M.J. and Chapanis, A. (1977) Limited vocabulary natural language dialogue. *International Journal of Man–Machine Studies*, 9, 479–501.
Läubli, Th., Hünting, W. and Grandjean, E. (1981) Postural and visual loads of VDT workplaces. II Lighting conditions and visual impairment. *Ergonomics*, 24, 933–944.
Litterick, I. (1981) QWERTYUIOP – dinosaur in a computer age. *New Scientist*, 89, 66–68.
Loveless, N.E. (1962) Direction-of-motion stereotypes: A review. *Ergonomics*, 5, 357–383.
Luce, P.A., Feustel, T.C. and Pisoni, D.B. (1983) Capacity demands in short-term memory for synthetic and natural speech. *Human Factors*, 25, 17–32.
McEwing, R.W. (1977) Touch displays in industrial computer systems. In *Displays for Man–Machine Systems*. London: IEE.
Martin, A. (1972) A new keyboard layout. *Applied Ergonomics*, 3, 48–51.
Mayer, R.E. (1975) Different problem solving competencies established in learning computer programming with and without meaningful models. *Journal of Educational Psychology*, 67, 725–734.
Mayer, R.E. (1976) Some conditions of meaningful learning for computer programming: Advance organizers and subject control of frame order. *Journal of Educational Psychology*, 68, 143–150.
Mayer, R.E. (1979a) A psychology of learning BASIC. *Communications of the ACM*, 11, 589–593.
Mayer, R.E. (1979b) Can advance organizers influence meaningful learning? *Review of Educational Research*, 49, 371–383.

Mayer, R.E. (1981) The psychology of how novices learn computer programming, *Computing Surveys*, 13, 121–141.
Michaelis, P.R. (1980) An ergonomist's introduction to synthesized speech. In D.J. Oborne and J.A. Levis (eds) *Human Factors in Transport Research, Volume I*. London: Academic Press.
Michaelis, P.R., Chapanis, A., Weeks, G.D. and Kelly, M.J. (1977) Word usage in interactive dialog with restricted and unrestricted vocabularies. *IEE Transactions on Professional Communication*, 20, 214–221.
Morgan, C.T., Cook, J.S., Chapanis, A. and Lund, M. (1963) *Human Engineering Guide to Equipment Design*. New York: McGraw-Hill.
Morton, J., Barnard, P., Hammond, N. and Long, J.B. (1979) Interacting with the computer: A framework. In E. Boutmy and A. Danthine (eds) *Teleinformatics '79*. Amsterdam: North Holland.
Norman, D.A. and Fisher, D. (1982) Why alphabetic keyboards are not easy to use: Keyboard layout doesn't much matter. *Human Factors*, 24, 509–519.
Noyes, J. (1983a) The QWERTY keyboard: A review. *International Journal of Man–Machine Studies*, 18, 265–281.
Noyes, J. (1983b) Chord keyboards. *Applied Ergonomics*, 14, 55–59.
Oborne, D.J. (1982) *Ergonomics at work*. Chichester: John Wiley.
Oborne, D.J. (1985) *Computers at Work: A Behavioural Approach*. Chichester: John Wiley.
Ochsman, R.B. and Chapanis, A. (1974) The effects of 10 communication modes on the behaviour of teams during co-operative problem-solving. *International Journal of Man–Machine Studies*, 6, 579–619.
Pfauth, M. and Priest, J. (1981). Person–computer interface using touch screen devices. *Proceedings of the 25th Annual Meeting of the Human Factors Society*. Baltimore: HFS.
Pike, K.L. (1972) General characteristics of intonation. In D. Bolinger (ed.) *Intonation – Selected Readings*. Harmondsworth: Penguin.
Pisoni, D.B. (1981) Speeded classification of natural and synthetic speech in a lexical decision task. *Journal of the Acoustical Society of America*, 70, 598.
Pisoni, D.B. and Hunnicutt, S. (1980) Perceptual evaluation of MITalk: The MIT unrestricted text-to-speech system. *Proceedings of IEEE International Conference on Acoustics, Speech and Signal Processing*. New York: IEEE.
Radl, G.W. (1980) Experimental investigations for optimal presentation-mode and colours of symbols on the CRT screen. In E. Grandjean and E. Vigliani (eds) *Ergonomic Aspects of Visual Display Terminals*. London: Taylor and Francis.
Rayner, K. (1978) Eye movements in reading and information processing. *Psychological Bulletin*, 85, 618–660.
Rey, R.P. and Meyer, J.J. (1980) Visual impairments and their objective correlates. In E. Grandjean and E. Vigliani (eds) *Ergonomic Aspects of Visual Display Terminals*. London: Taylor and Francis.
Sauter, S.L., Gottlieb, M.S., Jones, K.C., Dodson, V.N. and Rohrer, K.M. (1983) Job and health implications of VDT use: Initial results from the Wisconsin –NIOSH study. *Communications of the ACM*, 26, 284–294.
Seibel, R. (1964) Data entry through chord, parallel entry devices. *Human Factors*, 6, 189–192.
Shneiderman, B. (1976) Exploratory experiments in programmer behaviour. *International Journal of Computing and Information Sciences*, 5, 124–143.
Shneiderman, B. (1980) *Software Psychology*. Cambridge: Winthrop Publishing Inc.

Shneiderman, B. and Mayer, R. (1979) Syntactic/semantic interactions in programmer behavior: A model and experimental results. *International Journal of Man–Machine Studies, 8,* 219–238.
Simpson, C.A. and Hart, S.G. (1977) Required attention for synthesized speech perception for two levels of linguistic redundancy. *Journal of the Acoustical Society of America,* Supplement 1, S7/D3.
Simpson, C.A. and Williams, D.H. (1980) Response time effects of alerting tone and semantic context for synthesized voice cockpit warnings. *Human Factors, 22,* 319–330.
Smith, S.L. and Thomas, D.W. (1964) Colour versus shape coding in information displays. *Journal of Applied Psychology, 48,* 137–146.
Stevens, G.C. (1983) User-friendly computer systems? A critical evaluation of the concept. *Behaviour and Information Technology, 2,* 3–16.
Stewart, T.F.M. (1976) Displays and the software interface. *Applied Ergonomics, 7,* 137–146.
Stewart, T.F.M. (1980) Communicating with dialogues. *Ergonomics, 23,* 909-919.
Thimbleby, H. (1980) Dialogue determination. *International Journal of Man–Machine Studies, 13,* 295–304.
Tinker, M.A. (1965) *Legibility of Print.* Iowa: Iowa State University Press.
Usher, D.M. (1982) A touch sensitive VDU compared with a computer-aided keypad for controlling power generating plant. Paper presented to IEE Conference on Man/Machine Systems. London: IEE.
Wasserman, A.I. (1973) The design of idiot-proof interactive systems. *American Federation of Information Processing Societies Conference Proceedings, 42,* M34–M38.
West, L.H.T. and Fensham, D.J. (1976) Prior knowledge or advance organizers as effective variables in chemistry learning. *Journal of Research in Science Teaching, 13,* 297–306.
Wilson, J. and Grey, S. (1983) The ergonomics of laser scanner checkout systems. In K. Coombes (ed.) *Proceedings of the 1983 Ergonomics Society Annual Conference.* London: Taylor and Francis.

THE PSYCHOLOGICAL INFLUENCES OF TELEVISION
Barrie Gunter

Television today is a virtually universal feature of modern households in the West. A recent national survey revealed that 97 per cent of people in Britain said they had at least one set at home, and 54 per cent said they had more than one (IBA, 1986). On average, UK viewers watch television for nearly three and a half hours a day (BARB, 1985). Furthermore, the shape of television viewing is changing. Watching television is no longer simply a family occasion in the main living room; nearly one in four viewers admits to having a set in the main bedroom, (IBA, 1986). Expanded television schedules mean that many millions of people every week watch television not only in the evenings, but also over breakfast and throughout the day.

In view of the prevalence of television, it is not surprising that interest and concern about its social and psychological influences are as strong now as they have ever been. Most discussion has focused on supposedly harmful effects of television. There is concern, for example, that violence on television can enhance levels of interpersonal aggressiveness among viewers and contribute more broadly to levels of crime and violence in society. Of late, there has been growing concern also about the negative impact of over-regular television watching on the early cognitive development of children, which may be reflected later in impaired educational achievement.

Unfortunately, it is not uncommon that the debates carried on in public about the psychological influences of television are overly emotional, reveal a poor grasp of what the research evidence actually says and misrepresent the facts. There is now a wealth of information on uses and effects of television and the literature continues to grow at an accelerated rate. So much so, that it is difficult even for the most interested and vigilant student of this field to keep up with everything that is going on. As with much social science, for each hypothesis about the nature of an influence that is thrown up, a counter-hypothesis can be found; for each finding that reveals a particular effect, evidence for a reverse effect exists somewhere, and for all the numerous times a study may be repeated, the body of evidence may be demolished with the identification of a single but fundamental methodological flaw.

In this chapter, an attempt is made to provide a broad overview of research concerned with various psychological influences of television. Given limitations of space and the amount of ground there is to cover, some sections will of necessity be brief. Full reference sources will be provided throughout, however, so that readers may follow up the literature in each case in more detail for themselves.

One important function of this chapter is to point out particular methodological limitations to research on television's psychological influences. In broad terms, perhaps the two most fundamental problems in television research concern the inference of causality from correlational evidence and the generalizability to real life of experimental findings derived from contrived research settings. It is important for the reader to bear in mind throughout that the validity of the research evidence is to a large extent only as good as the validity of the methods used to obtain it. Each of the above and other methodological shortcomings is discussed in more detail at appropriate points in the chapter.

BEHAVIOURAL EFFECTS

Television and antisocial behaviour

Without doubt the most controversial, widely discussed and extensively researched television-effects issue is that concerned with the relationship between television violence and social violence. Does violence on television contribute significantly to criminal and antisocial behaviour in society? Do individuals who watch a great deal of programming containing violence become desensitized not simply to the violence they see on the screen but also, through a process of generalization, to violence in real life? Or does regular exposure to televised violence teach viewers, especially young ones, how to use violence to solve problems and provide justification for doing so? These are all questions which have concerned politicians, broadcasting policy makers, campaigners against television violence and social scientists for many years.

The research can be conveniently divided up according to the dominant research methodologies. Some studies have examined immediate or short-term effects of exposure to televised scenes of violence, while others have been concerned more with long-term relationships between television viewing patterns and antisocial behaviour. Researchers have used both experimental and survey procedures to investigate the effects of television violence and these can be categorized into:

- Laboratory experiments
- Field experiments
- Correlational surveys
- Panel surveys.

Laboratory experiments

Among the earliest laboratory studies directly concerned with measuring the effects of exposure to film violence were ones designed to investigate the notion that individuals can vicariously discharge their aggressive impulses via fantasy media content (Feshbach, 1961). This catharsis hypothesis has received only limited empirical support since that initial demonstration (Feshbach and Singer, 1971; Biblow, 1973; Loye, Gorney and Steele, 1977) and has been much disputed.

Berkowitz (1964) suggested a guilt-inhibition hypothesis to account for Feshbach's (1961) fantasy–catharsis findings. According to Berkowitz, watching fantasy violence did not produce a cathartic discharge of impulses but facilitated guilt, leading the individual to inhibit any overt expression of anger. More recently, some writers have suggested that a cathartic response may occur to fantasy media material, but that it depends on the ability of individuals to engage in fantasy (see Copeland and Slater, 1981, 1985; Gunter, 1980*a*).

In a paradigm used extensively by Berkowitz and his colleagues, in which aggression was operationalized in terms of delivery of electric shocks, angered college students were found to become more aggressive against someone who had earlier annoyed them after they had been shown a violent film clip than if they had seen a non-violent clip. This effect could be magnified in a number of ways. For instance, telling viewers that the victim of the violence in the film clip deserved his beating facilitated even stronger aggressive responding than if they were told that the beating was not justified (Berkowitz and Rawlings, 1963). Describing a violent scene as a realistic event also caused it to have a more powerful effect on viewers' subsequent aggressiveness (Berkowitz and Alioto, 1973).

The main problem with the Berkowitz paradigm is its artificiality. These experiments are unrepresentative of reality in their settings, their samples and in their measure of behavioural aggression. The validity of the electric shock procedure as an indicator of aggression in real life must be seriously doubted. Further, the norms governing what is acceptable or unacceptable behaviour in the laboratory differ from those in the outside world. The subject is invited to deliver an electric shock to another person and complies, feeling that this is what the experimenter expects. The experimenter assumes responsibility for any harmful or distressing consequences the subject's actions may have for the victim, and there is no threat of punishment or retaliation contingent on the subject's 'violent' behaviour. Indeed, the question of whether subjects actually perceive their behaviour in that context as deviant or antisocial is not investigated. And yet for most people this is an important factor detemining whether or not they behave violently in real life.

Another famous series of experiments conducted during the same period investigated the premise that media portrayals of violence can provide young viewers with examples of antisocial conduct which they may choose to copy. In the first of these studies, Bandura and his colleagues showed children a film portrayal of an actor attacking a large plastic doll. When placed in a playroom filled with toys and the same doll afterwards, many of the children imitated the actions of the film model against the doll (Bandura, 1965; Bandura, Ross and Ross, 1963).

Later research found that imitative aggression could be facilitated by a filmed example against a human clown figure as well as against an inanimate doll (Hanratty, O'Neal and Sulzer, 1972; Savitsky et al., 1971). Other studies have indicated, however, that not all children are equally likely to exhibit imitative aggressive responding after seeing a filmed example of such behaviour. Imitation is mediated by social class (Kniveton and Stephenson, 1972) and may be weakened when children are given prior experience with the modelled toys and play setting (Kniveton and Stephenson, 1970).

Another process investigated by laboratory experimentation is desensitization. With repeated exposure to television violence there is concern that young viewers will show not simply blunted emotional responses to violence as shown on the screen but also, through a process of generalization, to that occurring or encountered in real life (see Cline, Croft and Courrier, 1973; Drabman and Thomas, 1974; Thomas et al., 1977). Evidence for this effect has emerged from several laboratory studies.

Thomas et al. (1977), for example, found that children and college students who had seen violent drama material were found to be less emotionally aroused by scenes of real life newsfilm violence than were those who saw non-violent footage. This was taken as evidence for desensitization to real-life violence. One must question, however, whether this study really demonstrates enhanced tolerance to real violence or merely to film footage of violence which is described as real.

Field experiments

These studies represent an attempt to improve on the artificiality of laboratory studies by measuring television viewing and social behaviour patterns under, what are for the subjects under study, more natural surroundings. Such studies have the advantage over laboratory experiments of allowing subjects to watch complete programmes instead simply of clips from them, and changes in behaviour which may be contingent on viewing diet are measured unobtrusively in subjects' normal living environment. Field experiments, however, have usually been carried out among institutionalized children and adolescents who can be readily observed for most of the time in the homes where they live. The samples are therefore not representative of the general population and in some cases consist of young people with a record of delinquency.

Feshbach and Singer (1971) found that institutionalized adolescent boys who were shown a diet of mainly violent programmes for one week became *less* aggressive than those who saw mainly non-violent fare. This result has been questioned, however, (Freedman, 1984) and is not supported by other similar field experiments. Parke *et al.* (1977) carried out three field studies in the United States and Belgium and found that a week-long diet of television violence increased aggressiveness among teenage male juvenile delinquents residing in minimum security institutions. In the Belgian study, however, only boys who were already classed as aggressive types exhibited this reaction to violent programming.

One problem with field experiments is that the viewing diets for some groups are carefully controlled by the researchers. This means that programmes which the subjects normally might be able or would want to watch are not available to them, at least for the duration of the experiment. Removal of normal viewing choices may cause frustration, especially if favourite programmes are taken off the menu for the week. This factor alone can produce mood and behaviour changes, quite apart from any influence of the particular viewing diet different groups are fed.

Correlational surveys

These take a cross-sectional look at relationships between television viewing habits and attitudes or behavioural predispositions towards aggression among usually large samples of individuals at one point in time (for example, Dominick and Greenberg, 1972; McIntyre and Teevan, 1972; McLeod, Atkin and Chaffee, 1972).

Whilst correlational surveys improve on experimental studies in terms of the size and representativeness of their samples, they often fall down in terms of the accuracy and validity of their measures. Respondents are questioned typically only once and a great deal of faith is placed in personal estimates of television viewing. Respondents may have to recall from lists of programme titles the ones they think they have seen or say which they like best. On occasion, more effective diary measures of viewing are used, but even then assumptions are made about the violent content of programmes respondents claim to have seen that are hardly ever backed up by empirical evidence. Whilst these doubts exist about the efficacy of measures of exposure to television violence, then there must also be doubts about the validity of any television-effects conclusions relating to that content. More significant still is the fact that correlations cannot prove causation; they can simply provide indications of pairs of variables between which cause–effect relations may exist. Typically, correlational evidence is interpreted as showing that exposure to television violence increases propensities towards aggression among viewers. Equally consistent with these data, however, is the reverse hypothesis that viewers actively seek out and enjoy watching television violence, and that such preferences are especially strong among those individuals with existing aggressive predispositions (Gunter, 1983).

Belson (1978) interviewed over 1,500 adolescent boys in London, obtaining a great deal of information from them about their television viewing habits and the extent of their aggressive behaviour. The degree of association between television viewing and aggressiveness was assessed by dividing the sample into those high and those low on one factor and obtaining a mean score for the two groups on the second factor. Results indicated that boys who claimed to watch more often those programmes on television designated violent tended to report committing more violent acts than did boys who volunteered watching less violence on television.

Belson reported that earlier television violence viewing was more important to later aggressiveness than earlier aggressiveness was to later viewing of violence. But out of four measures of aggression, this fact was true with respect to only one total number of serious violent acts. Another difficulty is that total television viewing was more significant than violence viewing alone. In addition, viewing of non-violent television was just as significant as violent television watching. Therefore, it is difficult to separate out the effects of watching violent programmes from those of viewing television in general. The study also relied heavily of self-reports for measures of aggressiveness as well as of Television viewing, which raises the possibility that the boys were not entirely accurate in their descriptions of their own behaviour (see Freedman, 1984).

Panel studies

Perhaps the best method of examining causal relationships between television viewing and social behaviour under natural conditions is to follow people's viewing habits and behaviour patterns over time. This is what the longitudinal panel study attempts to achieve. This involves testing the same group of people on two or more occasions over a period of years to find out if the type of television programme they watch at one time is related to their behavioural tendencies later on. Results from panel studies, however, have so far still not been entirely in agreement. Some researchers claim to have found a strong link between early levels of exposure to television violence and subsequent development of aggressive behavioural tendencies among children and adolescents, while others using similar procedures have concluded differently.

Eron et al. (1972) obtained measures of television viewing and aggression from children at the age of 8 and again at 18 years. The findings revealed that television viewing at 8 years was significantly correlated with aggression both at 8 and again at 18 years. Aggression at an early age was related to later television viewing. Putting this result in context, however, it was found only for boys and then only with one out of three measures of aggression at 18 years. Huesmann (1982) surveyed children over a two-year spell and found that television viewing and aggression were related at different individual points over time, but no evidence was reported to show a stronger relationship between early television viewing and later aggression than early aggressive propensities and later television favourites.

Milavsky et al. (1982) examined the relationship between early and later aggression and early and later television viewing and reported that the unique contribution of early watching of television violence to later aggression among children and teenagers was very small (accounting for only about one per cent of the variance in aggression) when the effects of early aggression were controlled.

Finally, a study by Atkin et al. (1979) of a panel of children found no evidence that early television violence viewing was significantly related to later aggressiveness, but early aggressiveness was related to later preferences for violent programming even in the presence of controls for sex, school grade and initial viewing patterns. These results suggest that a portion of the basic relationship between television viewing and aggressiveness which has been reported in numerous single-wave field surveys may be attributable to selective exposure rather than to the reverse interpretation of a television influence on violent dispositions.

Television and prosocial behaviour

If its violent content can supposedly encourage or teach people to behave antisocially, can television, through the portrayal of altruistic, socially-constructive actions, increase the general level of prosocial behaviours? An expanding body of research has shown that televised examples of good behaviour can encourage children and adults alike to behave better. Evidence for prosocial effects of television has come from laboratory studies with educational broadcast materials and with popular entertainment programmes, and from field correlation studies in which amounts of watching prosocial television content have been related to prosocial behavioural tendencies.

Perhaps the most widely watched television production with educational aims has been *Sesame Street*. Whilst *Sesame Street* has proved to be very popular, what evidence is there that it and other similar types of show have prosocial influences on young viewers? Silverman (1977) found that many four-year-olds and almost all seven-year-olds who viewed versions of *Sesame Street* edited to emphasize cooperative behaviour understood the message of most 'cooperation segments'.

In a study with a different programme, Friedrich and Stein (1975) found that kindergarten children shown four episodes of *Mister Rogers' Neighbourhood*, depicting characters attempting to understand and help a stranger, were better able to correctly answer questions about prosocial behaviour than a control sample shown four neutral television programme episodes.

The programmes investigated in the studies cited above were specially designed to impart socially constructive examples and lessons to young viewers. Most children's viewing, however, consists of popular entertainment programmes. Action-adventure shows have been accused of supplying children with examples of antisocial conduct. But to what extent might popular dramas which depict prosocial actions encourage children to behave in socially desirable ways?

Rubinstein *et al.* (1976) found that children aged 5–6 years who saw an example of a boy helping a dog in an episode of *Lassie* chose to help puppies in distress more quickly and for a considerably longer time than did children who watched a different episode from the same series or a family situation comedy. Can prosocial content occurring in popular television dramas also have more general effects on viewers' helpful behaviours? Sprafkin and Rubinstein (1979) found that the less television a child watched and the more 'prosocial' his or her favourite programmes were, the more the child was likely to behave in a prosocial manner in school.

In a comparison of the relative influence of prosocial versus violent viewing, correlations obtained between viewing habits and prosocial behaviour were lower than those obtained between viewing habits and aggressive behaviour. However, there are several reasons for this which point to limitations in the current state of research in this field and offer a number of potential lines of inquiry for future study. First, children learn quite early than they should help or share, and thus television's prosocial content only reiterates what they already know. Aggressive behaviour, on the other hand, is generally punished in a child's home and school environment, and seeing it performed with frequent success on television contrasts with its treatment in reality. It may be useful for future studies to find out the extent to which children of various ages clearly differentiate prosocial and antisocial behaviours and their outcomes in reality and in television's fictional drama and to obtain measures of the relative salience and attractiveness of these behaviours for the child. A second point also concerns the manner in which prosocial and aggressive behaviours are presented on television. Prosocial behaviours are very often subtle and verbally mediated, whereas aggressive behaviours are blatant and physical. Because young children learn better from simple, direct and active presentations, they may be more likely to learn from violent than prosocial portrayals customarily shown on television. At present, no evidence is available to show that these differential portrayal characteristics produce differences in perception and learning of prosocial versus violent content.

Finally, content analysis has shown that televised prosocial behaviours are predominantly performed by female and non-white characters and that aggressive behaviours are most often performed by white males who are also the most successful and powerful character-type in television drama (Donagher *et al.*, 1975; Gerbner *et al.*, 1979). Thus, the relative influence of prosocial and violent behaviours may be compounded with the types of characters who normally portray them. It is important for further research to assess the relative amounts of prosocial and violent behaviours performed by specific leading characters. If it is to be assumed that their preferential production treatment makes their presence and activities more salient than those of less successful characters, not only their violent but also their prosocial actions may provide sources of learning and behavioural influence for young viewers.

COGNITIVE EFFECTS

Television and sex stereotyping

Does the way the sexes are portrayed on television influence public attitudes and beliefs about men and women? Research on sex portrayals on television has suggested that there may be such an influence. Descriptive analyses of programming have indicated that televison seems to be characterized by pronounced patterns of sex-stereotyping. This is manifested in a number of subtle ways. First, women are numerically grossly outnumbered by men in many categories of programmes (Gerbner and Gross, 1976; Miles, 1975; Signorielli, 1984). Second, even in programmes where the numerical balance is restored, women appear to enjoy a much narrower range of roles than do men (Butler and Paisley, 1980; Tuchman, 1978). Third, certain personality characteristics tend to be overemphasized for women, and others for men, with the latter usually judged to be the more flattering or favourable (Downing, 1974; Long and Simon, 1974; Manes and Melnyk, 1974; Tedesco, 1974; Greenberg, Richards and Henderson, 1980; Butler and Paisley, 1980).

It has been argued that sterotyped media portrayals condition sex stereotypes and restrict the range of opportunities girls believe to be open to them when they grow up. At the same time, they cultivate similar beliefs among boys, who grow up to believe that women are unsuited to many occupational and professional roles (Tuchman, 1978). Thus runs the argument of some critics of the way television portrays the sexes. Is there any sound evidence that television portrayals can have this sort of influence?

Survey and experimental techniques have been employed to understand better whether television has any influence on viewers' sex-role perceptions. The most often cited studies have been surveys which examined relationships between reported amounts of television watching in total and beliefs about the sexes. Concern about the stereotyping influence of television among children has led much research effort to focus on young viewers. Several such studies have reported relationships between claimed amount of television viewing and strength of traditional sex-role beliefs (Beuf, 1974; Frueh and McGhee, 1975; McGhee and Frueh, 1980). There are uncertainties about the measures and about the interpretations placed by these researchers on their data. For example, the authors do not establish for sure that television was the causal rather than the dependent variable (see Durkin, 1985).

Morgan (1982) examined relationships over two years between measures of television exposure (hours viewed on the 'average day') and acceptance of sex-role stereotypes and educational or occupational aspirations. There was evidence that heavier early television viewing was related to stronger sex-stereotyping at a later date, but only among girls. Among girls also, the effects of television were greater among the middle classes. Both working-class girls and boys generally were more sexist regardless of viewing levels.

There is evidence that pre-existing sex stereotypes among young viewers may distort their perceptions of and memory for television portrayals (Sprafkin and Liebert, 1976; Tan et al., 1980). When schoolchildren were shown a videotape of a male nurse and a female doctor and required to identify photographs and names of the characters afterwards, most youngsters up to the age of 12 tended to select male pictures and names for the doctor and female equivalents for the nurse (Drabman et al., 1981). These findings have been supported further by Durkin (1983) and Williams, La Rose and Frost (1981). Meanwhile, research among adults has indicated that people may not always be convinced by the portrayals of the sexes they see on television (Gunter and Wober, 1982). Both male and female viewers have been found to make distinctions between the way women and men are portrayed on television and how they are seen to be in everyday life, indicating that viewers recognize that television is different from reality (Gunter, 1986).

Television and race-role stereotypes

Similar criticisms have been made of television's portrayal of ethnic minorities as have been raised against its portrayal of women. Content analysis research has indicated that racial minority groups tend to be numerically under-represented on television in relation to their numerical presence in the real world population. Trends have changed over the years, however, and numerical representation has been found to vary across different racial groups. Dominick and Greenberg (1970) and Lemon (1978) observed, for example, that blacks on prime-time network television programming had achieved parity between their television and real world numbers. Other groups, however, such as the Hispanics and orientals, did not (Greenberg, 1980). There has been some disagreement between researchers on this matter, however. Signorielli (1984) claimed that orientals were the only ethnic minority to be over-represented in US prime-time television relative to their numbers in the US population.

Even when numerical presence improved, characterizations often did not. Thus, blacks have tended over the years to be portrayed most often in low status jobs (Northcott et al., 1975), even though they may be depicted as industrious, competent and law-abiding (Hinton et al., 1973). Subsequently, Greenberg (1980) observed that an early trend of portraying blacks as law-breakers seemed to have passed. Even recent studies have recorded that blacks tend generally to enjoy a lower professional and material status than whites on prime-time television (Baptista-Fernandez and Greenberg, 1982). Although less extensively researched in this country, similar charges of under-representation of ethnic minorities were levelled against British television broadcasters just a few years ago following a six-week analysis of British television programming across the end of 1978 and beginning of 1979 (Anwar and Shang, 1982).

What is the impact of black portrayals on television on white and black members of the audience? Are children and adults both affected by stereotypic depictions of ethnic minority groups? Television's importance as a source of information about nationality groups has been noted more than once. Lambert and Klineberg (1967) found that white American children reported obtaining most of their information about other nationalities (for example Africans, Chinese, Russians and Indians) from either their parents or from television. As the viewer's age increased, there was a greater reliance on television as the information source to go to about foreign groups.

Research has shown that more tolerant attitudes towards ethnic minority groups can be cultivated to some extent among young viewers by educationally-oriented television programmes (Bogatz and Ball, 1971; Gorn, Goldberg and Kanungo, 1976).

Quite apart from educational programmes, there is some evidence that children's racial attitudes can be modified by the appearance of black people in popular entertainment programmes. Graves (1975) found that just one exposure to a cartoon featuring black people enhances positive racial attitudes among six to eight-year-old children. Subsequently, Leifer, Graves and Phelps (1976) and Phelps (1976) reported similar findings.

Research with adults has indicated that pre-existing racial attitudes affect viewers' responses to black people shown on television. Research on the popular US situation comedy 'All in the Family' revealed that viewers did not perceive the programme to be a satire on bigotry (Surlin, 1974; Vidmar and Rokeach, 1973). Instead, highly prejudiced persons reported more frequent viewing of the series than did low-prejudiced persons. More prejudiced persons reported greater identification with the central, bigoted character Archie Bunker and were less likely to see anything wrong with his use of racial and ethnic slurs than did less prejudiced people (Lear, 1971).

What do black people think about the way they are portrayed on television? Do they identify with black characters on the screen more than with any others? Are they happy with the way television shows their own people? Some evidence suggests that black children may be more accepting of a white than of a black role-model on television. Neely, Heckel and Lechtman (1973) reported that the black pre-schoolers imitated the white models more often than they imitated equally or more attractive black models. Indeed a punished white model was copied about as much as the rewarded black model. In this study, the importance of the model's race outweighed what had been previously found to be a potent mediator of modelling effects – whether the model is rewarded or punished for his or her actions.

Age-role stereotyping

US findings have indicated an association between amount of television viewing and audience conceptions of the elderly, the strength of which varied with amount of viewing. Heavy viewing was related to a negative image of the elderly and the quality of their lives, but was never associated with any positive images of older people (Gerbner et al., 1980).

In Britain, Wober and Gunter (1982) found no evidence for a relationship between amount of general television viewing and public images of the elderly in real life. Comparing viewers' perceptions of the elderly in reality with perceptions of how the elderly are depicted in different categories of programming, however, revealed that these two sets of perceptions were significantly correlated by only with respect to reality programming (for example news, documentaries and quiz/game shows, but not situation comedies or action dramas). These findings indicated the need to examine more closely how viewers differentially respond to fictional and non-fictional television portrayals since this may determine whether and to what extent they incorporate information derived from each into their existing knowledge structures about social entities.

Perceptions of crime

Following analyses of public survey data on the US during the second half of the 1970s, Gerbner and his associates reported that heavy viewers of television in the US tended to endorse different beliefs about the world in which they live from individuals who were relatively light television viewers (Gerbner and Gross, 1976; Gerbner et al., 1978, 1979, 1980). One of their major findings was that heavy viewers (more than four hours television watching daily) tended to exhibit exaggerated beliefs about the occurrence of crime and violence in society, greater fear of personal victimization, greater mistrust of other people and less hope for the future compared with light viewers (that is those who viewed less than two hours daily). These results were interpreted as evidence of an appreciation effect of television viewing.

Research of a similar kind among British viewers, however, has so far provided only equivocal support for Gerbner's results. In two initial surveys which posed questions on the perceptions of social danger derived from versions originally worked in America, no relationships were found between self-reported reported estimates of amount of television viewing and perceptions of threat to personal safety (Piepe, Crouch and Emerson, 1977; Wober, 1978).

This discrepancy may mean that the US results do not travel well. Some researchers, even in the US, have revised Gerbner et al.'s measures and the way viewers were categorized into light and heavy types, (Hirsch, 1980; Hughes 1980). Another possible interpretation is a 'third variable' hypothesis which states that both social perceptions and television viewing may be effects of some additional factor not previously taken into account. Doob and Macdonald (1979), for example, reported that fear of environmental crime among residents of Toronto, Canada was related more closely to actual levels of such crime than to television viewing. But in addition to making people more fearful, high local crime rates might encourage them to stay indoors and watch more TV.

In a further British study, Wober and Gunter (1982) examined relationships between viewing behaviour and perceived threat to personal safety and mistrust, controlling for a 'third variable' – Rotter's (1965) internal-external locus of control dimension. Results showed that there was no significant relationship between television viewing and fear of crime when locus of control was controlled. The authors argued that future research in this area should take into account such individual difference factors which may be important to the way people see the world around them and underlie television viewing preferences.

Elsewhere, researchers have argued that since many television dramas end with the bad guys being caught and punished by the good guys, another message – that the world is really a safe place where justice ultimately prevails – may be conveyed by popular entertainment programming on television (Zillmann, 1980). Several recent American studies have supported this argument (Bryant, Carveth and Brown, 1981; Wakshlag, Vial and Tamborini, 1983; Tamborini, Zillmann and Bryant, 1984). Further support for this argument has emerged from a British survey by Gunter and Wober (1983) who found that high scorers on Rubin and Peplau's (1975) belief in a just world scale tended also to be heavier viewers of action adventure programmes and US television series with just endings.

Television and world knowledge

Survey research evidence has repeatedly indicated that people say that television is their major source of information about national and world affairs (Roper Organisation, 1983; IBA, 1986). It is the news source which is most trusted (Roper Organisation, 1983; Lee, 1975) and the supply of news in perceived to be among the most important functions of television (Levy, 1978; Rubin, 1984). Recent reviews of the research literature, however, have indicated that these subjective claims and evaluations about television news often are not matched by the extent to which viewers actually remember and understand the news presented on television (see Gunter, 1986; Gunter, Berry and Clifford, 1982; Berry, Gunter and Clifford, 1981, 1982; Robinson and Levy, 1986).

There is some evidence among both adults and children that those who claim more frequent attention to the news on television also have a greater knowledge of political and current affairs (Atkin and Gantz, 1978; Conway, Stevens and Smith, 1975; Furnham and Gunter, 1983; Gunter, 1985). There is further evidence that television may enhance public affairs knowledge only superficially, however (Benton and Frazier, 1976), and that television may be a less effective learning medium than newspapers (Furnham and Gunter, 1985; Gunter, Furnham and Gietson, 1984; Patterson, 1980; Wilson, 1974).

The early domination of sociological perspectives in mass communications research meant that much of the research on retention of broadcast news until fairly recently focused principally on the role of audience variables such as class, education and claimed interest in the news (for example Gunter, 1985; Neuman, 1976). With the growing interest in this field among psychologists (particularly those working in cognitive psychology) a growing body of recent research literature has begun to pay more detailed attention to the shape and content of the stimulus materials – the programmes themselves. The result of this effort has been the identification of numerous programme factors, often including routine features of news production, which have been demonstrated to affect memory and comprehension of the news in significant ways.

Researchers have found that irrelevant film footage can impair memory for news narratives (Edwardson, Grooms and Pringle, 1976; Gunter, 1979; 1980b). The organization of stories is also important. Consecutive stories about similar topics in news bulletins can be mutually interfering (Gunter, Clifford and Berry, 1980; Gunter, Berry and Clifford, 1981).

Television and intellectual growth

Increasingly in the last few years, attention has been given to the potential of television to impair or to enhance intellectual growth and educational performance. On the down side, television has been blamed for decreasing reading scores and intellectual competence, and for poorer attention and enthusiasm in school. Some research findings have suggested that heavy television viewing at an early age may not only affect academic *effort*, but even more seriously may affect *ability* to learn in formal educational settings (see Gunter, 1983). Displacement of reading by television viewing may have particularly acute and long-lasting consequences if it occurs during early school years when the child is first learning to read and needs to practise reading to develop the basic linguistic skills necessary for more advanced intellectual growth in later years.

Recent evidence on the impact of television viewing on reading skills emerged from a study with over six hundred 11 to 14-year-olds in New Jersey (Morgan and Gross, 1980). Amongst this sample, children with lower IQs tended to watch more television than the children with higher IQs. Lower IQ children also had poorer reading skills. However, on statistically controlling for the effects of IQ, there remained still a significant negative relationship between amount of television normally viewed and reading performance. Heavier viewers, regardless of IQ, tended to exhibit poorer reading. In following up a group of children over a three-year period, Morgan and Gross also found evidence for a television displacement effect on reading. That is, those children who viewed more over time read less, and those who viewed less tended to read somewhat more.

In another study, Zuckerman, Singer and Singer (1980) looked at relationships between television viewing, reading ability, reading habits and general school performance among US 10–11-year-olds. Children who spent more time reading tended to be the ones with higher IQs and highly educated fathers, and also watched fewer fantasy, violent action programmes such as *The Incredible Hulk*, *The Six Million Dollar Man* and *Wonder Woman*. But television's often violent adult dramas were not the main offenders here. Zuckerman and associates found that very few of their children watched relatively 'hard core' violent programmes, such as *Hawaii Five-O* or *Starsky and Hutch*. The children most enjoyed watching programmes featuring fantastic super-human characters and fast moving action-packed sequences. These programmes, it seemed, had come to replace adventure books, comics and other popular children's reading material as a source of entertainment and satisfaction of fantasy needs. The authors argued that unlike reading, however, viewing of fantasy television content does not stimulate the active imaginative mental processes so important for advanced intellectual growth.

Encouraging reading through television

In view of the prevalence and popularity of television today, it would be an enormously difficult task to prevent children from watching any at all. In any case, there are good arguments for not wanting to do so, since television can have many beneficial consequences for viewers, young and old, as a ready source of amusement, companionship and edification. In recent years, researchers have increased their efforts to explore ways in which television might be used to promote enthusiasm for reading and learning in general. Early results have been quite promising. Television has been used successfully to model pro-reading behaviours (Bogatz and Ball, 1981). Much of the effectiveness of television programmes as such, however, depends on how explicit encouragement and modelling examples are. It may be necessary for examples to have characters explicitly portrayed as engaged in reading (Almeida, 1978).

PSYCHOLOGICAL MEDIATORS OF TV EFFECTS

For many years the predominant model in television-effects research was one that emphasized the direct impact of television on viewers. Viewers, it was assumed, watched television in a passive way and were changed by what they saw. More recently, however, accumulating research evidence has indicated that this model does not tell the whole story. Viewers act on television material as much as it acts on them. And television's impact on viewers, young and old, is often neither as simple nor direct as the 'hypodermic' model would have us believe.

Instead, there is a growing awareness among television researchers that viewers in a very distinct psychological sense are both active and selective in their viewing behaviour and the ways they respond to the things they see on the screen (see Zillmann and Bryant, 1985). Lack of space does not allow a full review of this new wave of research here. But the significance of psychological mediators can be illustrated quite well through reference to two particular sets of variables – developmental processes and personality factors.

Cognitive developmental processes

Recently, several investigators have suggested that basic research into cognitive processing of television may reveal significant factors that mediate the effects of television. Collins (1979, 1981, 1983) has argued that the effects of television content interact in complex ways with the viewer's background, cognitive skills and social goals such that a clear picture of television effects cannot emerge without a detailed analysis of factors underlying the selection, interpretation and retention of television programming.

More recently, however, an alternative notion about children's attention and comprehension of television has emerged which has suggested that young viewers' understanding of television is more active and sophisticated and occurs at an earlier stage than the reactive theory indicates. Anderson and his colleagues have proposed that young children's visual attention to television is actively strategically-guided by their attempts to comprehend programmes. Children learn early on to monitor the audio track of television programmes for cues predictive of comprehensible content. Such cues elicit attention, whereas cues that lack any meaning for the child come to inhibit attention. Attention to the screen is therefore comprehension-driven and is maintained in so far as the content can be understood and is not overly predictable (see Anderson, 1979; Anderson and Lorch, 1983; Anderson and Smith, 1984). These findings have important implications for the study of the impact of television, since there is some evidence that as children become more sophisticated in the judgments they make about television, the less influence it may have on them.

Personality factors

In the long running debate about the effects of television violence, the simple cause–effect model which has predominated posits that exposure to violence on the small screen leads to enhanced aggressiveness among viewers. Viewers are changed through exposure. Recently, though, some writers have begun to question whether this model does not over-simplify and even misrepresent the nature of this television influence. Much of the correlational data, for instance, is consistent with the interpretation that viewers who are already aggressive seek out and enjoy violent programmes on television. Experimental research, meanwhile, has indicated that viewers' reactions to violent television content may depend on the psychological dispositions which they bring with them to the viewing situation (Gunter, 1980a, 1983; Copeland and Slater, 1985; Zillmann and Bryant, 1985).

Meanwhile, field research also has indicated that pre-existing aggressive disposition may boost preferences for watching violent television programmes. Atkin *et al.*, (1979) used a two-wave panel design with interviews conducted over a one-year lag. They found that viewers who had early aggressive attitudinal predispositions were heavier viewers of television violence one year later than were less aggressive individuals. However, early violence viewing was not related to the development of later aggressiveness.

Finally, at a perceptual level, Gunter (1985) has reported that individuals who exhibit physically aggressive tendencies rated violent programme excerpts featuring fist-fights as more exciting and less disturbing or less violent than did individuals with less aggressive tendencies. These findings imply a complex relationship between personal aggressiveness and viewing preferences where people characterized by particular kinds of aggressive tendencies react differently to certain types of television violence than do other people.

RESEARCH DEVELOPMENTS FOR THE FUTURE

In this final section I look briefly at two particularly interesting and important research initiatives which have implications for television-effects research. The first of these concerns attempts to find out about the way people actually watch television at home. The second is concerned with the development of an educational course about television which can be taught in schools.

Watching people watch television

Much of the evidence on the impact of television rests on the validity of assumptions about and operational measures of television viewing. One of the most common methods of assessing television viewing is through self-reports. Any indication that such evidence, reliant as it is upon viewers' potentially fallible memories for what they have seen on television, might be inaccurate would throw considerable doubt on the meaning and validity of inferences drawn about television effects on the basis of them.

Perhaps the only way to be really sure of how people watch television is actually to monitor them while doing it. Observational studies of families viewing at home have indicated that many of the assumptions about the nature of viewing embodied in standard research measures do not reflect accurately the way in which people actually watch television.

Three studies have emerged from the United States which have used unobtrusive methods of monitoring family viewing patterns in the home. Each one has involved a time-lapse photographic or continuous video recording technique of observation. Allen (1965) used a time-lapse camera mounted in the main television viewing room which photographed the family watching television at regular intervals. Going a step further, Bechtel, Achelpohl and Akers (1972) installed video cameras and microphones in the homes of 20 families for six-day periods. This equipment was switched on whenever the television set was turned on and a recording was made both of the family while watching and of the programmes they watched. In the most substantial published study so far, Anderson and his colleagues installed video-recording equipment in the homes of 99 families. This equipment was activated automatically when the television was switched on and recorded one video frame every 1.2 seconds. Over a 20-month period, 4,672 hours of recordings were obtained (Anderson et al., unpublished manuscript).

Bechtel et al. (1972) compared observational measures of television viewing with viewers' self-reports of their television watching, measures of the sort frequently used by academic and commercial researchers. They found that the per cent agreement between viewing diaries and observed visual attention ranged from 92 per cent in the best case to 54 per cent in the worst, with the average agreement being 71 per cent. Over-reporting of amount of viewing was far more common than under-reporting. Unfortunately, Bechtel et al. did not provide data sufficient to determine whether the under-reporting was due to the family members defining 'watching television' as simply being present when the set was on (as against being present and actually watching television). If so, the families may have accurately reported their presence but not their attention.

Anderson et al. found that the viewing room was empty 15 per cent of the time the set was turned on. They also found that parents who kept viewing diaries for their children produced fairly accurate records of how much television their youngsters watched when diary records were matched against presence in the room when the set was in use. If the criterion of viewing was taken as visual attention to television, however, then the diaries overestimated children's television viewing by 53 per cent.

Teaching about television

The last decade has seen the growth of a research effort to which psychologists have a contribution to make. This concerns the development of courses to teach children to understand more about television. Television literacy projects both in the USA and UK have found that such courses are welcomed by teachers and pupils and that they can have quite rapid and profound effects on awareness of specific aspects of television, such as how programmes and advertisements are made, and of more global aspects of the medium, such as the economics and politics of the television industry and about the potential influences television can have on intellectual development, attitudes and behaviour. It is usually intended that through enhanced understanding of television, children will become more critical and discerning viewers and less susceptible to television influences. Teaching about television is considered by many television researchers one of the most important practical developments in the last few years, and one that needs to be explored further.

Examples of television literacy projects

In the USA, a number of research groups have experimented in recent years with the idea of teaching television as a subject in schools (for example Idaho State Department of Education, 1978; Media Action Research Centre, 1979; Singer, Zuckerman and Singer, 1980). Courses have been developed that incorporate teacher-taught lessons, specially produced documentary and instructional programmes and practical assignments in the actual making of programmes by students themselves. Results have, in the short term at least, generally been promising. In the UK, although increasing use has been of television in schools, there has been relatively little experimentation with the concept of teaching television literacy as a formal school subject. Some writers have suggested detailed frameworks for the development and teaching of television literacy in schools (for example Buscombe, 1977; Masterman, 1980), but what has been missing until recently is systematic field testing of these ideas.

Kelley, Gunter and Kelley (1985), however, described a course carried out among 14–15-year-old children, aimed at explaining television production techniques and encouraging more critical and thoughtful viewing of news and drama on television. The course involved analysis of specific broadcasts and the planning, preparation and production of video programmes by the pupils themselves. Detailed course evaluation by pre- and post-testing of experimental and control groups demonstrated clear improvements of children's understanding of television following a two-month period of classroom tuition and practical field assignments.

CONCLUSION

Concern about the impact of television on the lives of viewers, especially the young, has existed since broadcasts began. For a long time the predominant assumption was that television acted upon viewers, whose behaviours and outlook on life were changed through passive exposure. However, there is a growing awareness that television does not influence people in this simple fashion. For all the publicity given to potentially harmful effects of the media, recent research findings are beginning to show that television can produce beneficial effects and that it can be turned to educational advantage as a tool for instruction, a source of information about the world and as a subject matter in its own right. Furthermore, children's natural interest in television may function as a powerful motivating force, which can be used to facilitate rapid learning about the medium itself and to encourage youngsters to practice reading, writing and critical thinking, which they normally face up to only with reluctance. It is easy enough to join those who criticize television for its destructive social and cognitive influences, but rather more imagination and effort is required to utilize the medium for its socially and educationally constructive value. The theoretical and practical research skills which psychologists possess provide perhaps the best investigative equipment through which to understand the real nature of television's impact and the socially useful purposes to which it may be put in the future.

REFERENCES

Allen, C. (1965) Photographing the TV audience. *Journal of Advertising Research*, 14, 2–8.

Almeida, P. (1978) Children's television and the modeling of proreading behaviours. In C.M. Pierce (ed.) *Television and Education*. Beverly Hills, Ca.: Sage.

Anderson, D.A. (1979) Active and passive processes in children's television viewing. Paper presented at American Psychological Association annual meeting, New York.

Anderson, D.A. and Lorch, E.P. (1983) Looking at television: Action or reaction? In J. Bryant and D.R. Anderson (eds) *Children's Understanding of Television: Research on Attention and Comprehension*. New York: Academic Press.

Anderson, D.R. and Smith, R. (1984) Young children's TV viewing: The problem of cognitive continuity. In F. Morrison, C. Lord and D. Keating (eds) *Advances in Applied Developmental Psychology*, Vol. 1. New York: Academic Press.

Anderson, D.R., Lorch, E.P., Field, D.E., Collinns, P.A., and Nathan, J.G. (1986) Television viewing at home: Age trends in visual attention and time with TV. (Unpublished manuscript.)

Anwar, M. and Shang, A. (1983) *Television in a Multi-Racial Society*. London: Commission for Racial Equality.

Aronoff, C. (1974) Old age in prime time. *Journal of Communication*, 24, 86–87.

Atkin, C. and Gantz, W. (1978) Television news and political socialisation. *Public Opinion Quarterly*, 42, 183–197.

Atkin, C., Greenberg, B., Korzenny, F. and McDermott, S. (1979) Selective exposure to televised violence. *Journal of Broadcasting*, 23, 5–13.

Bandura, A. (1965) Vicarious processes: A case of no-trial learning. In L. Berkowitz (ed.) *Advances in Experimental Social Psychology*, Vol. 2. New York: Academic Press.

Bandura, A., Ross, D. and Ross, S. (1963) Imitation of film-mediated aggressive models. *Journal of Abnormal and Social Psychology*, 66, 3–11.
Baptista-Fernandez, M. and Greenberg, B. (1980) The context, characteristics and communication behaviours of blacks on television. In B. Greenberg (ed) *Life on Television*. Norwood, N.J.: Ablex.
BARB (1985) *Trends in Television*. London: Audits of Great Britain/Broadcasters Audience Research Board.
Bechtel, R., Achelpohl, C. and Akers, R. (1972) Correlates between observed behaviour and questionnaire response on television viewing. In E. Rubinstein, G. Comstock and J. Murray (eds) *Television and Social Behaviour. Volume 4: Television in Day-to-Day Life: Patterns of Use*. Washington, D.C.: US Government Printing Office.
Belson, W.A. (1978) *Television Violence and the Adolescent Boy*. Farnborough: Saxon House.
Benton, M. and Frazier, P.J. (1976) The agenda-setting function of the mass media at three levels of information holding. *Communication Research*, 3, 261–274.
Berkowitz, L. (1964) The effects of observing violence. *Scientific American*, 21, 35–41.
Berkowitz, L. and Alioto, J.T. (1973) The meaning of an observed event as a determinant of its aggressive consequences. *Journal of Personality and Social Psychology*, 28, 206–217.
Berkowitz L. and Rawlings, E. (1963) Effects of film violence on inhibition against subsequent aggression. *Journal of Abnormal and Social Psychology*, 66, 405–412.
Berry, C. and Clifford, B.R. (1986) Learning from Television News: Effects of Presentation and Knowledge on Comprehension and Memory. (Unpublished manuscript).
Berry, C., Gunter, B. and Clifford, B.R. (1981) Memory for televised information: A problem for applied and theoretical psychology. *Current Psychological Reviews*, 1, 171–192.
Berry, C., Gunter, B. and Clifford, B.R. (1982) Research on television news. *Bulletin of The British Psychological Society*, 35, 301–304.
Beuf, F.A. (1974) Doctor, lawyer, household drudge. *Journal of Communication*, 24, 110–118.
Biblow, E. (1973) Imaginative play and the control of aggressive behaviour. In J.L. Singer (ed.) *The Child's World of Make-Believe*. New York: Academic Press.
Bogatz, G.A. and Ball, S. (1971) *The Second Year of Sesame Street: A Continuing Evaluation*. Princeton, N.J.: Educational Testing Service.
Buscombe, E. (1977) *Television in Schools and Colleges*. London: Independent Broadcasting Authority.
Butler, M. and Paisley, W. (1980) *Women and the Mass Media* New York: Human Sciences Press.
Bryant, J., Carveth, R. and Brown, D. (1981) Television viewing and anxiety: An experimental examination. *Journal of Communication*, 31, 106–119.
Cline, V.B., Croft, R.G. and Courrier, S. (1973) Desensitisation of children to television violence. *Journal of Personality and Social Psychology*, 27, 360–365.
Collins, W.A. (1979) Children's comprehension of television content. In E. Wartella (ed.) *Children Communicating*. Beverly Hills, Ca: Sage.
Collins, W.A (1982) Cognitive processing and television viewing. In D. Pearl, L. Bouthilet and J. Lazar (eds) *Television and Behaviour: Ten Years of Scientific*

Progress and Implications for the Eighties. Washington, D.C.: National Institute for Mental Health.
Collins, W.A. (1983) Interpretation and influence in childrens' television viewing. In J. Bryant and D.R. Anderson (eds) *Children's Understanding of Television.* New York: Academic Press.
Conway, M.M., Steven, A.J. and Smith, R.G. (1975) The relation between media use and children's civic awareness. *Journalism Quarterly, 8,* 240-247.
Copeland, G.A. and Slater, D. (1981) Catharsis and fantasy. Paper presented at the meeting of the Speech Communication Association, Anaheim, Ca.
Copeland, G.A. and Slater, D. (1985) Television, fantasy and vicarious catharsis. *Critical Studies in Mass Communication, 2,* 352–362.
Donagher, P.C., Poulos, R.W., Liebert, R.M. and Davidson, E.S. (1975) Race, sex, and social example: An analysis of character portrayals on interracial television entertainment. *Psychological Reports, 37,* 1023–1034.
Dominick, J. and Greenberg, B.S. (1970) Three seasons of blacks on television. *Journal of Advertising Research, 10,* 21–27.
Dominick, J. and Greenberg, B.S. (1972) Attitudes towards violence: Interaction of television, social class and family attitudes. In G. Comstock and E. Rubinstein (eds) *Television and Social Behaviour. Vol. 3, Television and Adolescent Aggressiveness.* Washington, D.C.: US Government Printing Office.
Doob, A.N., and Macdonald, C.E. (1979) Television viewing and fear of victimization: Is the relationship causal? *Journal of Personality and Social Psychology, 37,* 170–179.
Downing, M. (1974) Heroine of the daytime serial. *Journal of Communication, 24,* 130–139.
Drabman, R.S. and Thomas, M.H. (1974) Does media violence increase children's toleration of real life aggression? *Developmental Psychology, 10,* 418–421.
Drabman, R.S., Robertson, S.S., Patterson, J.N., Jarvie, C.J., Hammer, D. and Cordua, G. (1981) Children's perception of media portrayed sex roles. *Sex Roles, 7,* 379–389.
Durkin, K. (1983) Sex roles and children's television. A report to the Independent Broadcasting Authority. Available from the Social Psychology Research Unit, University of Kent, Canterbury.
Durkin, K. (1985) *Television, Sex Roles and Children.* Milton Keynes: Open University Press.
Edwardson, M., Grooms, D. and Pringle, P. (1976) Visualisation and TV news information gain. *Journal of Broadcasting, 20,* 373–380.
Eron, L.D., Huesmann, L.R., Lefkowitz, M.M. and Wlader, L.O. (1972) Does television violence cause aggression? *American Psychologist, 27,* 253– 263.
Feshbach, S. (1961) The stimulating versus cathartic effects of a vicarious aggressive activity. *Journal of Abnormal and Social Psychology, 63,* 381–385.
Feshbach, S. and Singer, J. (1971) *Television and Aggression.* San Francisco: Jossey-Bass.
Freedman, J.L. (1984) Effect of television violence on aggressiveness. *Psychological Bulletin, 96,* 227–240.
Friedrich, L.K. and Stein, A.H. (1975) Prosocial television and young children: The effects of verbal labeling and role playing on learning and behaviour. *Child Development, 46,* 27–38.
Frueh, T. and McGhee, P.E. (1975) Traditional sex-role development and amount of time spent watching television. *Developmental Psychology, 11,* 109.

Furnham, A. and Gunter, B. (1983) Political knowledge and awareness in adolescents. *Journal of Adolescence*, 6, 373–385.

Furnham, A. and Gunter, B. (1985) Sex, presentation mode and memory for violent and non-violent news. *Journal of Educational Television*, 11, 99–105.

Furu, T. (1962) *Television and Children's Life: A Before–After Study.* Tokyo: Japan Broadcasting Corporation.

Furu, T. (1971) *The Function of Television for Children and Adolescents.* Tokyo: Sophia University Press.

Gerbner, G., Gross, L., (1976) Living with television: The violence profile. *Journal of Communication*, 26, 173–199.

Gerbner, G, Gross, L., Jackson-Beeck, M., Jeffries-Fox, S. and Signorielli, N. (1978) Cultural indicators: Violence profile no 9. *Journal of Communication*, 28, 176–207.

Gerbner, G., Gross, L., Signorielli, N., Morgan, M. and Jackson-Beeck, M. (1979) The demonstration of power: Violence profile no 10. *Journal of Communication*, 29, 177–196.

Gerbner, G., Gross, L., Morgan, M. and Signorielli, N. (1980) The mainstreaming of America: Violence profile no 11. *Journal of Communication*, 30, 10–29.

Gerbner, G., Gross, L., Signorielli, N. and Morgan, M. (1980) Aging with television: Images on television drama and conceptions of social reality. *Journal of Communication*, 30, 34–47.

Gorn, G.I., Goldberg, M.E. and Kanungo, R.N. (1976) The role of educational television in changing intergroup attitudes of children. *Child Development*, 47, 277–280.

Graves, S.B. (1975) Racial diversity in children's television: Its impact on racial attitudes and stated programme preference. Unpublished doctoral dissertation, Harvard University.

Greenberg, B.S. (ed) (1980) *Life on Television.* Norwood, N.J.: Ablex Press.

Greenberg, B.S., Richards, M. and Henderson, L. (1980) Trends in sex-role portrayals on television. In B. Greenberg (ed.) *Life on Television.* Norwood, N.J.: Ablex Press.

Gunter, B. (1979) Recall of television news items: Effects of presentation mode, picture content and serial position. *Journal of Educational Television*, 5, 57–61.

Gunter, B. (1980a) The cathartic potential of television drama. *Bulletin of The British Psychological Society*, 33, 448–450.

Gunter, B. (1980b) Remembering televised news: Effects of visual format on information gain. *Journal of Educational Television*, 6, 8–11.

Gunter, B. (1982) Does television interfere with reading development? *Bulletin of The British Psychological Society*, 35, 232–235.

Gunter, B. (1983) Do aggressive people prefer violent television? *Bulletin of The British Psychological Society*, 36, 166–168.

Gunter, B. (1985) News sources and news awareness: A British survey. *Journal of Broadcasting and Electronic Media*, 29, 397–406.

Gunter, B. (1985) *Dimensions of Television Violence.* Aldershot: Gower.

Gunter, B. (1986) *Poor Reception: Miscomprehension and Forgetting of Broadcast News.* Hillsdale, N.J.: Lawrence Erlbaum Associates.

Gunter, B. (1986) *Television and Sex Role Stereotyping.* IBA Research Monograph. London: IBA and John Libbey.

Gunter, B., Berry, C. and Clifford, B. (1981) Release from proactive interference with television news items: Further evidence. *Journal of Experimental Psychology: Human Learning and Memory*, 7, 480–487.

Gunter, B., Berry, C. and Clifford, B. (1982) Remembering broadcast news: The implications of experimental research for production technique. *Human Learning*, 1, 13–29.

Gunter, B., Clifford, B. and Berry, C. (1980) Release from proactive interference with television news items: Evidence for encoding dimensions with televised news. *Journal of Experimental Psychology: Human Learning and Memory*, 6, 216–223.

Gunter, B., Furnham, A. and Gietson, G. (1984) Memory for the news as a function of the channel of communication. *Human Learning*, 3, 265–271.

Gunter, B. and Wober, M. (1982) Television viewing and perceptions of women's roles on television and in real life. *Current Psychological Research*, 2, 277–288.

Gunter, B. and Wober, M. (1983) Television viewing and public trust. *British Journal of Social Psychology*, 22, 174–176.

Hanratty, M.A., O'Neal, E. and Sulzer, J.L. (1972) The effects of frustration upon the imitation of aggression. *Journal of Personality and Social Psychology*, 21, 30–34.

Himmelweit, H.T., Oppenheim, A.N. and Vince, P. (1958) *Television and the Child: An Empirical Study of the Effects of Television on the Young*. London: Oxford University Press.

Hinton, J.L., Seggar, J.F., Northcott, H.C. and Fontes, B.F. (1973) Tokenism and improving the imagery of blacks in TV drama and comedy: 1973. *Journal of Broadcasting*, 18, 423–432.

Hirsch, P.M. (1980) The 'scary world' of the non-viewer and other anomalies: A reanalysis of Gerbner *et al.*'s findings on cultivation analysis. *Communication Research*, 7, 403–456.

Hughes, M. (1980) The fruits of cultivation analysis: A re-examination of some effects of television watching. *Public Opinion Quarterly*, 44, 287–302.

Huesmann, L.R. (1982) Television violence and aggressive behaviour. In D. Pearl, L. Bouthilet and J. Lazar (eds) *Television and Behaviour: Ten Years of Scientific Progress and Implications for the Eighties. Vol. II, Technical Reviews*. Rockville: National Institute of Mental Health.

IBA (1986) *Attitudes to Broadcasting in 1985*. London: Independent Broadcasting Authority.

Idaho State Department ,of Education. (1978) *The Way We See It: A Programme to Improve Critical Viewing Skills*. Idaho: Idaho State Department of Education.

Katz, E., Adoni, H. and Parness, P. (1976) Remembering the news: What the picture adds to recall. *Journalism Quarterly*, 54, 231–239.

Kelley, P., Gunter, B. and Kelley, C. (1985) Teaching television in classroom: Results of a preliminary study. *Journal of Educational Television*, 11, 57–63.

Kniveton, B.H. and Stephenson, G.M. (1970) The effect of pre-experience on imitation of an aggressive film model. *British Journal of Social and Clinical Psychology*, 9, 31–36.

Kniveton, B.H. and Stephenson, G.M. (1972) An examination of individual susceptibility to the influence of aggression film models. *British Journal of Psychiatry*, 122, 53–56.

Lambert, W.E. and Klineberg, D. (1967) *Children's Views of Foreign Peoples: A Cross-National Study*. New York: Appleton-Century-Crofts.

Lear, N. (1971) As I read how Laura saw Archie . . . *New York Times*, October 10.

Lee, R. (1975) Credibility of newspaper and TV news. *Journalism Quarterly*, 55, 282–287.

Lee, R. (1980) Prime time in the classroom. *Journal of Communication, 30,* 175–180.
Leifer, A.D., Graves, S.B. and Phelps, E. (1976) Monthly report of Critical Evaluation of Television Project. Unpublished manuscript, Centre for Research in Children's Television, Harvard University.
Lemon, J. (1978) Women and blacks on prime time television. *Journal of Communication, 27,* 70–74.
Levy, M.R. (1978) The audience experience with television news. *Journalism Monographs,* no 55.
Long, M. and Simon, R. (1974) The roles and statuses of women and children on family TV programmes. *Journalism Quarterly, 51,* 107–110.
Loye, D., Gorney, R. and Steele, G. (1977) Effects of television. An experimental field study. *Journal of Communication, 27,* 206–216.
Manes, A. and Melnyk, P. (1974) Televised models of female achievement. *Journal of Applied Social Psychology, 4,* 365–374.
McGhee, P. and Frueh, T. (1980) Television viewing and the learning of sex-role stereotypes. *Sex Roles, 2,* 179–188.
McIntyre, T. and Teevan, J. (1972) Television violence and deviant behaviour. In G. Comstock and E. Rubinstein (eds) *Television and Social Behaviour. Vol. 3, Television and Adolescent Aggressiveness.* Washington, DC.: US Government Printing Office.
McLeod, J., Atkin, C. and Chaffee, S. (1972) Adolescents, parents and television use. In G. Comstock and E. Rubinstein (eds) *Television and Social Behaviour. Vol. 3, Television and Adolescent Aggressiveness.* Washington, DC.: US Government Printing Office.
Masterman, L. (1980) *Teaching about Television.* (London, MacMillan).
Media Action Research Centre. (1979) *Television Awareness Training.* (New York, Media Action Research Centre).
Milavsky, J.R., Stripp, H., Kessler, R. and Rubens, W. (1982) *Television and Aggression: A Panel Study.* New York: Academic Press.
Miles, B. (1975) Channeling children: Sex stereotyping as primetime TV. Princeton, N.J.: Women on Words and Images.
Morgan, M. (1982) Television and adolescents' sex role stereotypes: A longitudinal study. *Journal of Personality and Social Psychology, 43,* 947–955.
Morgan, M. and Gross, L. (1980) Television and educational achievement and aspirations. In D. Pearl, L. Bouthilet, and J. Lazar (eds) *Television and Behaviour: Ten Years of Scientific Progress and Implications for the Eighties.* Washington, DC: US Government Printing Office.
Murray, J.P. and Kippax, S. (1978) Children's social behaviour in three towns with differing television experience. *Journal of Communication, 28,* 19–29.
Neely, J.J., Heckel, R.V. and Leichtman, H.M. (1973) The effect of race of model and response consequences to the model on imitation in children. *Journal of Social Psychology, 89,* 225–232.
Neuman, W.R. (1976) Patterns of recall among television news viewers. *Public Opinion Quarterly, 40,* 115–123.
Northcott, H.C. (1975) Too young, too old – age in the world of television. *The Gerontologist, 15,* 184–186.
Parke, R.D., Berkowitz, L., Leyens, J.P., West, S.G. and Sebastian, R.J. (1977) Some effects of violent and non-violent movies on the behaviour of junevile delinquents. In L. Berkowitz (ed.) *Advances in Experimental Social Psychology, Vol. 10.* New York: Academic Press.
Patterson, T. (1980) *The Mass Media Election.* New York: Praeger.

Phelps, E. (1976) Analysis of Phase II attitude data. Unpublished manuscript, Harvard University.
Piepe, A., Crouch, J. and Emerson, M. (1977) Violence and television. *New Society*, 41, 536–538.
Pingree, S. and Hawkins, R.P. (1980) US programmes on Australian television: The cultivation effect. *Journal of Communication*, 31, 97–105.
Robinson, J.P. and Levy, M.R. (1986) *The Main Source. Learning from Television News*. Beverly Hills, Ca: Sage.
Roper Organisation (1983) *Trends in Attitudes Towards Television and Other Media: A Twenty Year Review*. New York: Television Information Office.
Rotter, J.B. (1965) Generalised expectancies for internal versus external control of reinforcement. *Psychological Mongraphs*, 80(1) (whole no 609).
Rubin, A. (1984) Ritualised and instrumental television viewing. *Journal of Communication*, 34, 67–77.
Rubin, Z. and Peplau, I. (1975) Who believes in a just world? *Journal of Social Issues*, 31, 65–89.
Rubinstein, E.A., Liebert, R.M., Neale, J.M. and Poulos, R.W. (1976) Assessing television's influence on children's prosocial behaviour. Stony Brook, NY: Brookdale International Institute.
Savitsky, J.C., Rogers, R.W., Izard, C.E. and Liebert, R.M. (1976) Role of frustration and anger in the imitation of filmed aggression against a human victim. *Psychological Reports*, 29, 807–810.
Schramm, W., Lyle, J. and Parker,. E. (1961) *Television in the Lives of our Children*. Stanford: Stanford University Press.
Signorielli, N. (1984) The demography of the television world. In G. Melischek, K.E. Rosengren and J. Stappers (eds) *Cultural Indicators: An International Symposium*. Vienna, Austria: Austrian Academy of Sciences.
Silverman, L.T. (1977) Effects of Sesame Street programming on the cooperative behaviour of preschoolers. Unpublished doctoral dissertation, Stanford University.
Singer, D.G., Zuckerman, D.M., and Singer, J.L. (1980) Helping elementary children learn about TV. *Journal of Communication*, 30, 84–93.
Sprafkin, J.N. and Rubinstein, E.A. (1979) Children's television viewing habits and prosocial behaviour: A field correlational study. *Journal of Broadcasting*, 23, 265–276.
Stauffer, J., Frost, R. and Rybolt, W. (1978) Literacy, illiteracy and learning from television news. *Communication Research*, 5, 221–232.
Stauffer, J., Frost, R. and Rybolt, W. (1980) Recall and comprehension of radio news in Kenya. *Journalism Quarterly*, 57, 612–617.
Stauffer, J., Frost, R. and Rybolt, W. (1983) The attention factor in recalling network television news. *Journal of Communication*, 33, 29–37.
Surlin, S.H. (1974) Bigotry on air and in life: The Archie Bunker case. *Public Telecommunications Review*, 212, 34–41.
Tamborini, R., Zillmann, D. and Bryant, J. (1984) Fear and victimization: Exposure to television and perceptions of crime and fear. In R. Bostrom (ed.) *Communication Yearbook, 8*. Beverly Hills, Ca: Sage.
Tan, A., Raudy, J., Huff, C. and Miles, J. (1980) Children's reactions to male and female newscasters' effectiveness and believability. *Quarterly Journal of Speech*, 63, 201–205.
Tedesco, N. (1974) Patterns in prime time. *Journal of Communication*, 24, 119–124.
Thomas, M.H., Horton, A.W., Lippincott, E.C. and Drabman, R.S. (1977)

Desensitisation to portrayals of real life aggression as a function of television violence. *Journal of Personality and Social Psychology*, 35, 450–458.

Tuchman, G. (1978) The symbolic annihilation of women by the mass media. In G. Tuchman, A. Daniels and J. Benet (eds) *Hearth and Home: Images of Women in the Mass Media*. New York: Oxford University Press.

Vidmar, N. and Rokeach, M. (1973) Archie Bunker's bigotry: A study in selective perception and exposure. Paper presented at the annual meeting of the Eastern Psychological Association, Washington, DC.

Wakshlag, J., Vial, V. and Tamborini, R. (1983) Selecting crime drama and appreciation about crime. *Human Communication Research*, 10, 277–242.

Werner, A. (1971) Children and television in Norway. *Gazette*, 16, 133–151.

Williams, F., La Rose, R. and Frost, F. (1981) *Children, Television and Sex-Role Stereotyping*. New York: Praeger.

Wilson, C.E. (1974) The effect of medium on loss of information. *Journalism Quarterly*, 51, 111–115.

Wober, M. (1978) Televised violence and paranoid perception: The view from Great Britain. *Public Opinion Quarterly*, 42, 315–321.

Wober, M. and Gunter, B. (1982) Television and personal threat: Fact or artifact? A British survey. *British Journal of Social Psychology*, 21. 239–247.

Zillmann. D. (1980) Anatomy of suspense. in P. Tannenbaum (ed.) *Entertainment Functions of Television*. Hillsdale, N.J.: Lawrence Erlbaum Associates.

Zillmann, D. and Bryant, J. (eds) (1985) *Selective Exposure to Communication*. Hillsdale, N.J.: Lawrence Erlbaum Associates.

Zuckerman, D.M., Singer, D.C. and Singer, J.L. (1980) Children's television viewing, racial and sex role attitudes. *Journal of Applied Psychology*, 10, 281–294.

INDEX

ACCOMMODATION, speech 119–20
action
  and emotion 71
  and identity 95
advertising, and health 131–3
affect
  and cognition 59–62, 66–9, 70
  and hypnosis 65
  influence on memory 65
affective primacy 66–9
age-stereotyping, and television 287
agency, and identity 104
aggression
  and catharsis 277–9
  imitative 278
agnosias 174
alcohol, and memory disorders 185
amnesia
  hypnotic 245–7
  organic 178–9, 182–7
  source 242
animal liberationists 218–9
animals
  moral status of 220
  use in psychology experiments 2–3, 140–41, 218–31
anorexia nervosa 140
antisocial behaviour, and television 276–83
assimilation—accommodation, and identity 101–2, 106
attitudes
  and health 122–3
  and language 120
  and non-standard speech 118
attribution
  and depression 61–2
  and emotion 57–8, 61–2
  and mood 20
auditory systems, and spatial frequency 3–5
autonomic arousal, and emotion 57

BASE-RATE FALLACY 80
behaviour
  and adaptation 195–6

altrustic, evolution of 203–5
  cooperative, evolution of 202–3
  and genetic determinism 194
  selfish, evolution of 200–1
  spiteful, evolution of 205–6
behavioural effects of television 276–83
behavioural processes, and computer hardware 256–9
belief bias 83
biasing effects, and reasoning 79–80, 83
body-weight set-points 145–7
brain injury, and face recognition 32–6, 45
bulimia nervosa 140, 162

CATHARSIS, and aggression 277–9
certainty in psychology 14–15
clinical hypnosis 249–51
cognition
  and affect 59–62, 66–9, 70
  effects of emotion on 65–6
  and emotion chapter 3 *passim*
  and identity 102–3
  and reasoning 74
cognitive appraisal, and emotion 60–1, 67
cognitive compatibility, and computers 267
cognitive control, and eating 151, 164
cognitive effects of television 284–91
cognitive systems
  and face recognition 48
  and hypnosis 248
  and information technology 256, 263–5
colour, and computer design 269
communication
  and health 121–3
  human—computer 265–6
  see also language
compliance, and speech 118
computational modelling, and face recognition 49
computer design
  and colour 269
  and eye movements 268–9
  and movement compatibility 270–71
  and speed of presentation 270
computer models of reasoning 77–8

305

computer programming
  and learning 263-4
  and memory 264-5
computer simulations
  of emotion 71
  of reasoning 82
computers
  and cognitive compatibility 267
  and communication 265-6
  hardware, and behavioural processes 256-9
conditioned satiety, and eating 160-61
configuration, and face recognition 39
conjunction fallacy 80
contextual knowledge, and reasoning 76
continuity, and identity 103-4
convergence
  linguistic 126
  speech 119
crime, and television 287-8
cross-cultural concepts of identity 107-8
cross-cultural studies of emotion 57
Cruelty to Animals Act (1876) 220, 229
cultural differences, and eating 153

DARWIN, CHARLES, theory of emotion 11-12
depression
  and attribution 61-2
  and instrumental failure 23-4
  and learned helplessness 19-20, 61-2, 231
  and life events 20-23
  and social loss 23-44
desensitization, and television 278
development, and television 281-2, 290-2
developmental changes, and identity 108
dietary restraint, and eating 147-53
dieting, and eating disorders 161-3
divergence
  linguistic 126
  speech 119
dualism, and identity 128
dysphasias 174

EARLY LEARNING, and eating 153-5
eating
  animal studies 140-41
  anthropological studies 141
  and cognitive control 151, 164
  and conditioned satiety 160-61
  and cultural differences 153
  and dietary restraint 147-53
  and dieting 161-3
  and early learning 153-5
  and emotional arousal 154-5
  and food selection 156-8
  and instrumental conditioning 160, 161
  and internal cues 142-7
  and learning experiences 153-60
  and measures of satiety 163-4
  and mother—baby interaction 155
  and nutrition 158-60
  and personal beliefs 152
  and ponderostat 147
  and predictability of weight gain 152-3
  and set-points 145-7
  and sex differences 153, 156, 162
eating disorders 140
Eliot, George 9
emotion
  and action 71
  and attribution 57-8, 61-2
  and autonomic arousal 57
  and cognitive appraisal 56, 57, 60-61, 67
  computer simulations of 71
  cross-cultural studies 57
  Darwin's theory of 11-12
  defined 55-6
  effects on cognition 65-6
  and facial expression 56, 57, 58, 63-4
  and heuristics 69
  and hypnosis 65-6
  and information processing 57, 63-4, 66-9
  and learned helplessness 61-2
  and overt behaviour 56
  psychophysiological approaches 56, 59
  and psychophysiological approaches 64-5
  and social cognition 68-9
  social construction of 70-1
  special process theories of 63-5
emotional arousal, and eating 154-5
episodic memory
  disorders of 177-9
  and hypnosis 246
ergonomics, and information technology 255
errors in reasoning 83, 84
ethical authority, and scientific method 219
ethnic minorities, and health 123
ethnolinguistic identity theory 124-7
evaluation, and identity 101-2, 106
evolutionary stability 198-9, 201-11
evolutionary theory
  and social behaviour 192, 200-11
  and social organization 212
experiment design, and psychology 276
experimental science, psychology as 13-15
experimentation, and psychological method 1-9
externality theory of obesity 141-5

FACE PROCESSING, and babies 29–30
face recognition
  and accessing information 43–4
  and brain injury 32–6, 45
  and classification 28, 30, 37
  and cognitive system 48
  and computational modelling 49
  differences in ability in 44–6
  disorders of 28
  familiar vs unfamiliar 39–41, 47
  functional models of 47–9
  importance of understanding 28–9
  and inversion 30–2, 36
  and lipreading 46
  and prosopagnosia 36–38, 45, 46, 176–7
  and representations 38–42
  and saliency 39
  and semantic priming 42–3
  and spatial frequency 38–9
  special process in 30–8
  as three-dimensional structures 49–50
face recognition units 40, 42
facial expression
  and emotion 56, 57, 58, 63–4
  recognition of 45
food deprivation, and experimental method 224
food selection, and eating 156–8
Fourier analysis 3–5
frontal lobe lesions, and memory disorders 179–81

GENETIC DETERMINISM, and behaviour 194
group conflict, and individualism 127–9

HEALTH
  and advertising 131–3
  and attitudes 122–3
  and communication 121–3
  and ethnic minorities 123
  and language 115
  models of 129–30
  and social class 122–3
  and social pluralism 127–9
  and social support 130
  and stereotypes 121–3
health education 130
helping behaviour, psychological studies of 12–13
heuristics
  and emotion 69
  and problem solving 199
  and reasoning 76, 78–80, 87–8
hidden observer, and hypnosis 248
historical social psychology 106–7
hunger, development of concept 154
hypnosis
  and affect 65
  and amnesia 245–7
  clinical 249–51
  experimental methods 237, 240–2, 244
  and extraordinary feats 238–40
  and hidden observer 248
  neo-dissociation theory 243–45
  non-state theory 235–7, 239, 248–9, 251
  and pain 247–9
  physiology of 238
  simulated 239, 241–2
  and source amnesia 242
  state theory 234–5, 239, 248–9, 251
  and susceptibility 250–51
  and trance logic 240

IDENTITY
  and action 95
  and agency 104
  and assimilation—accommodation 101–2, 106
  and cognition 102–3
  contextual features of 105–6
  and continuity 103–4, 104
  cross-cultural concepts 107–8
  differentiated from self-concept 94–9
  and distinctiveness 104–5
  and dualism 128
  and evaluation 101–2, 106
  and information processing 102–3
  and language 124–7
  processes of 101–3
  research methods 108–9
  and salience 105
  and self-esteem 103
  social 127–9
  stucture of 100–101
  and transition 105–6
  and universality 106–8
identity theory, ethnolinguistic 124–7
image enhancement 2–8
individualism, and group conflict 127–9
inference rules, and reasoning 76–8, 81–2, 87, 89
information processing
  and emotion 57, 63–4, 66–9
  and face recognition 43–4, 48
  and identity 102–3
  and memory disorders 171–4
information technology
  and cognitive systems 256
  and ergonomics 255
insight, defined 9–10
instrumental conditioning, and eating 160, 161
instrumental failure, and depression 23–4
instrumental learning, and scoliosis 231

intellectual growth, and television 290–2
intelligence, and language 123–4
interactionists
  processual 97–9
  structural 97–9
intergroup theory 116

JAMES, WILLIAM 57, 59

KNOWLEDGE
  compared to insight 10
  status of psychological 13–14

LANGUAGE
  and attitudes 118, 120
  and health 115
  and identity 124–7
  and intelligence 123–4
  and prejudice 120
  and psychological health 119–20
  and reality 129
  as social marker 116–19
  and stereotypical beliefs 118
language attitudes 117
learned helplessness
  and depression 61–2, 231
  and emotion 61–2
learned helplessness and depression 19–20
learning
  and computer programming 263–4
  and systematic desensitization 230
learning experiences, and eating 153–60
life events and depression 20–3
linguistic divergence 126
linguistic convergence 126
lipreading, and face recognition 46
logic, propositional 75, 76

MATCHED GUISE TECHNIQUES 116–7
matching bias 85
media, and health education 131–3
memory
  and computer programming 264–5
  influence of affect on 65
  organic disorders, groups of 170
  and reasoning 79, 80–2, 85–7
  and self-concept 101–2
see also hypnosis
memory disorders
  and alcohol 185
  and contextual knowledge 184–6
  and encephalitis 175
  and frontal lobe lesions 179–81
  selective 174–8
  semantic vs episodic 177–9
  short-term 171–4

storage vs retrieval 177–9
see also amnesia, organic
mental health, and social support 24
mental models, and reasoning 89
methodology, scientific 1
methodology of social sciences 15–19
models, mental 82–3
modus tollens 76–7
mother—baby interaction, and eating 155

NATURAL SELECTION, and sociobiology 192–3
neuropsychology 32–6, 45, 46, 47
  and memory disorders 170–1

OBESITY, externality theory of 141–5

PAIN
  and hypnosis 247–9
  as reinforcer 225–6
parental care, and sex differences 206–11
Pavlov, Ivan 2
peas, mechanical energy of 10
perseveration, and memory disorders 181
personality, and voice type 117–8
personality factors, and television 292–3
physiology of hypnosis 238
political limitations to applications of psychology 9
ponderostat, and eating 147
prejudice, and language 120
primates, use in psychology 223
probability, reasoning about 78–80
problem solving, and heuristics 199
process, and reasoning 77
processual interactionists 97–9
propositional logic 75, 76
prosocial behaviour, and television 282–3
prosopagnosia 36–8, 45, 46, 176–7
psychological health, and language 119–20
psychological knowledge, status of 13–14
psychology
  and experiment design 276
  experimental approach 1–9
  funding of research 228
  limitation of natural science paradigm 17–18
  limits to applications of 9
  methodology 1, 14–15
  and relevance 229–31
  usefulness 2
psychology as experimental science 13–15
psychophysiological approaches to emotion 56, 59, 64–5

RACIAL STEOREOTYPING, and television 285–6
reasoning
  and biasing effects 79–80, 83

computer models of 77–8
and computer simulations 82
and contextual knowledge 76
errors in 75, 77, 83, 84
explicit *vs* implicit 74–5
and heuristics 76, 78–80, 87–8
and inference rules 76–8, 81–2, 87, 89
and memory 79, 80–2, 85–7
and mental models 89
and probability 78–80
and process 77
real-life studies 85–7
and relevance 88
and representation 77, 82–3
and schemas 80–2, 88–9
and scientific methodology 75
semantic theories of 76
syntactic theories of 76
received pronunciation 117
representation, and reasoning 77, 82–3
representativeness, and reasoning 78–80
response prevention 231
restraint, dietary, and eating 147–53

SACCADIC EYE MOVEMENTS, and computer design 268–9
sadism, and psychological research 227–8
saliency, and face recognition 39
satiety, measures of, and eating 163–4
schemas, and reasoning 80–2, 88–9
science, uses of 1, 9
scientific method 1
and ethical authority 219
and replication 228
use of models 195
and reasoning 75
self-concept
and identity 94–9
and memory 101–2
self-esteem, and identity 103
semantic memory, and hypnosis 246
semantic memory disorders 177–9
semantic priming, and face recognition 42–3
semantic theories of reasoning 76
sex differences
and eating 153, 156, 162
and parental care 206–11
sex-stereotyping, and television 284–5
selection task, Wason 84–9
social behaviour
cost-benefit analysis 199
and evolutionary theory 192, 200–11
social class, and health 122–3
social cognition, and emotion 68–9
social construction of emotion 70–1
social identity 98, 116, 124–9

socila loss, and depression 23–4
social marker, language as 116–19
social organization, and evolutionary theory 212
social pluralism, and health 127–9
social psychology
historical 106–7
and hypnosis 237
social sciences
methodology of 15–19
and status quo 129
sociobiology, and natural selection 192–3
source amnesia, and hypnosis 242
spatial frequency
and auditory/visual systems 3–5
and face recognition 38–9
speech, non-standard, and attitudes 118
speech accommodation 119–20
speech input/output, and computers 260–1, 262–3
statistical theory, and induction 75
stereotypes
function of 123–4
and health 121–3
and language 118
and television 284–6
stress, psychological studies of 2–3
structural interactionists 97–9
syntactic theories of reasoning 76
systematic desensitization, and learning 230

TECHONOLOGY, and experimental method 14–15
television
and age-stereotyping 287
behavioural effects 276–83
cognitive effects 284–91
and crime 287–8
and desensitization 278
and development 281–2, 290–1
as information source 289
and intellectual growth 290–2
and learning 294–5
and personality factors 292–3
and prosocial behaviour 282–3
and racial stereotyping 285–6
and sex-stereotyping 284–5
viewing behaviour 291–3
Tit for Tat 202–3
trance logic, and hypnosis 240
transition, and identity 105–6
truth conditions, and mental models 83

UNIVERSALITY, and identity, 106–8

VDUs, and health hazards 261–2

verification bias 85
Verstehen 15–17
vision
   and computer design 269
   and spatial frequency 3–5

WASON SELECTION TASK 84–9